ink & wash

in the garden

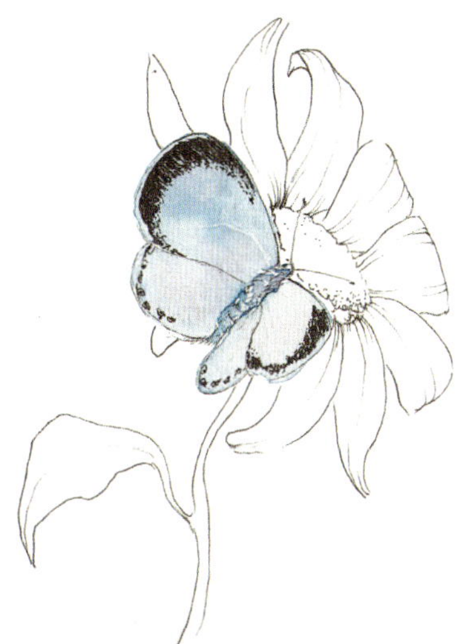

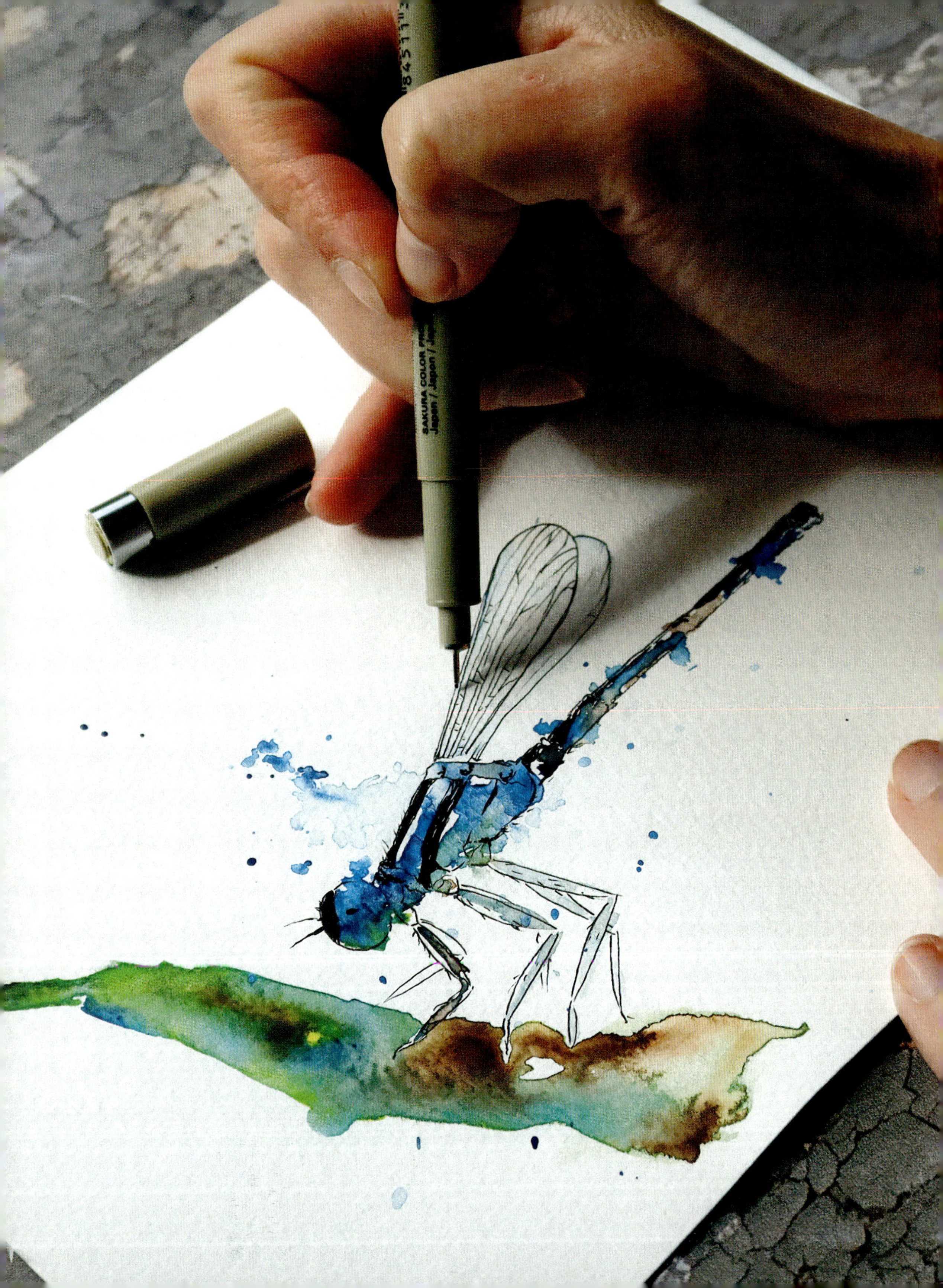

ink & wash
in the garden

Watercolor & Ink Birds, Insects, Wildlife & More

camilla damsbo brix

author of *Ink & Wash Florals*

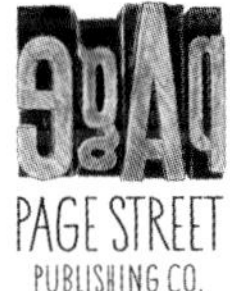

PAGE STREET
PUBLISHING CO.

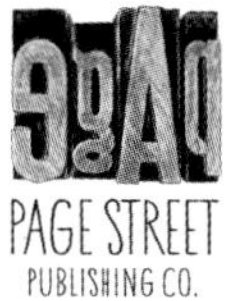

PAGE STREET
PUBLISHING CO.

First published in 2024 by

Page Street Publishing Co.

27 Congress Street, Suite 1511

Salem, MA 01970

www.pagestreetpublishing.com

Distributed by Macmillan, sales in Canada by The Canadian Manda Group.

28 27 26 25   2 3 4 5 6

ISBN-13: 979-889-0-03991-0

Library of Congress Control Number: 2023936750

Edited by Aïcha Martine Thiam and Sadie Hofmeester

Cover and book design by Emma Hardy for Page Street Publishing Co.

Photography and artwork by Camilla Damsbo Brix; author photo on page 185 by Line Kongsted

Printed and bound in China

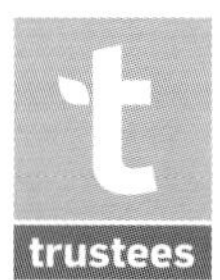

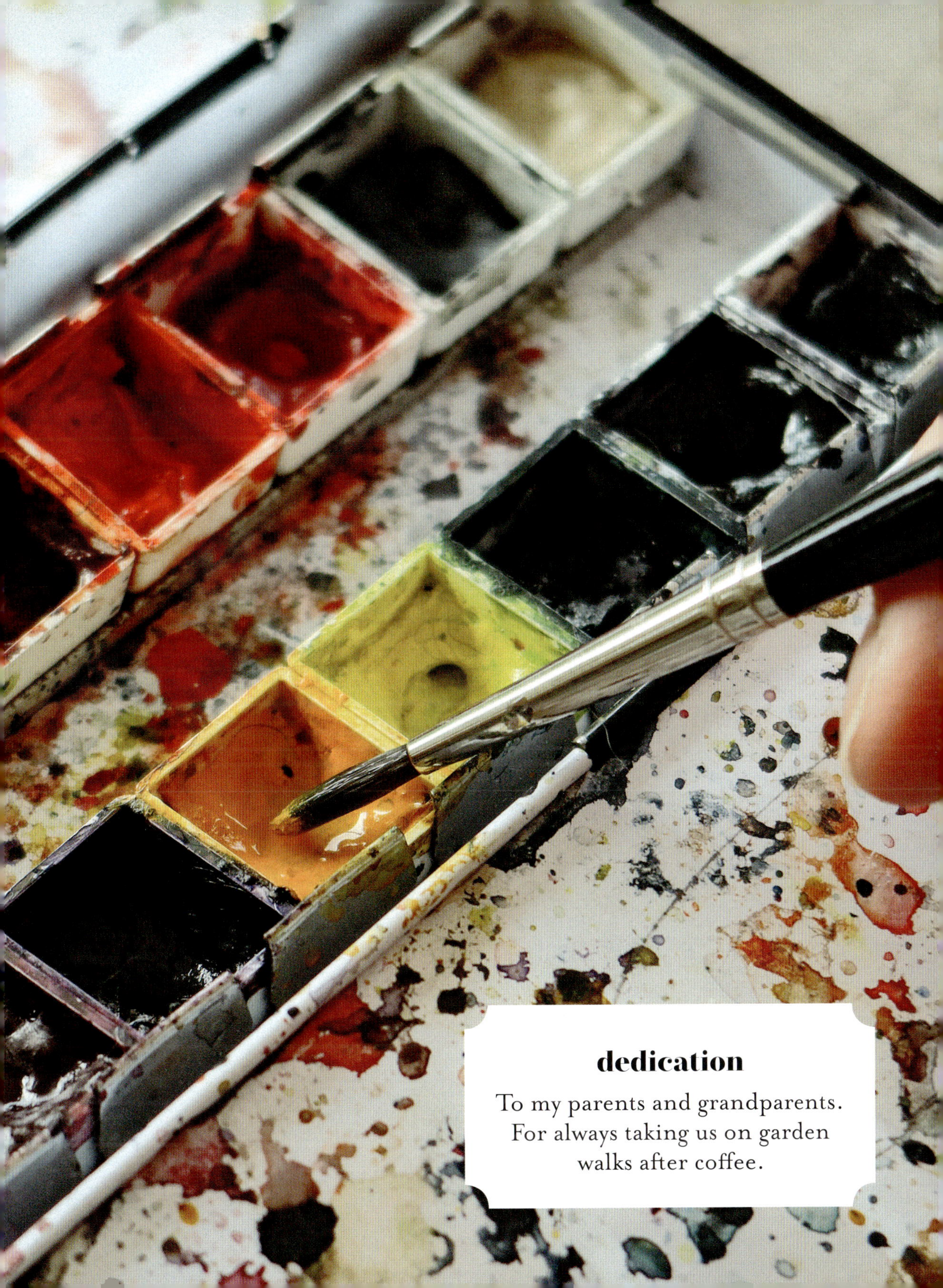

dedication

To my parents and grandparents.
For always taking us on garden
walks after coffee.

contents

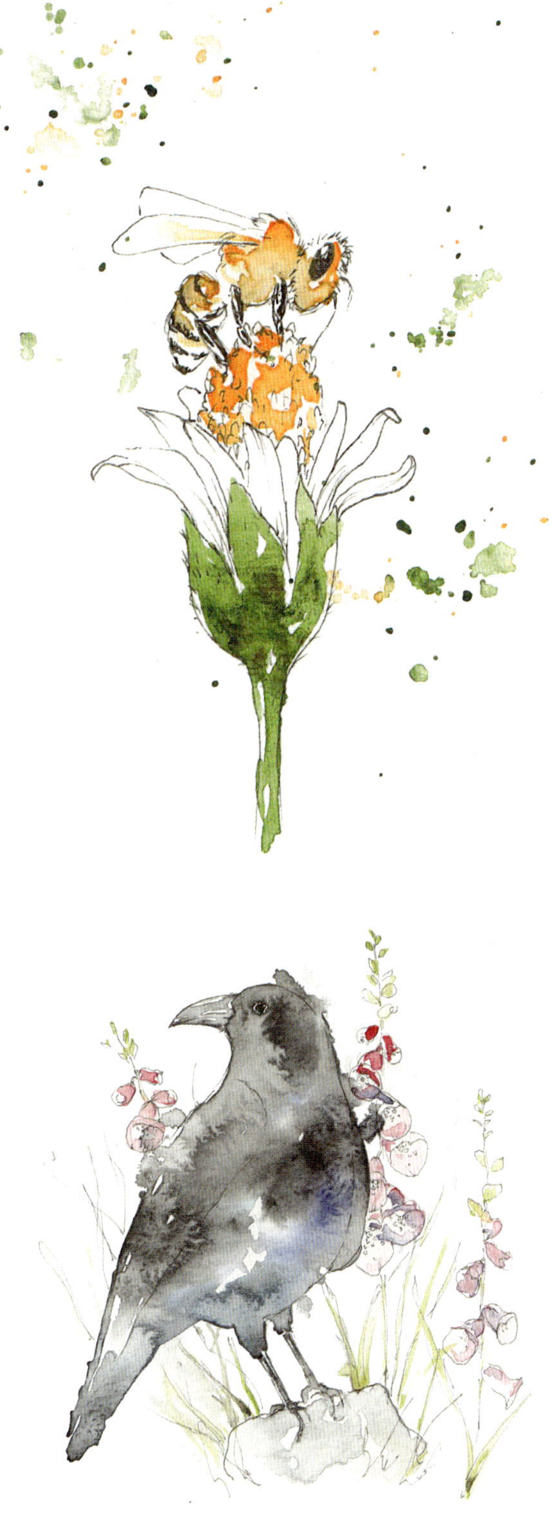

welcome!

A grand big welcome to you, my friend! I am beyond excited to have you here, with this book in your hand.

I absolutely love ink and wash. You know—that style where you combine watercolor and fineliner in elegant sketches. To me, it's the perfect way of relaxing, letting go of expectations and perfectionism and getting into a flow—even when we only have a short amount of time after doing the laundry and before cooking dinner. I would say that this is the perfect technique for the modern, busy person.

And yes, I know I promise a lot, but stay with me here. The reason why ink and wash can do all that is because it's fast and not at all centered around the outcome but, instead, the process. And that means it can be truly enjoyed even if you only have twenty minutes for yourself.

In fact, the sketches in this book are a prime example because none of them were planned or practiced ahead of time but intuitively created in the present. I actually created flower sketches in my first book like this as well. Therefore, each sketch shows different approaches to ink and wash where you don't follow an exact technique but mostly go with flow and intuition. And yes, I do show a suggested course of action here in the book, but as you grow in confidence, you can definitely play with the rules.

This book is centered around the garden and all the beautiful winged wildlife out there. I think it's so relaxing to just watch the birds eat at the bird feeders and enjoy the butterflies as they dance from flower to flower. This is when the garden comes to life. And this is also one of the main reasons why our garden looks like it does. Each year we find new blooms fit for insects so we can get even more life and joy in the garden. And of course, if you want inspiration to sketch florals, I know just the book for you. My first book, *Ink & Wash Florals*, is the perfect companion to this one. After all, flowers, birds and insects are really part of the same story.

And now I want to give you a quick guided tour around the book.

We start with Fundamentals of Watercolor & Ink (page 11). First, we'll go over the supplies used in the book. For more beginner advice on supplies, check out my first book. Then, we move on to some basic watercolor and ink techniques. There are tons more techniques out there, but these are the ones being used in the book. If you are excited to learn more, you can go to my YouTube channel (www.youtube.com/camilladamsboart), where there is even more to explore.

Then we start with the wonderful wildlife. I am not a scientist, so I will take you through a very basic—we aren't in an anatomy class—lesson about how birds and insects are built. Then we will work on making the animal the star of the sketch (page 23) when surrounded with flowers, leaves, branches and more. And that is it for the technical stuff.

Then we grab our fineliners and brushes and turn the page to embellishments (page 25). Because, just like when you are pregnant and getting all the baby stuff prepared ahead of time, we want to be ready for the animals with some things to surround them: bird feeders, picket fences, wildflowers and more. And then you are set for when the wildlife arrives.

Now it's finally time! I have chosen birds from my own garden and some that are so bright and colorful they just had to be included as well. After all, garden birdies vary so much around the globe. The birds are closely followed by eleven cute insects. Butterflies, beetles, bees and more are ready to be sketched. And don't worry, I didn't include any creepy ones. After all, I don't want to scare you away.

Finally, you are ready to fly on your own. So, after the step-by-steps, I've included a chapter—Finding Your Own Style (page 183)—on how to develop your own style (this chapter may surprise you) and how you can go out into the wild like a regular Steve Irwin to find even more wildlife.

One final note: I would be thrilled to see your sketches from this book! So, when you share them on social media, make sure to use #inkandwashgarden and tag me @camilla_damsbo_art so I can see it.

Have fun, my friend!

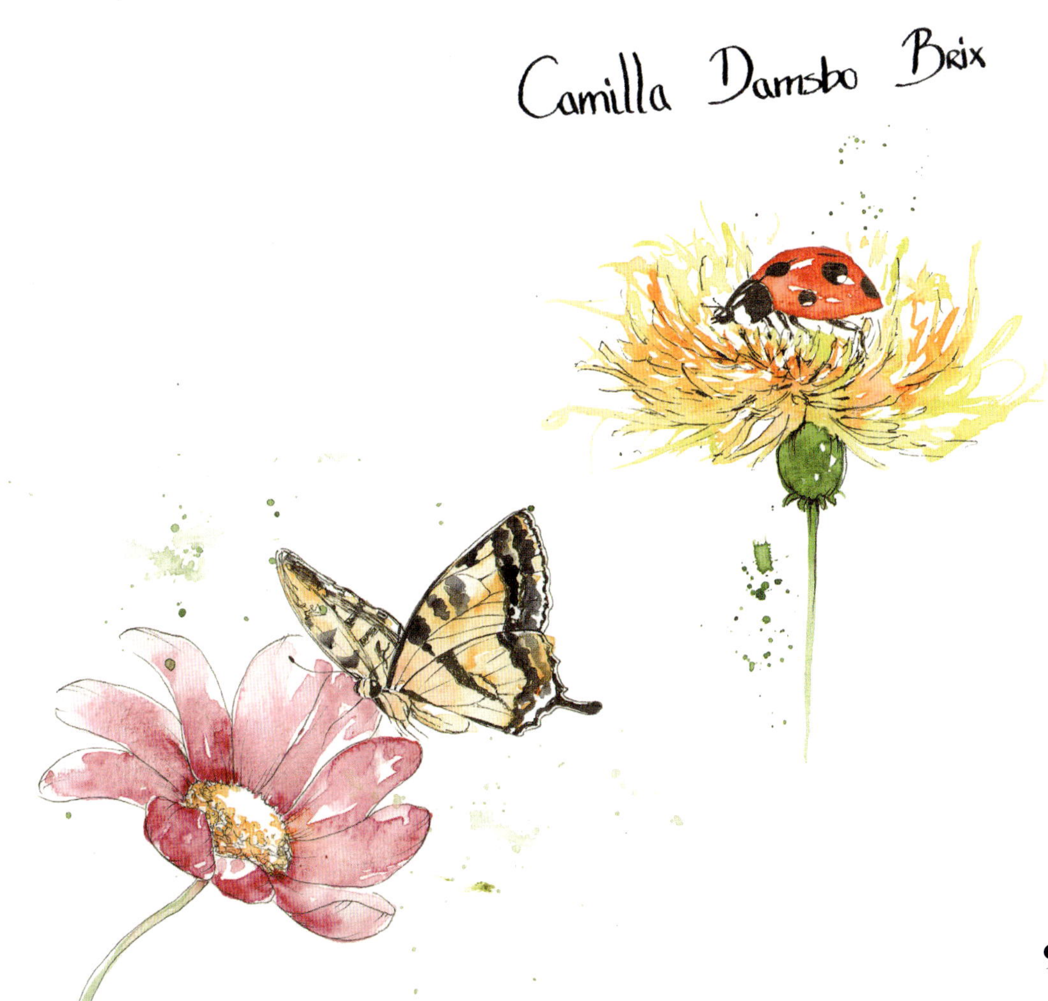

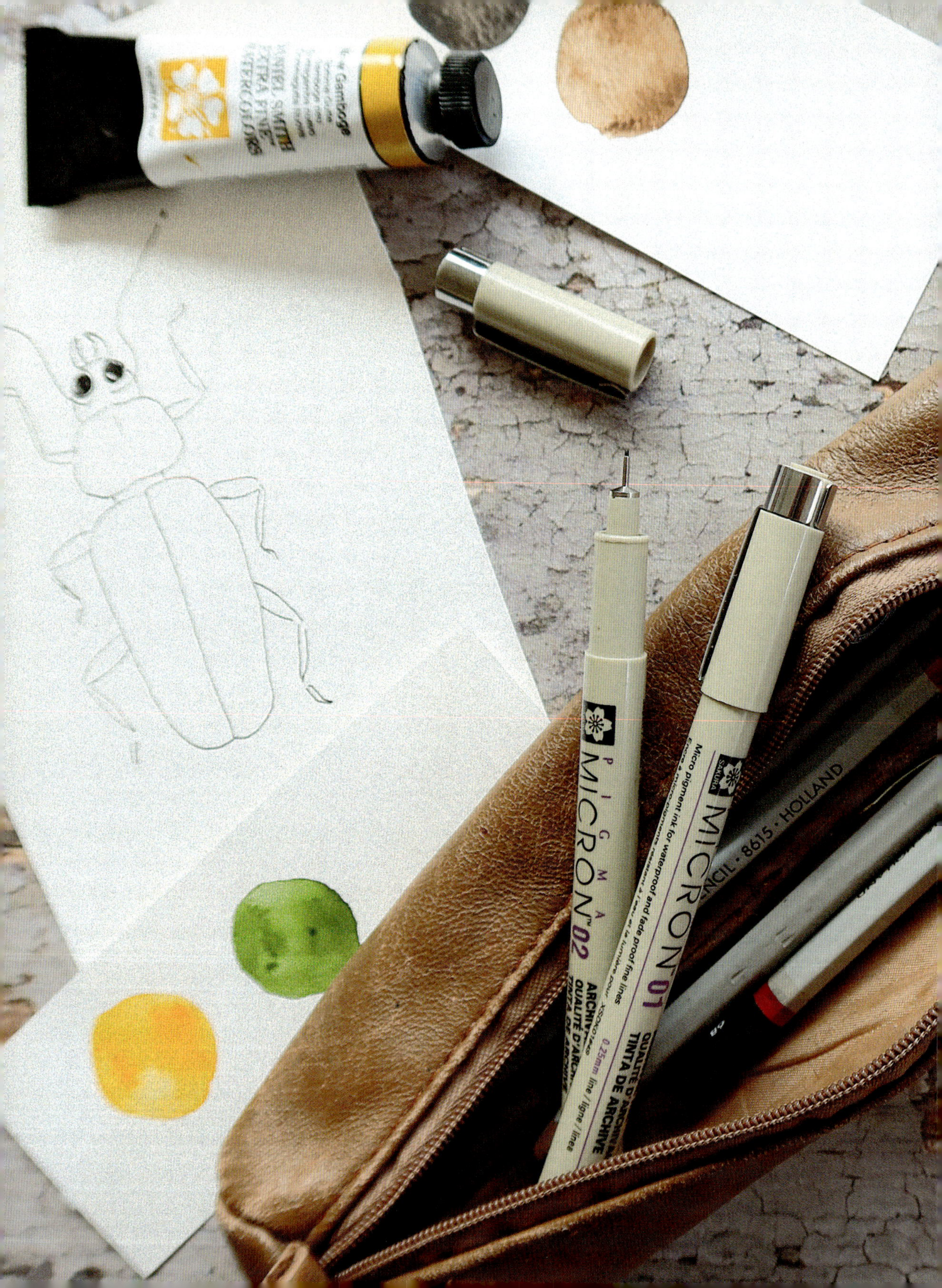

part I
fundamentals of watercolor & ink

In this first chapter, we will prepare for the upcoming projects. You will gather your supplies and learn a few watercolor and ink basics so you are all set to sketch like a pro.

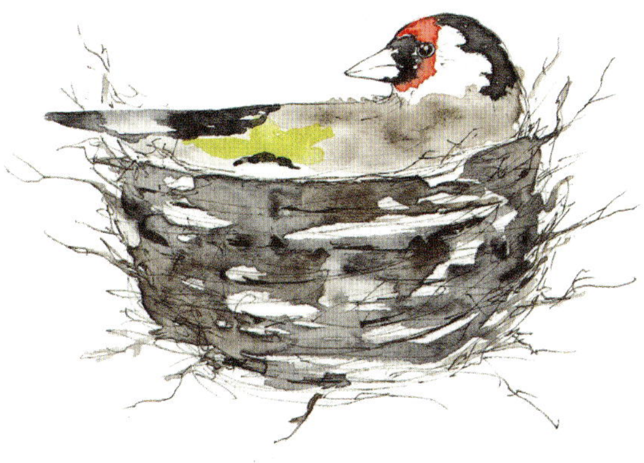

Supplies

Before we dive into all the techniques, I just want to make sure you have your supplies all set and ready. So here is an overview of what is used in the book. And by the way, one of the wonderful things about ink and wash is that you don't need much. You actually need so few things that you can easily gather them and drag them out in the garden to find real winged friends. ("When you finish the book, of course," the teacher says while looking over the top of her glasses.)

Fineliners

I love fineliners because they give the soft and playful watercolor a graphic edge with their crisp black line. Contrasts just work—on paper as well as in real life. In short, a fineliner is just a pen with a tip made of fibers or plastic that is filled with pigment-based ink. When you look for fineliners, make sure they are waterproof and lightfast so they don't fade in the sun over time. The brand is really not super important because they work similarly, but in this book, I use Pigma Micron® and Staedtler® Fineliners in sizes 005, 01 and 02.

Brushes

I only use four different brushes in this book, all round (sizes 1, 4, 7 and 9). I use fine-tip synthetic brushes from Betty Hayways® and Panart® for watercolor as well as gouache. I want you to treat your brushes like dear friends. (Tip: No one puts his friends headfirst into a jar of water. Just saying.)

Paint

To me, the most important supply is the paint. This is where you get color, texture and flow, so choose wisely. I use Daniel Smith® tube paints squeezed into pans to dry. And of course, you don't have to splurge on this brand, but look for paints with a nice amount of pigment, and it's always lovely if they granulate. I recently fell in love with the handmade paints from Art to Basic, and you can also look for Winsor & Newton® for a great starter paint.

I also use a tube of white gouache from Winsor & Newton. This is an opaque watercolor paint, which makes it perfect for white details on a dark surface. And by the way, if someone tells you that using gouache is cheating because the white in watercolor is supposed to be the white paper, tell them that the teacher says there is no such thing as cheating in art. Period!

Just like in my first book, I wanted to give you a list of the colors I use here in this book, along with some alternatives if you don't have the others in your stash (see the chart on the next page).

Paper

Sketches with few layers, like the ones we are doing, don't need too fancy a paper. I would go with something like a 300gsm (140lb) cold-press cellulose paper. The difference between hot-press and cold-press papers is mostly texture: Hot press is super smooth and cold press has a delicious texture. We use 300gsm (140lb) because it holds all the water you need; we use cold press because the texture is wonderful; and we use cellulose because you don't need more expensive cotton paper for these smaller sketches. Here in the book, I used Canson Montval® and constantly stuck to around size A5 for each illustration.

Colors I Use	Alternatives
Sap Green (warm earthy green)	Olive Green, or mix this shade by using a bright Hooker's Green with a bit of red
Green Gold (cool green)	Mix this by using a warm green and a bit of cool yellow
Hansa Yellow Light (cool yellow)	Lemon Yellow or Winsor Yellow
New Gamboge (warm yellow shade)	Cadmium Yellow Deep, Sunflower Yellow or other warm yellows
Quinacridone Sienna (warm earthy orange)	Burnt Sienna or Transparent Red Oxide
Quinacridone Rose (cool red)	Permanent Rose, Carmine or Rose Madder
Pyrrol Scarlet (warm red)	Vermilion or Perylene Scarlet
Dioxazine Violet (cool violet)	Mix this by using Phthalo Blue and slowly adding magenta until you get the shade you like
French Ultramarine (warm granulating blue)	Ultramarine Blue or Cobalt Blue
Phthalo Blue (cool blue)	Prussian Blue, Cyan Blue or Cerulean Blue
Prussian Blue (cool blue)	Winsor Blue or Ultramarine Blue
Neutral Tint (dark)	Lamp Black or other black watercolor
Payne's Gray (gray with a blue tint)	Mix this by using Ultramarine Blue and Burnt Sienna or by using a Lamp Black with a bit of blue
Van Dyke Brown (cool brown)	Mix this by using brown and a bit of Lamp Black
Burnt Umber (warm brown)	Sepia or Burnt Sienna
White Gouache	White gel pen

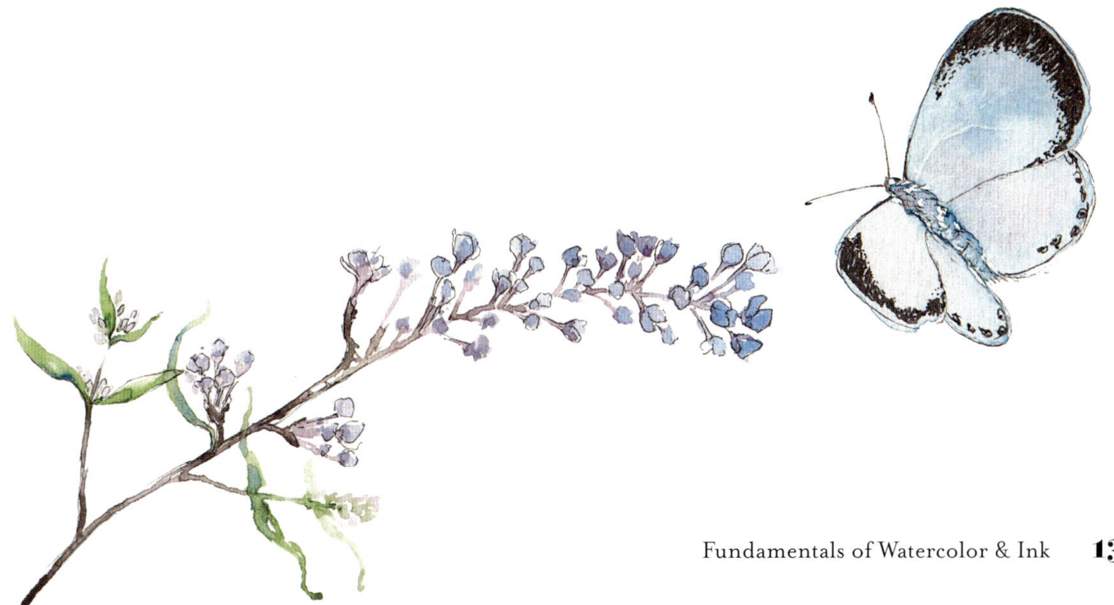

Pencil and Eraser

We use pencil in almost all the illustrations in the book to create guides to paint or ink afterwards. Choose a regular school pencil, which would be around HB or maybe up to a 2B in softness. I use the pencils from Bruynzeel® in this book. Don't push your pencil too hard, and it can be a good idea to not sharpen it too much. This helps avoid the risk of holes or grooves in the paper.

When searching for an eraser, you want to look for a regular soft rubber eraser. I use one from Staedtler and I love it. Just make sure that the watercolor and ink on the paper is completely dry before softly erasing lines to avoid the paper breaking. Sometimes the eraser can remove a bit of the ink. If you experience that, carefully redo the ink lines.

Other: Palette, Water, Cloth and Mist Spray Bottle

It's always nice to have a palette close by when going into a project—either for mixing or just for putting the color down to pour a bit of water in it. If you can get your hands on a ceramic palette, that's great, but a white ceramic plate from the kitchen will do just fine.

Then, of course, you want a jar of water. Make it a big one! We are working with dark and bright colors, so the water will quickly become muddy. Also, place it far away from your drinking cup so you don't accidentally drink it or dip your brush in your menthe tea. A pro tip is to place your painting water by your brush hand and your beverage to the other side. Take this advice from someone who knows the taste of painting water and who really prefers tea.

When working with water, it's always great to have something to dab your brush with. I always use a cotton cloth for this. If you don't have anything laying around, you can also just use a paper towel, but for the sake of the environment, I would go with something that does not have to be thrown out (like a kitchen cloth).

Finally, we are playing with something really fun when we get to sketching the Hummingbird (page 111): a small mist spray bottle! Yes, it is just as fun as it sounds! It mists water onto the paper so you get a nice, uneven surface of water droplets for the paint to play around in. Watching the process is almost like observing the paint go on an adventure, exploring droplet after droplet. It's so wonderfully satisfying.

Essential Watercolor Techniques

Wet-on-Dry

This might be the simplest of all the techniques, so we will start here. For wet-on-dry, you paint wet paint on dry paper. It's just like drawing with your brush, really. This is perfect for smaller details like beaks, feathers and so on. It can look a bit flat, but remember that as long as the paint is wet you can keep adding color (also called charging). That way, you can create color variation and even texture and blooms if you add paint that is wetter than the drying surface.

Wet-on-Wet

I am such a fangirl of the wet-on-wet technique. It gives so much character and movement. In this book, we mostly use wet-on-wet as the first layer. You wet an area with clean water and drip in the paints you like. Let the water do the work and sit back to enjoy the flow. I know you have to give up some control here but I promise it's all worth it.

Bridging Colors

Sometimes you want to have two bright colors next to each other without them mixing too much. That is where bridging comes in handy. You paint two areas of wet paint close to each other and make small bridges of clean water between the two areas. Then the paint will only mix where you make the bridges. I use this when painting birds with different colors that would not benefit for the colors to mix too much.

White Space

White space is the breathing space for your sketch. And you want to make sure to keep plenty of it. This helps define areas with feathers and texture; it shows highlights and emphasizes texture.

In your wet-on-wet washes you can do this by adding less paint in some of the wet areas, letting it naturally stay white or light. If you are doing wet-on-dry, you just don't paint in some areas. Super easy.

And if you accidently painted something that you want to keep white, take a damp brush or a kitchen towel and dab the paint you want to remove. Easy peasy.

Using Gouache

In this book, we use a bit of white gouache, which is a wonderful opaque watercolor. We use it especially for eyes and highlights on beaks to make sure we have the light we need. You just dip the tip of your brush in the paint and paint wet-on-dry. If you are uncomfortable with the brush, you can also use a white gel pen. It can look a bit harsh with a very bright white, so if you want to dim it down a bit just tap it softly with a finger while it's still wet. That way you can actually make it transparent like the rest of the sketch.

Wet-on-Dry

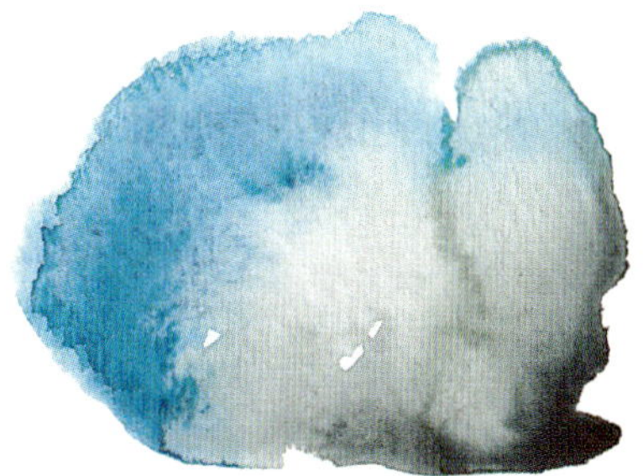

Wet-on-Wet

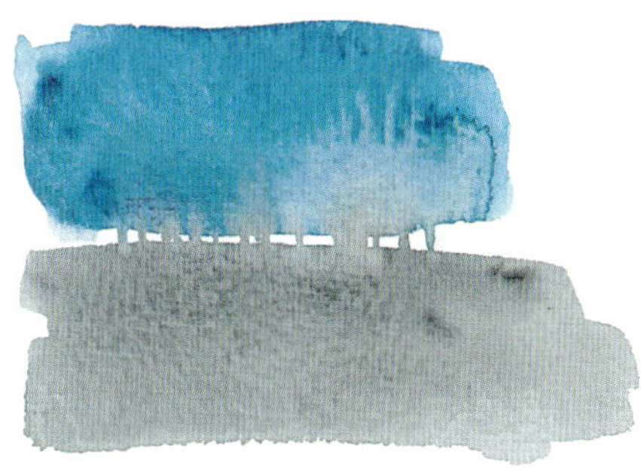

Bridging

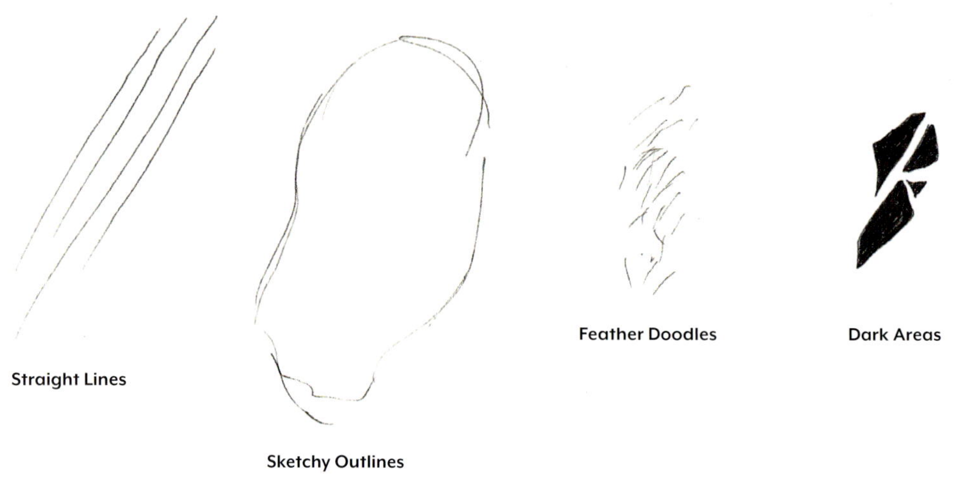

Straight Lines

Sketchy Outlines

Feather Doodles

Dark Areas

Basic Inking Techniques

Perfectly Imperfect Lines

When we are working with a loose style (like in this book) you have to set your mindset right. There is no such thing as perfection. And you really want to see the fast, sketchy imperfect lines as the closest you will get to perfection.

Keep your lines quick and light. Hold your fineliner loosely, and don't grab it too tightly. That way you get beautiful lines and don't risk straining your wrist.

Creating a Focal Point with the Fineliner

We want to guide people to the important part of our sketch. When it comes to animal sketches, that is usually the eye and face. When inking your focal point, you move your fineliner slower, making the lines more "perfect" and with more detail. Then when you move away from the face, you start becoming faster and looser. This way the increase in texture and variation in looseness will draw the viewer in.

Different Types of Line

A line is not just a line. It can do so many things. Here are a few ways we are going to use lines in the book.

- Straight lines (for example, long feathers)
- Sketchy outlines
- Feather doodles
- Dark areas (for example, spots on butterfly wings)

The Importance of Drying Times

When mixing watercolor, pencil and ink, there is of course a bit to say about drying times. You want to make sure the layers of either ink or watercolor are completely dry before proceeding to the next. This also applies when erasing pencil lines. Before removing any pencil lines, make sure that the ink is dry; when using watercolor first, wait for the paint to dry completely before adding ink and erasing any pencil lines.

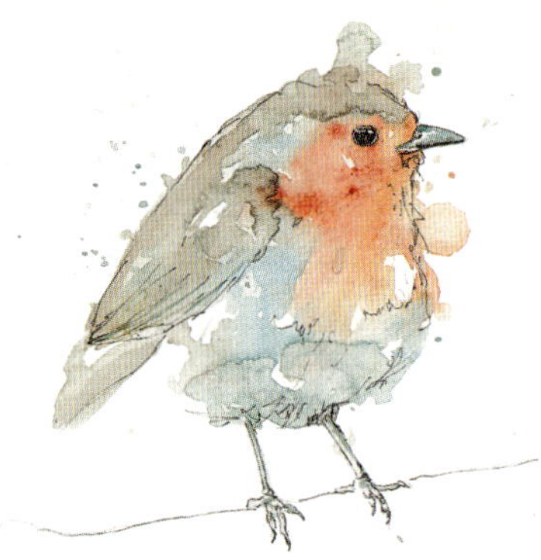

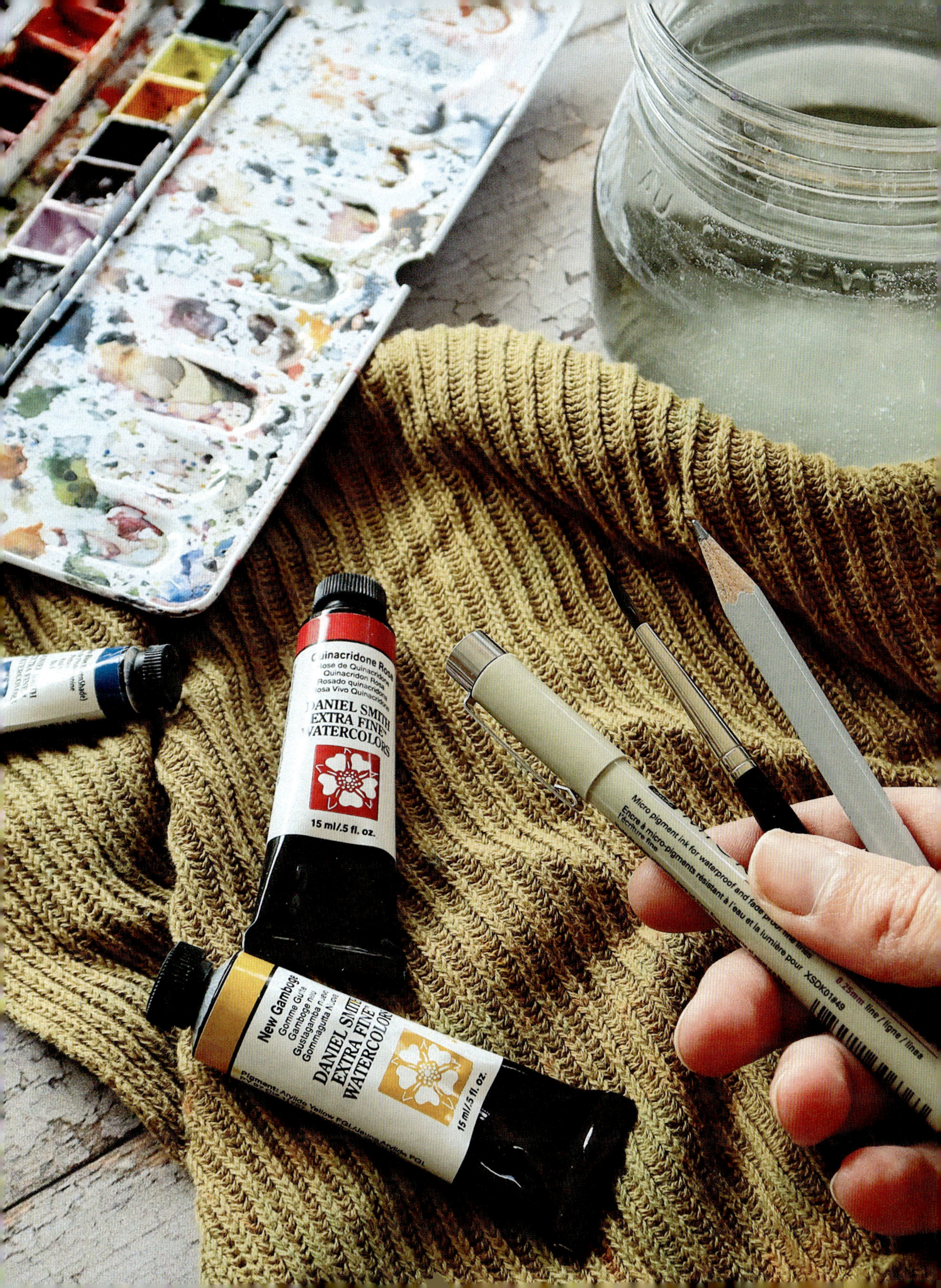

Quinacridone Rose
Rose de Quinacridone
Quinacridon Rosa
Rosado quinacridona
Rosa Vivo Quinacridona
DANIEL SMITH
EXTRA FINE
WATERCOLORS
15 ml/.5 fl. oz.
New Gamboge
Gomme Gutte
Gustagamba Pu
Gomaguta N.
DANIEL SMITH
EXTRA FINE
WATERCOLORS
15 ml/.5 fl. oz.
Micro pigment ink for waterproof and fade
Encre à micro-pigments résistant à l'eau et à la lumière pour
l'écriture fine
0.25mm line / ligne / linea
XSDK01849

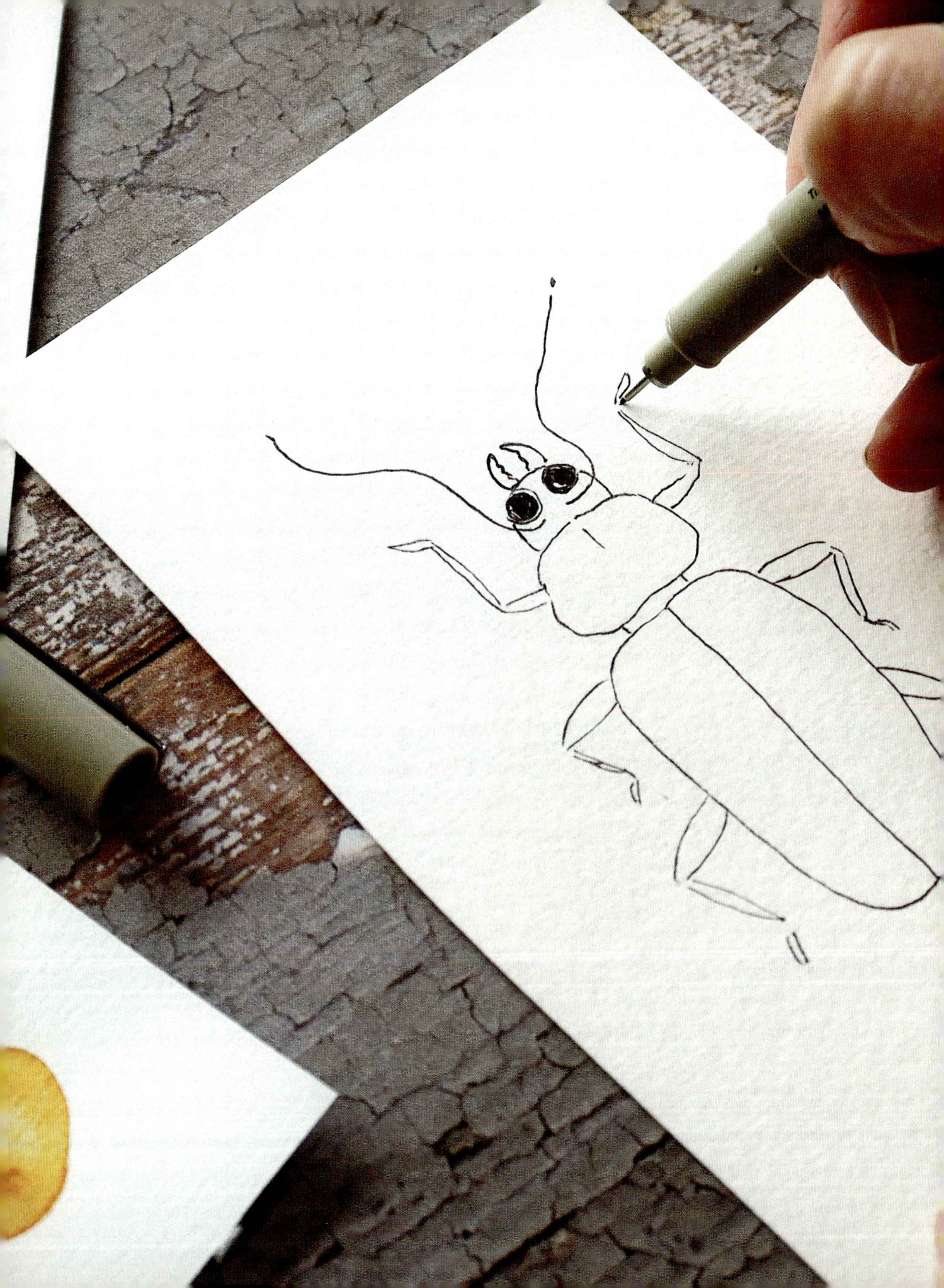

part II
sketching wildlife

Animals can be a bit scary to sketch. That might be because there is very little room for error, especially when it comes to facial features. The animal quickly looks goofy, tired or even drunk. So, to take away some of that fear, I am throwing on my professor hat and sharing a small anatomy class with you. And then you can practice some of the more challenging parts like the eye, beak and feet to get more familiar with them.

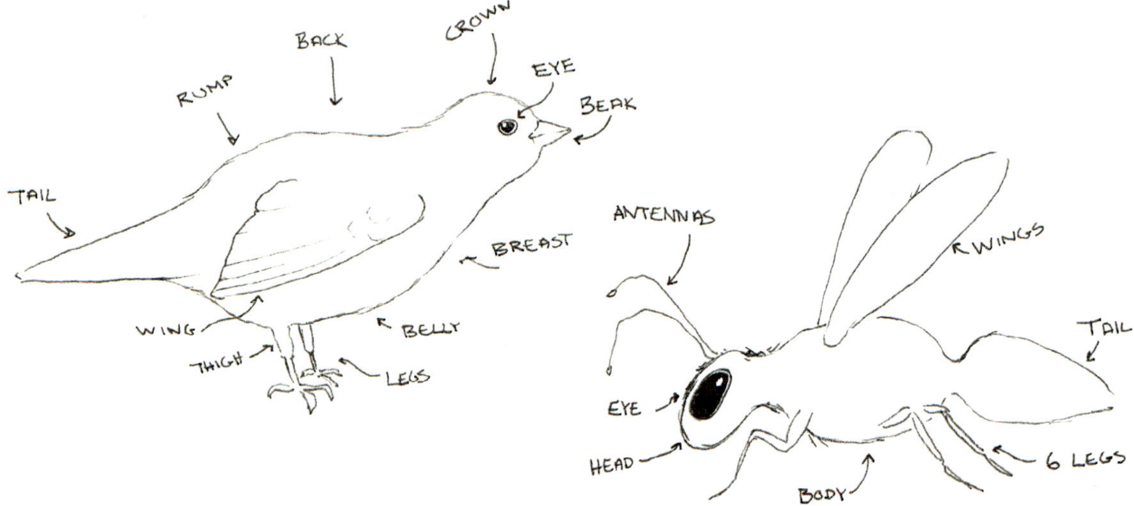

Anatomy of Winged Wildlife

There is, of course, a lot of science as to how birds and other winged lovelies are built. And don't worry, I won't go into detail. But I think we need to review a few of the terms so you know what I'm talking about in the step-by-steps. So here, I've included a few drawings with some of the most important features. I just want to put a big disclaimer here: Since I am not a scientist, I stayed away from the Latin names and used names that are easier to remember.

Birds

First, we have the head of the bird. Here you have the eyes and the beak, and the top of the head is called the crown (yes, very royal indeed).

The body of a bird is made of the breast and belly. On the top of the birdie, we have its back that ends in a cute little rump and continues into a tail. Then of course, we have the wing and the feet. Sometimes the legs look like they are wearing shorts—that is not a fashion statement, but called the thigh.

Insects

A lot of bugs are actually very similar and only differ a bit between species.

In general, you can say that an insect's body is divided into three pieces: the head, the body and the tail. The head holds the antennas, eyes and mouthparts. Many insects have wings.

Insects all have six legs attached to the body. And those legs are divided into two parts and a foot, which means they have knees that bend around the middle.

Butterflies

The head of a butterfly has long antennas, big eyes and palps. The body is covered in fur, making it look very soft up close. Then of course, it has two wings with some kind of pattern. The wing patterns are made out of veins and cells. The bottom wing can, in some cases, be all dressed up like the Swallowtail (page 143) to have a small tail as well.

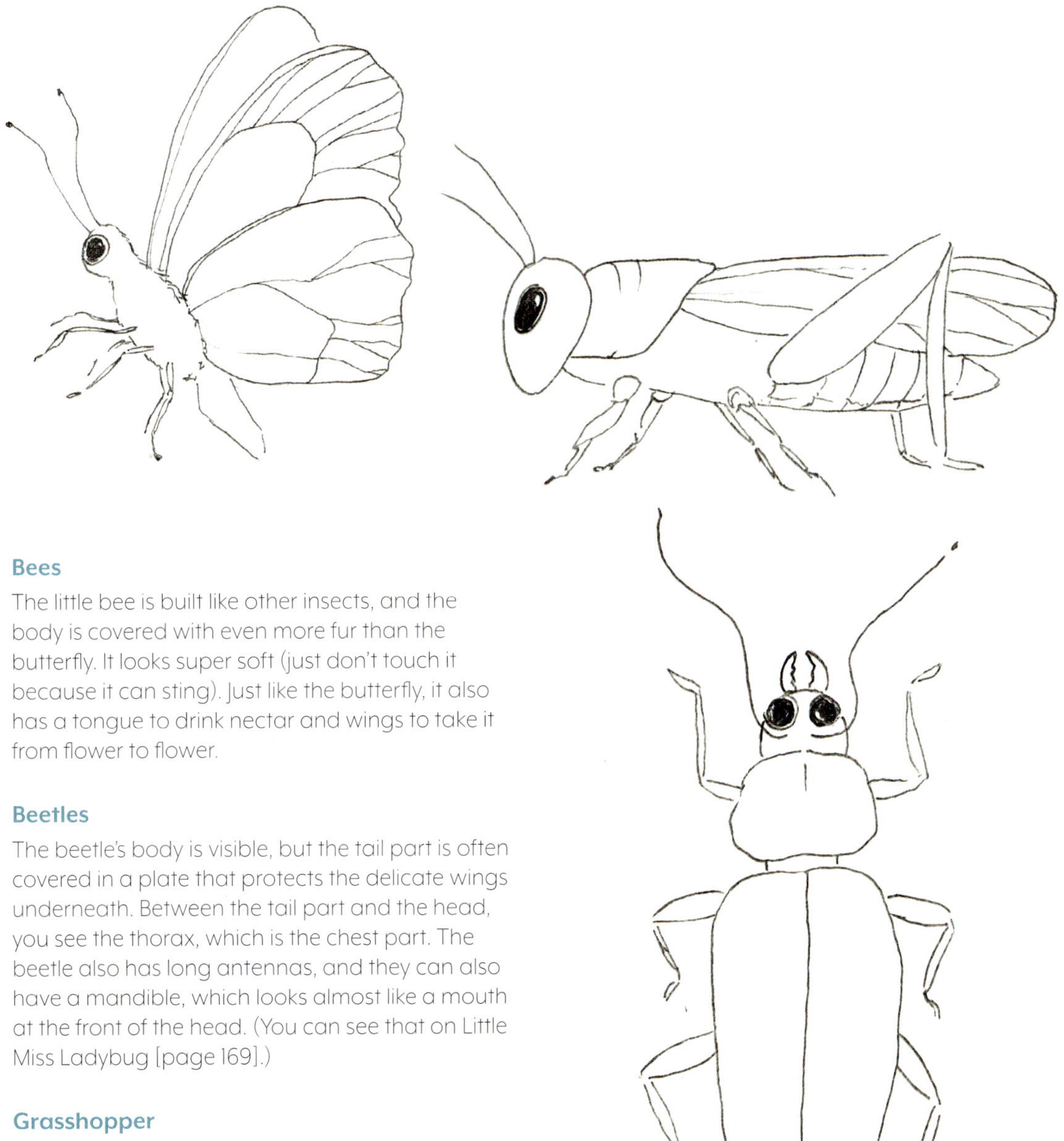

Bees

The little bee is built like other insects, and the body is covered with even more fur than the butterfly. It looks super soft (just don't touch it because it can sting). Just like the butterfly, it also has a tongue to drink nectar and wings to take it from flower to flower.

Beetles

The beetle's body is visible, but the tail part is often covered in a plate that protects the delicate wings underneath. Between the tail part and the head, you see the thorax, which is the chest part. The beetle also has long antennas, and they can also have a mandible, which looks almost like a mouth at the front of the head. (You can see that on Little Miss Ladybug [page 169].)

Grasshopper

The grasshopper is kind of on its own. A lot of the body is covered in armor, but what really sets it apart is the jumping legs. You will learn to sketch them on page 159.

A Few Sketching Tips for Our Birdie Friends

Here are a few things you can practice before diving in or if you just want to build your skills. As a warm-up before the step-by-steps, I recommend drawing a few eyes and legs. It's super fun, and you can get really good quickly when you focus on just one thing.

How to Draw Eyes

To sketch the eye on a bird, draw a circle. Then make a small circle on the side of the eye for a highlight. Fill in the area inside, leaving a white border between the first circle and the dark area. If you lose some of the highlight, use white gouache to paint it with a thin brush. (This process works for bugs as well.)

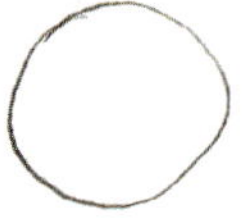 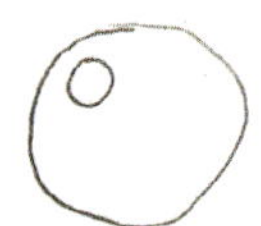 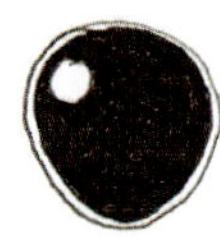

How to Draw a Beak

The beaks you see in this book can be divided into two categories: small and big. Some are narrow, some are wide and some are super long like for the Hummingbird (page 111). (Yes, I know it's like listening to a regular scientist here.)

Beak Seen from the Side

Draw the outline and then a line in the middle showing the upper and lower parts. Then you can add paint. Keep a white highlight at the top of the beak.

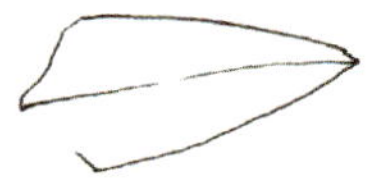 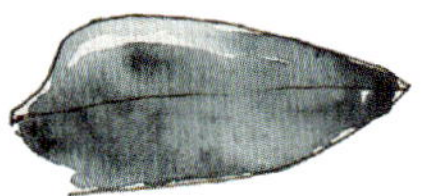

Beak Seen from the Front

The beak can have lots of different shapes. They can appear almost like a square with bended lines and round edges. Or like with the Blackbird (page 69), rounded at the top and almost like a bell. When seen from the front, the top part of the beak is most of what you see. The bottom part is barely visble below.

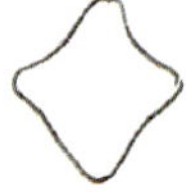 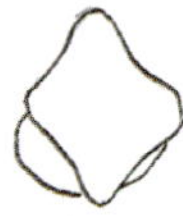 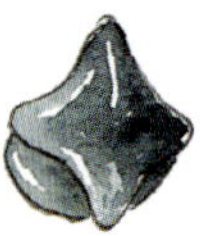

How to Draw Bird Feet

There is a lot of character in a bird's leg and foot. The leg starts at the body and is sometimes covered in a small, feathery thigh, and then it is very straight all the way down to the foot. The foot has three toes pointing forward and one pointing back. Each toe has a claw to hang on to stuff. When drawing a bird foot, you want to think about texture. The foot is often very wrinkled, especially where there are bends. You can create these wrinkles with a few lines across the toes and leg.

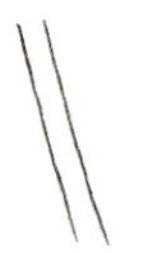 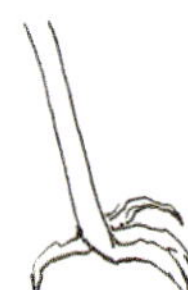 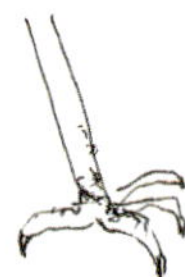

Making the Animal the Star of the Show

If your sketch is centered around an animal, you really want to keep in mind how to make that animal shine. Even Beyoncé would have a hard time shining if she was tucked in a crowd with a bunch of look-alikes.

When composing a sketch with an animal, you can do it in two ways. Well, tons of ways really, but let's keep it simple. You can sketch the animal alone on the page or with embellishments like flowers, bird feeders or more birds.

Shine Like a Diamond

When you put your birdie alone on the page, all of the focus is on it. And that's great. You can really explore the detail, colors and mood of the bird. You put the bird up on a pedestal. When you do this, I want to encourage you to add just a tiny bit of environment. Maybe it's a bit of earth or something else that will ground it on the paper. But other than that, you've got it!

In Its Right Environment

You can also decide to tell an entire story just by adding context. It can be a hungry bird resting at a bird feeder, or it can be a raven chilling out on the ground amongst the blooms.

Don't be scared to add environment. It's incredible! But make sure it stays cohesive and toned down; use it strategically to guide the viewer to the focal point.

Keep the Colors Cohesive

Let some of the colors from the animal shine through in the surroundings as well. It does not have to be all the colors; just a few will make it a cohesive color scheme. So, if you are using Van Dyke brown in the bird, you can also use it in the surroundings on a branch, a rock or on a picket fence. You can also let a color from a flower shine onto the animal. For example, the pink flower shining onto the wings of the Swallowtail (page 143).

Be Strategic about the Composition

You can use the environment to build a strong composition and strategically lead the viewer's eye towards the bird. Create the most detail and contrast on the animal. Then, when you move away from the star and into the surrounding background, you can slowly let the detail level decrease as you go farther towards the edge.

And that smoothly leads us to the next chapter, which is all about some of the beautiful things surrounding the animals in the garden.

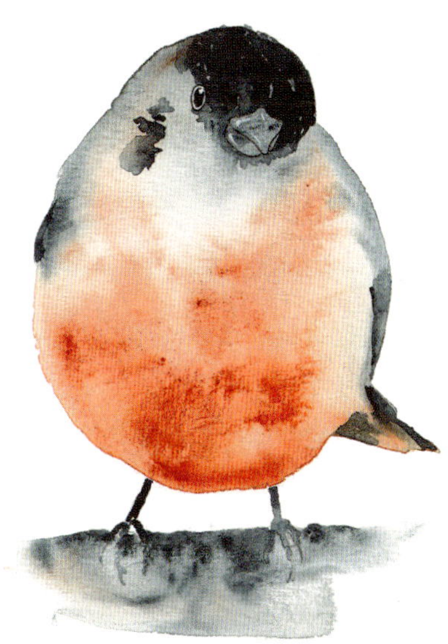

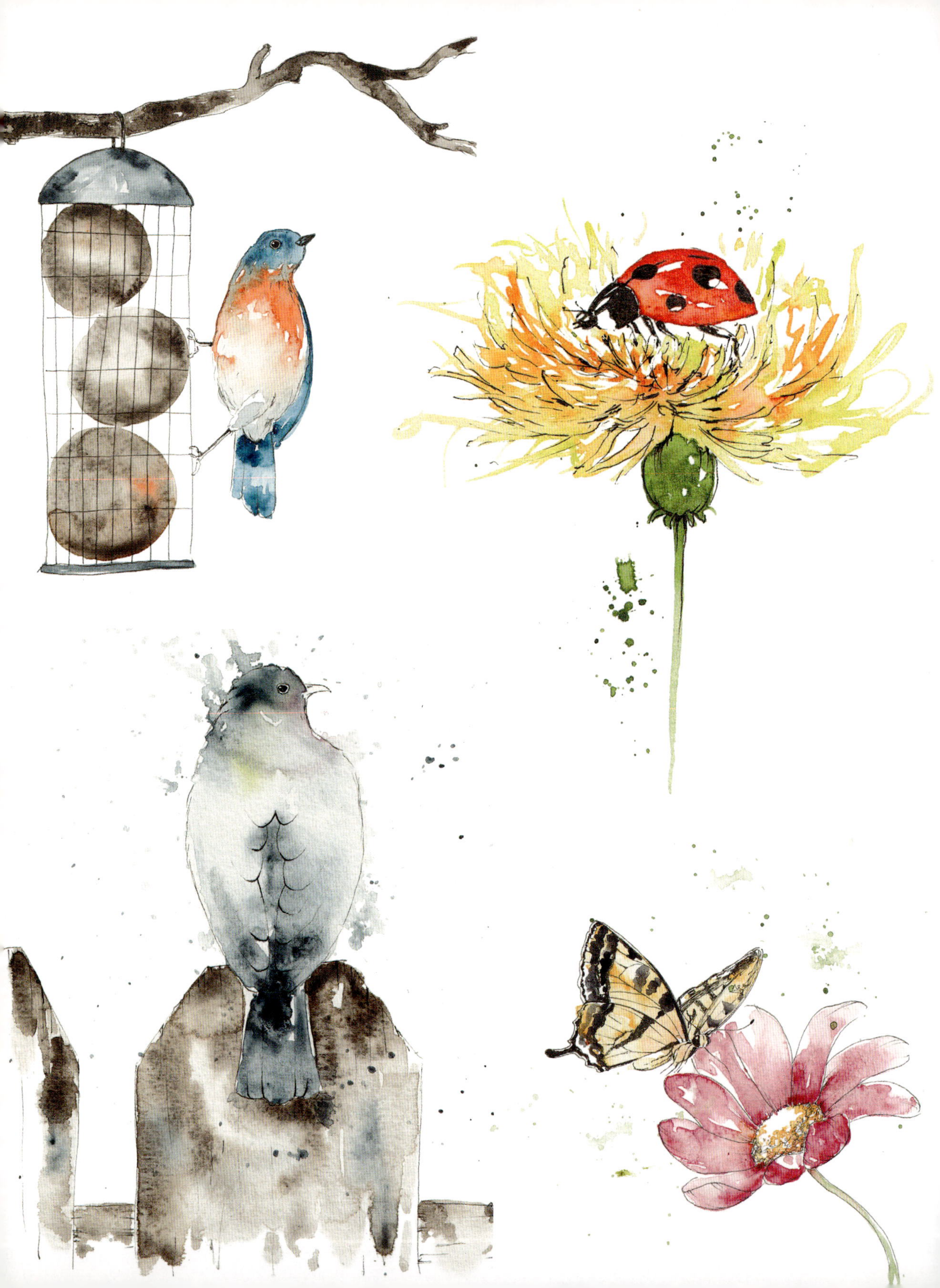

part III
composition embellishments

We are going to start off nice and easy, because here we will cover a few of those things you can use to surround your winged friends: their hangout places, favorite blooms and more. These are not meant to be full projects, but more like mini projects to accompany the birds and insects later on. You will see that these projects will be used throughout the book and vary in a lot of ways, so never think there is just one way of doing it. Just like with your favorite outfits, it's all up to you to mix and match.

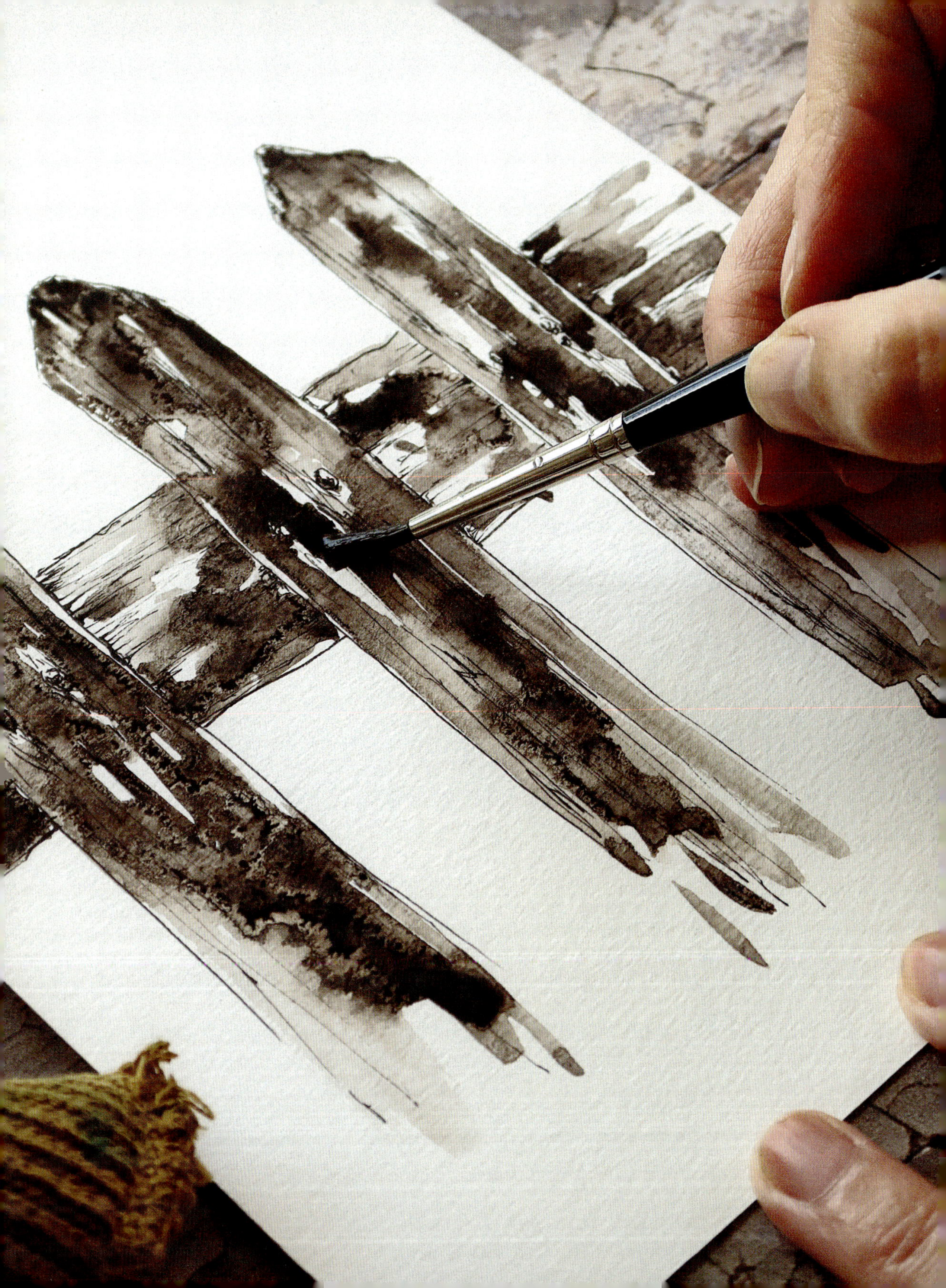

picket fence

It can be hard to find a garden without some kind of fence to keep out animals (Yes deer, I am looking at you!), surround flowerbeds or just be super pretty. And birdies love to rest on them. It's a hangout place almost as popular as the town square in the middle of summer. This is also a super-easy project with just one color, so it's a great starting point as well as a wonderful way to let your birdies and flowers shine.

Materials

Pencil and eraser
Paper: Canson Montval 300gsm (140lb) cold press
Fineliners: sizes 01, 005 and 02
Watercolor brush: size 7
Water and cloth
Palette

Color

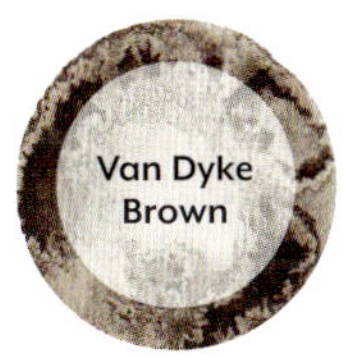

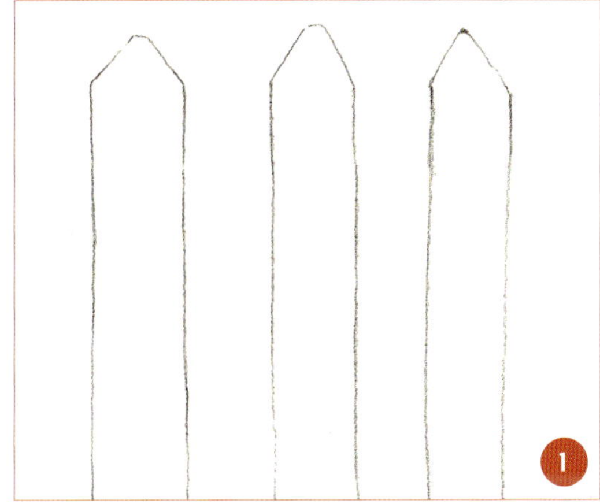

Step 1: Let's start out easy by grabbing your pencil and drawing the boards that point upwards. Shape them almost like a pencil with a flat tip at the end.

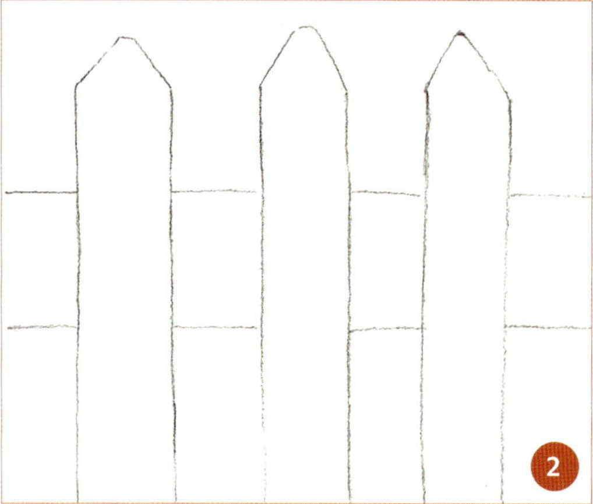

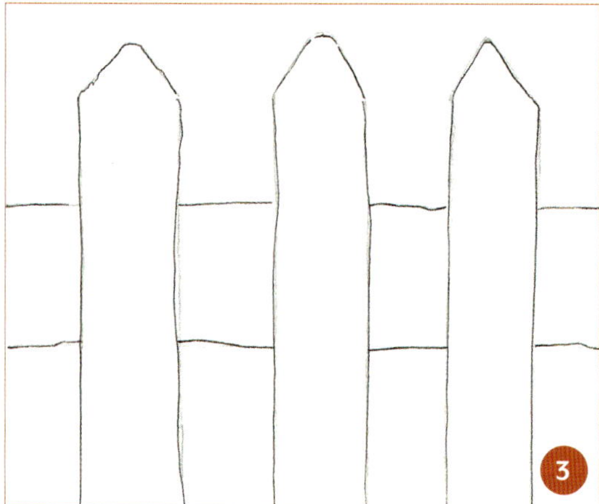

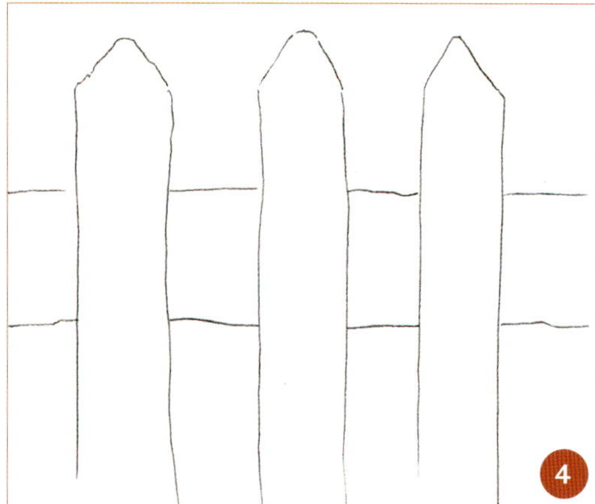

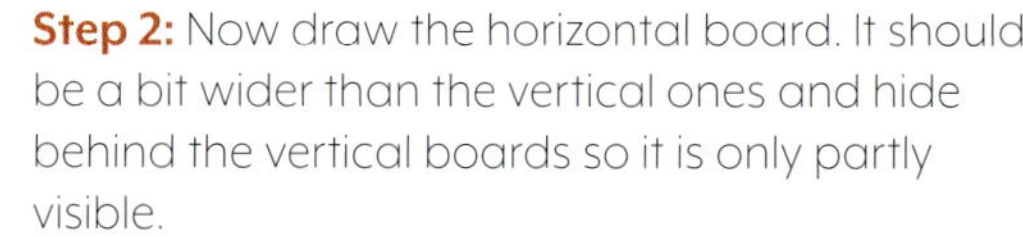

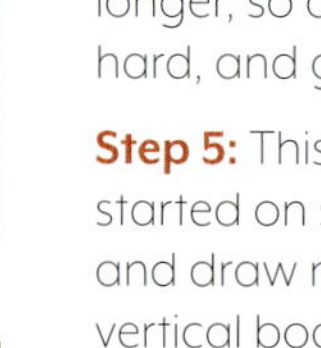

Step 2: Now draw the horizontal board. It should be a bit wider than the vertical ones and hide behind the vertical boards so it is only partly visible.

Step 3: Now, for the first time in this book, take your 01 fineliner and draw a rough outline on the boards. Keep it fast, and make the lines uneven—just like old wood.

Step 4: You don't need your pencil guidelines any longer, so carefully erase them. Don't push too hard, and go slowly so you don't break the paper.

Step 5: This still looks a bit unfinished, so let's get started on some details. Take the 005 fineliner and draw nails: two small, uneven ovals on each vertical board where it meets the horizontal one.

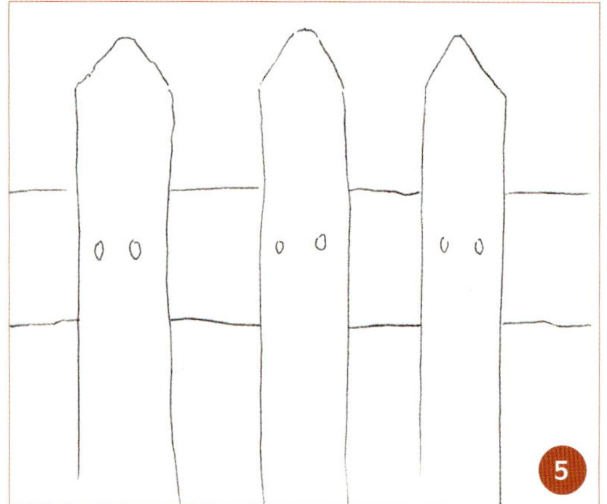

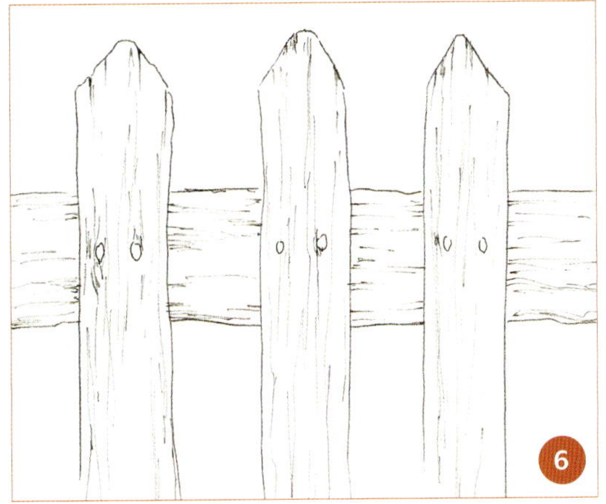

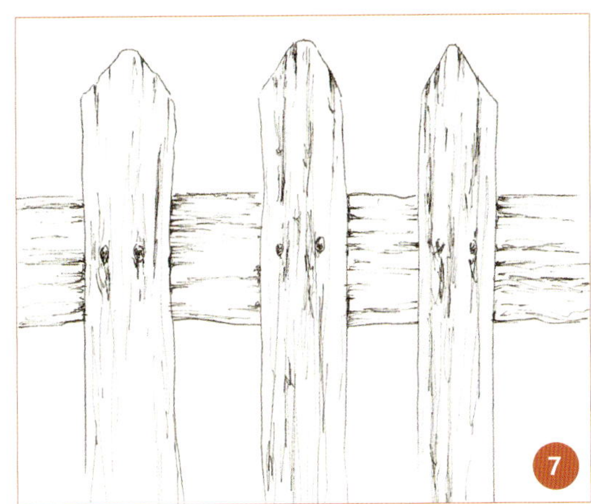

Step 6: Now the fun begins! Keep the 005 fineliner in your hand and start creating the texture of the aged wood. Vary the line length and follow the direction of the boards while moving around the nails. Move your hand fast to avoid overworking this step. At the top of the vertical boards, you can add a few cracks for even more character.

Step 7: Finally, finish the texture with a 02 fineliner to give a few darker details. Add a bit of darkness to the nails at the bottom of the ovals. Draw darker spots where you want the wood to have uneven cracks. At the end, add a few dark lines to the horizontal board where there might be shadow from the vertical ones.

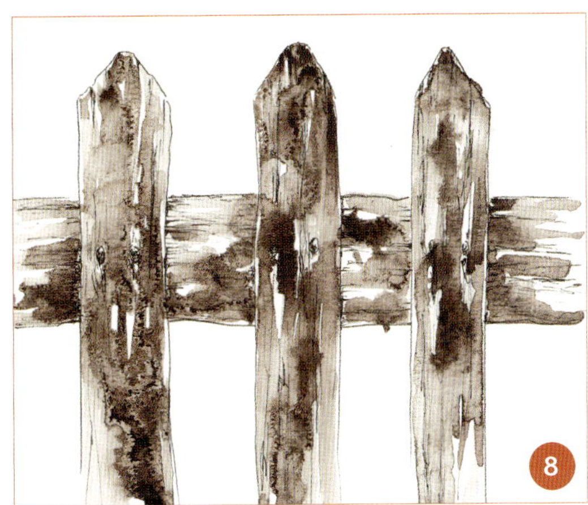

Step 8: When you are happy with your sketch, grab the size 7 brush and dip it in Van Dyke brown. Paint the boards wet-on-dry with plenty of white space. While it's wet, you can drip in clean water for more texture and charge the color with more paint to make the colors darker and more varied.

And that is it! Birds are now welcome to land and chill on this beautiful resting place. Use this sweet picket fence for the Blackbird on page 69 and the Pigeon on page 115.

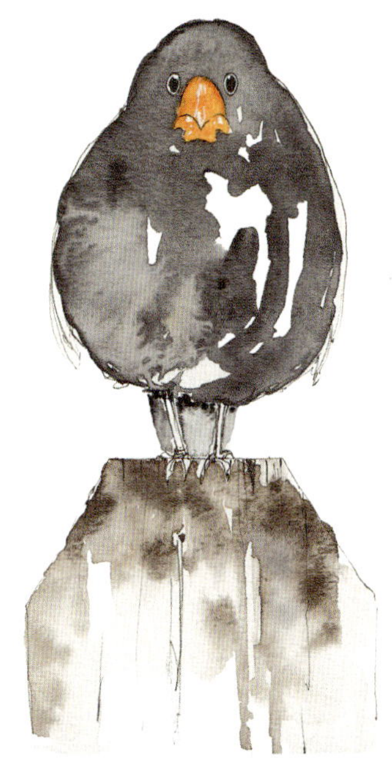

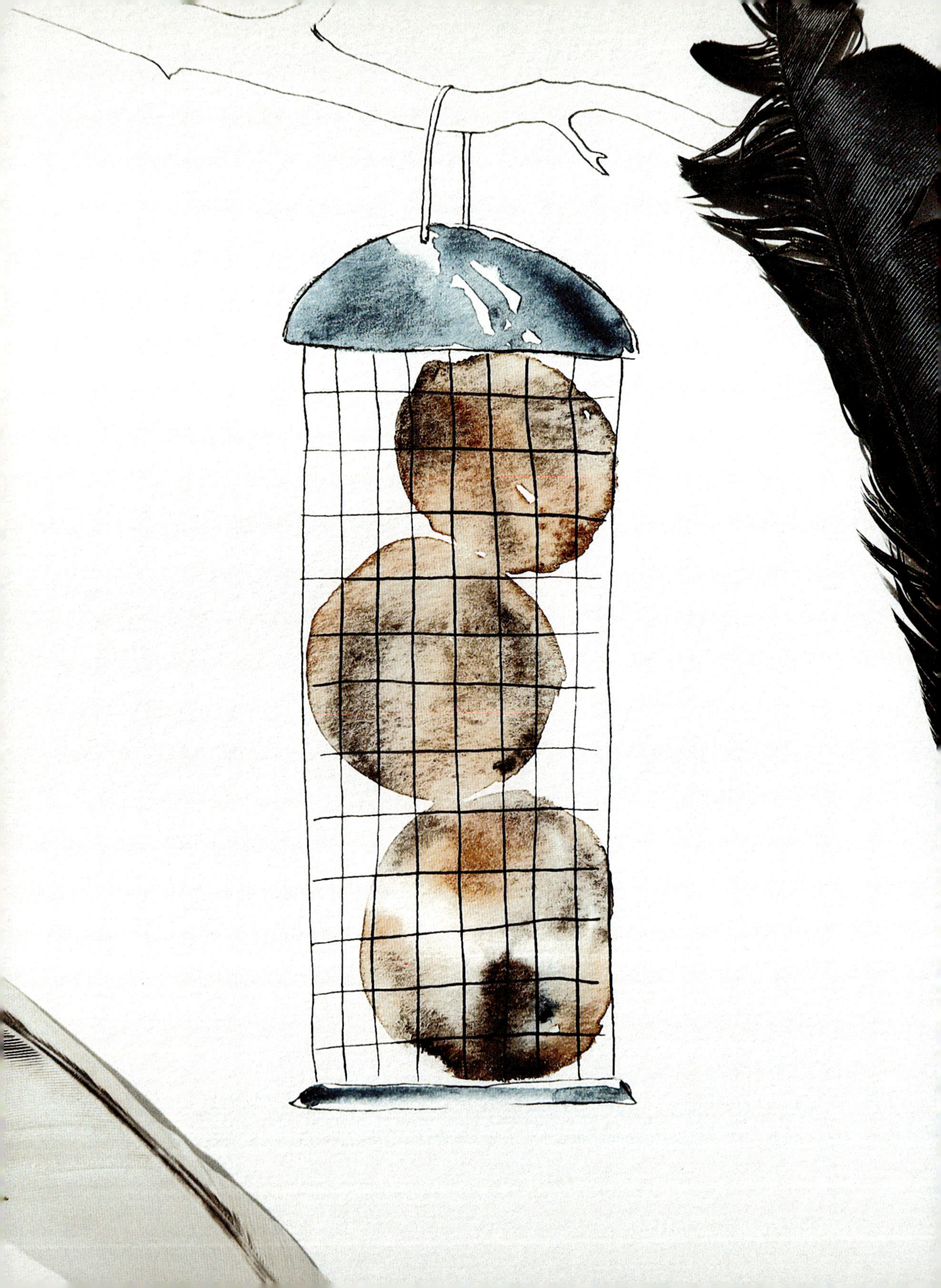

bird feeder

When the weather becomes cooler, we always hang out bird feeders in the apple tree in our garden. We can see it from the kitchen and it adds so much pleasure to our day. Suddenly the garden is not just winter-gray but filled with birds of all colors and shapes gathering to eat. I can't help but think of the feeders as a kind of birdie café, where they hang out, chat and eat. In this feeder, I have placed fat balls because we do that here in Denmark, but you can put whatever you like into the feeder. As an example, you could also fill it with seeds and then use the exact same method as I've shown here, but instead of big circles, make a lot of small ovals. You are fine as long as you keep the food behind the net.

Materials

Pencil and eraser

Paper: Canson Montval 300gsm (140lb) cold press

Watercolor brush: size 9

Water and cloth

Palette

Fineliner: size 01

Colors

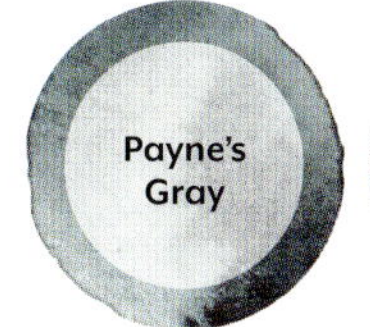

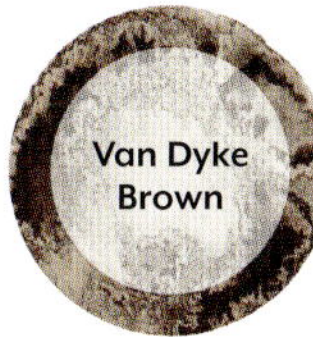

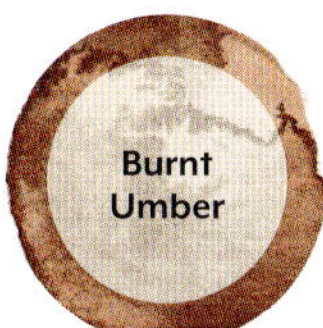

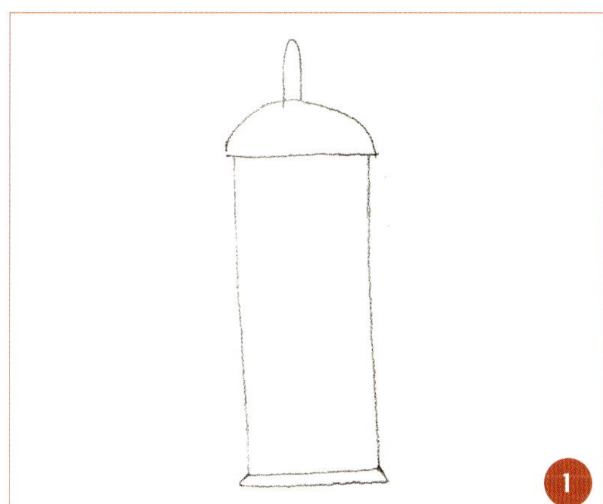

Step 1: Let's start with a pencil guide. Draw a high rectangle with a half circle as a hat and a flat foot. Draw a half oval on top where the line on the left is a bit longer than the right one crossing into the hat. This will be the string that holds the feeder.

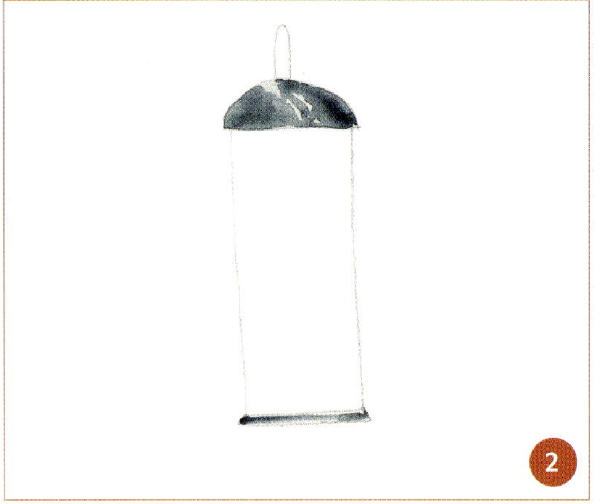

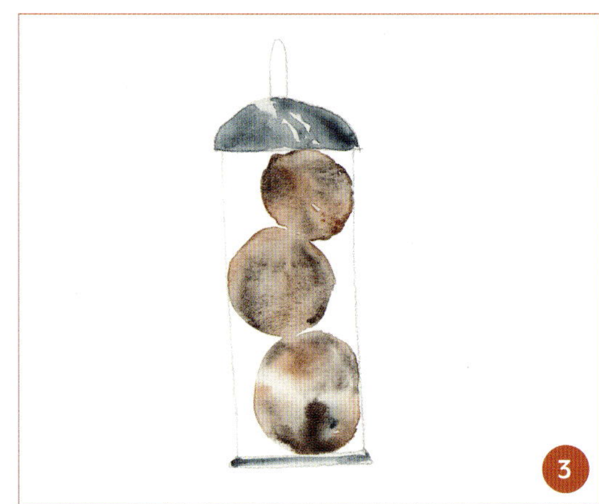

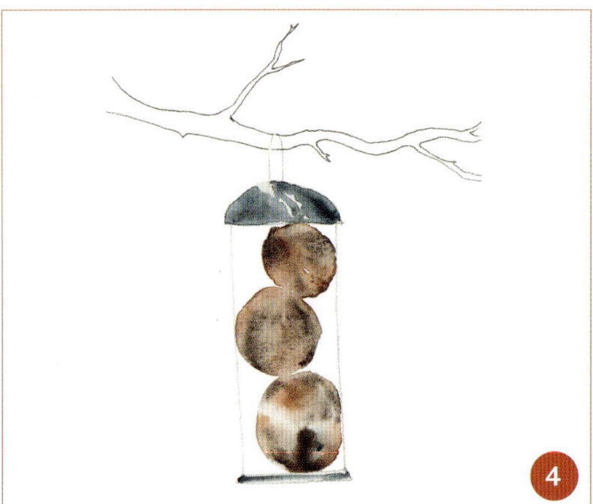

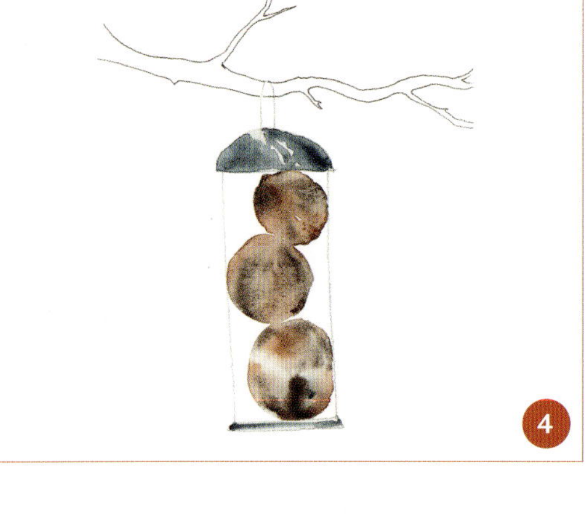

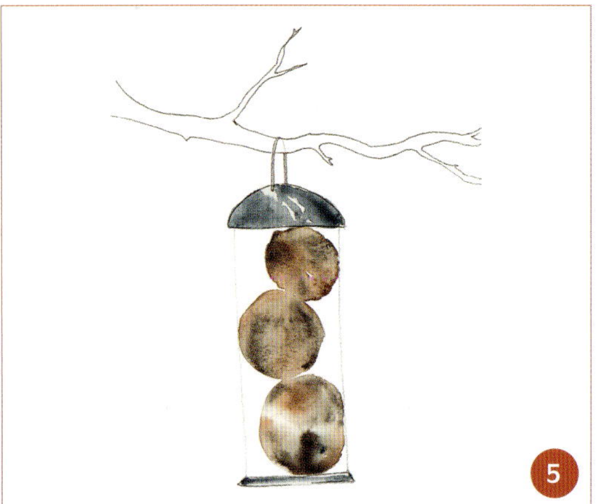

Step 2: Using the size 9 brush, paint the hat and foot wet-on-dry using Payne's gray. Make sure to keep white space in the direction of the curved surface to give an illusion of shiny metal.

Step 3: When the hat and foot are dry, paint the three fat balls using the same brush. Start by painting three circles in clean water on top of each other, keeping them within the pencil guide. A small tip: If you can't see where you placed the water, tilt your head a bit to see the shine. Drip the Van Dyke brown and burnt Umber into the water and let the paint mingle naturally.

Step 4: Draw a branch using the 01 fineliner. For more details on sketching branches, see Simple Branch on page 35. Make sure not to draw over the long line of the oval on the top of the hat.

Step 5: Draw the string that holds up the bird feeder with the fineliner. Draw the left side all the way across the branch and the right side hiding behind the branch. Draw the outline of the hat and foot.

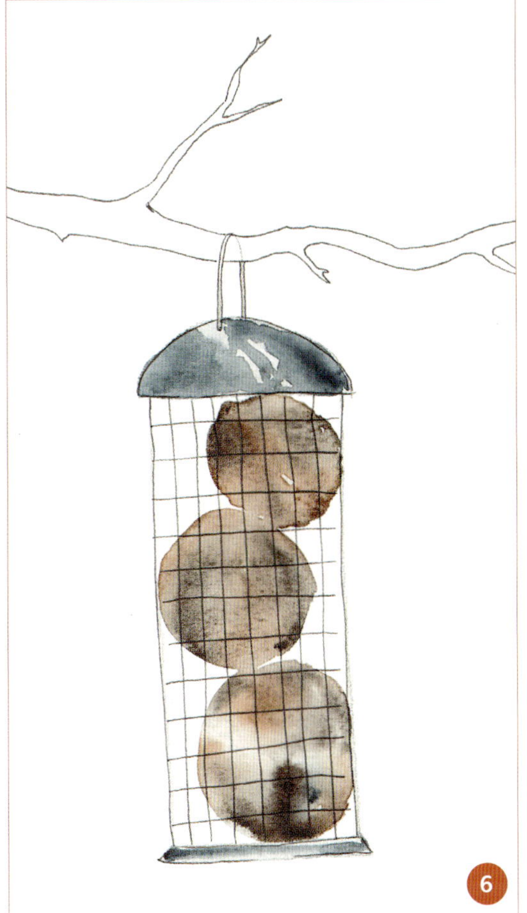

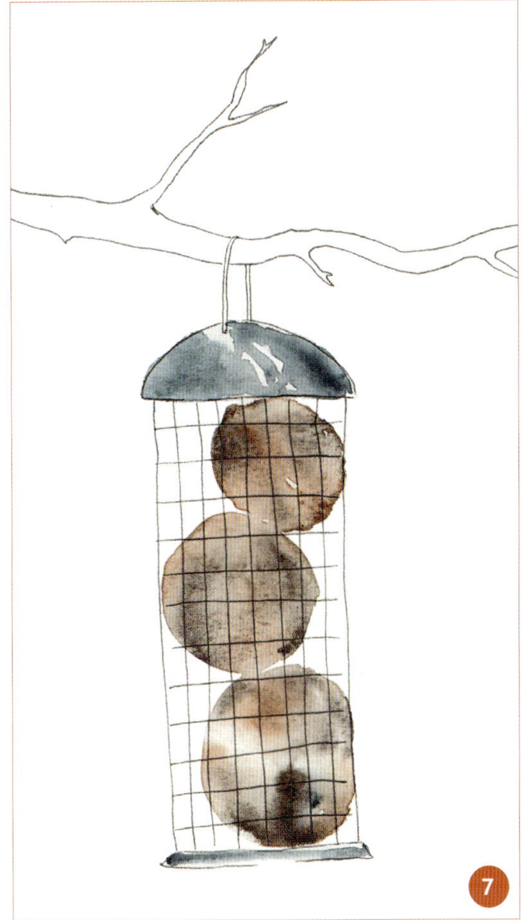

Step 6: With the fineliner, draw a grid using the pencil rectangle you drew in step 1 as a guideline. Start with the lines going vertical, and then draw the horizontal ones. You can vary this pattern however you like, but keep it fast and sketchy so you don't strain your wrist or overwork it.

Step 7: Finally, you can erase the pencil lines, and the bird feeder is now ready for the flocks of hungry birds. Well done you for feeding the birds!

Turn to page 95 or 119 if you'd like to try out this birdie restaurant with two of the birds in book. On page 95, you will find the Bluebird feeding while looking for his friends, and on page 119, you can paint the flying House Sparrow.

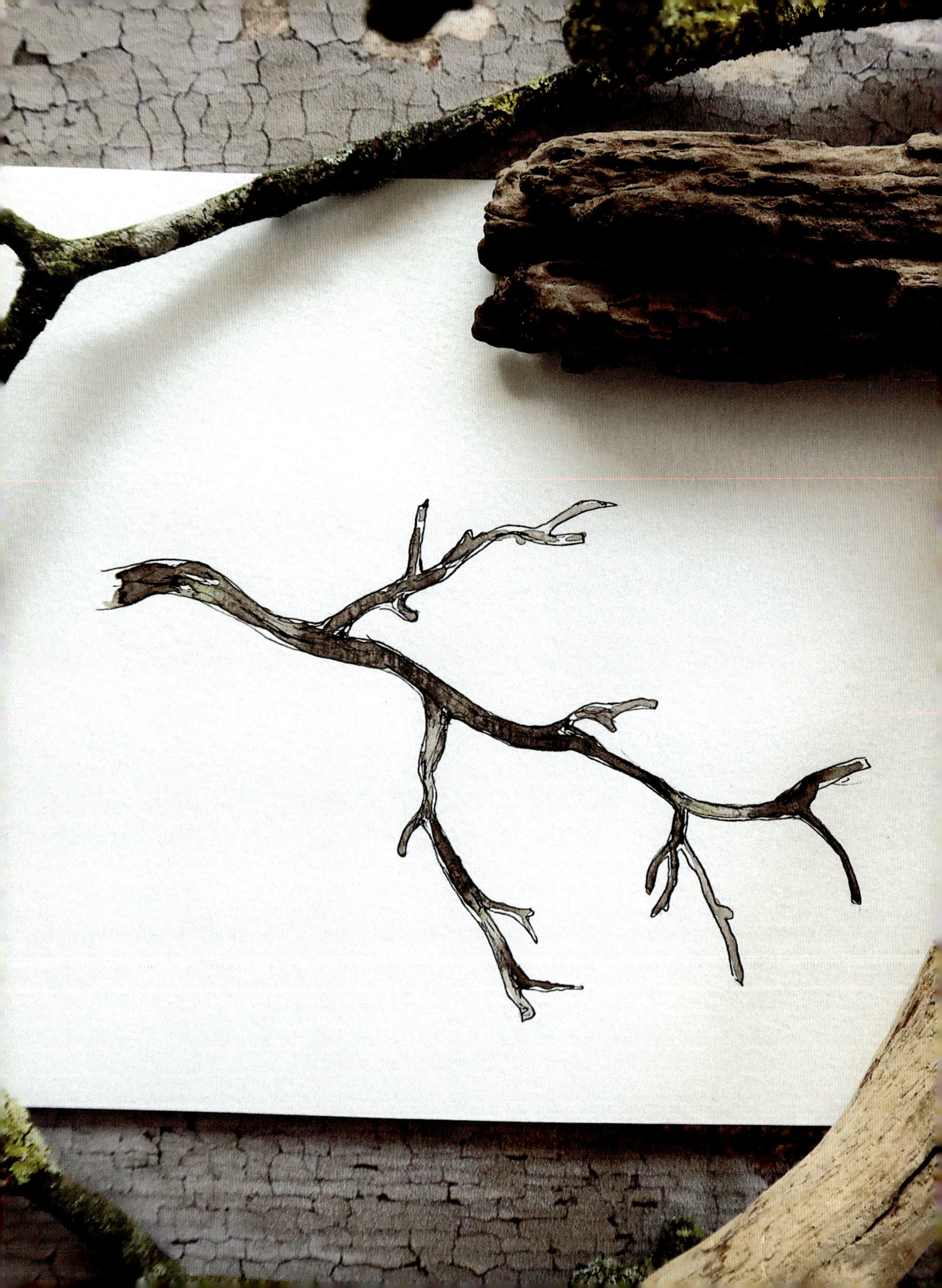

simple branch

Whereas fences and bird feeders are hangout places for our winged friends, trees and branches are their homes. This is where they build their nests and have friends over for a worm or two. Here you'll learn how to create a very simple branch as well as how to vary them depending on the type of tree you are drawing.

Materials

Pencil and eraser
Paper: Canson Montval 300gsm (140lb) cold press
Fineliners: sizes 01, 005 and 02
Watercolor brush: size 4
Water and cloth
Palette

Colors

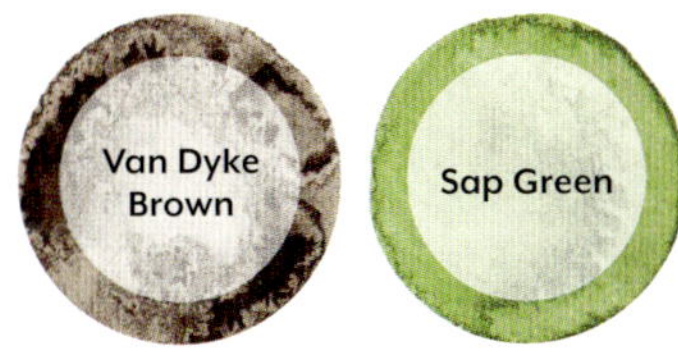

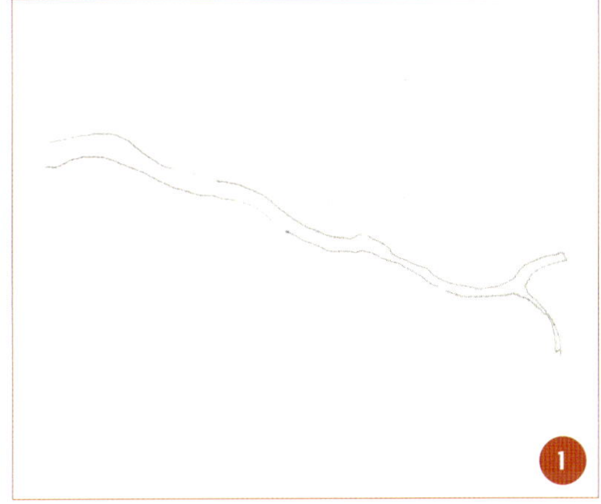

Step 1: A branch very often consists of a thick main branch and a bunch of thinner side branches. Sketch the main branch with pencil first. Leave small gaps in the line where you want to add side branches.

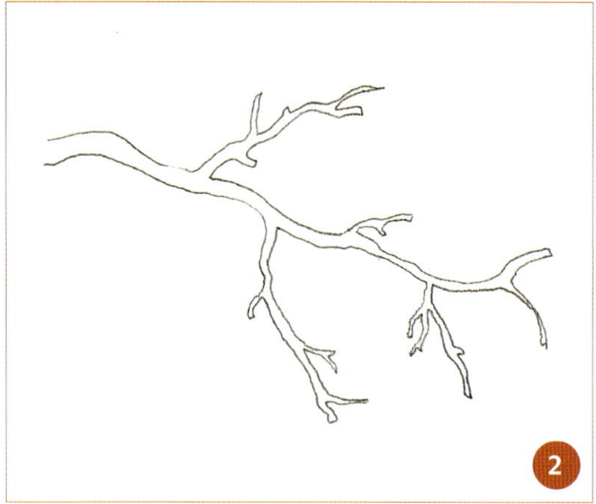

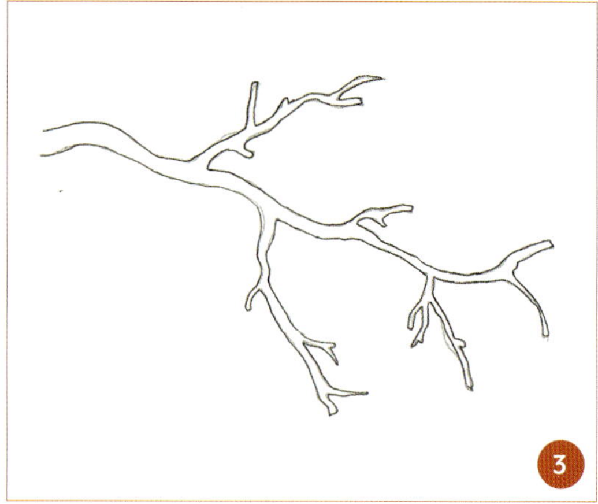

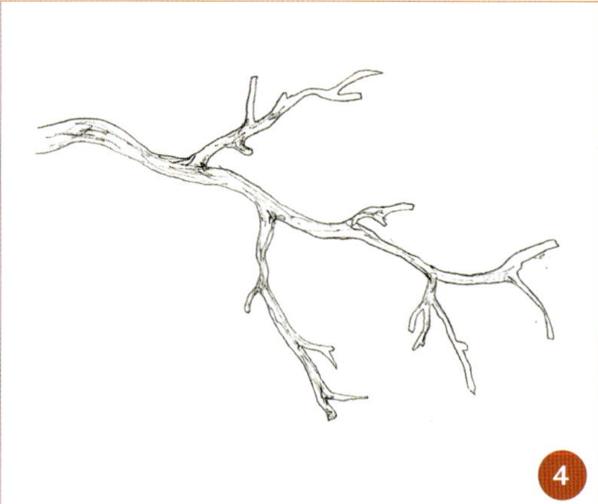

Step 2: Draw the side branches. Make some small and some bigger with even more side branches. You can see how you can just keep adding more and more. Let some of the branches end in a point and keep some a bit flatter.

Step 3: Now it's time to sketch a rough outline with your trusty 01 fineliner. Keep it fast and make sure that the main branch still has the most thickness and the smaller ones are thinner and getting even narrower towards the end. When you are happy, you can erase the pencil lines. If you accidentally remove some of the dark lines, go over them again with the fineliner afterward.

Step 4: Get your 005 fineliner and start giving your branch some texture with quick lines of varying lengths. Some should be straight in the direction of the branch, and some should crisscross and follow the curve of the branches.

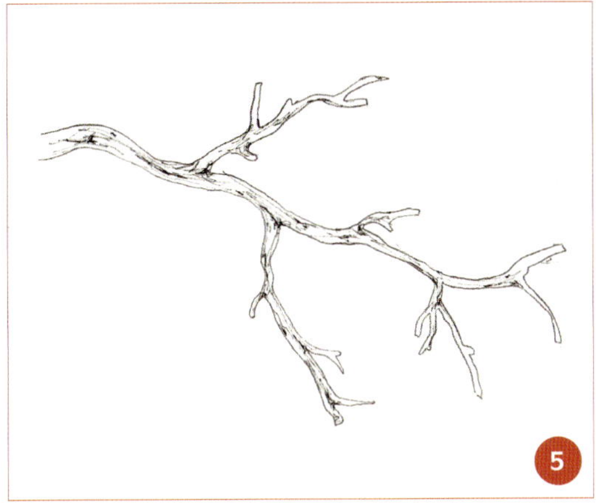

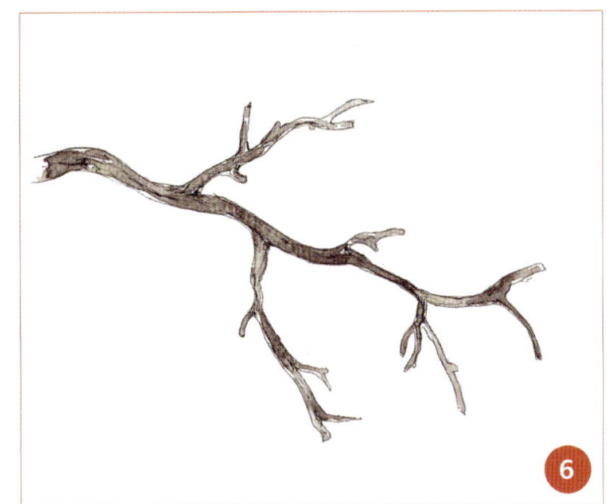

Step 5: You can now add a lot of character by giving the branch dark details with the 02 fineliner. Add dark to the places where the main branch splits out into side branches and a bit on the bark. A good rule of thumb is that the older the tree, the more wrinkles and dents (just like with people, really).

Step 6: Load your size 4 brush with Van Dyke brown and paint the branch wet-on-dry. Leave plenty of white space on the branch to create texture. While it's still wet, drip in another color to create interest. Here, I used sap green.

And now you have a delicate little branch for a bird or butterfly to land on. They are going to love it! In the next tutorial, I want to show you how you can dress up this simple branch by turning it into a floral haven. Branches are used in several of the projects, including the Nuthatch (page 83), House Sparrow (page 119) and Bluebird (page 95).

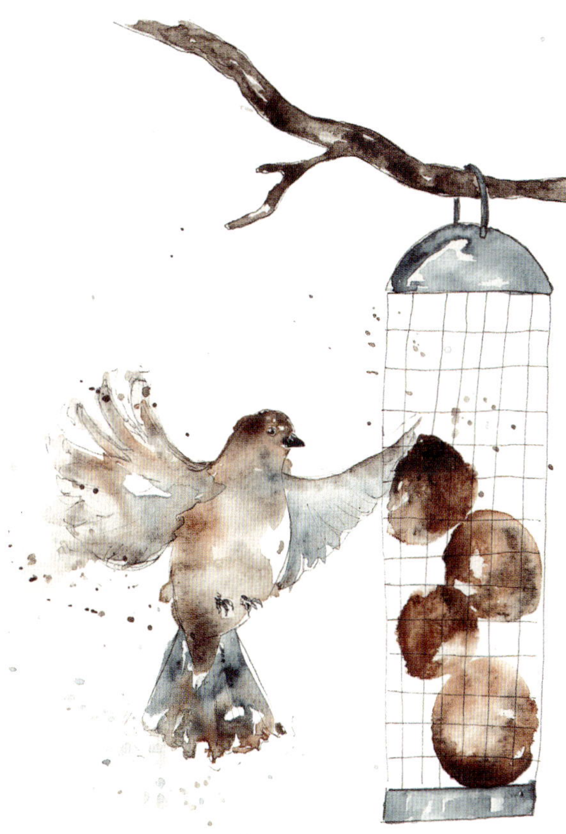

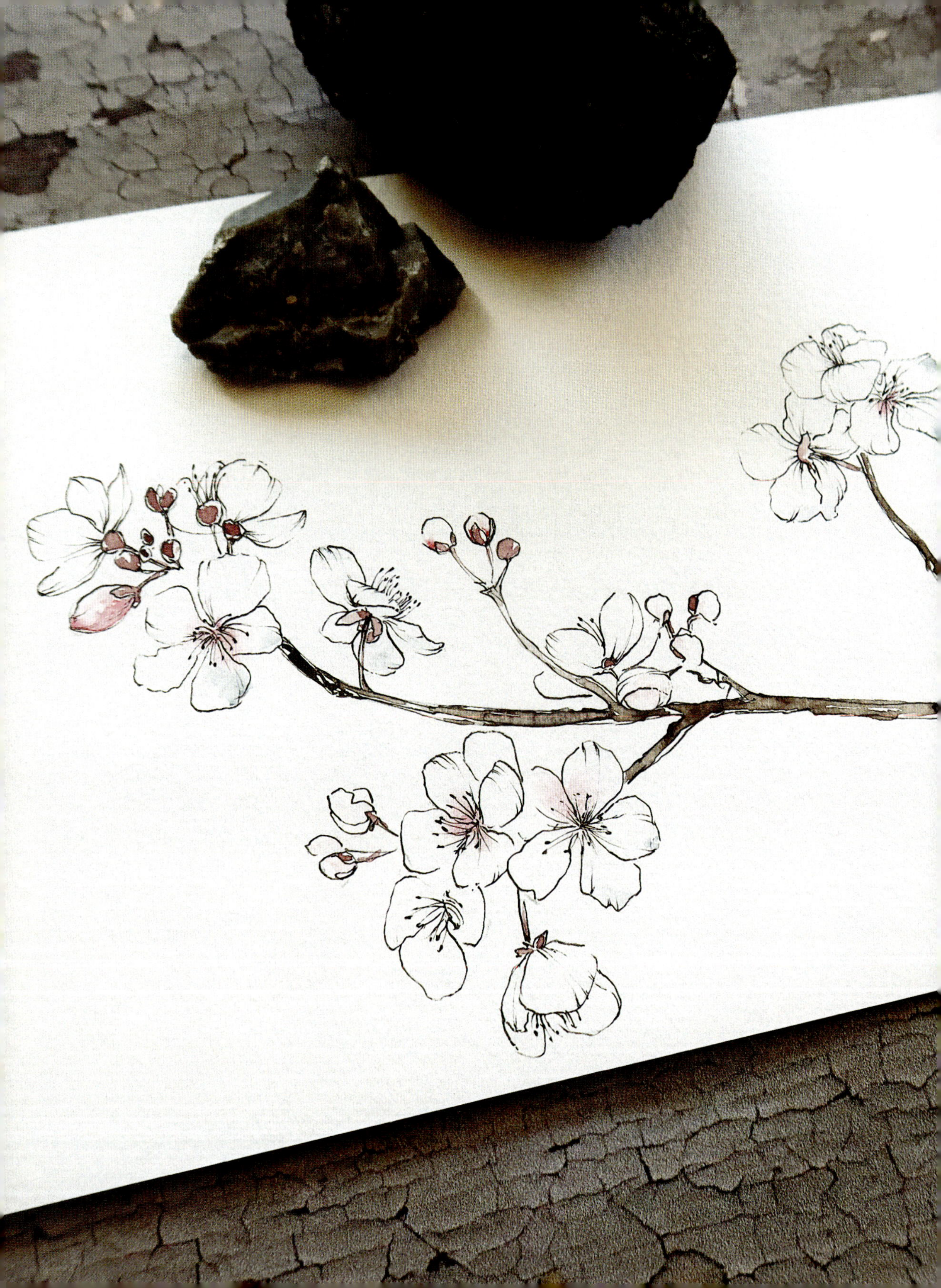

cherry blossom branch

Branches can be varied in many ways to create a diverse range of housing for our garden friends. One of the most beautiful ways in my opinion is a branch filled with blooms. And the most iconic blooming tree to me is the cherry blossom. Its pops of pink just scream spring and optimism after a dark and gray winter. I can't think of anything better than having a home in the middle of a cherry blossom, so why not create that for our flying friends?

Materials

Pencil and eraser
Paper: Canson Montval 300gsm (140lb) cold press
Fineliners: sizes 01 and 005
Watercolor brush: size 4
Water and cloth
Palette

Colors

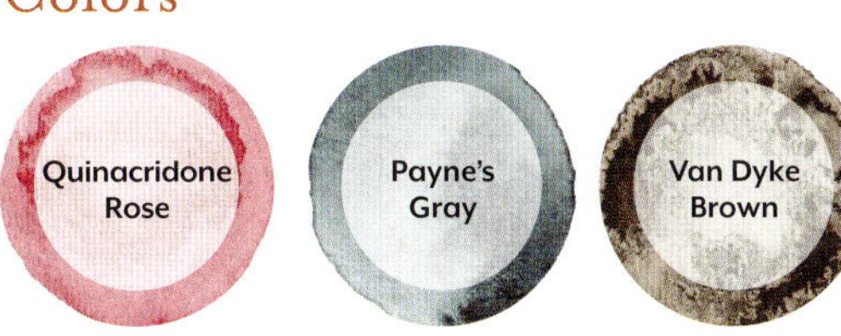

Mixes

To get the colors of the small buds, I mixed equal parts Van Dyke brown and quinacridone rose.

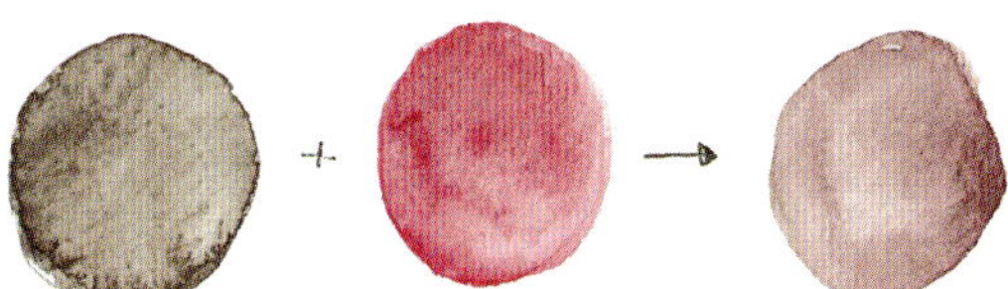

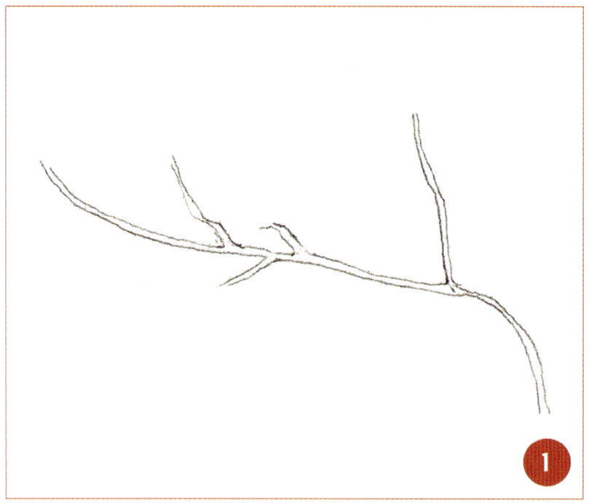

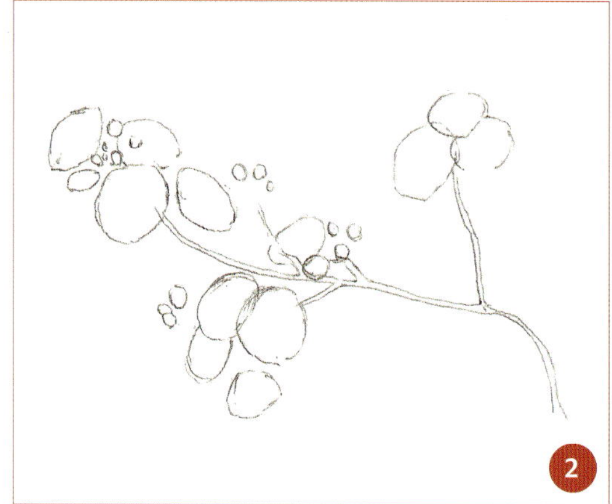

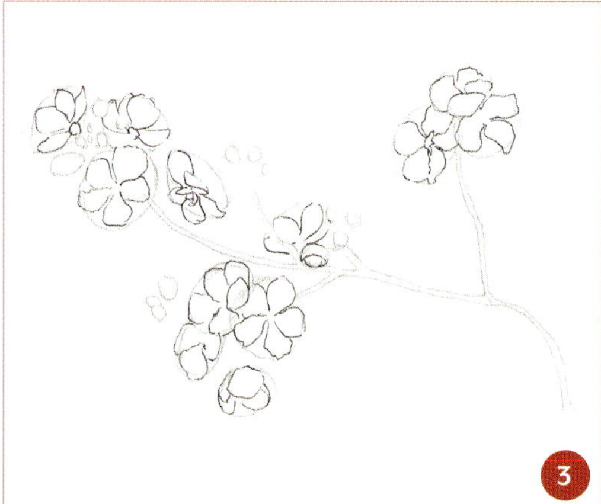

Step 1: Sketch a branch with a few side branches with the pencil. (For how to sketch branches, see Simple Branch on page 35.)

Step 2: And now we make it bloom! Start by adding lots of ovals and circles at the end of the different branches. The big ovals are guides for the big blooms, and the small circles will become the buds. Place them in clusters, with some completely round and others more oval. Also, tuck some of them behind others to create depth.

Step 3: Add petals to the big blooms with the 01 fineliner. Cherry blossoms have five teardrop-shaped petals and are attached at the center. From the side, you can only see a few petals and a small circle at the bottom for small leaves. Drawing these blooms can seem hard at first, but after a few blossoms you'll get it, so just keep going. I believe in you!

Step 4: With the same fineliner, continue to draw the round buds with small leaves at the bottom, small stems and the branch. Can you see how nicely it really comes together?

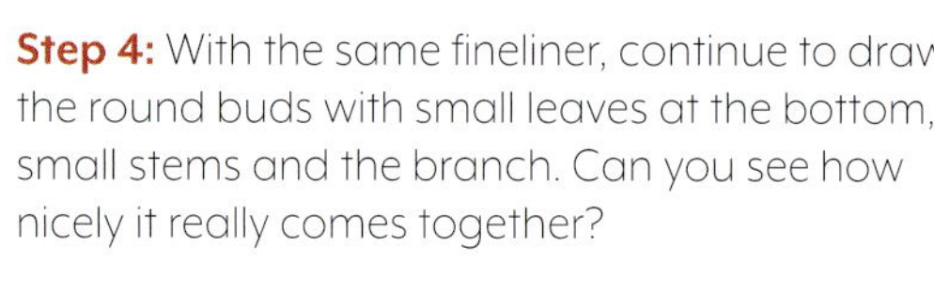

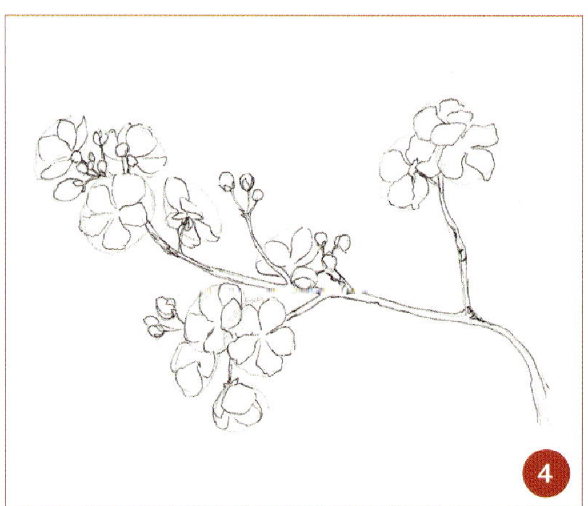

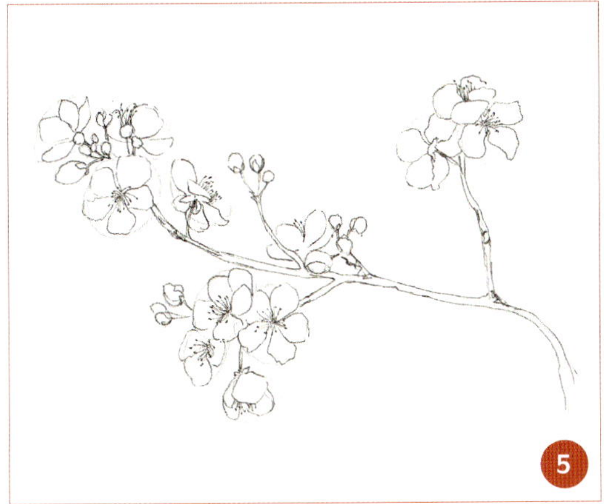

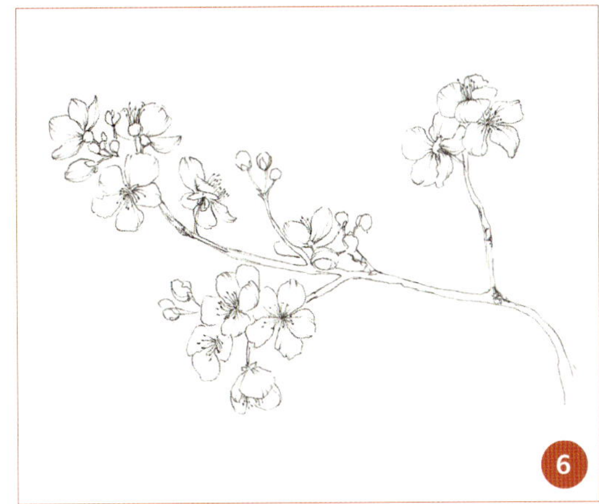

Step 5: Now we want to give the blossoms a bit of personality. Use the 005 fineliner to draw the small stamens using light C-strokes, and finish them with small ovals at the end. Now you have a wonderful sketch. Carefully erase the pencil lines.

Step 6: With the 005 fineliner, add details like bark (see page 37) and shaping lines in the petals. The shaping lines start from the center of the flower and move out into the petal. Some lines start at the edge of the petal, going in towards the center. You don't have to add details to all the petals. Actually, I think it's a lot more interesting if about half don't have details.

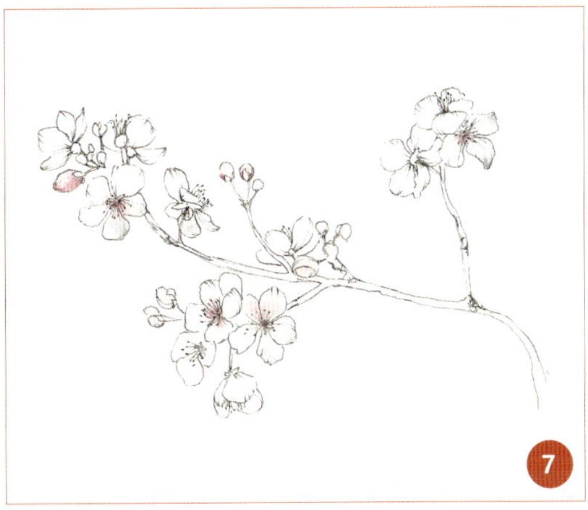

Step 7: Let's add a pop of color now. With the size 4 brush, wet the blossoms with clean water, and drip a bit of quinacridone rose in the center that will flow outwards. While still wet, drip a watery Payne's gray at the tip of some of the petals. Then paint the buds where you can see the white petals peek out with the same color. Again, don't do it with all the blooms—less is always more.

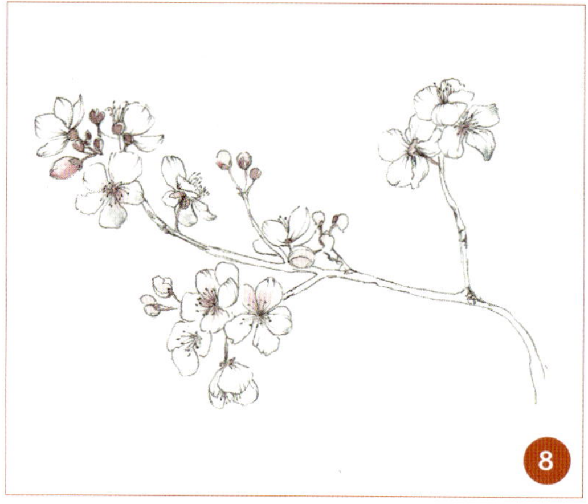

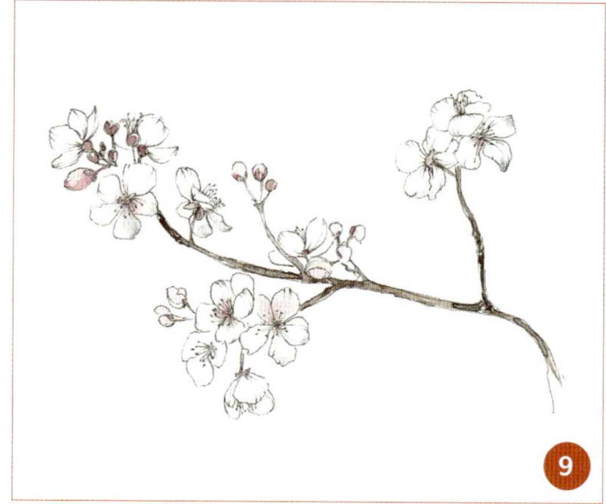

Step 8: Now you want to get your palette out and mix Van Dyke brown and quinacridone rose. Paint with the mix wet-on-dry on the closed buds as well as on the small circles below the side-view blooms. After that, you can add a bit of the same color mix to their thin stems.

Step 9: Finally, paint the branch using Van Dyke brown. While it's still wet, drip in a bit of Payne's gray to tie it all together nicely.

Phew, that was a bit challenging with all those blooms, but you did it! Now you deserve to go for a walk and look for our feathery friends outside. Say hello from me and have a great time! To put this branch in action, check out the Blue Jay on page 99..

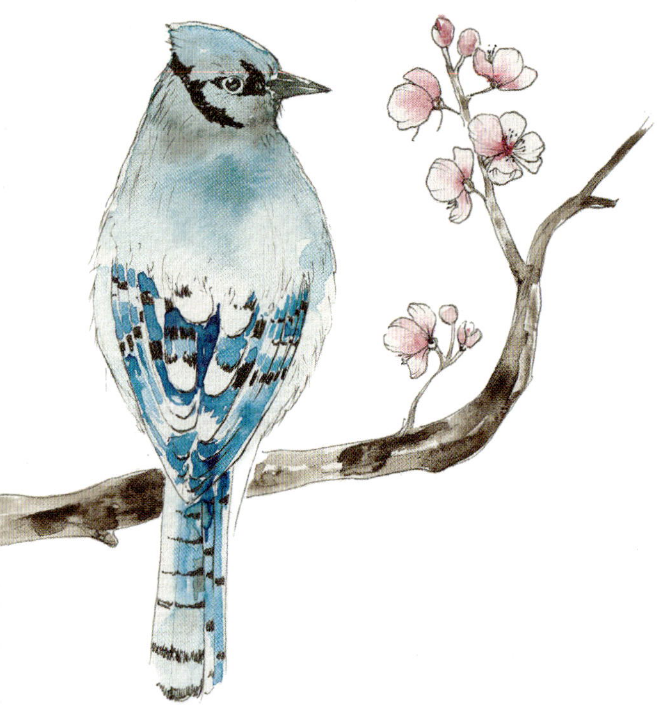

butterfly bush

My butterfly bush is the most magical place in my garden in the summer. There is always so much life! You can spot pops of orange, yellow, bright red and subtle blue just flying around everywhere. If there were no such thing as laundry, work or cleaning, I could just sit and observe this for hours. (And sometimes I do anyway with a sketchbook in hand.)

Here we utilize the power of watercolor, because when we are working with a bush with clusters of blooms, we don't want to overcomplicate our fineliner sketch.

Materials

Pencil and eraser
Paper: Canson Montval 300gsm (140lb) cold press
Watercolor brush: size 4
Water and cloth
Palette
Fineliner: size 01

Colors

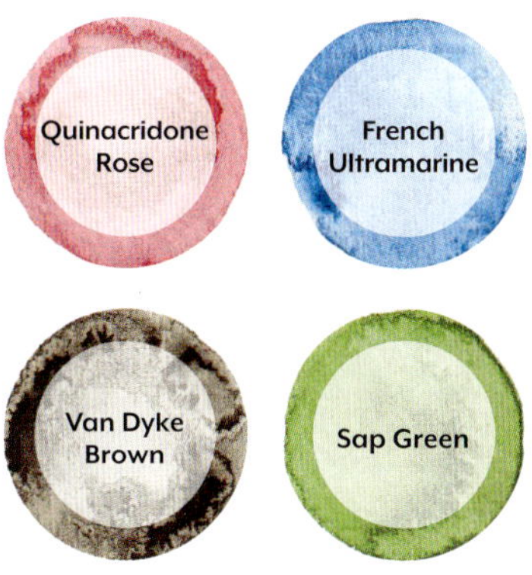

Mixes

The first mix for the outer petals on the small blooms is mostly French ultramarine with a hint of quinacridone rose.

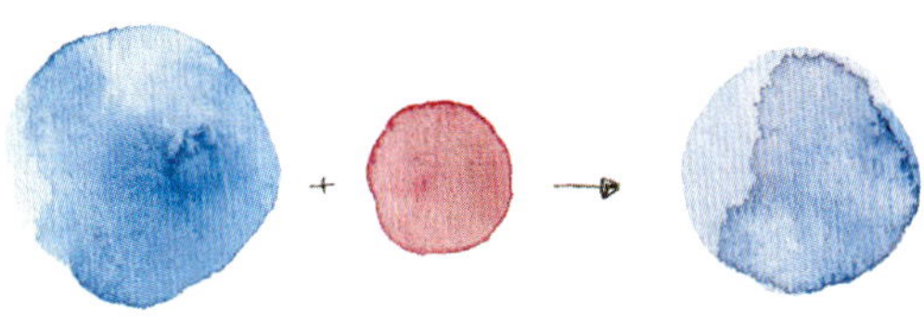

The second mix for the lower part of the blooms where they attach to the stem is equal parts French ultramarine and quinacridone rose.

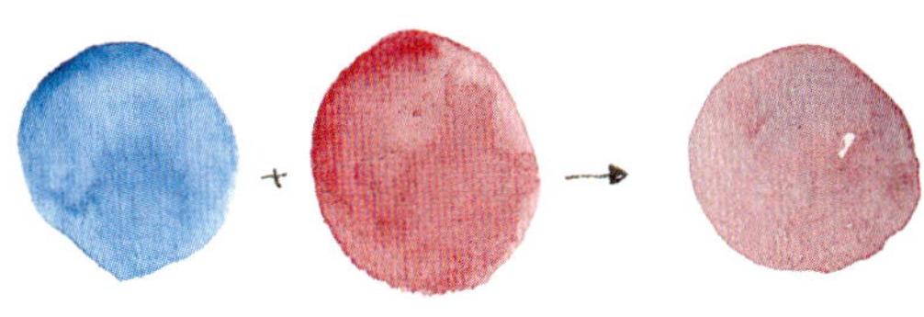

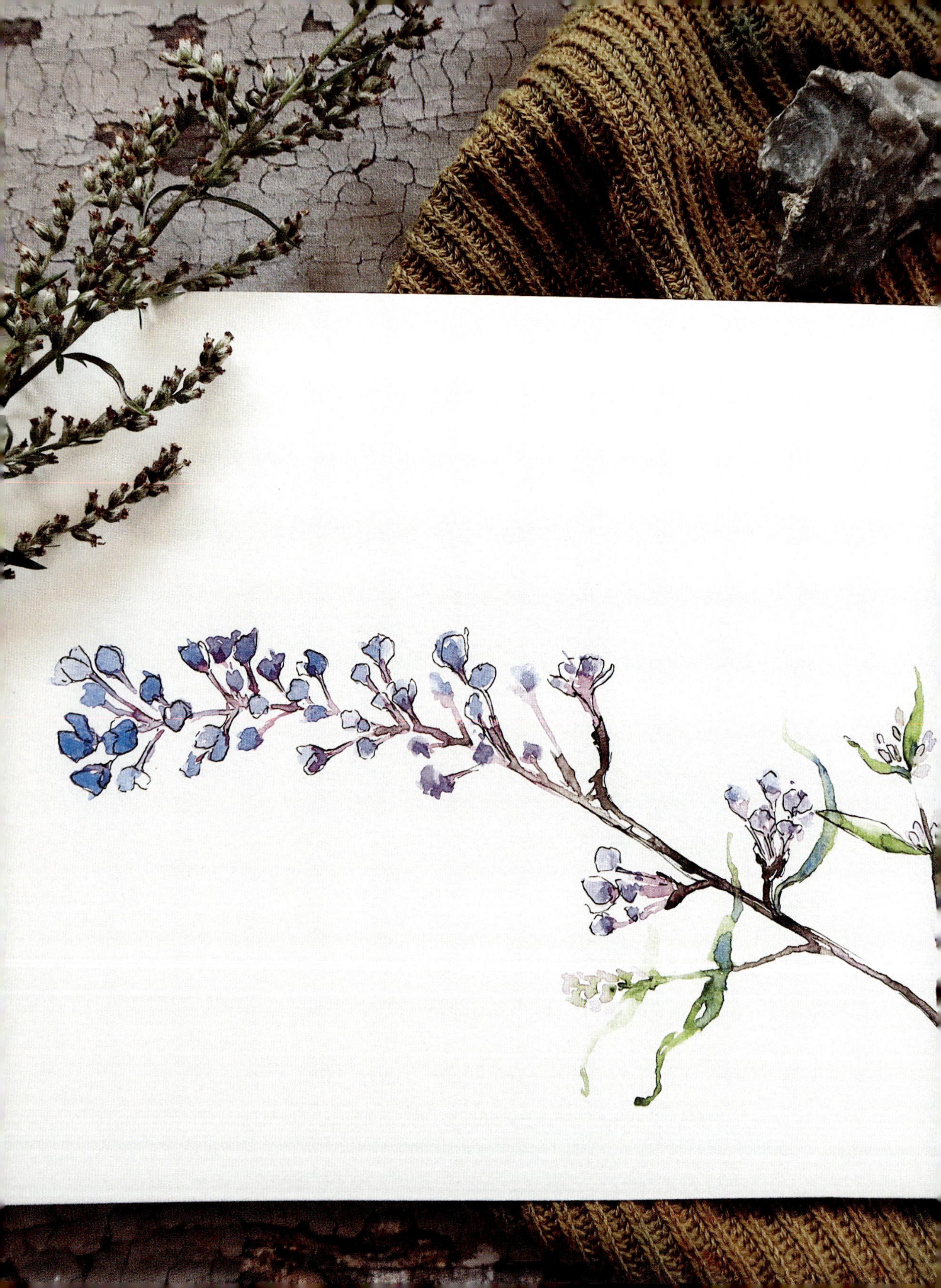

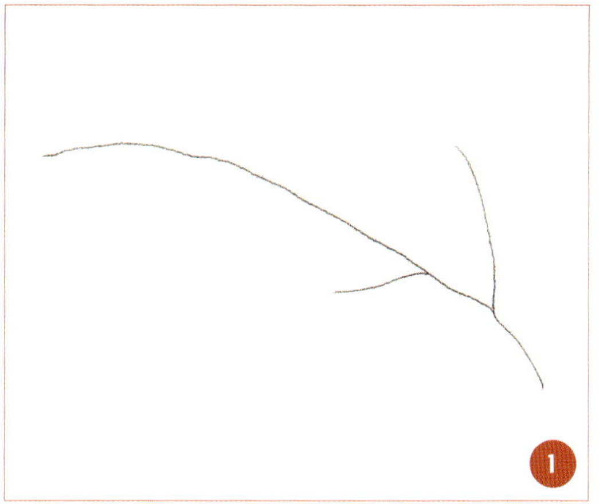

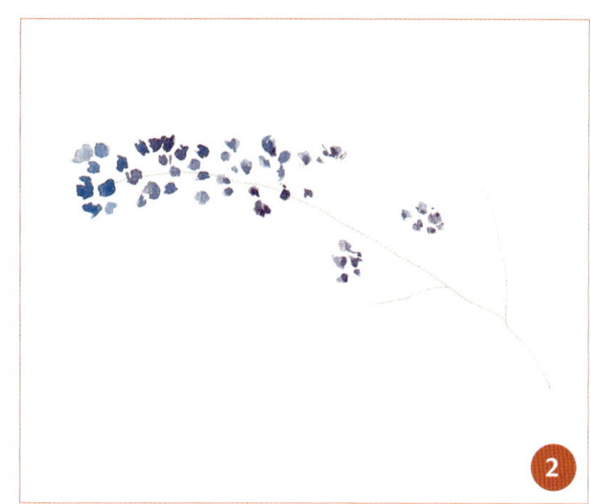

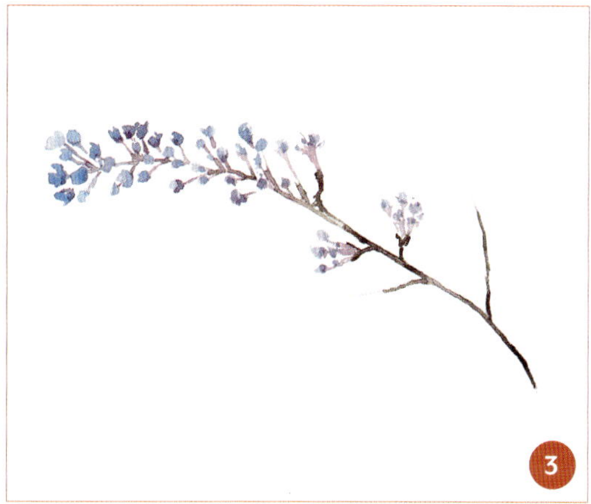

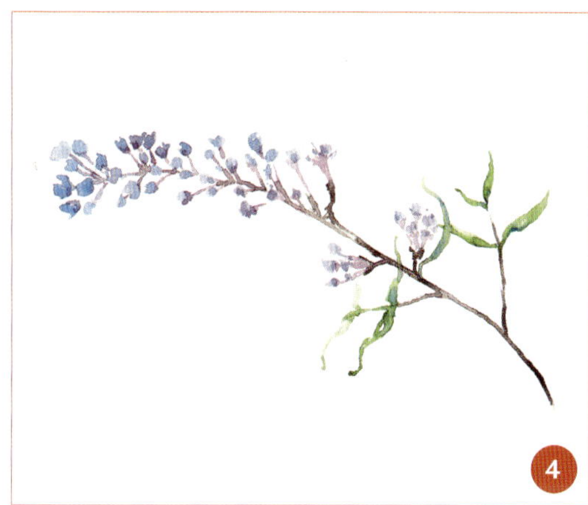

Step 1: Start with a super simple pencil sketch of a long, slightly bent line with two side branches.

Step 2: Use the first color mix to paint the small blooms with the size 4 brush. Make some big and some small, but keep them light. Have a big cluster at the top of the branch and then smaller ones towards the bottom. The flower shapes are irregular: Some are teardrop shapes; some are almost squares and some are ovals. The shapes do not matter too much because it's the number of blooms that gives the illusion of a floral cluster.

Step 3: Paint the branch in the middle using Van Dyke brown. Then paint the small stems that attach the blooms to the branch with the second color mix. If the Van Dyke brown isn't entirely dry when painting the stems, that is completely fine; that will just make the paints flow a bit into each other, creating a beautiful transition.

Step 4: Add leaves using sap green, and while it's still wet, drip in a bit of French ultramarine. (That is just so pretty!) Let the leaves vary in length, but have them all end in a fine tip. Let a few of them overlap for a sense of depth.

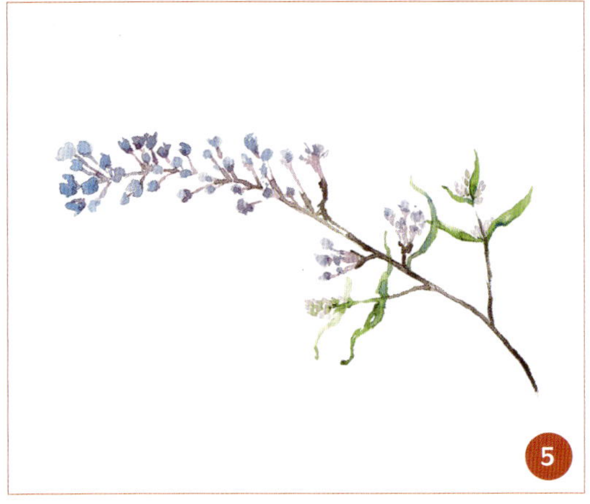

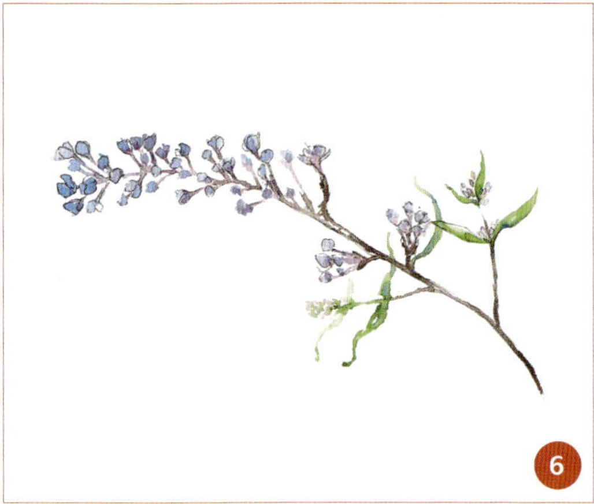

Step 5: Add a few small oval buds between the leaves. Keep them in the rosy mix, but add a bit of green to make them look younger than the other blooms. Now you can erase the pencil lines.

Step 6: Sketch outlines for the blooms and stems with the 01 fineliner. You don't need to add a lot of detail to the single blooms. The number of small blooms is more than enough to make an impression of the butterfly bush.

This is perfect! Now it's ready for the butterflies to dine. On page 135, you'll learn to paint the graceful Monarch Butterfly enjoying these blooms.

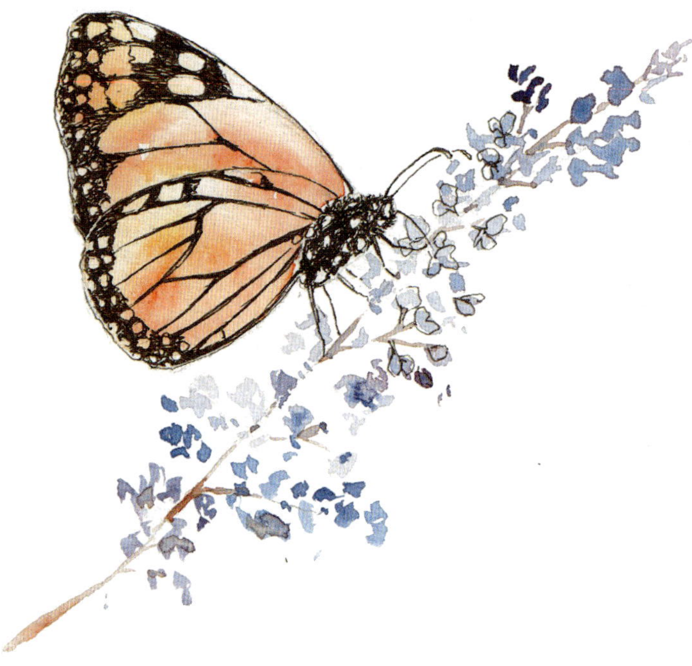

dandelion

There are a lot of different flowers in gardens across the globe. But some of the most important flowers to me are wildflowers because they appear out of the blue, need very little care and are the bread and butter for all our small winged friends. And our first wildflower in this book is the flower of growth, hope and healing, as well as a reason for a lot of frustration amongst gardeners because it pops up everywhere it's not supposed to be: the yellow dandelion.

Materials

Watercolor brush: size 4
Paper: Canson Montval 300gsm (140lb) cold press
Water and cloth
Palette
Fineliners: sizes 01 and 005

Colors

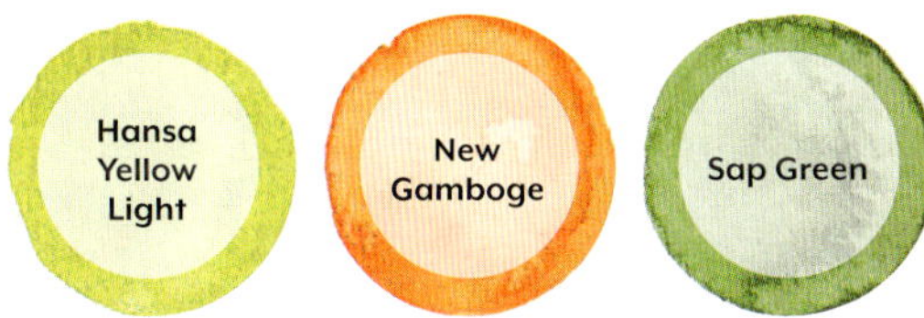

Step 1: Dip the size 4 brush in Hansa yellow light. Then paint small C-shaped strokes starting in the center and then turning upwards. While it's still wet, you can drip in a bit of new gamboge wet-on-wet to the lower part for a bit of warmth to the cool yellow.

Step 2: Paint longer C shapes using Hansa yellow light from the center and going out. Some will go in the same direction as before; some will point more down and a few can be tucked behind the center you painted in the first step. Keep white space between the strokes, and keep it light and flowy. Continue until the flower is the size you want.

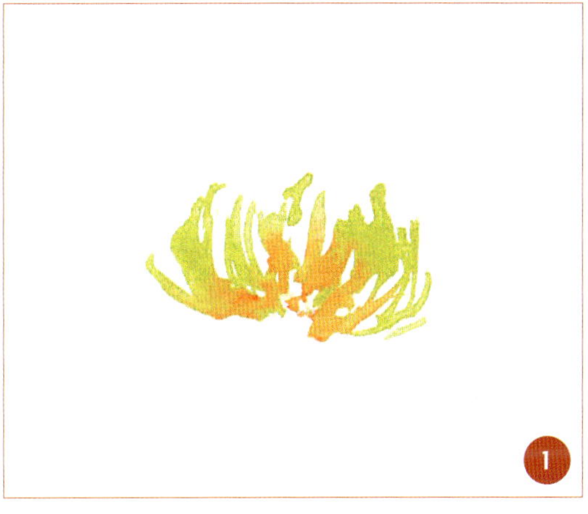

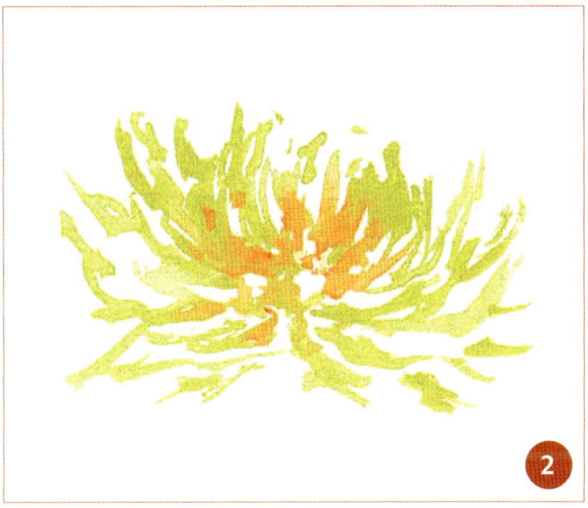

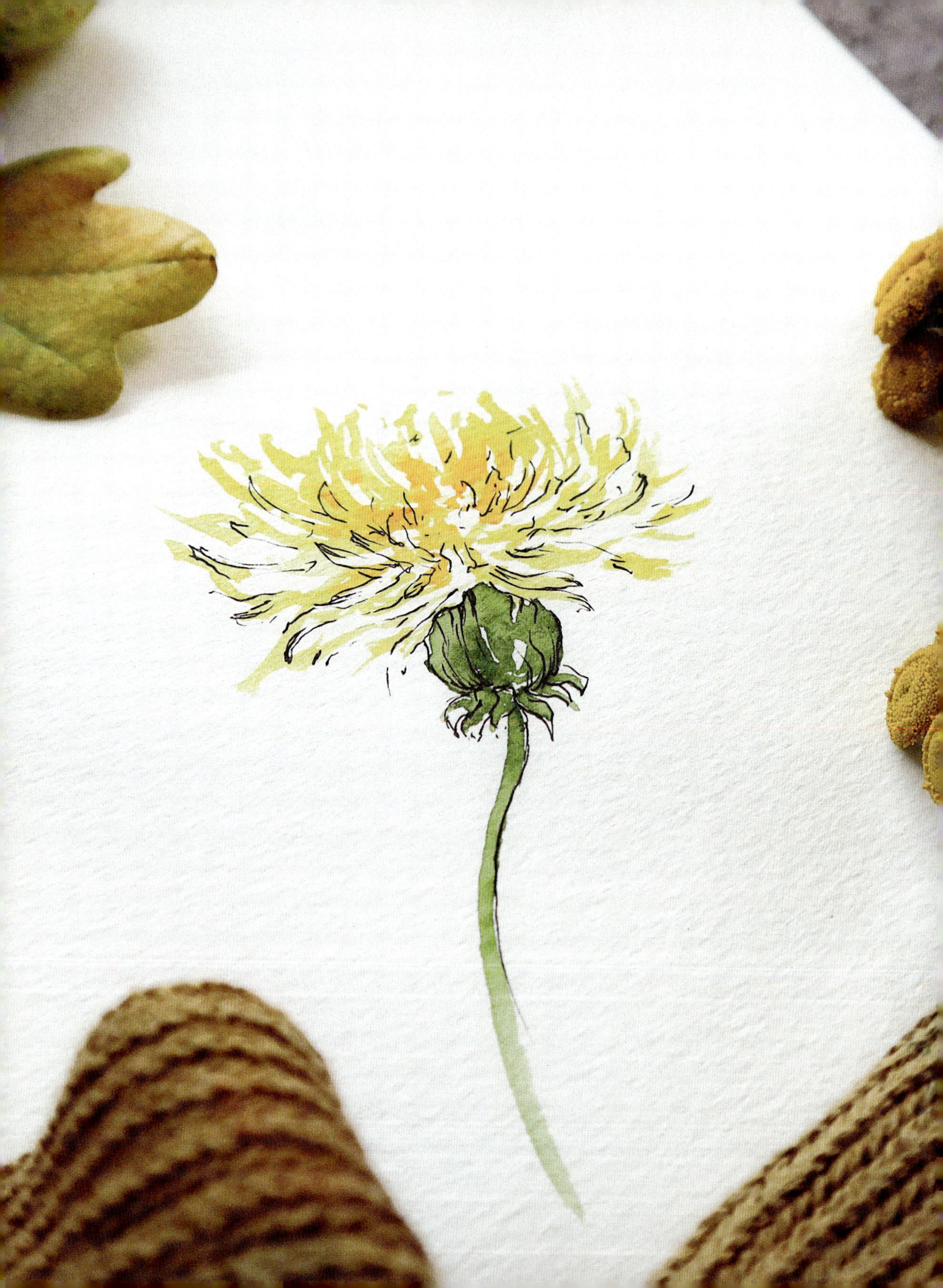

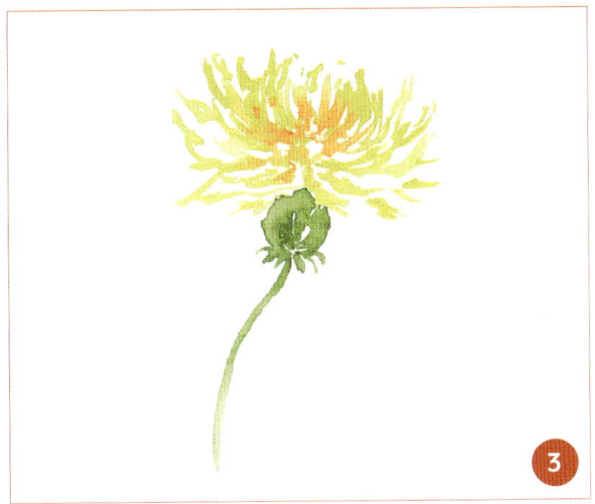

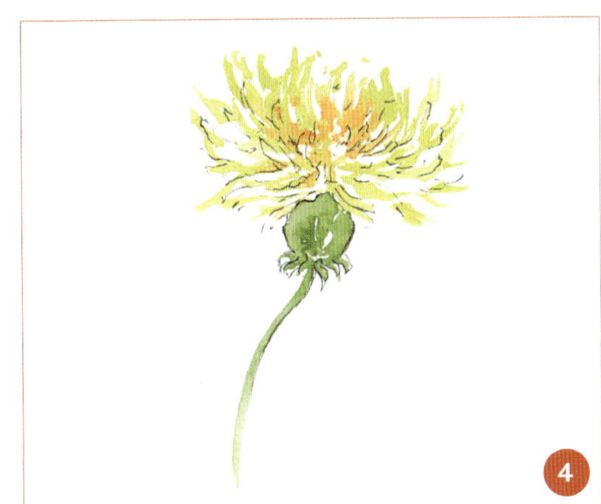

Step 3: Paint a bottom for the flower wet-on-dry using sap green. The bottom is in the shape of an oval that is tucked behind the yellow flowerhead. Keep white space when painting it, and drip in a denser sap green to give variation to the greens. At the bottom of the circle, you can paint small green leaves and a flowing stem.

Step 4: Use your friend the 01 fineliner to draw the outline of the bottom of the flower and to sketch some of the lower part of the flower petals. Keep the petals long and sketchy—you really don't want to overwork it. To keep it light, challenge yourself not to finish any of the lines. I know it's hard and messes a bit with our perfectionism, but I promise it works.

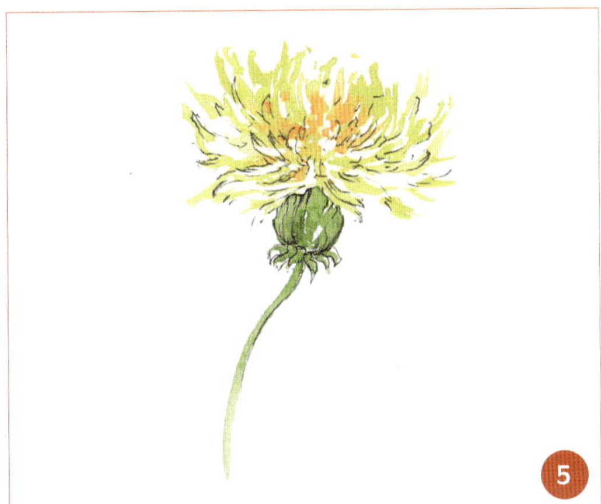

Step 5: Add a bit of texture to the greens with the 005 fineliner and a bit of direction to a few of the petals.

Here is our first wildflower ready to go! You can see how it can be used in the projects on page 149 with the Common Buckeye Butterfly and on page 169 where it serves as a beautiful resting place for Little Miss Ladybug. But this is a garden, and we want a sea of colors and nectar, so let's tackle another flower right away.

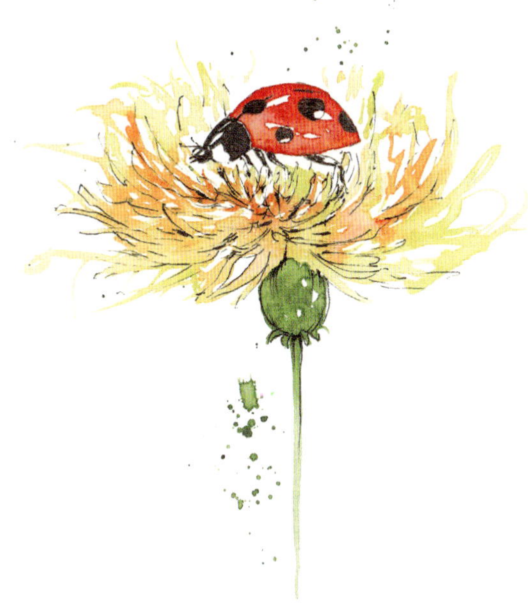

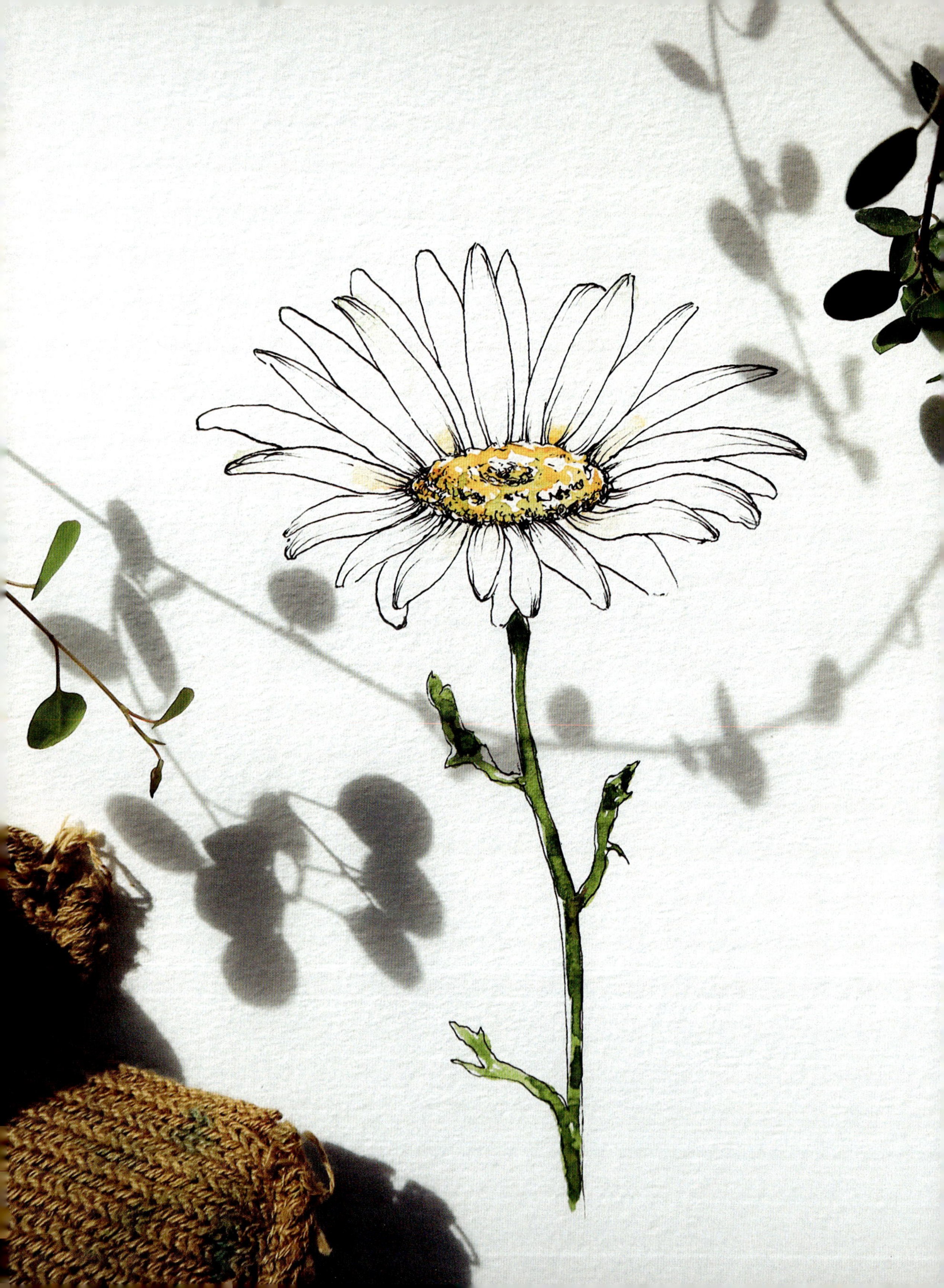

white oxeye daisy

One of the wildflowers we see so many of here in Denmark is the flower of patience: the white oxeye daisy. They are everywhere, and it's absolutely incredible! Their tall, floating grace adds so much to any garden.

The beauty of this particular bloom is its simplicity. And when you know how to ink and wash it, you can vary it to create so many other similar blooms with round centers surrounded by petals. It all comes down to the number of petals and the colors. Pretty cool, right?!

Materials

Pencil and eraser
Paper: Canson Montval 300gsm (140lb) cold press
Fineliners: sizes 005, 01 and 02
Watercolor brush: size 4
Water and cloth
Palette

Colors

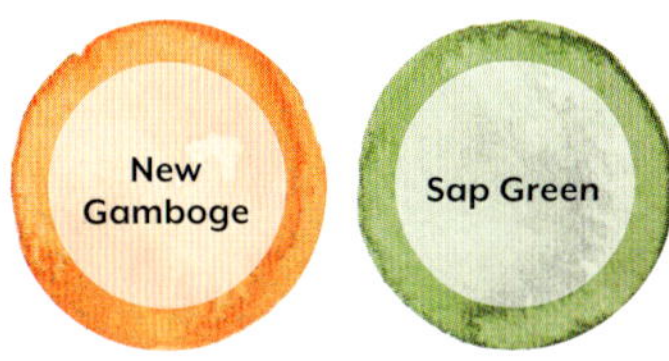

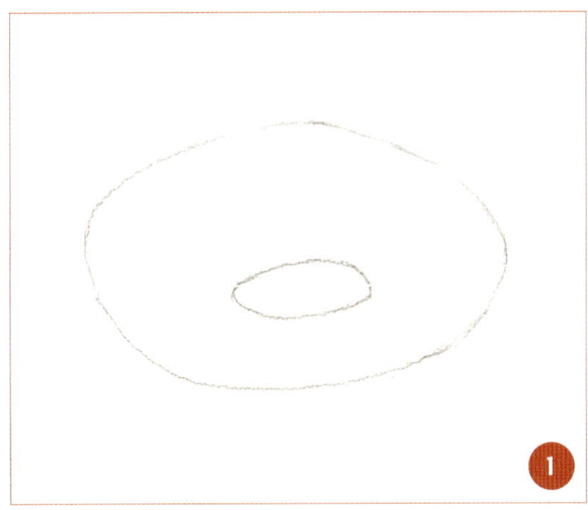

Step 1: Sketch two flat ovals, one inside the other, with the pencil. Have the little one float a bit towards the bottom of the big oval.

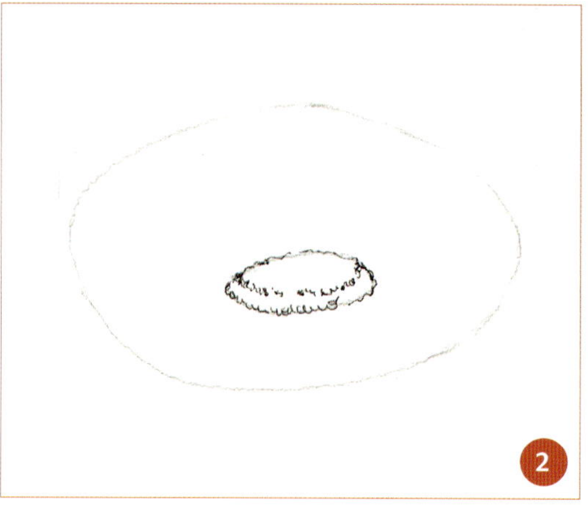

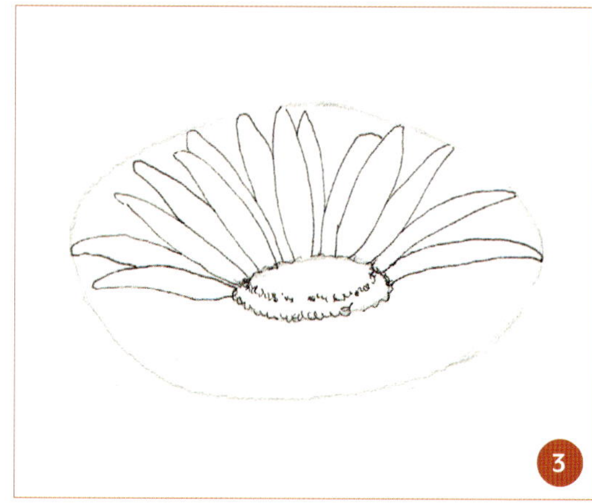

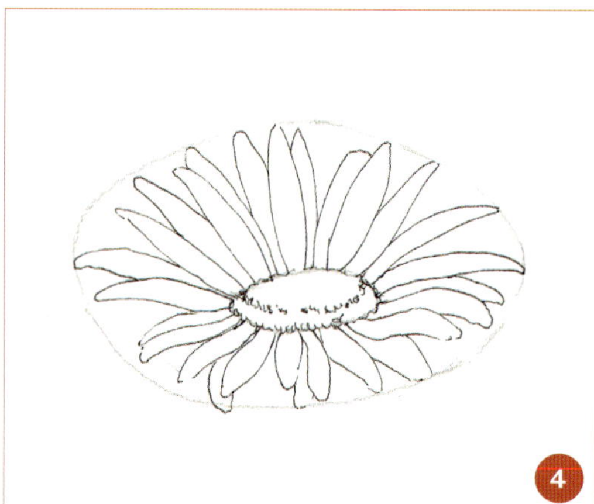

Step 2: Use your 005 fineliner to trace the small oval with curly scribbles. Use smaller curly scribbles to draw an even smaller oval within the small oval.

Step 3: Use your 01 fineliner to draw the top (or back) petals. They are full-length and shaped a bit like long, flat ovals. When you move towards the sides, the petals become thinner and a bit longer. Let the tip of the petals bend a little at the end to create some movement.

Step 4: Keep going with the 01 fineliner on the foreshortened petals in the front. These petals are shorter, thicker and more bent. If it's not looking right at the moment, don't worry—it will make sense as soon as we add the shaping lines.

Step 5: With the 01 fineliner, draw a long stem with a few quick leaves in random shapes.

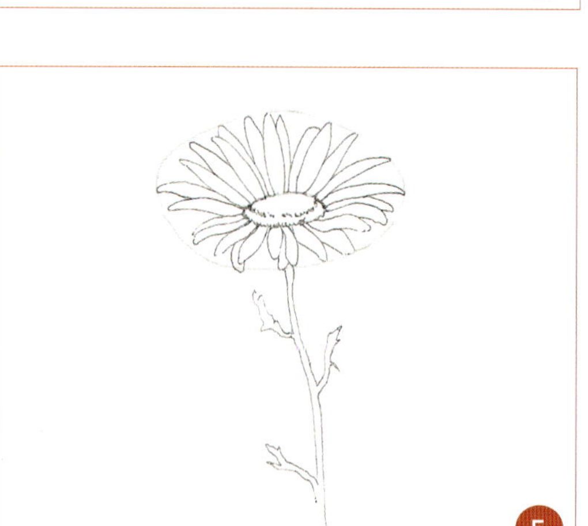

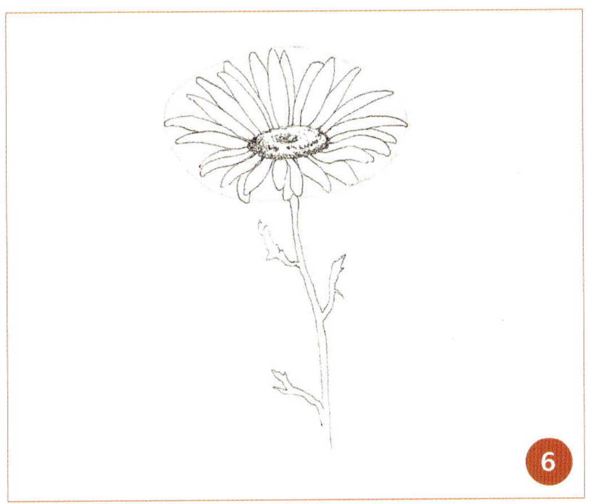

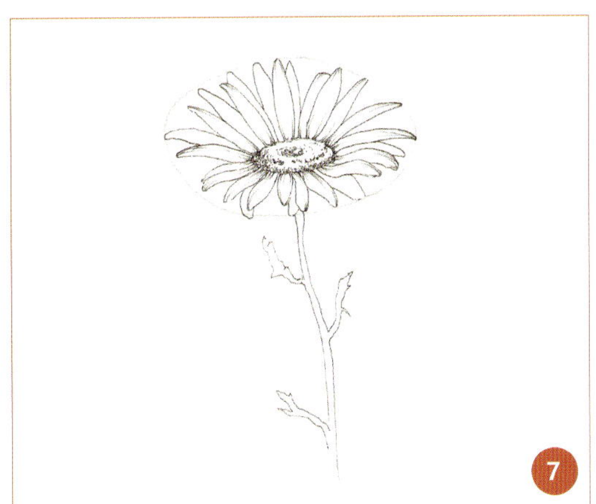

Step 6: Now we are getting started on the details. With the 005 fineliner, draw dots and scribbles to add texture to the middle and edge of the center.

Step 7: Then give some of your petals the shaping lines we used in step 6 of the Cherry Blossom Branch (page 41). Curve them along with the petals to show movement. It's especially important on the foreshortened petals in the front to make the illusion realistic. Isn't it incredible how little you need to make this look fabulous?

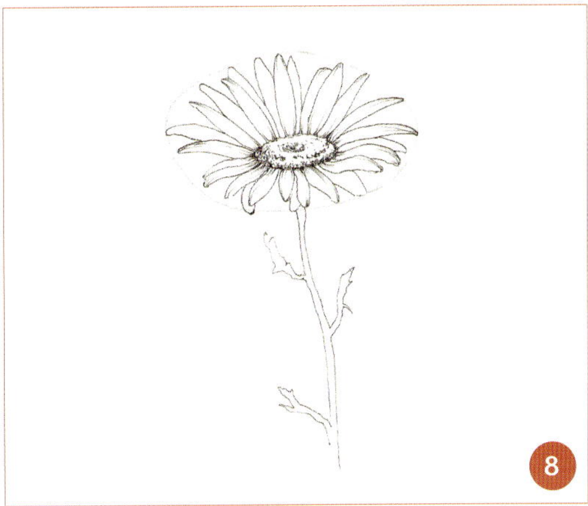

Step 8: Now use the 02 fineliner to give a few darker details where the center meets the petals. When you love it, you can erase the pencil lines and stand back to admire your beautiful sketch.

Step 9: When you feel ready to continue, grab the size 4 brush because we are going to add some color now. Paint the center wet-on-dry using new gamboge. Remember to leave plenty of white spots to make the flower breathe. While it's still wet, add a bit of sap green on the bottom part of the warm yellow and a tiny dab in the middle as well. Let it flow freely with the yellow to mingle.

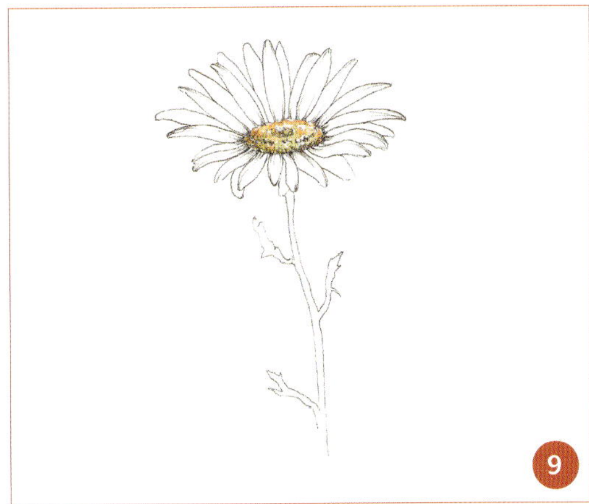

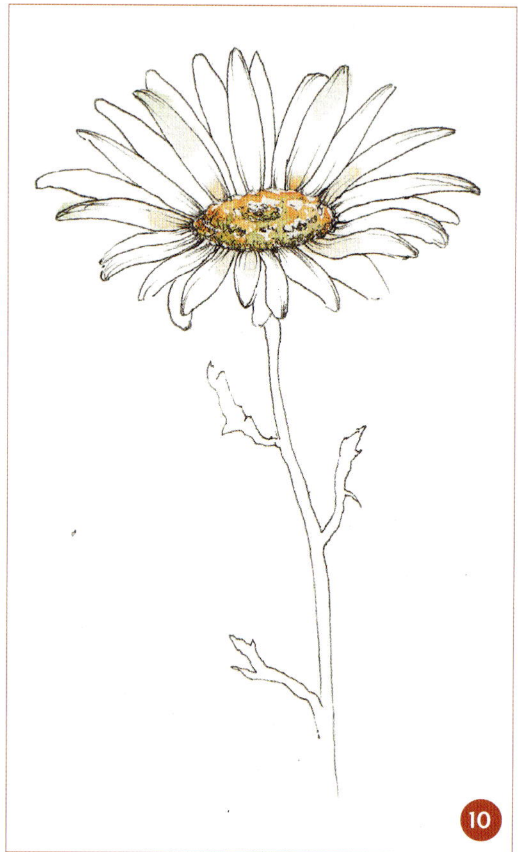

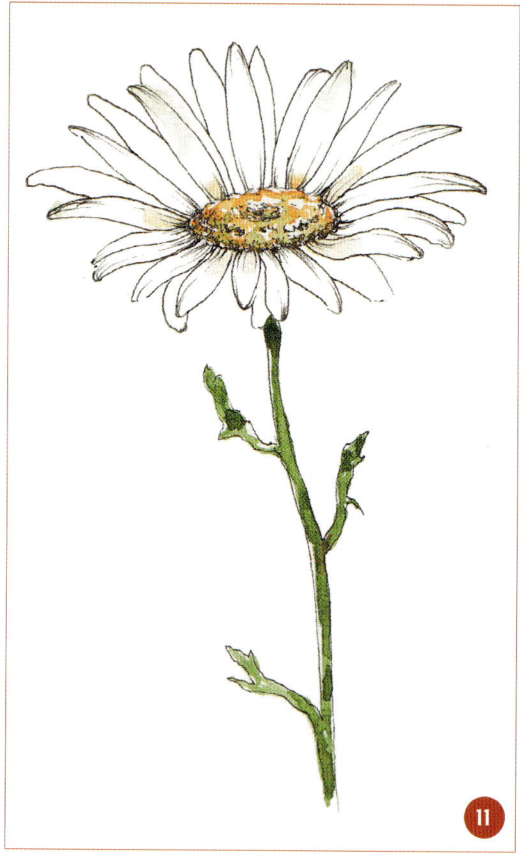

Step 10: With the brush, wet a few of the petals with clean water, softly kissing the middle. Then let the yellow run freely from the center and out into the wet petal. Drip in a bit of sap green on the tip of the wet petals as well to give it a young and fresh look.

Step 11: Now you just need the stem, and that's an easy one. Load your brush with sap green and paint it wet-on-dry. Who says things always have to be complicated?

Now you can sketch an oxeye daisy along with so many similar flowers, such as Gerberas, Cosmos and regular daisies, of course. This garden is starting to take shape!

This flower is actually used in quite a lot of places in this book because it can be changed up in so many ways. You can see it in action on page 139 with the Holly Blue Butterfly, the beautiful Swallowtail (page 143) and also the cute Honeybee (page 177).

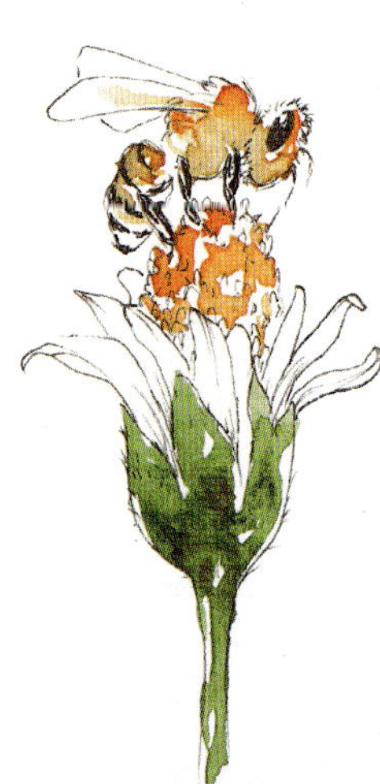

foxglove

The tall, colorful foxglove is always a welcomed surprise. I never know where they will appear, but it's always somewhere. Maybe this is why it's the flower of secrets, because it keeps to itself where it will bloom. The wonderful thing about the foxglove is how tall it gets. It's like a small tower of color in the middle of the flowerbed, and the insects just love it.

Here you will learn how to quickly sketch this delicate, cheeky flower so you have some nectar for our friends in the coming chapters.

Materials

Watercolor brush: size 4
Paper: Canson Montval 300gsm (140lb) cold press
Water and cloth
Palette
Fineliners: sizes 01, 005 and 02

Colors

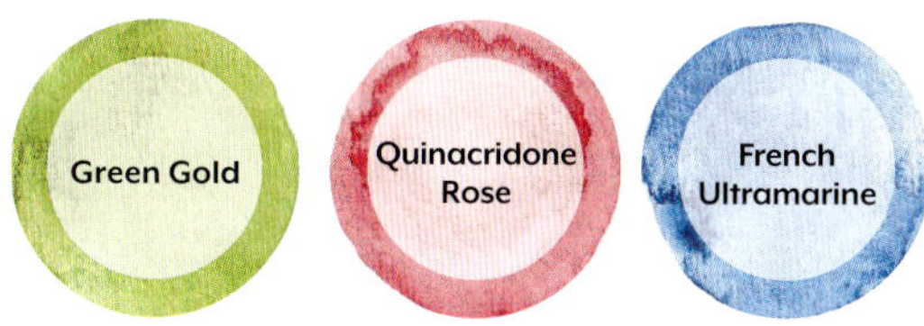

Mixes

Use a good amount of quinacridone rose along with a bit of French ultramarine until you get a nice purple hue. Add more or less of the colors to give variations while using it.

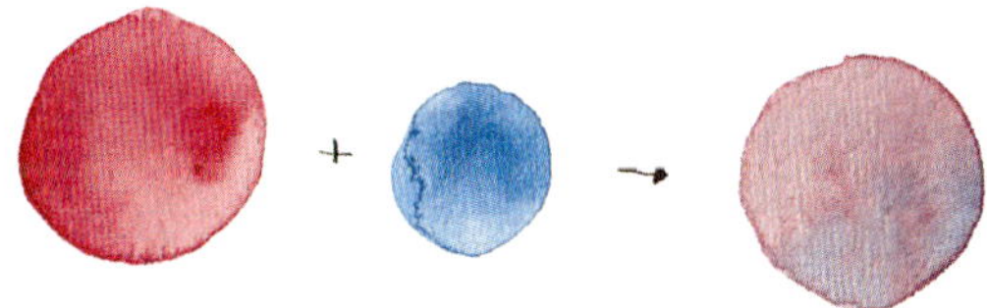

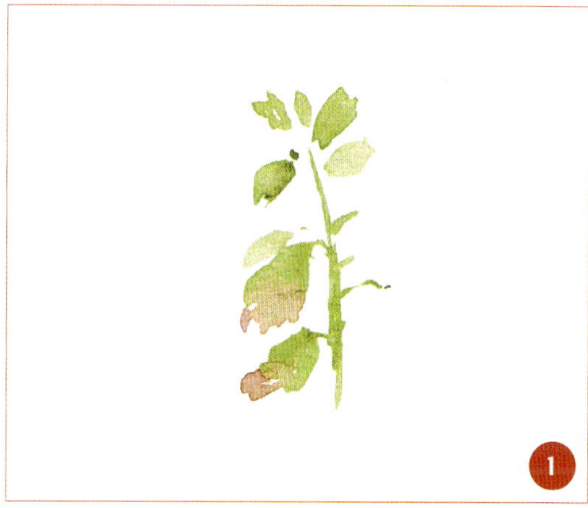

Step 1: Use a size 4 brush to paint the top of the foxglove using green gold. The small buds at the top are flat ovals, and they float a bit above the stem for an airy look. The bigger buds are more teardrop shaped with a small drip of quinacridone rose that flows into the green.

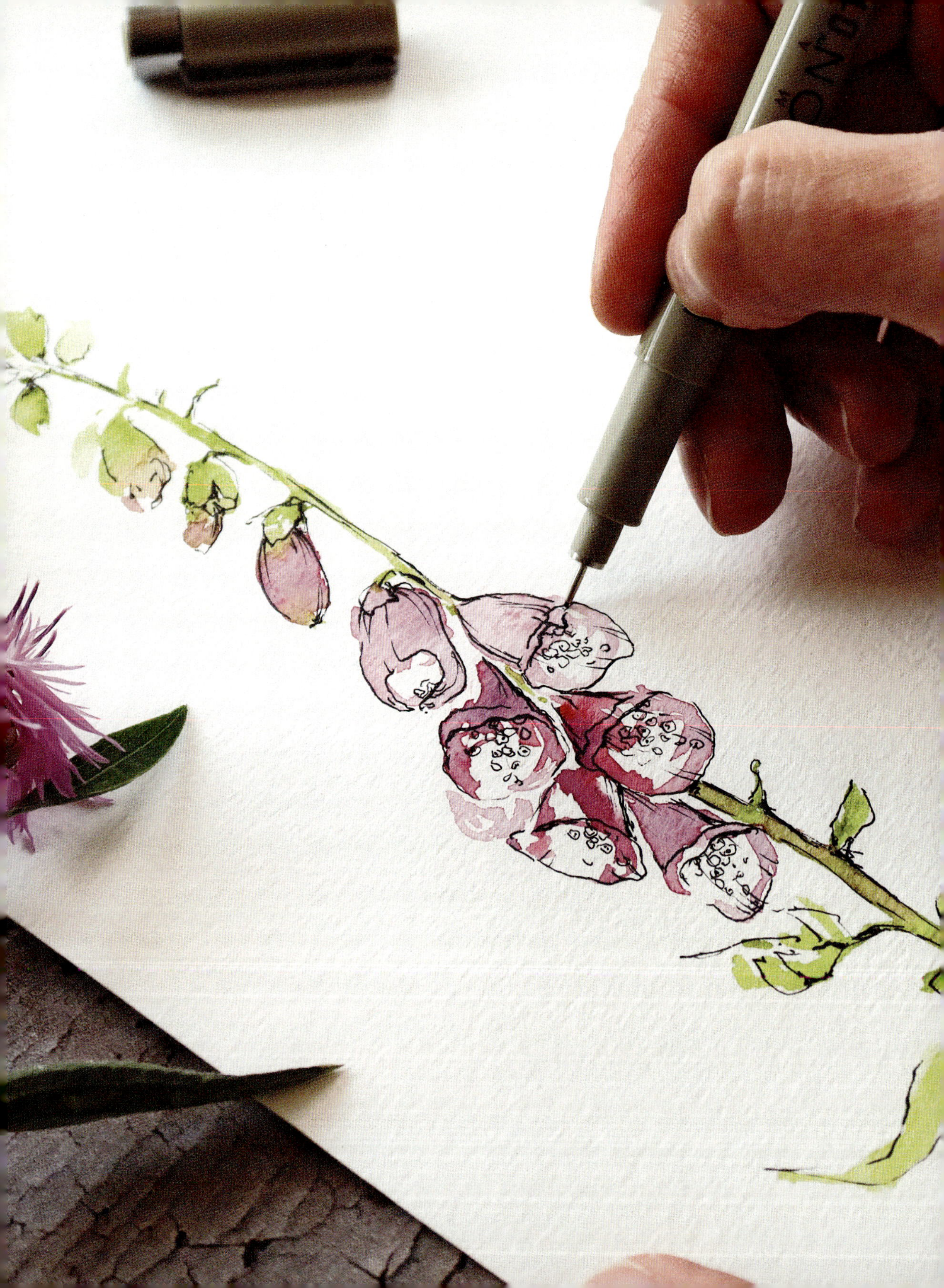

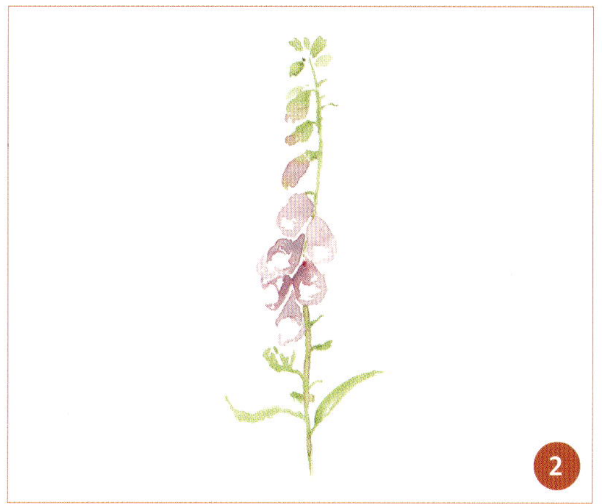

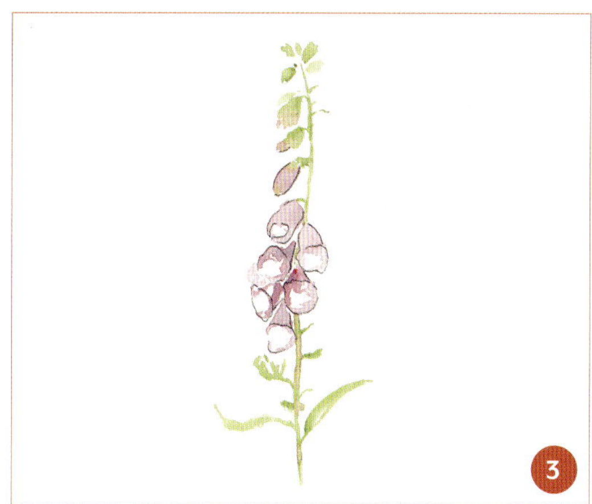

Step 2: Paint the bigger blooms using the quinacridone rose and French ultramarine mix. Make the top blooms ovals with round white spaces at the bottom. The blooms on the bottom are tucked between each other, so when you paint them, it will look almost like a cone shape with a white circle at the bottom. Finally, paint a stem using green gold with a few long leaves and a few short ones. Drip a bit of quinacridone rose into the green for an interesting hue.

Step 3: Use the 01 fineliner to add outlines to the big blooms showing the opening of the flower.

Step 4: Keep working with the 01 fineliner to add details to the stem, the leaves and the buds. Keep it light, and try not to outline everything.

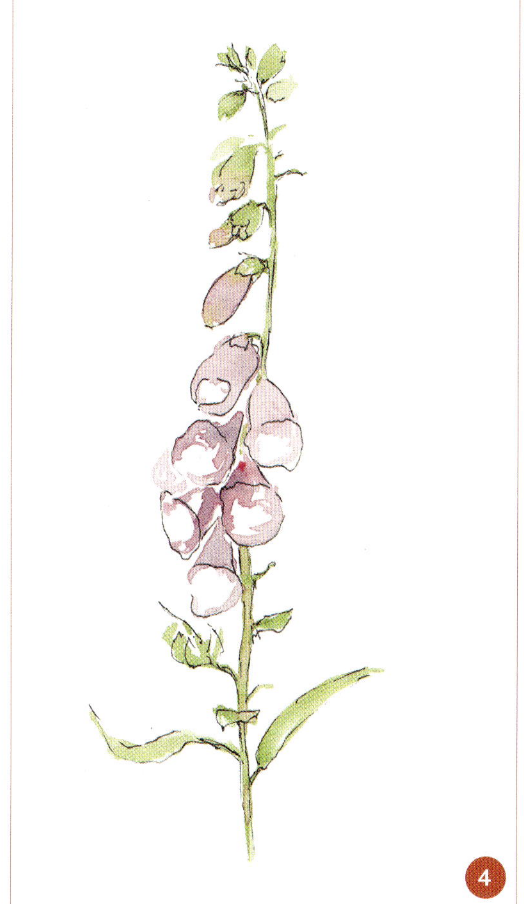

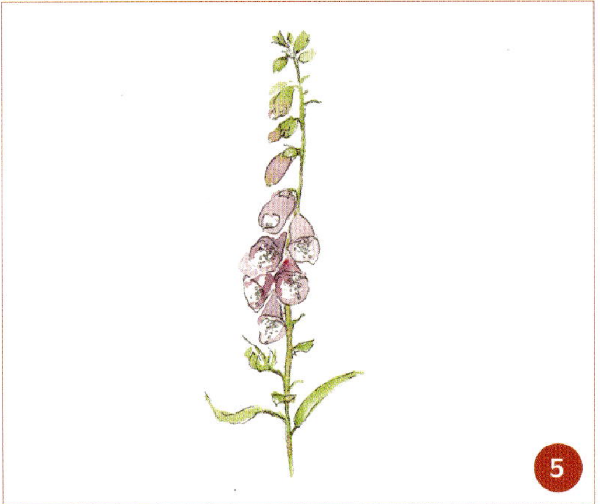

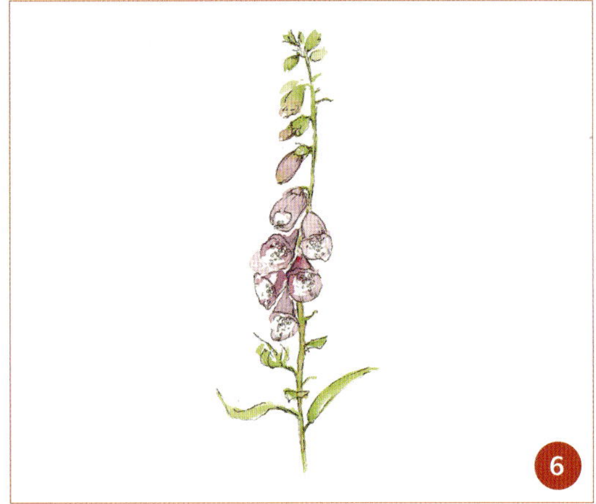

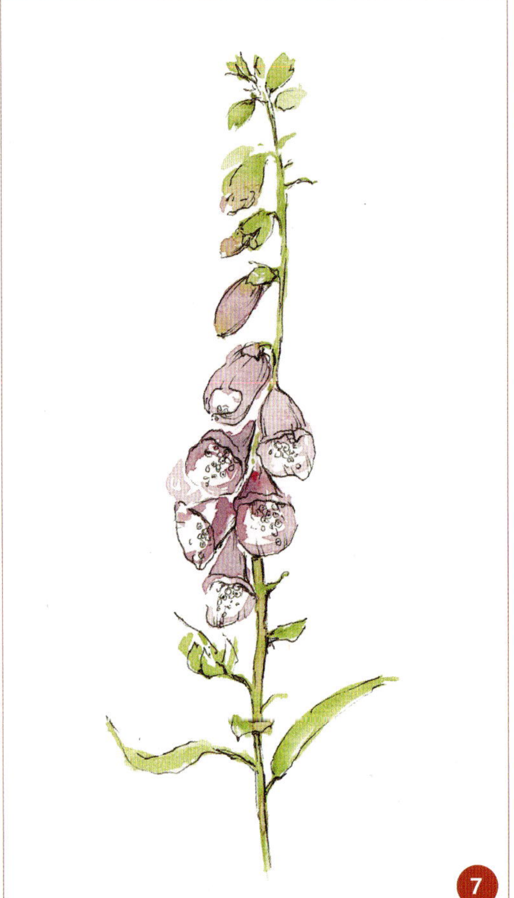

Step 5: Now get your 005 fineliner to add details inside the big blooms. Here we have small, uneven circles that start from the opening and move towards the edge of the bloom. .

Step 6: Add shaping details to the buds and the big blooms with the 005 fineliner.

Step 7: Finally, grab the 02 fineliner to add a few dark details at the bottom part of the bended edges in the big blooms, on the stem and on the leaves.

The foxglove can seem like a complicated flower, but you did it in just seven steps! Woo-hoo! Now you are ready to put it with a birdie or insect. For a bit of inspiration, check out the Raven (page 125) prancing around in a field of foxgloves or turn to page 111 to see the Hummingbird enjoying a sip of nectar

a cute bird's nest

The final project in this section is one of the most important birdie accessories: the nest, where birds lay their eggs, take care of them and raise their babies. I love the time of year where we can see the small birds fly from the nest to a tree branch and then back again—back and forth, just testing whether or not their wings will hold.

I kept this tutorial super simple so it's easy to mix it up. You could add moss, use bigger or smaller branches or add eggs like I did on page 109. Everything is possible when creating this little bird sanctuary. Just remember to place it far away from cats.

Materials

Pencil and eraser
Paper: Canson Montval 300gsm (140lb) cold press
Fineliners: sizes 01, 02 and 005
Watercolor brush: size 4
Water and cloth
Palette

Colors

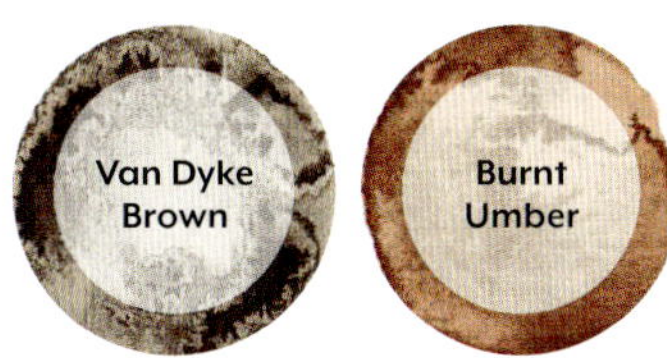

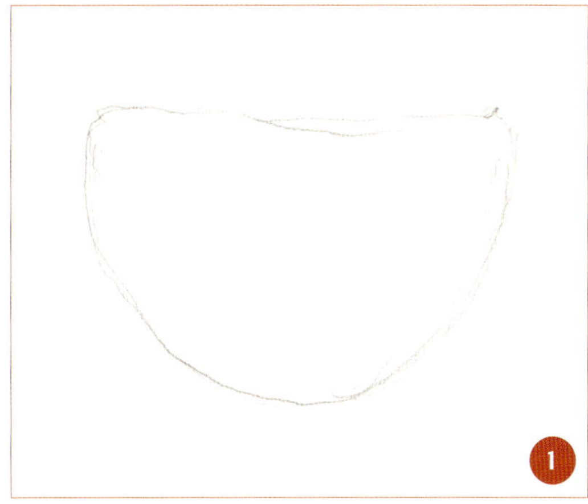

Step 1: Sketch the shape of the nest with a pencil. It's roughly a half circle.

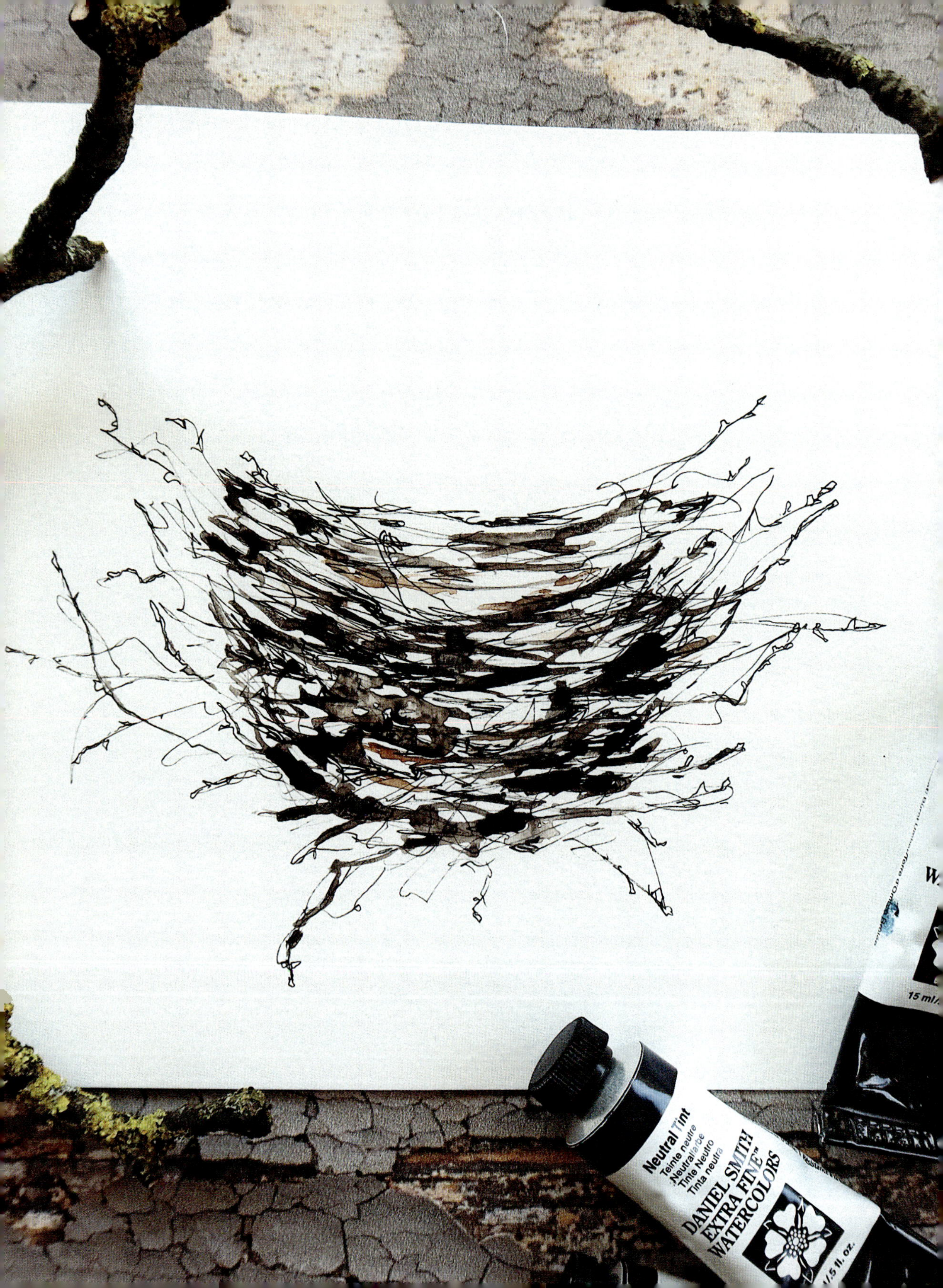

Neutral Tint
Teinte neutre
Neutralfarbe
Tinta Neutro
Tinta neutra
DANIEL SMITH
EXTRA FINE™
WATERCOLORS
15 ml/
1/5 fl. oz.

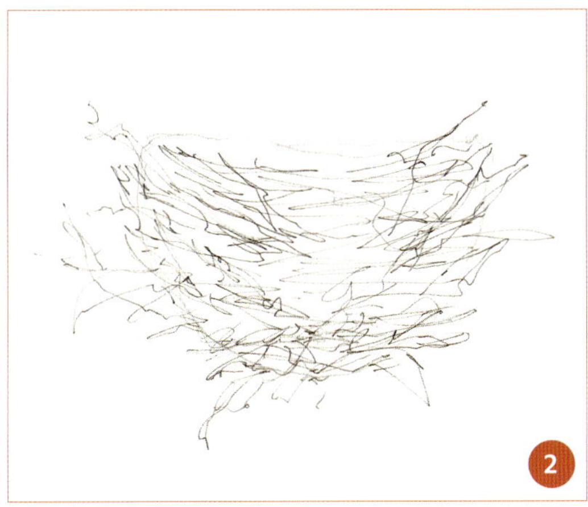

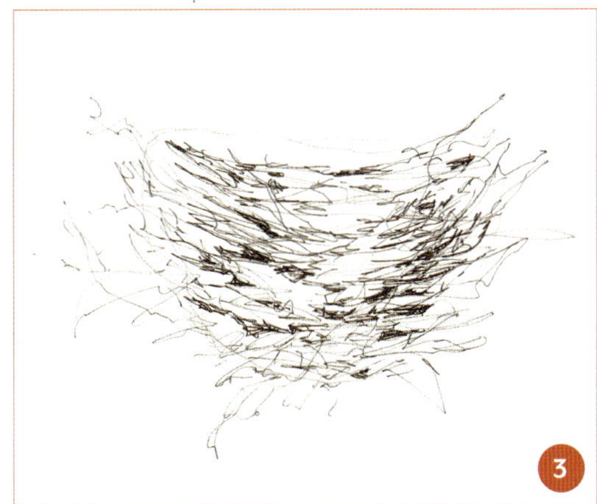

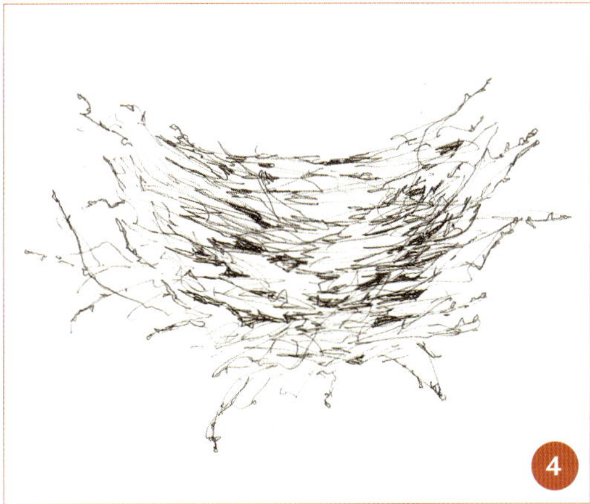

Step 2: Use the 01 fineliner to create a lot of branches. Look at it as a texture instead of single branches. Create marks in the direction of the nest—some long, some short. Have a few breaking free from the border of the nest.

Step 3: Use the 02 fineliner to create darker spots in the main area of the nest. Don't be scared of darks here as they will help emphasize the texture. When you feel like you have enough darks, you can erase the pencil lines.

Step 4: Take your 005 fineliner and add details to the floating branches outside the border. You can add small leaves and oval buds. Keep it very sketchy. You actually need very little here to make it look interesting.

Step 5: Load the size 4 brush with Van Dyke brown, and paint sweeping strokes wet-on-dry in the direction of the texture, leaving plenty of white space. While it's still wet, change to the burnt Umber and do the same. Add a bit of color to the floating branches too.

And that's it. Now we are ready for the family to move into the small villa. On page 106 you can see the Red Cardinal watching over his eggs and on page 90 the Goldfinch is relaxing while taking care of the little ones.

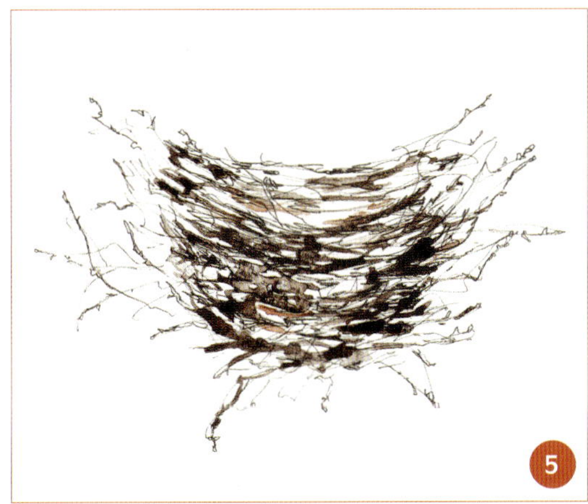

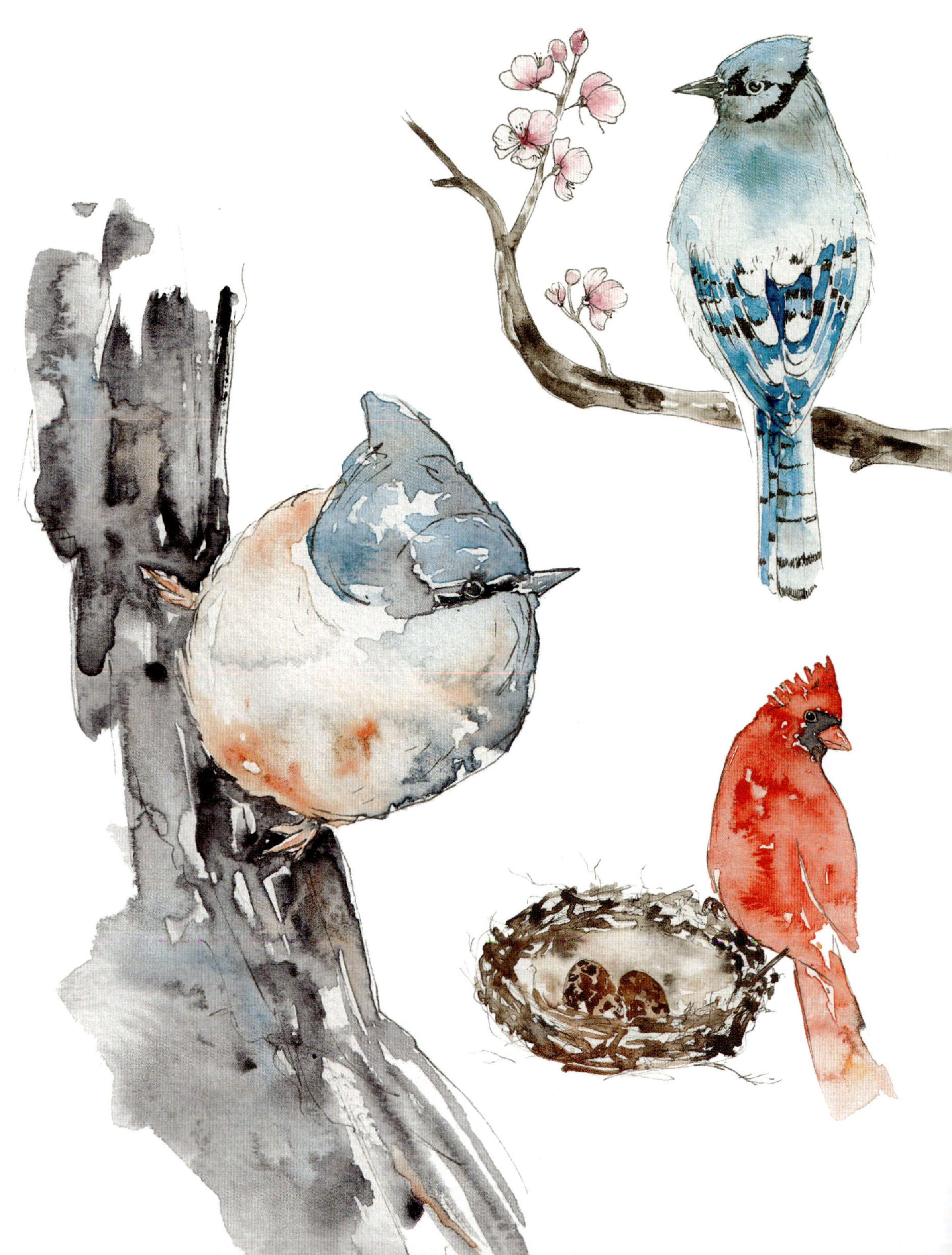

fourteen garden birdie tutorials in ink & wash

Tweet, tweet! Can you hear it? It's the sound of all the happy birdies in the next chapter just waiting for you to dive in! It's almost like those early hours of the morning when the birds wake up in the garden and all sing at the same time.

In this section, we go over thirteen different birds (along with a colorful egg tutorial), ranging from the small Hummingbird (page 111) to the big Raven (page 125). You will learn to make interesting textures, practice those scary features like beaks and eyes and then learn how to place the bird in a beautiful environment.

And the best part is that each and every time we sketch a bird or butterfly (any animal, really), they get a new look or emotion. We never know who will appear on the paper, and that is just magical.

But enough talk. Those birdies won't sketch themselves, right!? ;) Grab your brush and let's go.

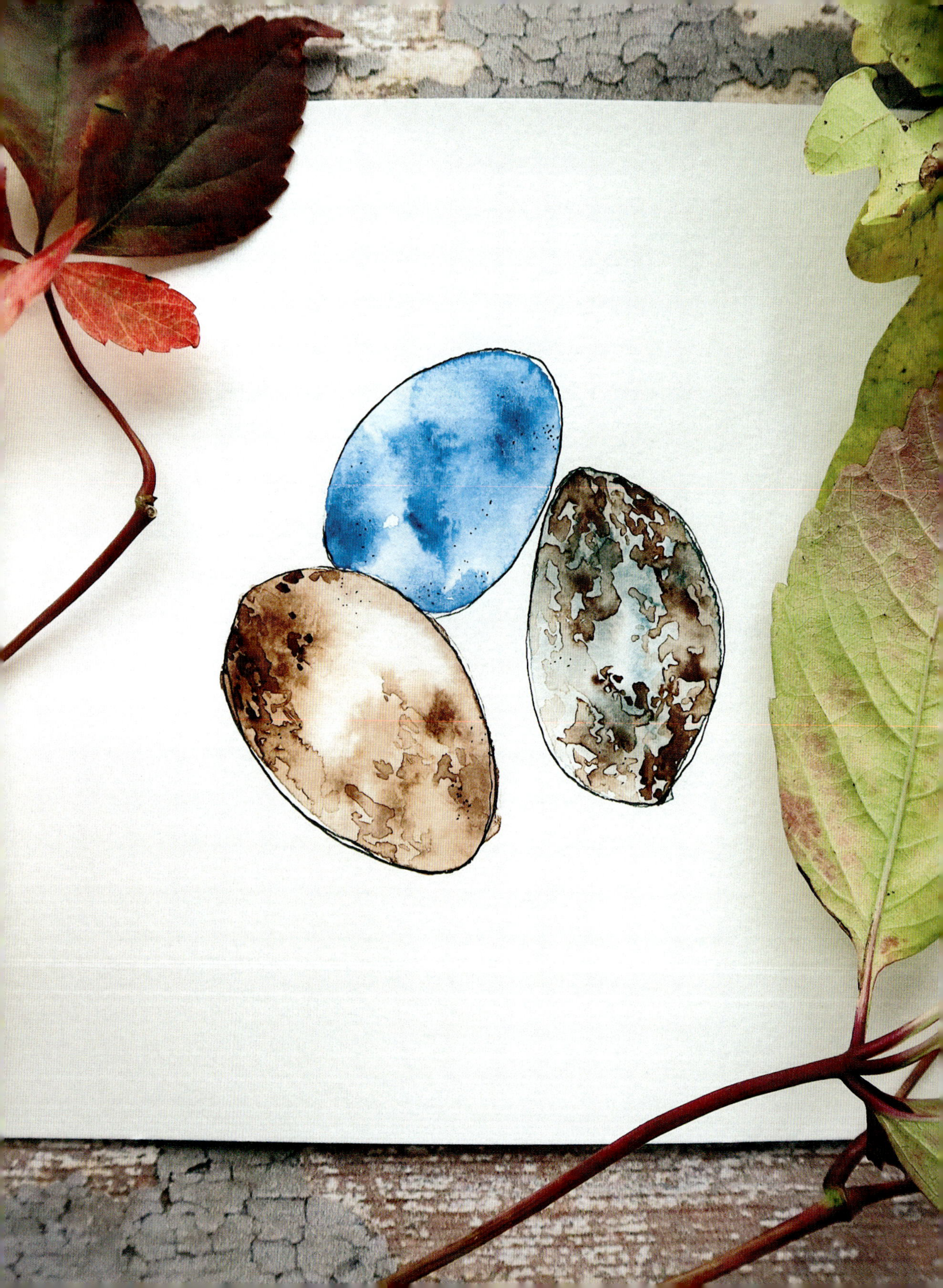

colorful bird eggs
where it all begins

What comes first: the chicken or the egg? Well, since neither philosophy nor science plays a big part in this book, I decided to let the eggs go first. It just seems right. Of course, different birds lay different eggs. Here I show you three variations: the eggs from a robin, a blackbird and a nuthatch. They differ in sizes, textures and colors so you can just play around. If you want to match the egg with the bird, just do an Internet search to see what the eggs look like. When you get the hang of it, you can start putting these eggs in nests next to their mommy or daddy.

Materials

Pencil and eraser
Paper: Canson Montval 300gsm (140lb) cold press
Watercolor brush: size 4
Water and cloth
Palette
Fineliners: sizes 01 and 005

Colors

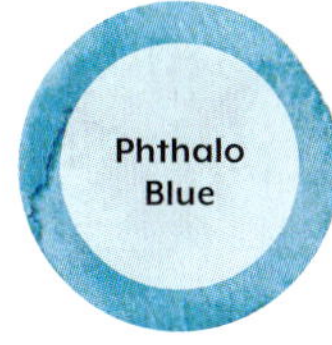

Mixes

To get the mix for the blueish egg, mix equal parts phthalo blue and burnt Umber. You will get beautiful variations in color if you don't mix it too much.

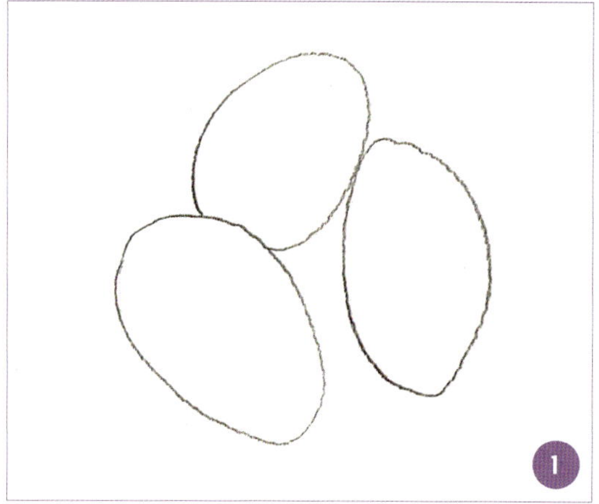

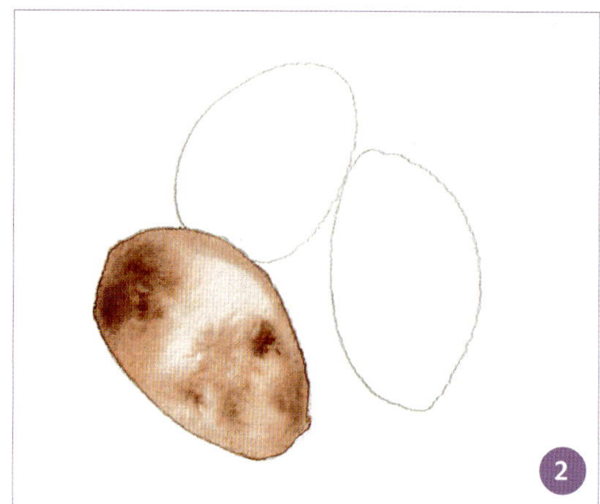

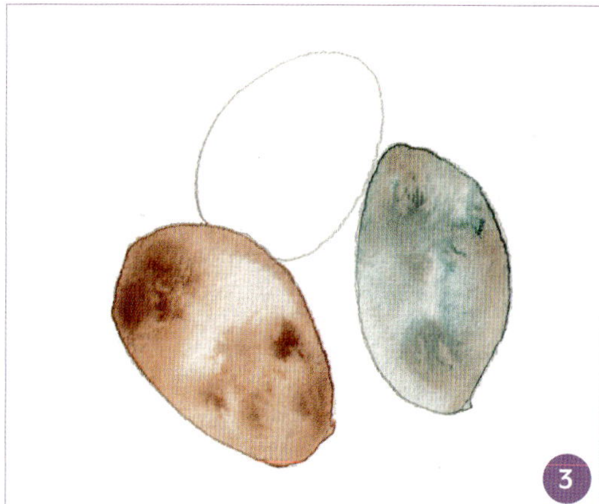

Step 1: With your pencil, draw three ovals. I tucked one behind to create a bit of depth.

Step 2: Wet the left oval and drip in burnt Umber with the size 4 brush. Leave white space and just play around with different tones of Umber flowing around in the water. This brown egg will become the nuthatch's.

Step 3: Wet the right egg and drip in the phthalo blue and burnt Umber mix. Just let the colors flow naturally and separate into both colors from the mix. You can drip in clean water if you would like to mix it up a bit. This will be a blackbird egg.

Step 4: Once the other eggs are dry, you're ready to start on your blue egg. For the middle egg, add clean water again and drip in pure phthalo blue. Just let it flow. As it dries, drip in a drop or two of clean water to get a nice texture. This stunning blue egg is going to grow up to be a beautiful robin.

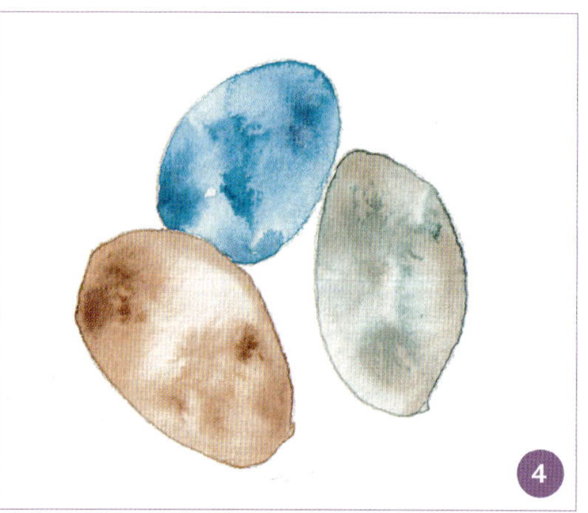

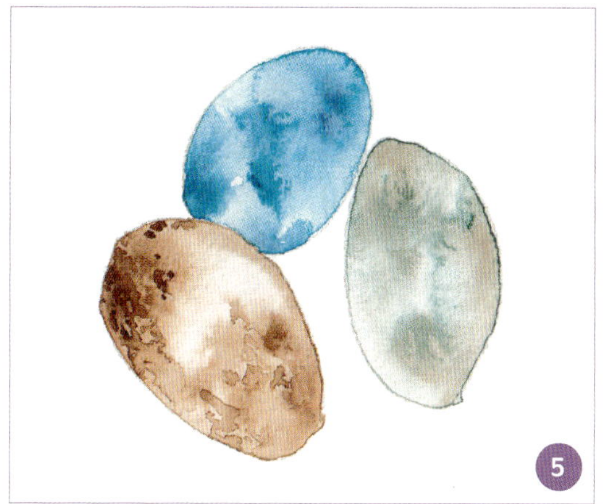

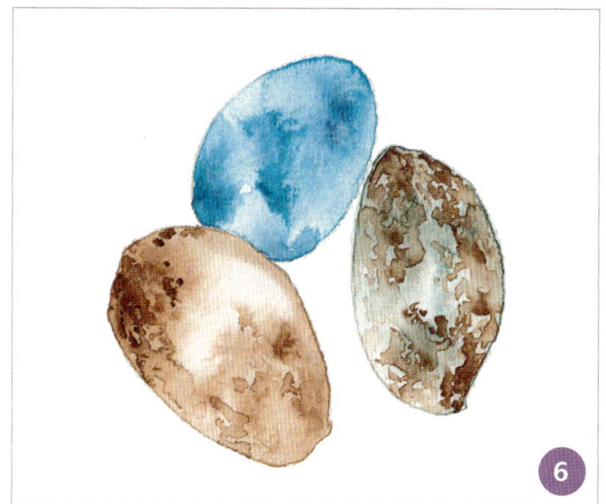

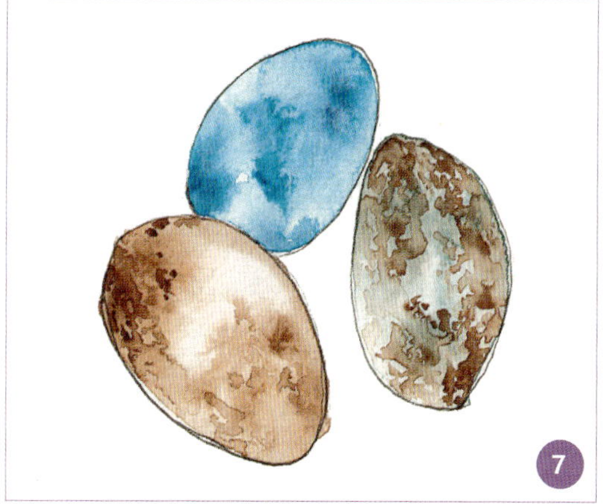

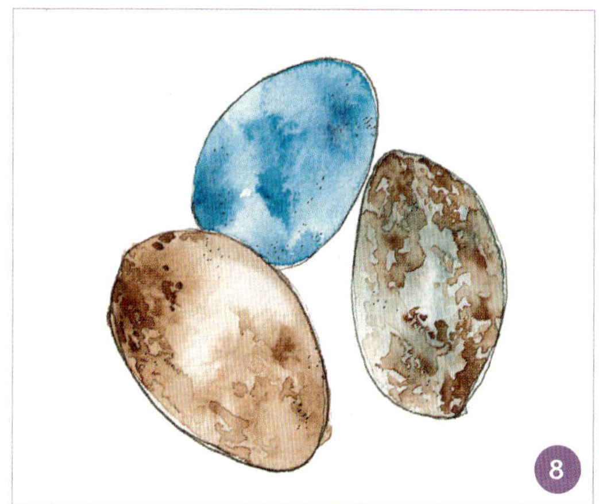

Step 5: When the eggs are dry, paint the left egg wet-on-dry using burnt Umber. Add doodle marks in different sizes. Before it dries completely, wet some of the edges with clean water to get it to run a bit and lose some of the hard edges.

Step 6: Do the same for the right egg, also using burnt Umber. I absolutely love that brown against the blue tones in this egg! Leave the middle egg as is. When you are done adding texture and everything is completely dry, you can erase the pencil lines.

Step 7: Quickly outline the eggs with your 01 fineliner. It's totally cool if the line does not follow the edge of the paint completely—this just adds to the charm of the style.

Step 8: When you look at eggs, you can see they very often have tiny dots. Draw a few of them in random spots with a 005 fineliner.

Now you just wait to see which feathered friends will come out of these beauties while you start your first birdie.

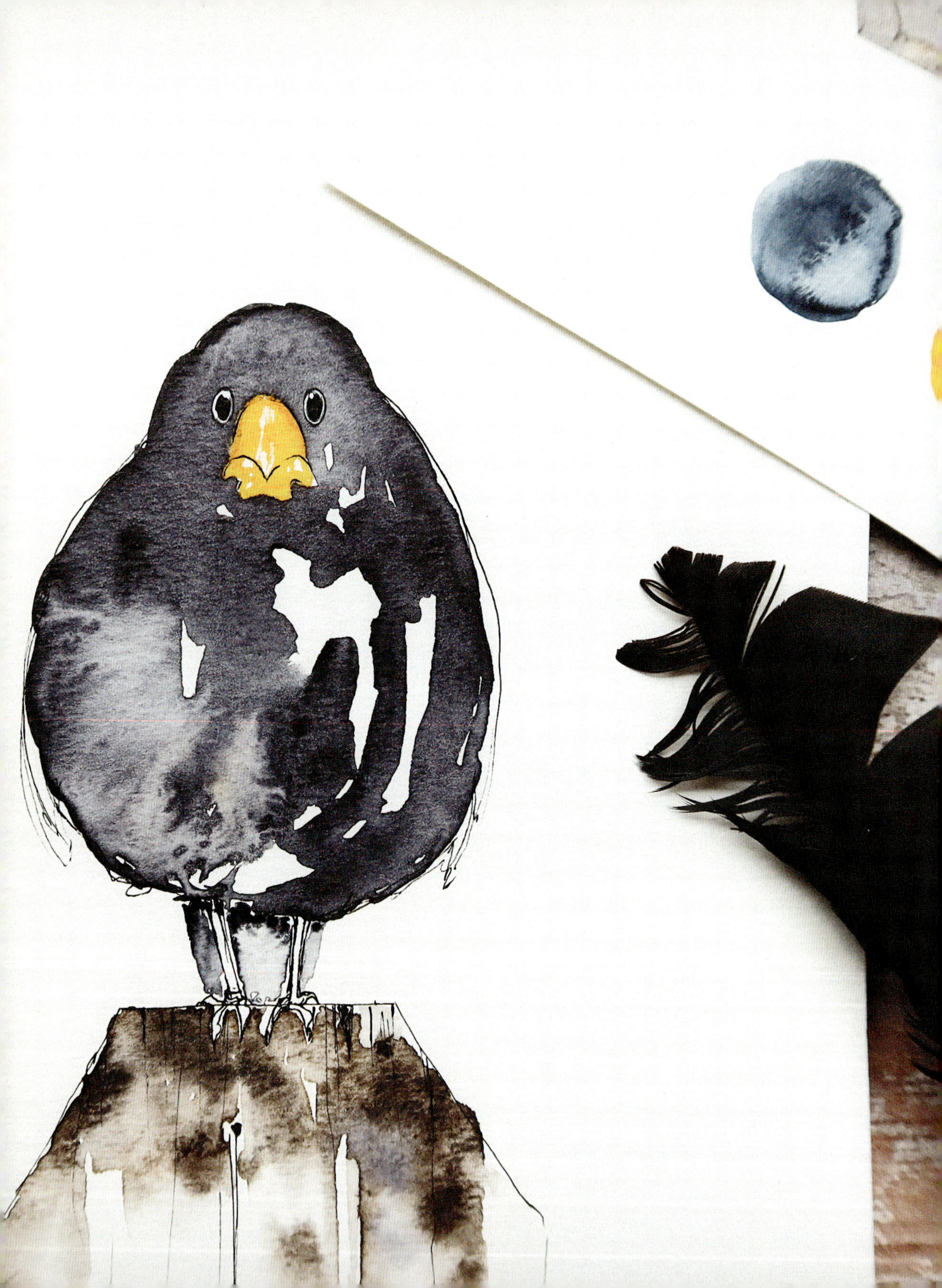

blackbird
a bird of wisdom and magic

The most common bird in my garden is the blackbird. They are everywhere, jumping around on the lawn looking for food. Often, they stop and look a bit grumpy—almost like they are thinking where on earth did the humans put those worms!

I wanted to start with the blackbird in order to introduce you to the easiest way of painting birds. Then we can scale up the difficulty levels a bit later. Here you will learn how to let the watercolor do its thing, and then just add enough detail to emphasize features and shape. I also introduce you to gouache—the wonderful miracle maker.

Materials

Watercolor brushes: sizes 4 and 9
Paper: Canson Montval 300gsm (140lb) cold press
Water and cloth
Palette
Fineliner: size 01

Colors

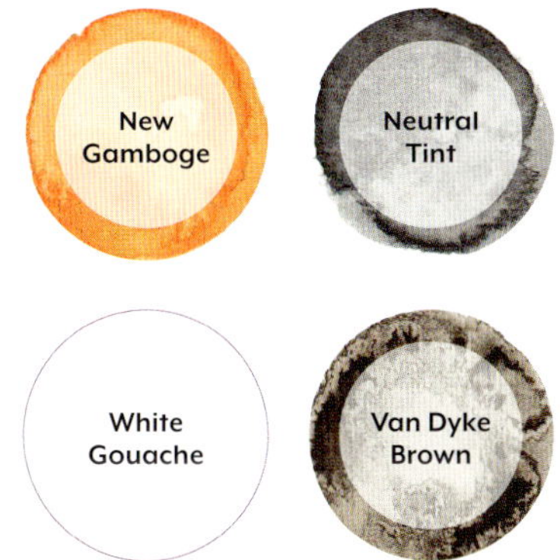

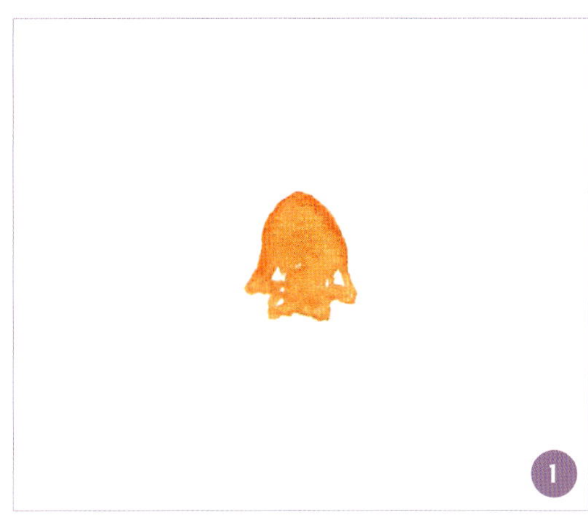

Step 1: With the size 4 brush, paint the beak using new gamboge. The beak looks a bit like a bell or a skirt. Leave some white space for highlights.

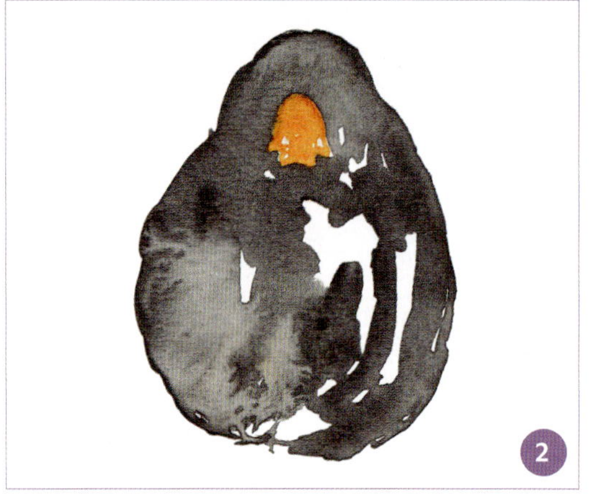

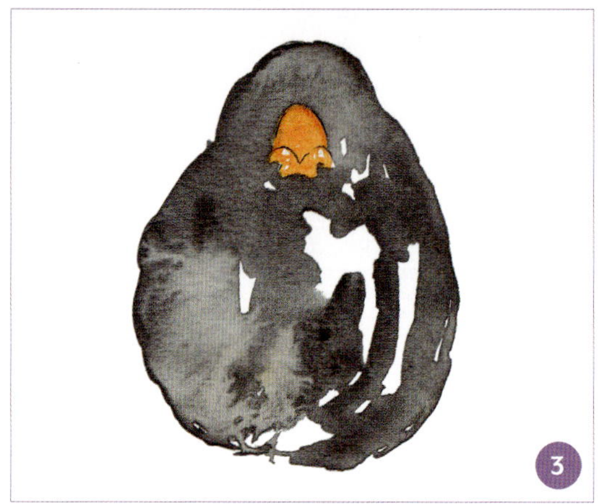

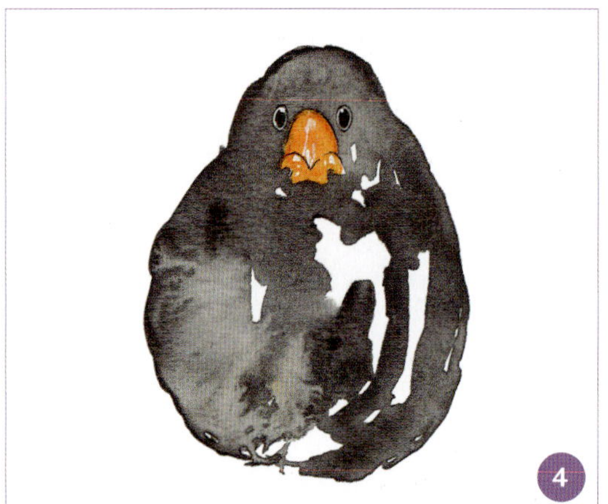

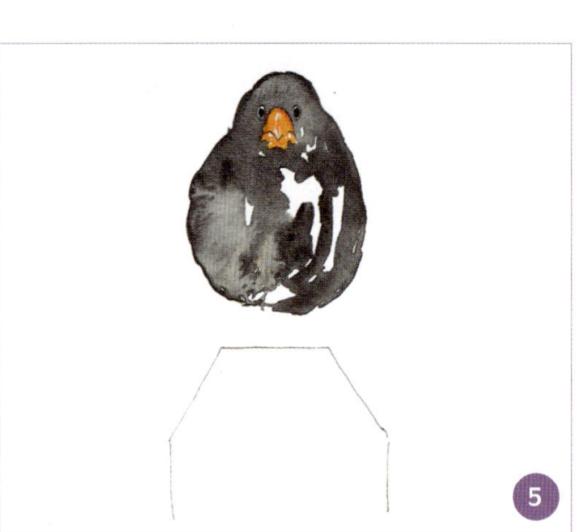

Step 2: Paint the head and body with the size 9 brush in one go using neutral tint. Make sure to keep white space even though the bird is black. This will help the body become less heavy. The shape is easy. It's just a half circle above the beak as the head and an oval body below. Drip in a bit of clean water for texture.

Step 3: After it has dried completely, add a few lines of 01 fineliner to the beak so that it gets a small outline and a separation in the middle that goes down into a point.

Step 4: Sketch the eyes with the fineliner. These are tall ovals because they are seen a bit from the side. (You can see in detail how it's done on page 22—A Few Sketching Tips for Our Birdie Friends.) Since you are drawing with black fineliner on dark watercolor, you need to add some white highlights. This is where our miracle maker comes in handy. Just add a bit of white gouache using the size 4 brush to make a highlight at the top of the eye and a circle around it.

Step 5: Sketch a fence floating below the blackbird with the fineliner, using the Picket Fence (page 27) as inspiration.

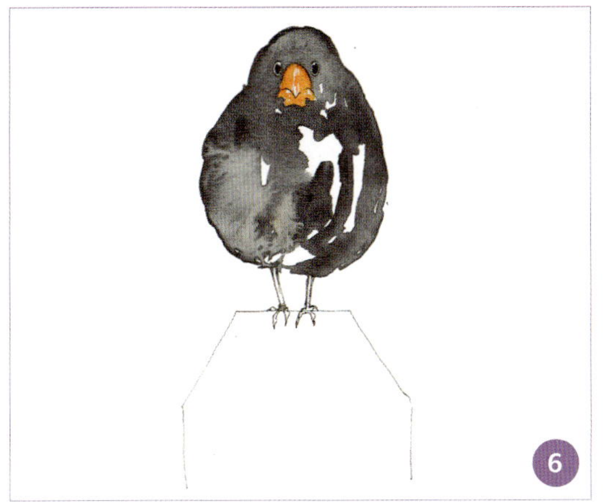

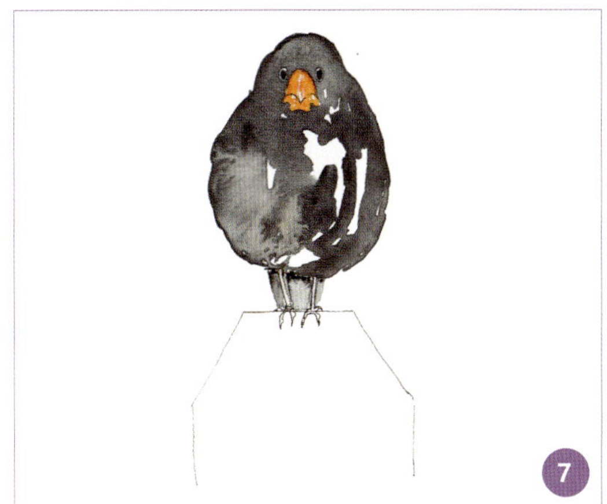

Step 6: Draw two legs with the 01 fineliner like shown on How to Draw Bird Feet (page 22). Wrap the toes around the fence.

Step 7: Paint a tail behind the bird and fence using a watery neutral tint. At the top, where the tail meets the body, you can drip in a bit more intense color.

Step 8: Quickly outline the body with the 01 fineliner, and then give it a small wing on each side. Finally, add a few details and colors to the fence. In my sketch, I used Van Dyke brown and a bit of neutral tint to tie the colors together.

And now you are already done with your first birdie! I'm so proud!

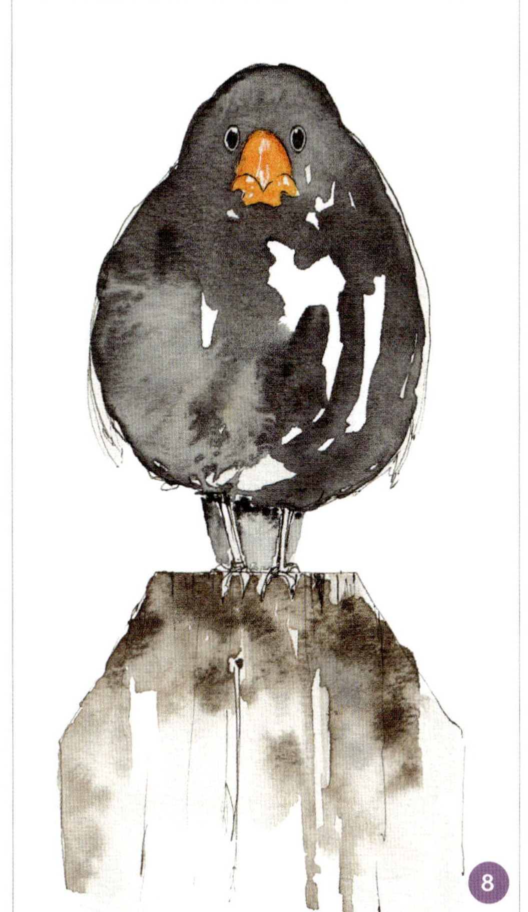

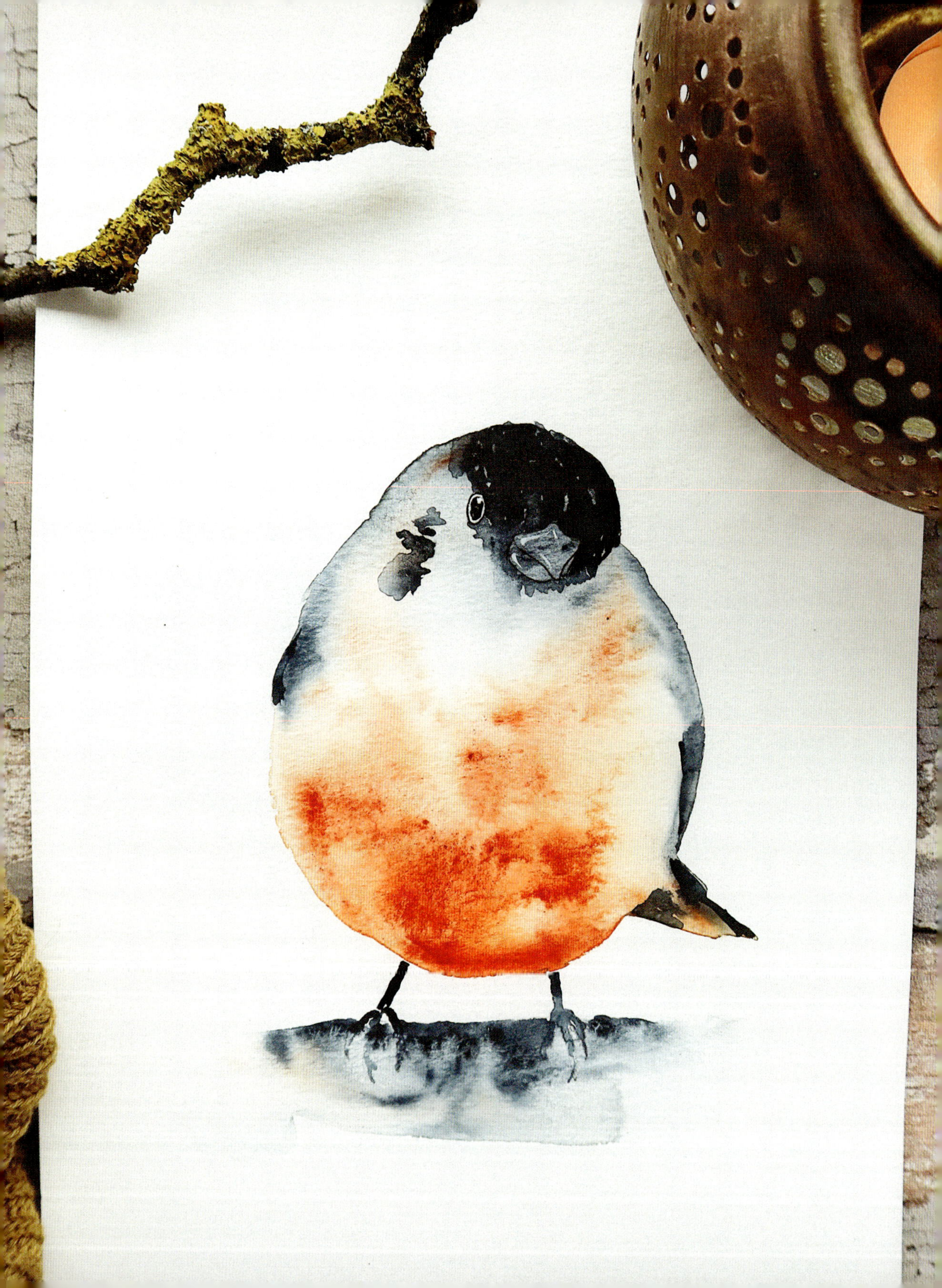

bullfinch

spreading hope and resilience in the garden

During the winter, when everything is kind of gray and boring in the garden, a bullfinch sighting is one of the most exciting things. You can just watch that little colorful fellow jump around on the branches forever. I can definitely see why it symbolizes hope and resilience. You could actually create a card featuring this small birdie for someone who needs a bit of hope in trying times. It might just be what that special person needs.

I am also going easy with you on this second birdie. We are testing out the wonders of the flowing watercolor and only playing around with three colors to really emphasize the warmth of this cute, red-bellied bird.

Materials

Pencil and eraser
Paper: Canson Montval 300gsm (140lb) cold press
Watercolor brushes: sizes 9 and 4
Water and cloth
Palette
Fineliner: size 01

Colors

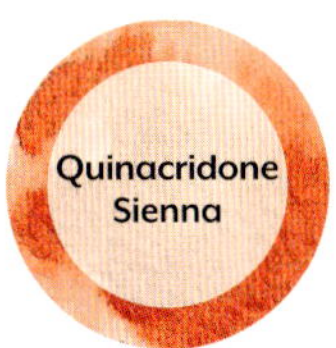

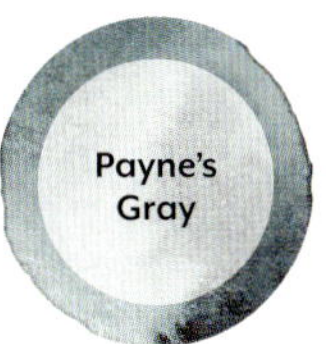

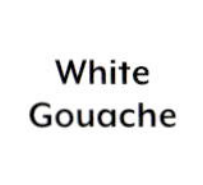

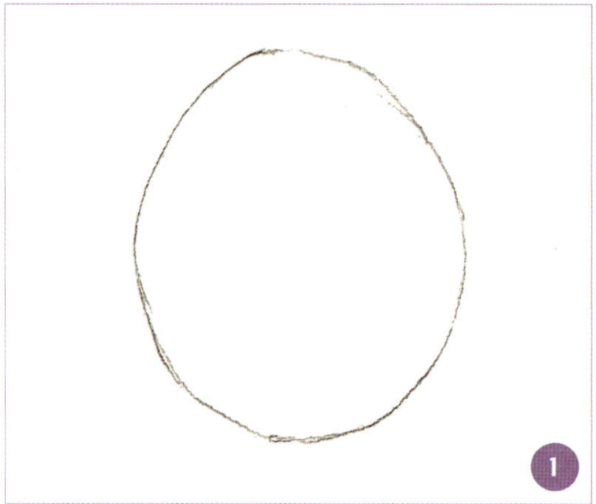

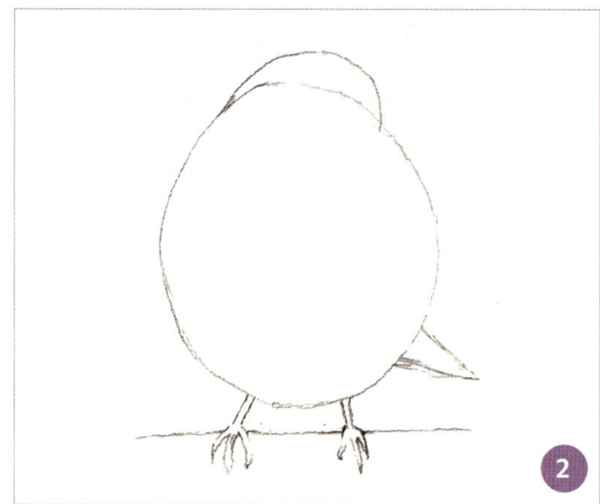

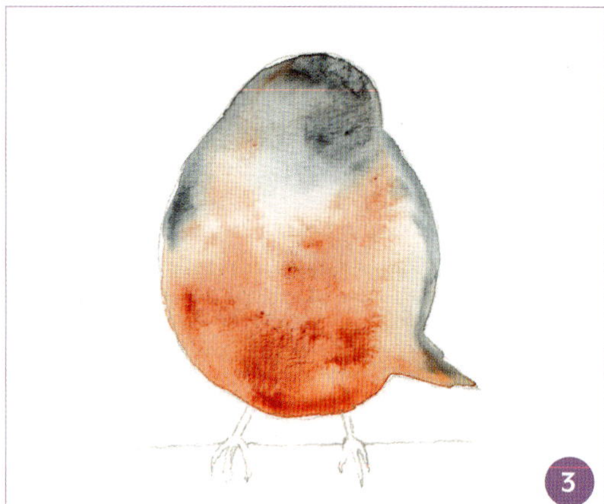

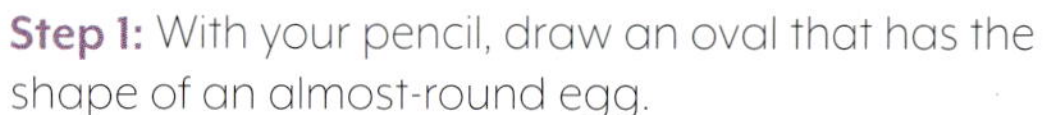

Step 1: With your pencil, draw an oval that has the shape of an almost-round egg.

Step 2: We will sketch a bird that is looking off a bit to the side. Sketch an oval head on top of the body oval that tilts a little to the right. Then sketch a tail triangle on the right side, two legs and a line below that will be the surface where the bird is standing. Sketch the middle toes the longest, and try to make the feet look like they are resting on the ground. When you like your sketch, you can erase the lines you don't need.

Step 3: With the size 9 brush, wet the entire bird except the feet with clean water. Start by dripping in quinacridone sienna on the body. Then add Payne's gray to the top of the head as well as on the wings. Let it dry completely.

Step 4: Sketch a beak and one eye with the 01 fineliner. You can start out with a pencil so it's not too intimidating. Make a narrow oval with a highlight at the top right for the eye. And the beak has the shape of a very soft diamond with a half circle below it.

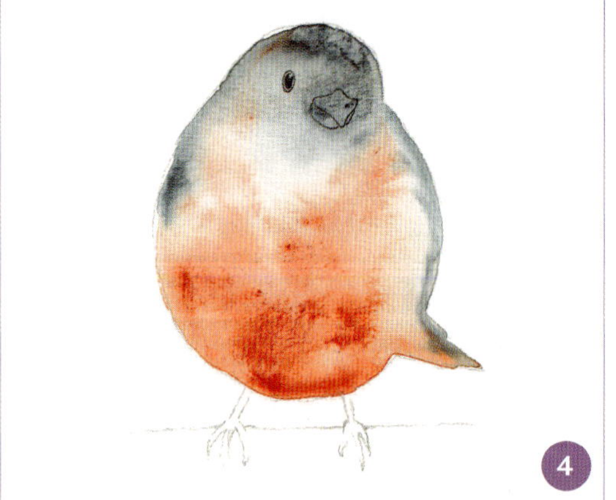

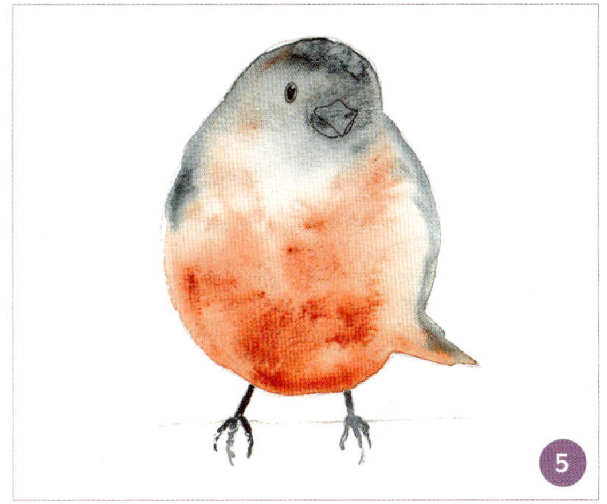

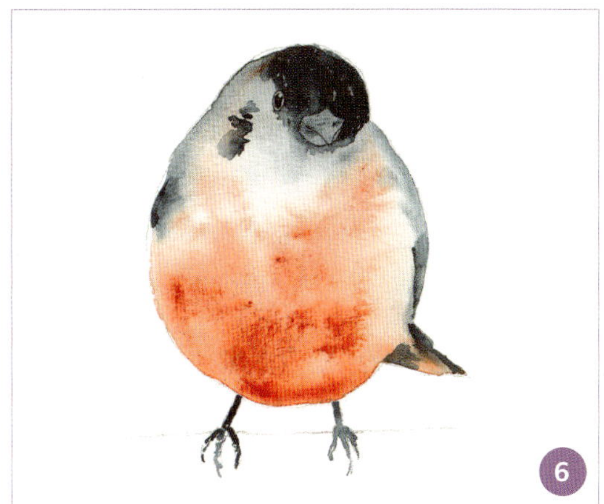

Step 5: Paint the feet using Payne's gray with the size 4 brush. Keep it darker towards the body for a bit of shadowing.

Step 6: Paint the dark areas on the bullfinch using Payne's gray with the size 4 brush. First paint the beak next to the eye and the top of the head. Keep white space and paint wet-on-dry with brushstrokes going in the direction of the feathers. Add a few marks to the left cheek as well. Keep it light and soften a few of the edges on the neck with clean water. Paint darker spots on the tail and a few dark areas at the tip of the wings.

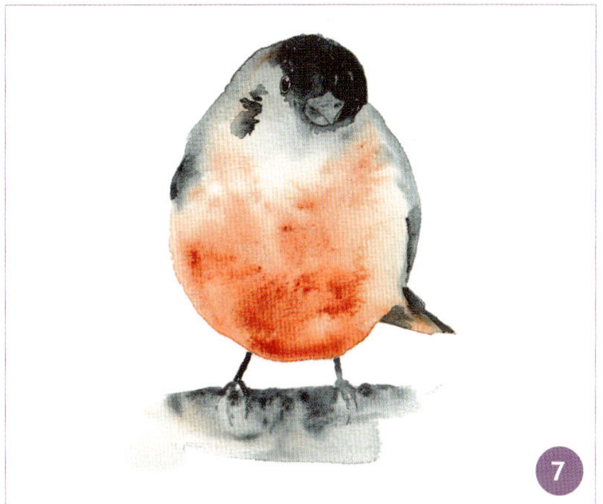

Step 7: Give the surface the bird is standing on a swoosh with the size 9 brush using Payne's gray. Drip in a bit of sienna and that is done.

Step 8: Paint white highlights with the size 4 brush in the eye with the white gouache. You can also give the beak a few lines of gouache as well, highlighting the shape.

Now the bullfinch is so ready to jump into the garden to spread winter cheer.

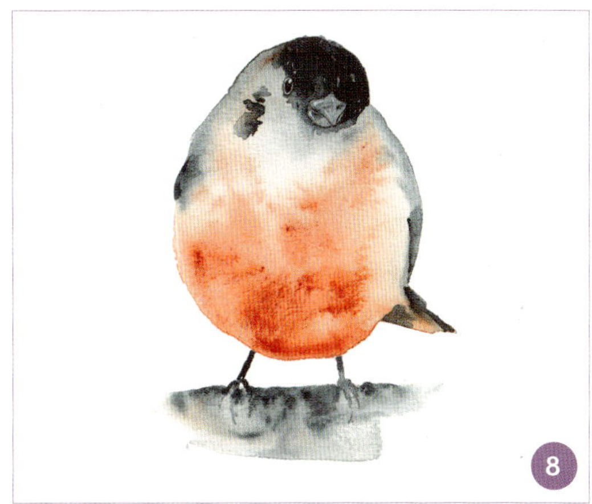

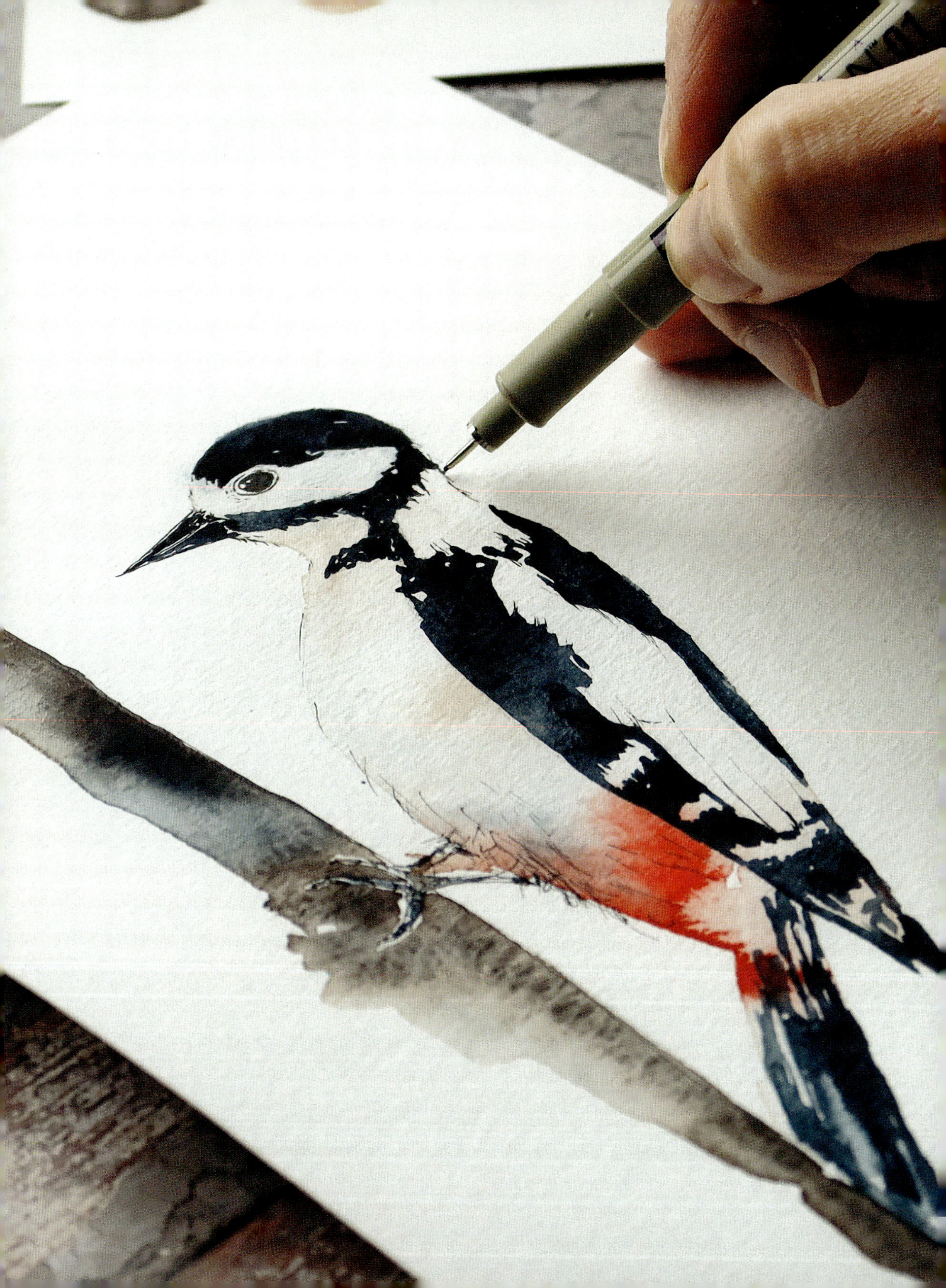

woodpecker
a bird of optimism and creativity

The woodpecker is the creative person's spiritual animal when you look at its symbolism. And to be honest, it IS a very creative individual. Here in the garden, I am constantly amazed by how tightly it can hold the bird feeder meant for the smaller birds and then eat all the seeds. It's a bit greedy but definitely both optimistic and very creative.

In this step-by-step, we are going a bit further along on the difficulty scale. We will work in layers and strengthen the wet-on-wet layer with wet-on-dry texture. This is going to be fun!

Materials

Pencil and eraser
Paper: Canson Montval 300gsm (140lb) cold press
Watercolor brushes: sizes 9 and 4
Water and cloth
Palette
Fineliners: sizes 005 and 01

Colors

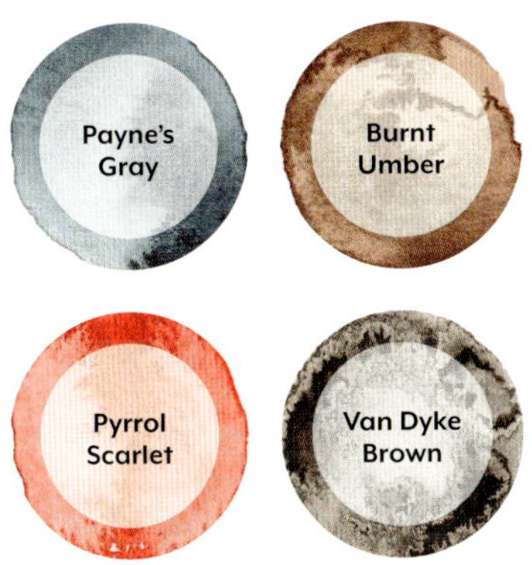

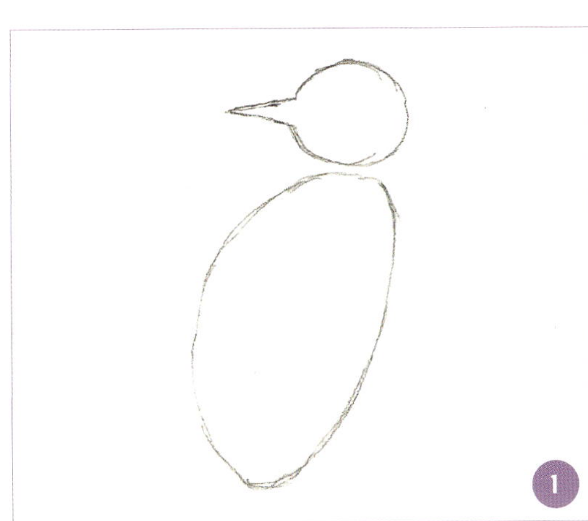

Step 1: With the pencil, sketch a pointy beak and an oval head turning to the left. Then draw an oval body tilting to the right.

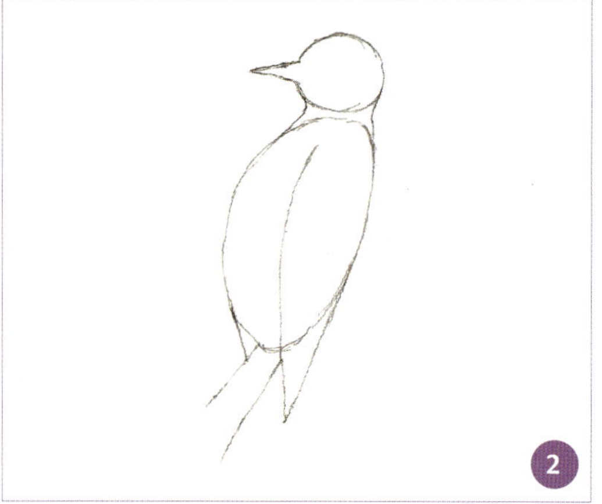

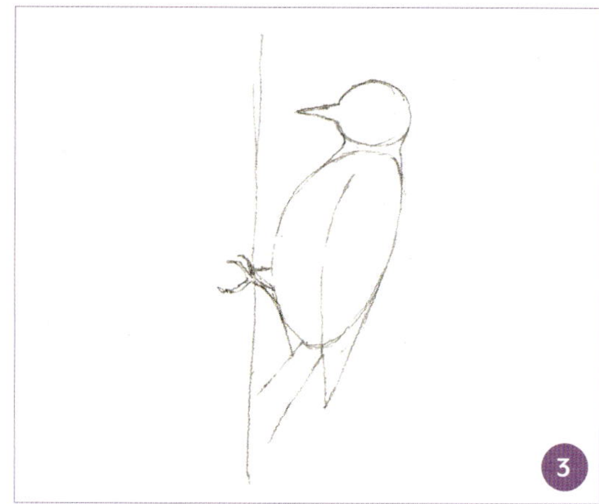

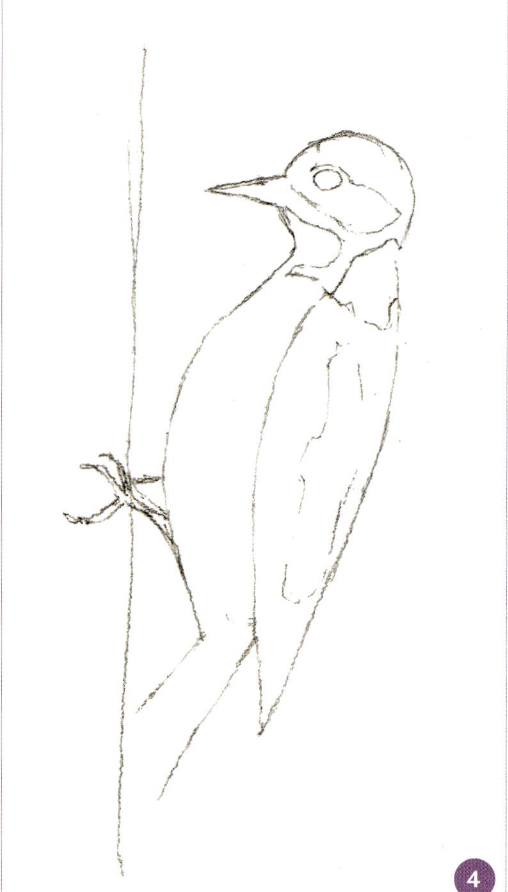

Step 2: Sketch the lines for the neck—attaching the head to the body—and a wing and tail tilting along with the body.

Step 3: To finish the main part of our pencil sketch, draw feet and a very simple line to resemble a tree. The front foot has three long toes: two pointing forward and one pointing back. The back leg is barely visible. When you are confident with your sketch, you can erase the lines you don't need.

Step 4: You actually need the pencil a bit more, because now you want to make guides for the dark marks on the head and wing. And while you are at it, draw in the oval eye as well. Now you are done and you can put down the pencil.

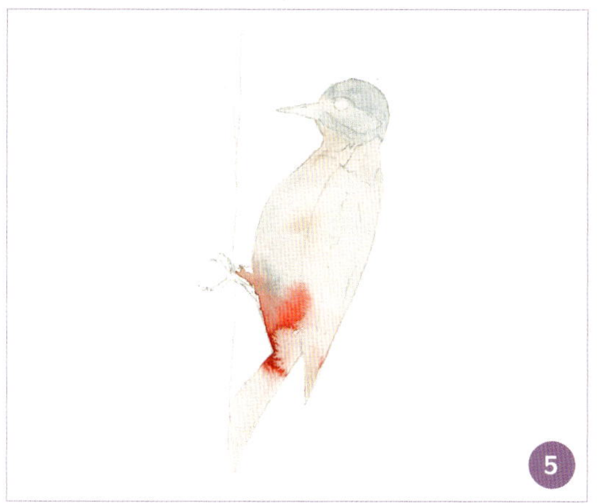

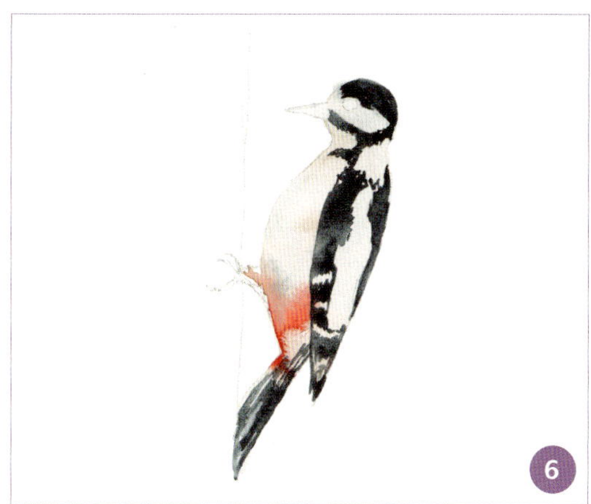

Step 5: With the size 9 brush, wet the entire body except the eye and beak. While it's wet, drip in Payne's gray and burnt Umber with the size 9 brush to the head and stomach. Keep it light. Then, count to twenty, and when it's not completely wet any longer, add a touch of pyrrol scarlet to the lower stomach. It will run a bit into the rest of the body, and that is totally cool. Let it dry completely before moving on. This can take a while, so a great activity would be to glance out the window for a while along with a cup of tea. You might get lucky and see a real-life woodpecker!

Step 6: When you've finished your tea, with your size 4 brush, paint a new layer covering the dark areas on the head, wing and tail using Payne's gray. Keep it uneven at the edges to show feather texture.

Step 7: With the 005 fineliner, outline the beak with a divider in the middle and draw the eye. Give the eye two highlights on the left side in two different sizes.

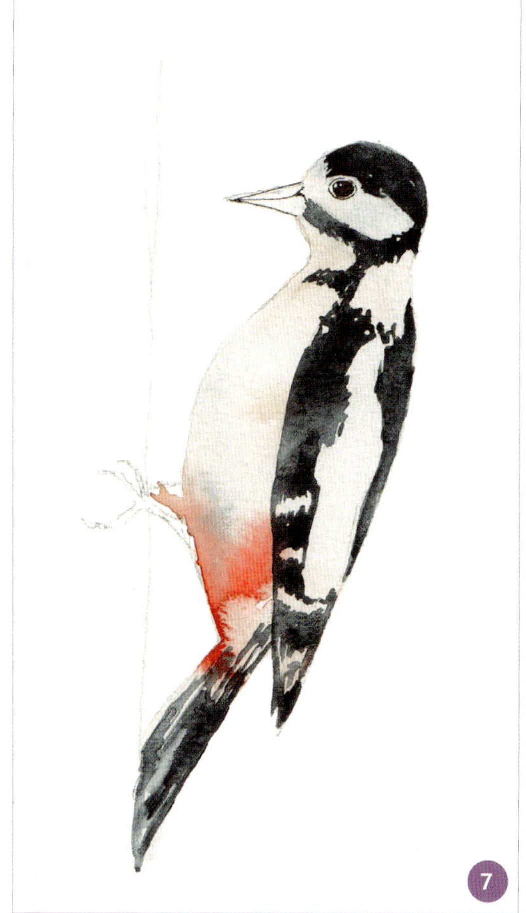

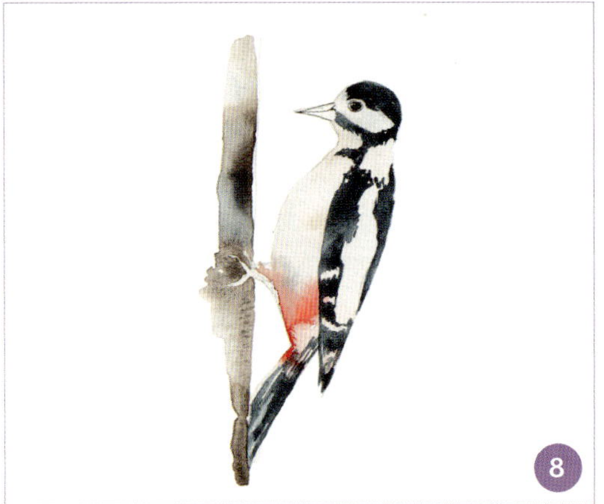

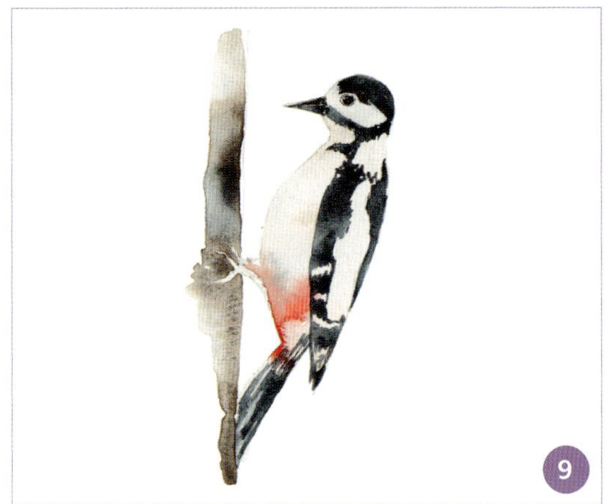

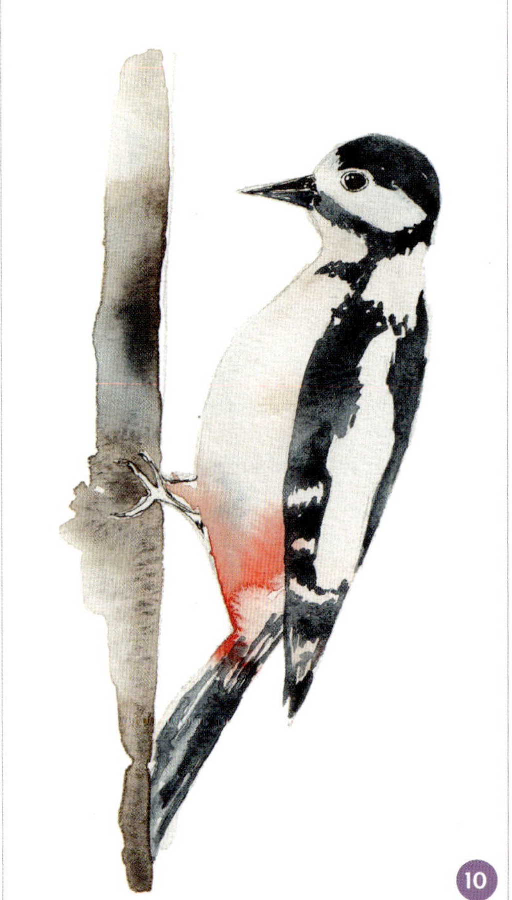

Step 8: With the size 9 brush, paint the tree in Van Dyke brown and Payne's gray. Try to stay clear of the feet so we can give them color a bit later.

Step 9: And now back to the woodpecker. With the size 4 brush, paint the beak using Payne's gray and a little burnt Umber. Leave a few white spots and a white line in the middle.

Step 10: Outline the feet with the 01 fineliner. When that is done, you can erase the pencil lines.

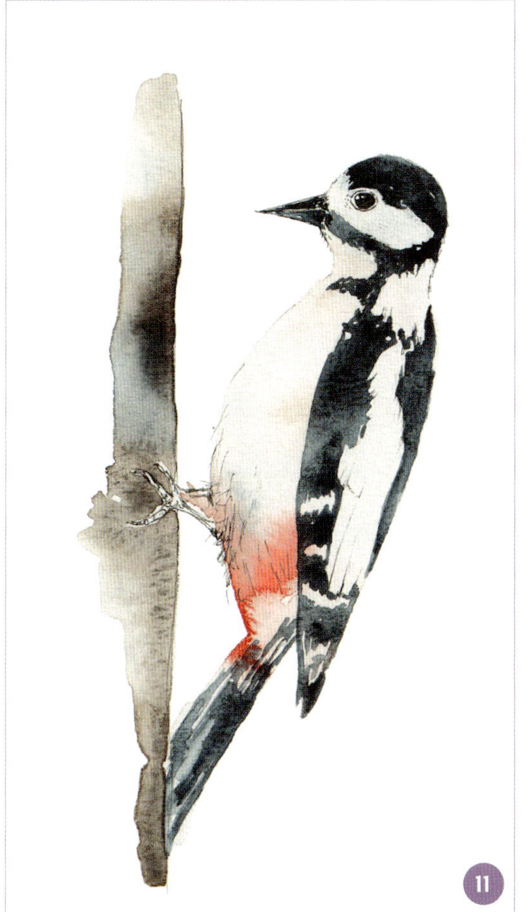

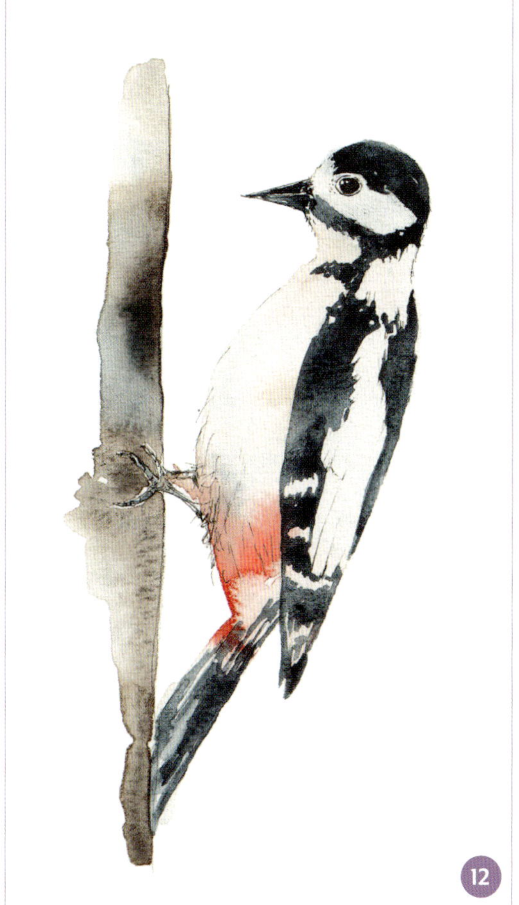

Step 11: Now it's time to grab your 005 fineliner and go crazy with some fast lines. Add details to the feathers, wings and feet. You can also give the tree a line to outline it.

Step 12: We're at the end here, but I think we should give the feet a bit more love. So, add a bit of color using Payne's gray and burnt Umber with the size 4 brush.

You now have a lovely, optimistic and creative birdie ready to play with. Maybe for your next sketch you could put him on a bird feeder. That would be cool, and I would love to see it!

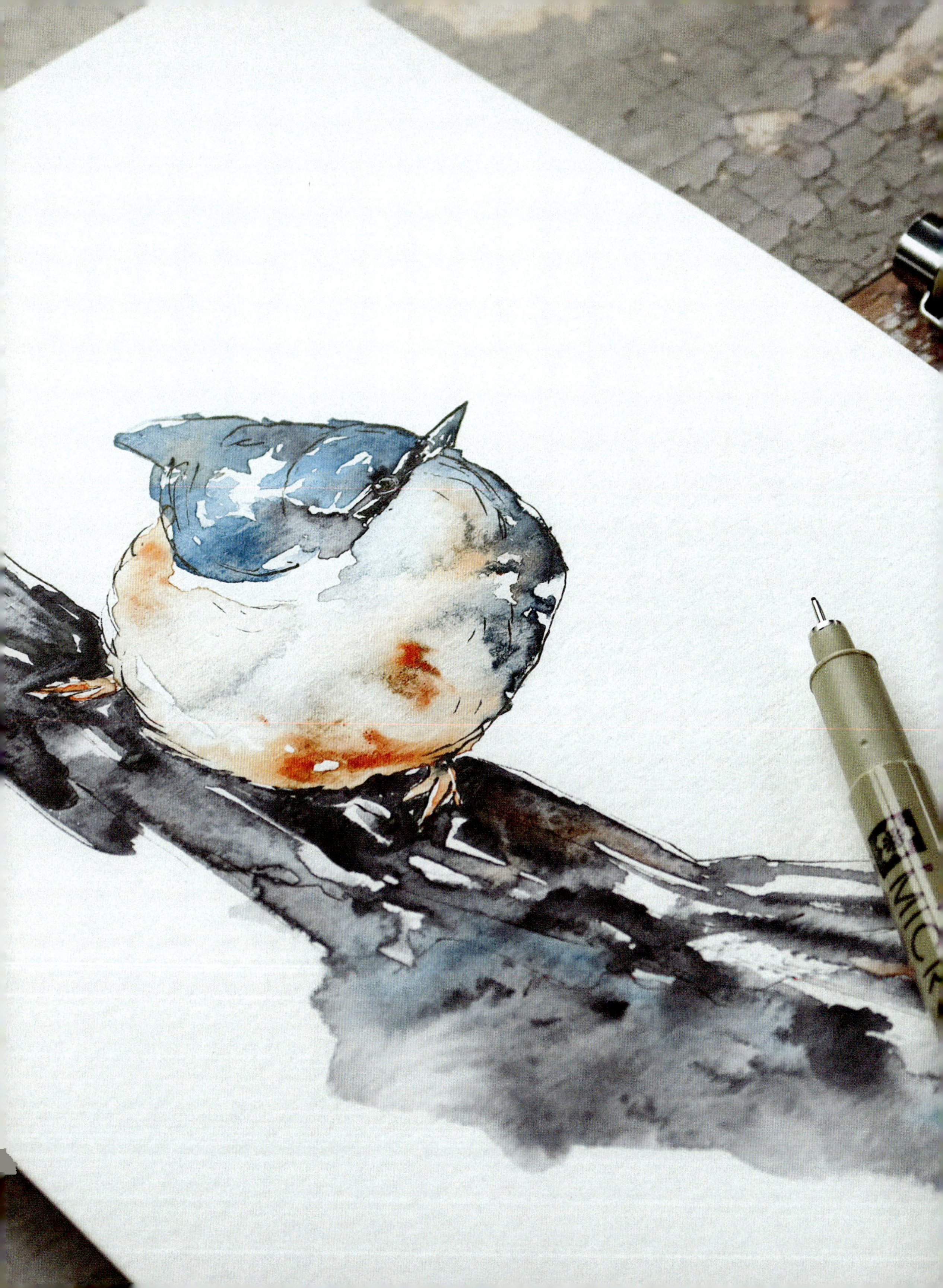

nuthatch
ready to take on even the biggest nuts

The nuthatch does not give up easily when looking for food. No nut is too tough, and I think we can all learn something from that kind of perseverance. I always love watching nuthatches in the garden. They always look so happy climbing up and down trees and running super-fast. It's so impressive how they can hang on like that. And speaking of tough nuts, I thought this would be a great tutorial to introduce bridging colors like I showed you on page 15. And don't worry; it's not as hard as you would think. It's more like a hazelnut in difficulty level.

Materials

Paper: Canson Montval 300gsm (140lb) cold press

Watercolor brushes: sizes 4 and 9

Water and cloth

Palette

Fineliner: size 01

Colors

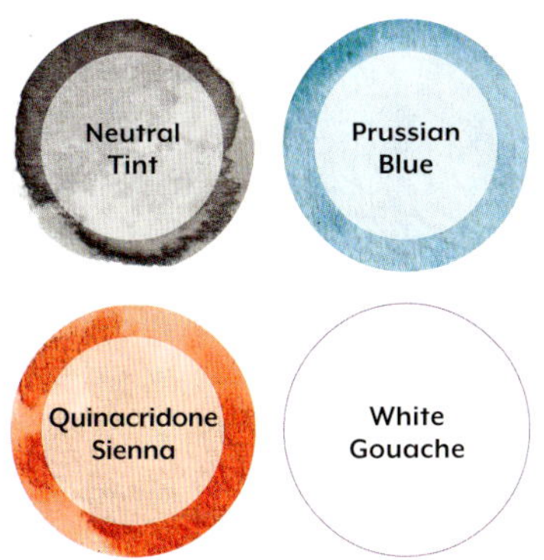

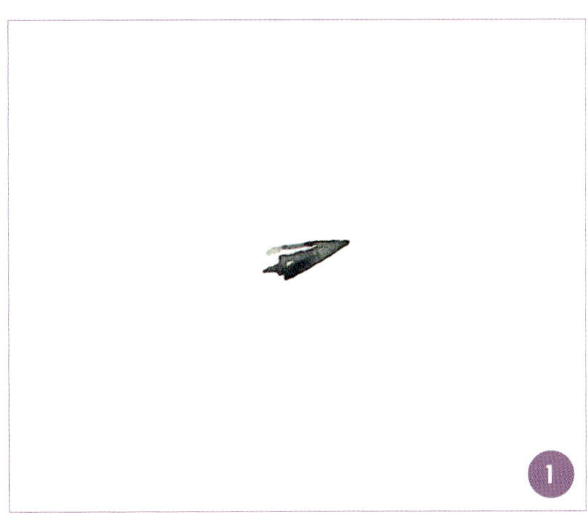

Step 1: With the size 4 brush, paint a small, narrow beak using neutral tint with a white highlight at the top. Point it to the right and a bit upwards.

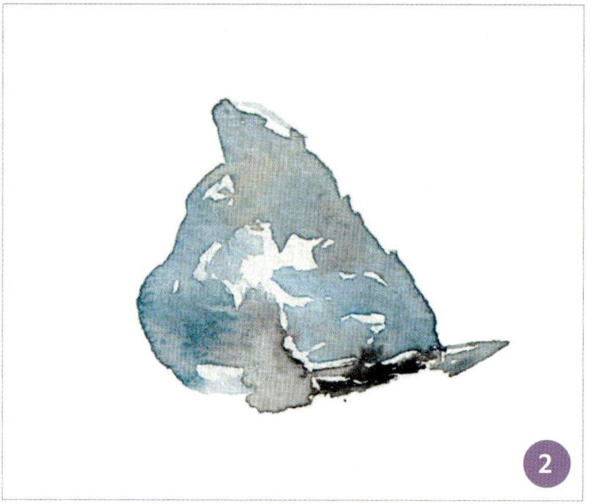

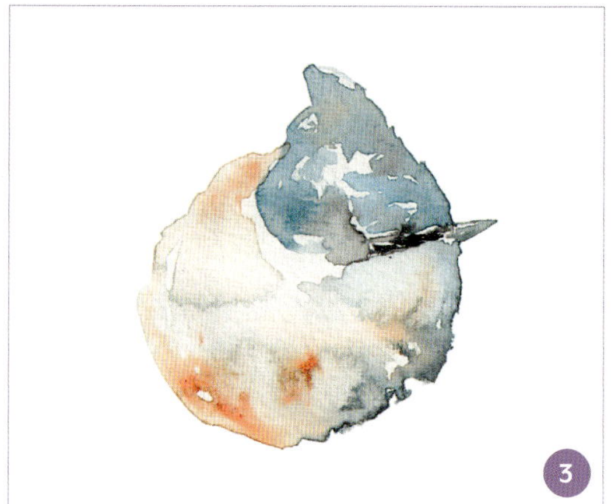

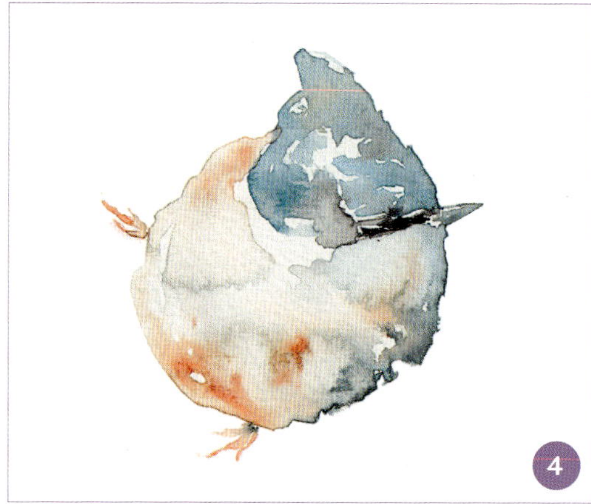

Step 2: With the same brush, paint the top of the head, the side of the wing and a tail in Prussian blue. Leave a bit of white space between the head and the wing, but make small bridges for the paint to flow in. (See Bridging Colors on page 15 for more details.) Right now—before adding fineliner—it looks like a bird with a shark fin, but don't worry, it will get better. Count to ten, and then add a line of neutral tint below the blue, starting from the beak. It's okay if the colors bleed a bit. Let this dry.

Step 3: With the size 9 brush, wet a big circle below the top part of the bird with clean water. Drip in a bit of the different colors and let them bleed: quinacridone sienna on the stomach all the way back to the tail and Prussian blue and neutral tint along the right side. Don't go overboard here.

Step 4: With the size 4 brush, add two feet pointing to the left with the quinacridone sienna. You can only see three toes on each foot. Drip in a bit of neutral tint where the feet meet the body for a bit of shadow.

Step 5: With your 01 fineliner, add an outline to the beak. Then draw the eye with the white gouache using the size 4 brush to create the highlight and a small circle around the pupil.

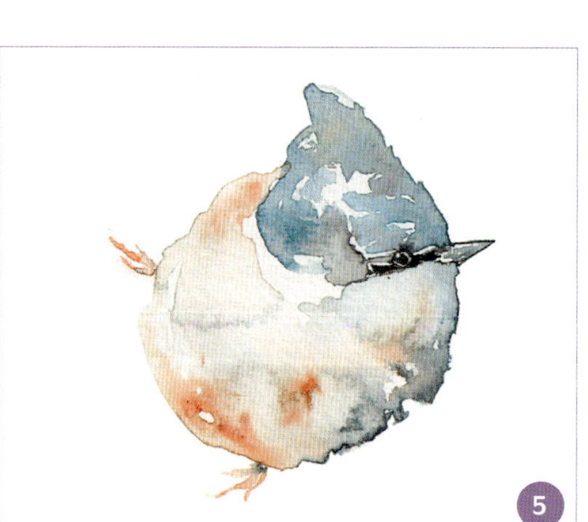

Step 6: Now it's time to add some definition and texture. Start by defining the top of the head, the wings and the tail with the 01 fineliner. Can you see how the weird shape suddenly makes sense? Then use the lines to show the direction of the feathers all the way around the body. Keep the belly clear of lines to create the illusion of a highlight.

Step 7: Use the fineliner to sketch a very quick tree branch. You can see this is a bigger variation than the one the Woodpecker (page 77) rests on, but the technique is the same. With the size 9 brush, paint the branch using mostly neutral tint along with some Prussian blue and quinacridone sienna. Keep the colors darkest below the bird for a bit of shadow.

While it's still wet, load the size 4 brush with neutral tint and paint a few lines from the branch that push into the stomach of the bird. This will emphasize the texture of the feathers against the dark branch.

Woo-hoo! You finished the lovely nuthatch. Congrats! Maybe you got inspired to step in its footsteps and try that tree climbing thing. As an old YMCA scout in Denmark, I gotta tell you that it's really fun!

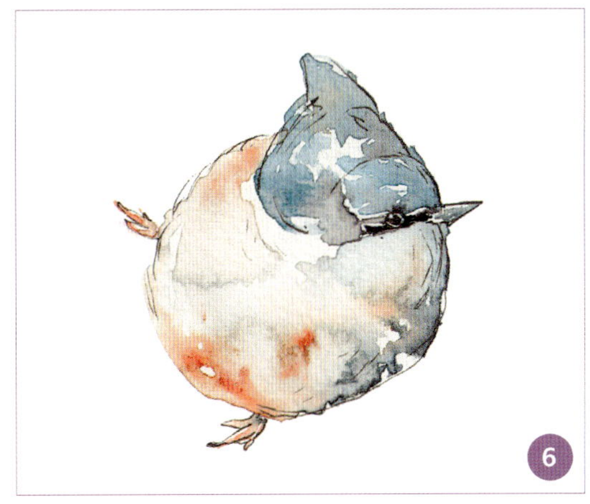

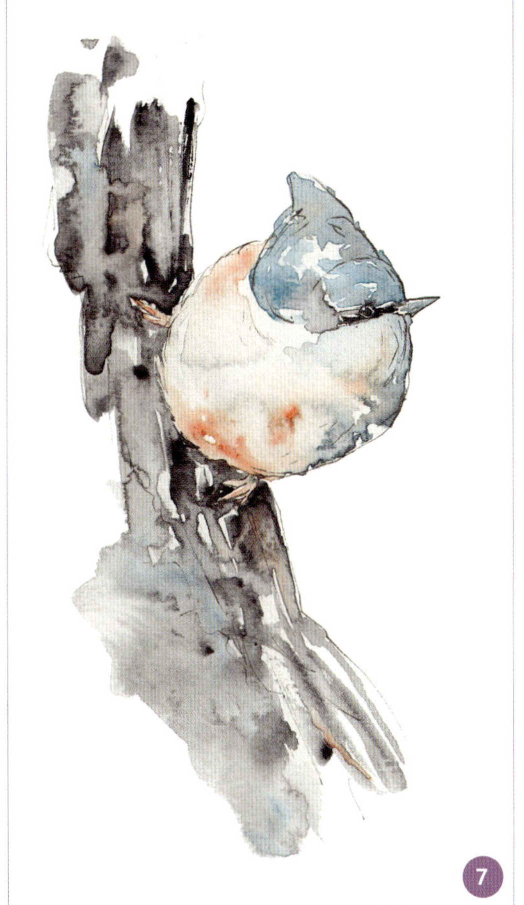

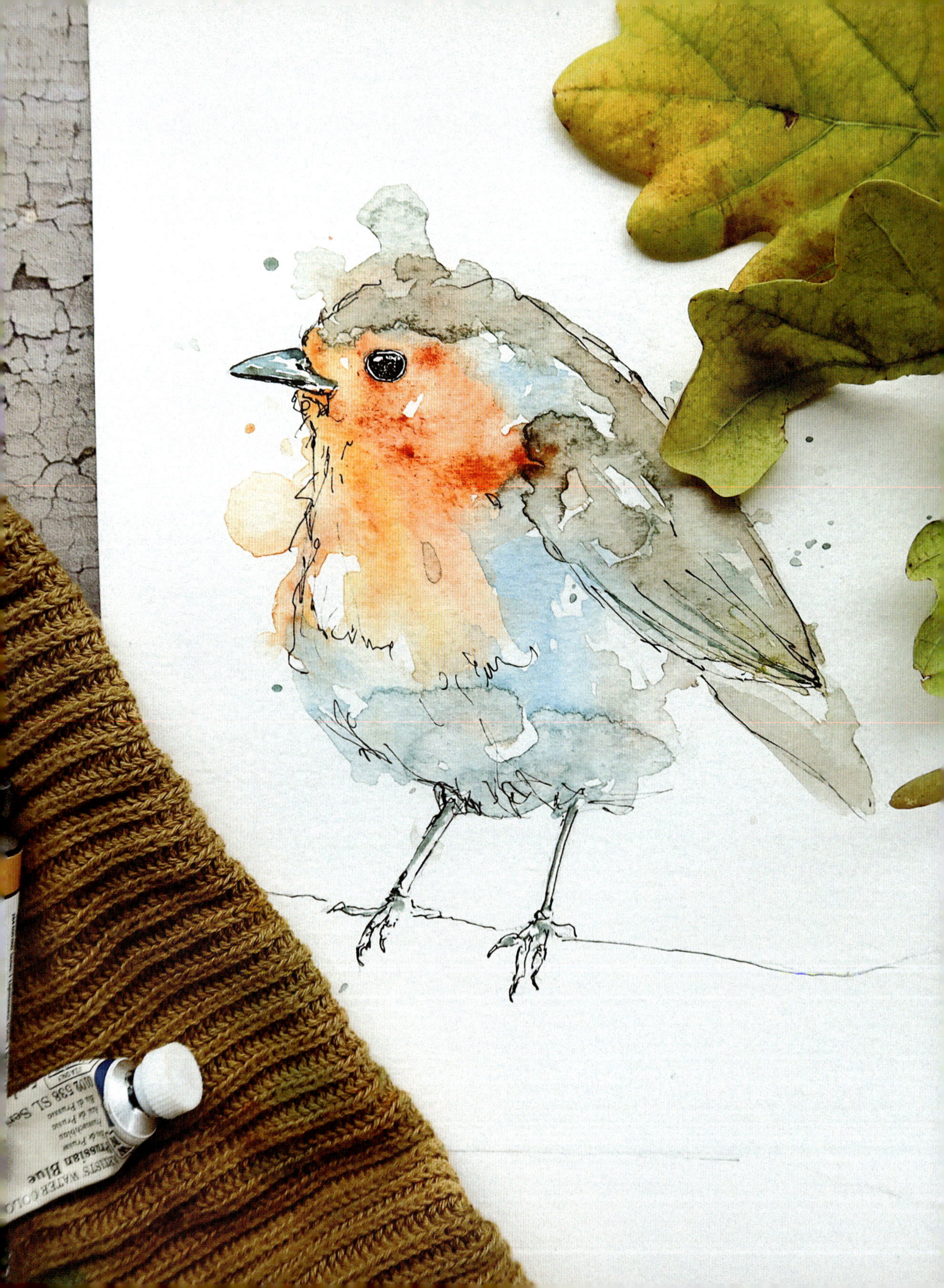

red robin
a colorful bird of joy

The robin is one of those birds that just lights up the grays and browns in my winter garden. The bright red chest makes it stand out and shine like a small lantern in the dark. That might be the reason why it is quite the celebrity amongst birds, being featured on thousands of winter holiday cards across the globe.

In this tutorial, you'll learn how to be very loose with your wash and let the fineliner shape the bird afterward.

Materials

Pencil and eraser

Paper: Canson Montval 300gsm (140lb) cold press

Watercolor brushes: sizes 9 and 1

Water and cloth

Palette

Fineliner: size 01

Colors

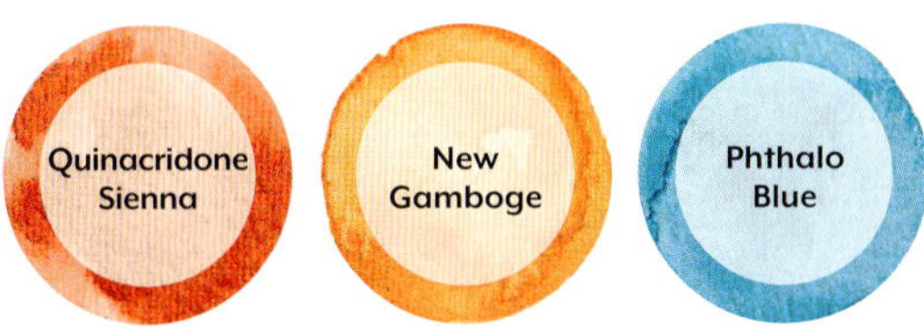

Mixes

To get all the pretty neutrals in the wing and tail, create an equal mix of quinacridone sienna and phthalo blue. Every time you dip your brush, you can vary the amount of either blue or sienna to get a lot of different but cohesive neutral browns.

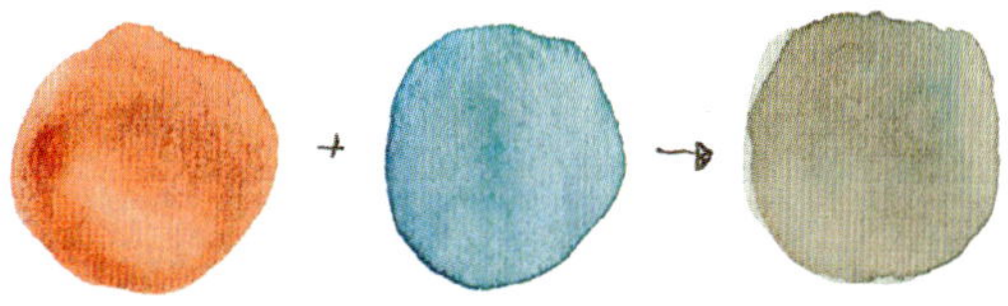

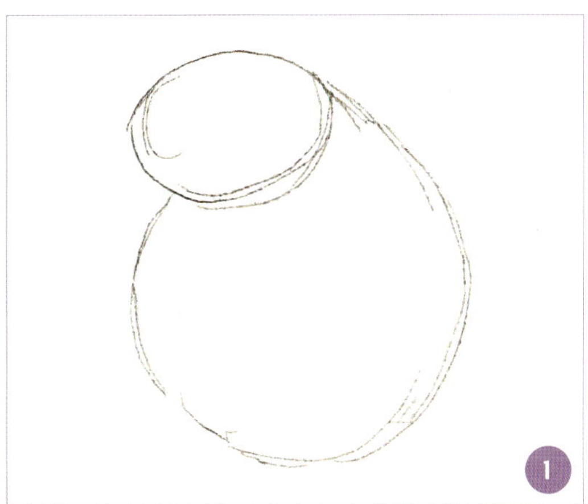

Step 1: When I look out my window and spot this little robin, I see the head as a small oval and the body as a bigger circle beneath. So, grab your pencil and sketch that. The right side of the circle should touch the neck and the left side should meet the oval at the bottom.

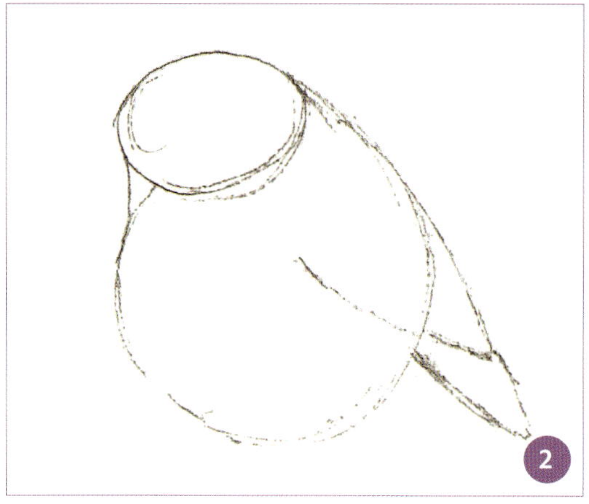

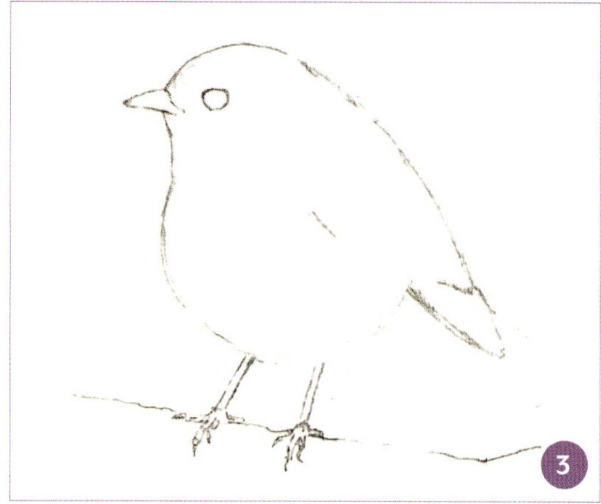

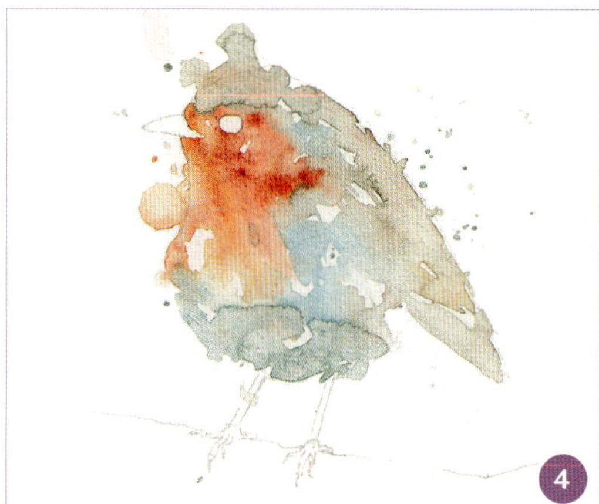

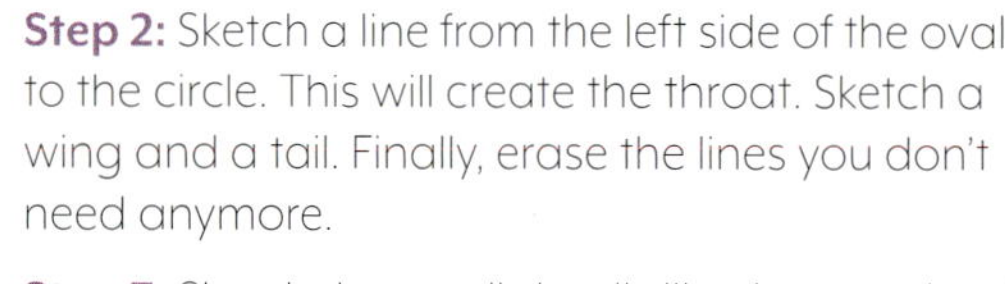

Step 2: Sketch a line from the left side of the oval to the circle. This will create the throat. Sketch a wing and a tail. Finally, erase the lines you don't need anymore.

Step 3: Sketch the small details like the eyes, beak and legs. The distinct thing about the robin is its big eye compared to the body and smallish beak. The feet have long claws grabbing onto a branch.

Step 4: Now you've come to the fun part! Start by wetting the area around the eye and beak (keeping the eye and beak dry) with the size 9 brush, all the way down the chest. Drip in quinacridone sienna and new gamboge and let it blend. Be careful not to paint too close to the eye and beak. Let this dry for a couple of minutes.

When it is shiny but not runny, you can add a watery phthalo blue around the edge of the sienna. Wet the rest of the bird with clean water and drip in the phthalo blue and sienna mix. On the wings you can drip in a bit of new gamboge as well. Don't be scared of pooled-up water— when it dries it creates beautiful blooms that are the perfect texture for this bird. Let the robin dry completely.

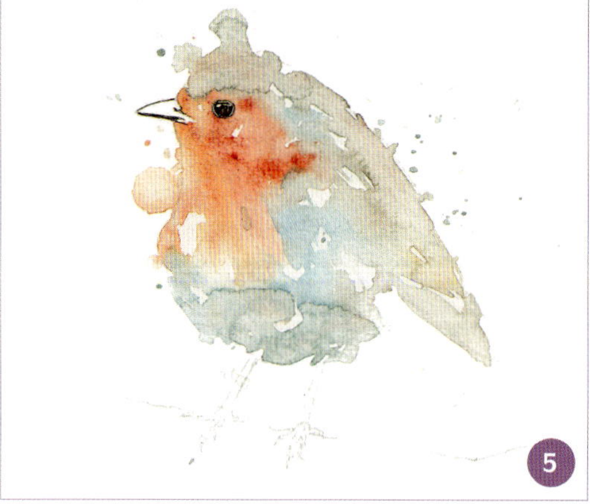

Step 5: With the 01 fineliner, carefully draw the beak and eye. When drawing the beak, you can doodle a small nostril with a half circle where the beak attaches to the head. Make sure to leave a highlight on the top of the eye. That way it gets a bit of shine. Also leave plenty of white space on the beak so we can add watercolor to it.

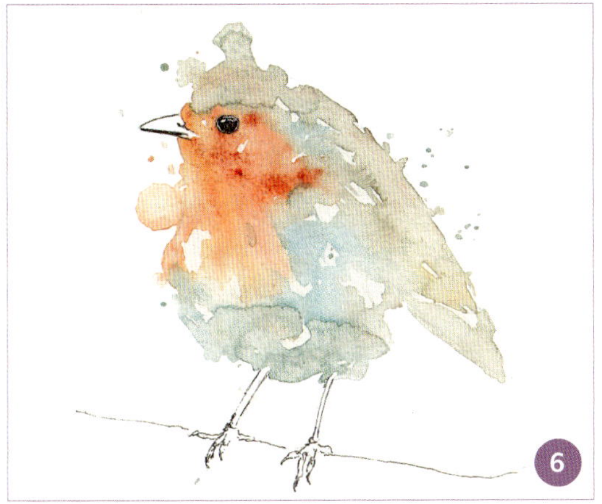

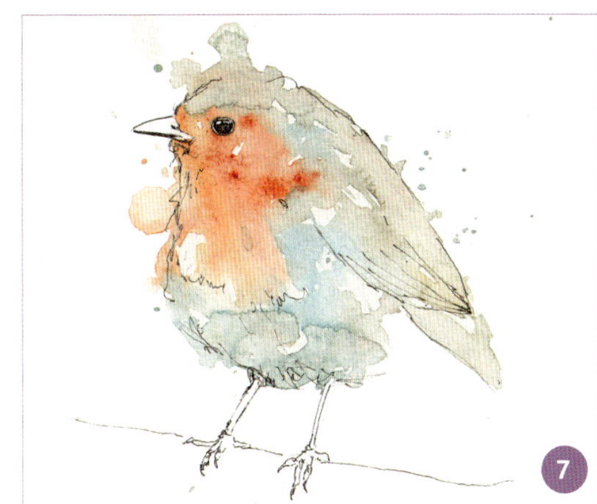

Step 6: Holding your fineliner with a very light touch, add the legs and feet as well as a branch for the birdie to rest on. You want these lines to look lighter and sketchier than the eye and beak.

Step 7: Finally, we can add some quick texture to the body with the fineliner. Going fast, hold the fineliner high on the handle and draw lines and doodles around the body. Give the wings a few straight lines to indicate the direction of the feathers. Remember, this is not an outline, so you don't have to go all the way around. Leaving areas without fineliner gives the sketch interest.

Step 8: You can now add a second layer of paint to darken the colors on the wings and the top of the head. Just use the quinacridone sienna and phthalo blue mix here. And then finally, add a bit of color to the beak and legs with the size 1 brush. The color is the same mix as before, just go a bit bluer than the mix for the feathers.

Yay! You just started preparing for the holidays ahead of time! You are now ready to sketch all the cards you need to send out. And I promise you—people will love it!

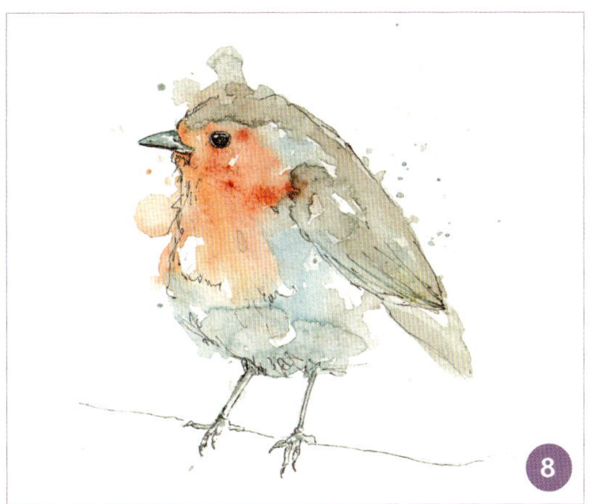

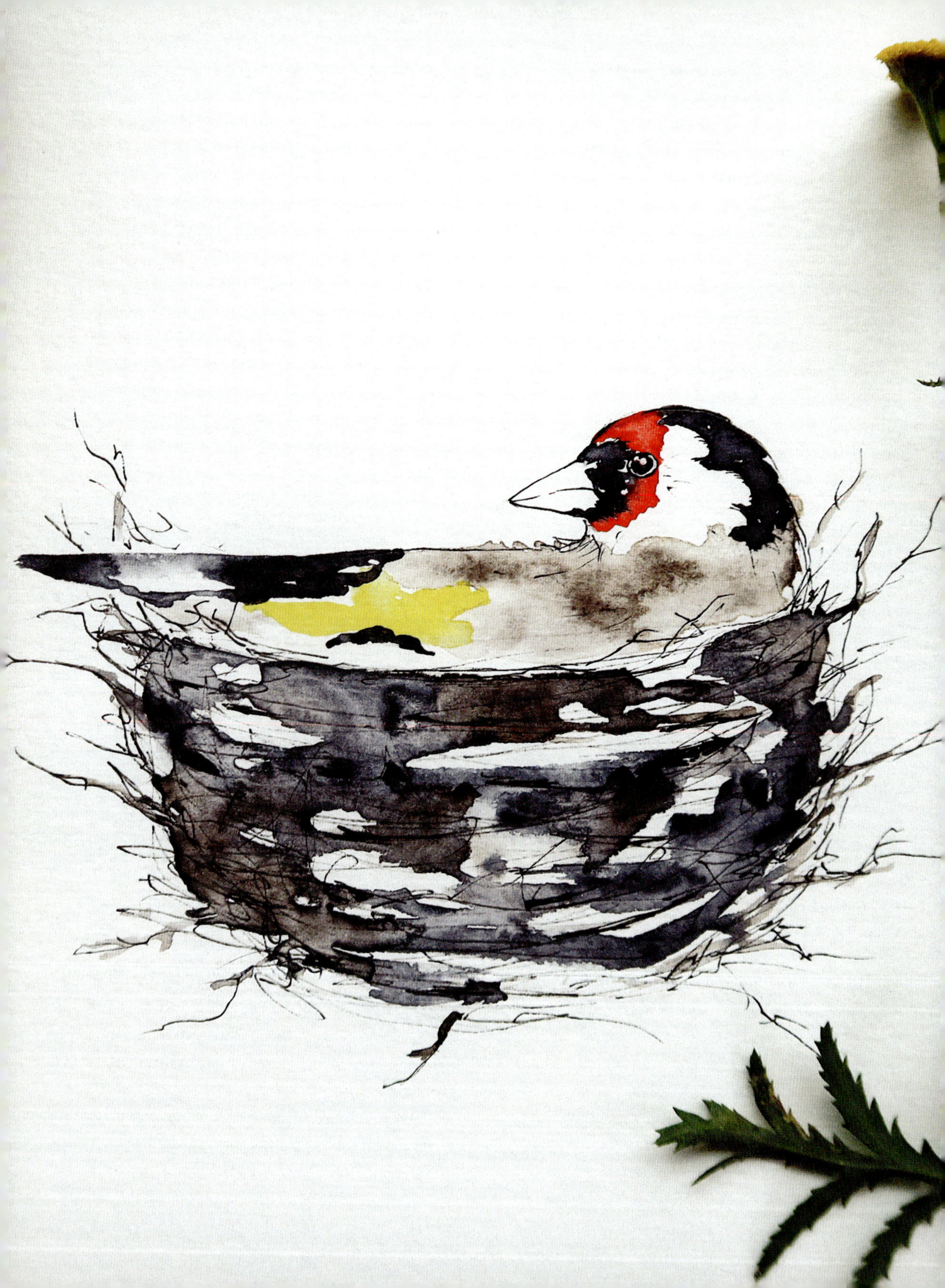

goldfinch
a bird of unbridled inspiration and motivation

Who doesn't love a bit of gold!? I am absolutely drawn to shiny objects and glitter. So, when a goldfinch flies by the window, I instantly look up. Not every bird can wear a strong colorful suit, but this birdie is killing it. In this tutorial, we are going to let the goldfinch take a bit of a rest. Maybe it's taking care of the little ones in the nest, or perhaps it's just watching the Tour de France on bird TV. That also means that you don't have to worry about legs and feet this time but can relax while creating the texture of the nest.

Materials

Pencil and eraser
Paper: Canson Montval 300gsm (140lb) cold press
Watercolor brush: size 4
Water and cloth
Palette
Fineliners: sizes 01, 005 and 02

Colors

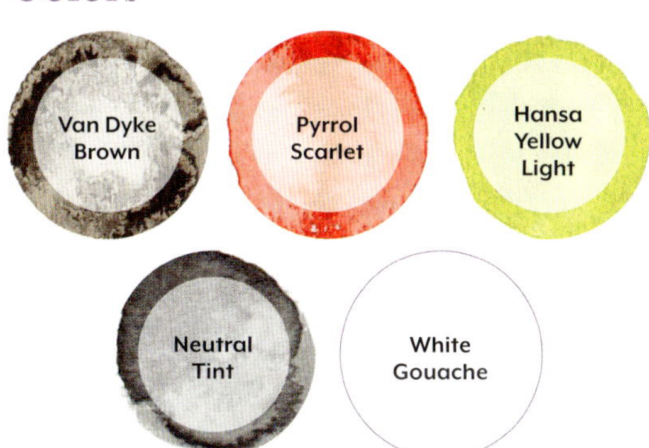

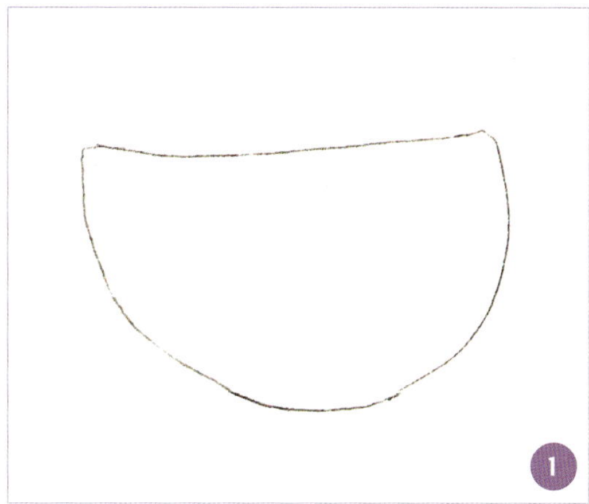

Step 1: Start by sketching a rough half circle for the nest with the pencil. Remember, you can find a guide for sketching the nest on page 59 (A Cute Bird's Nest).

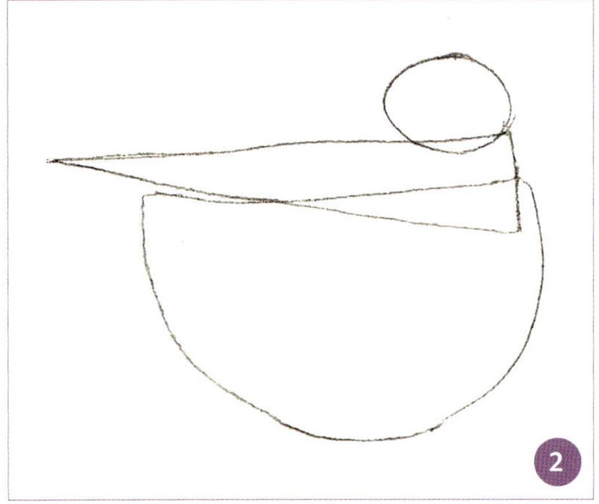

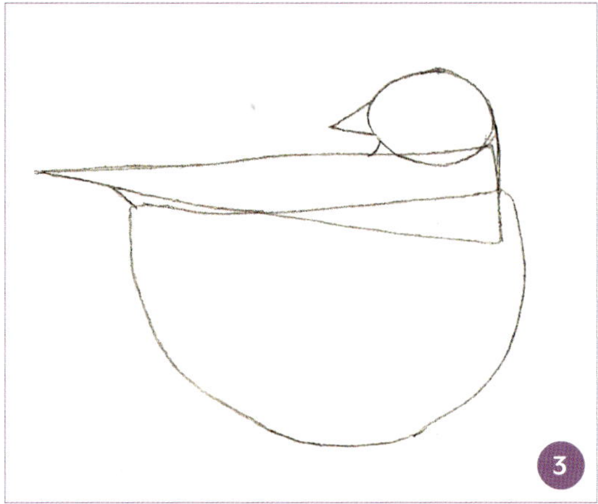

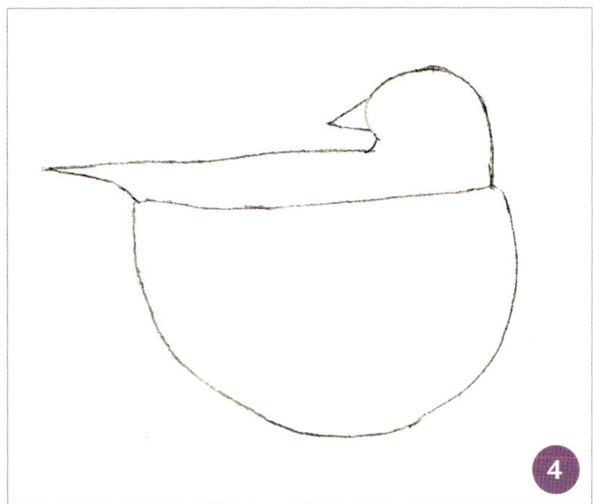

Step 2: We are going to draw this goldfinch resting in the nest while looking to the left. So, continue by sketching an oval head floating above the edge of the nest, and then sketch a long triangle below the head for the bird's back and tail.

Step 3: Draw a beak to the left of the oval head and small lines showing the neck, shoulder and the beginning of the bird's bottom.

Step 4: Carefully erase the pencil lines you don't need to make it look a bit more like a bird and not just an abstract sketch.

Step 5: With the size 4 brush, paint the neck, the breast and the back of the body using Van Dyke brown. Also, add a tiny bit below the tail. You can grab a nice cup of coffee while you wait for this to dry.

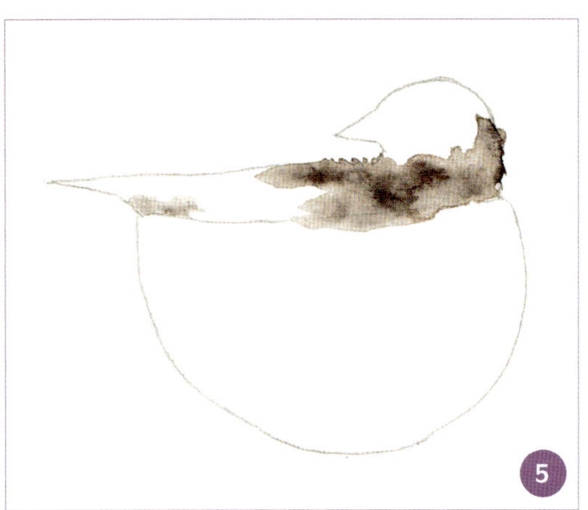

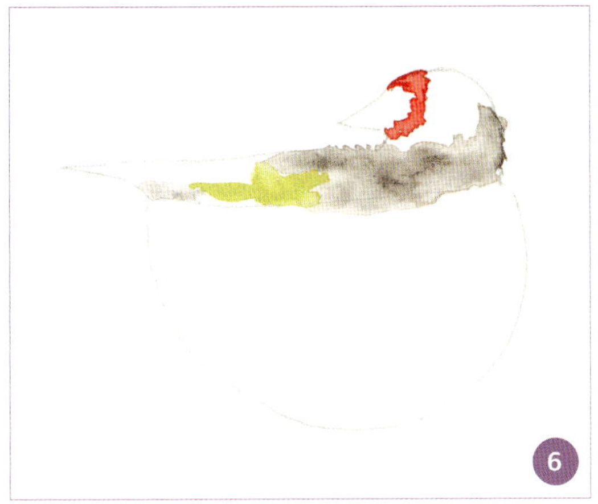

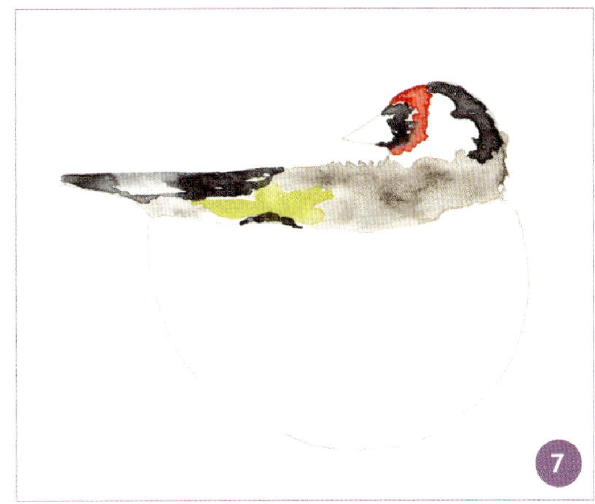

Step 6: Now we can dive into the bright colors. Paint wet-on-dry first using pyrrol scarlet around the beak and then using Hansa yellow light on the wing. Let these two colors dry completely to make sure they stay bright and beautiful.

Step 7: We are now going to add the contrasting darks. Paint the dark areas around the neck and around the beak using neutral tint. Then paint the tail and a small patch beneath the yellow. Vary the transparency to make it look lighter and not too heavy and dark. Isn't it incredible how the darks make the colors pop even more!?

Step 8: With the 01 fineliner, draw around the beak and draw an eye with two highlights and a white ring around it. You can let the white gouache do its part of the magic with the whites here.

Step 9: Now you can just quickly turn to A Cute Bird's Nest on page 59 to see how to finish the nest. I used neutral tint and Van Dyke brown for this one. When you are done with the nest, you can add a few short lines with the 005 fineliner to represent small feathers behind the eye. Finally, erase the pencil lines and you are finished. Well done, you!

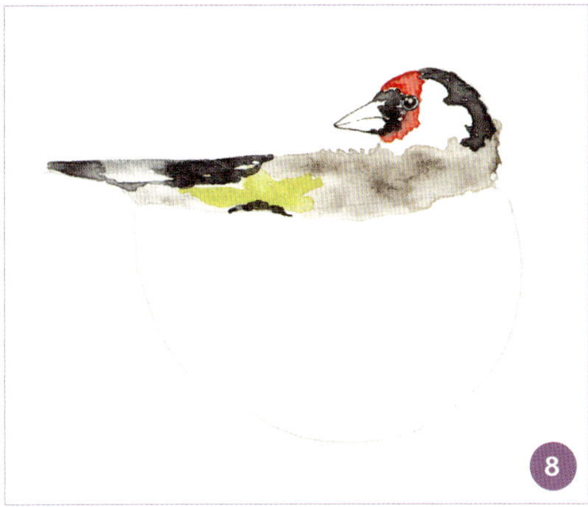

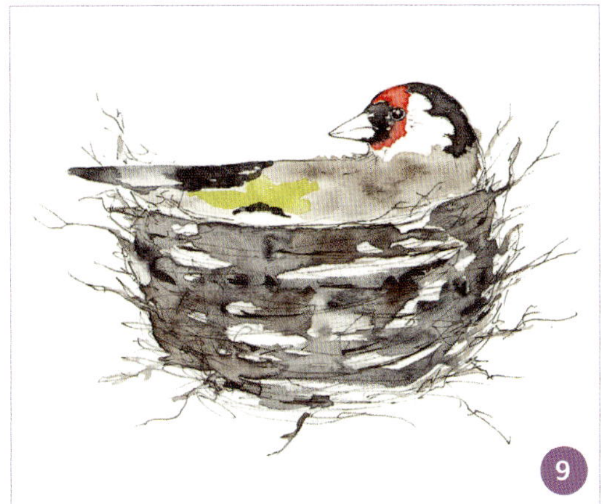

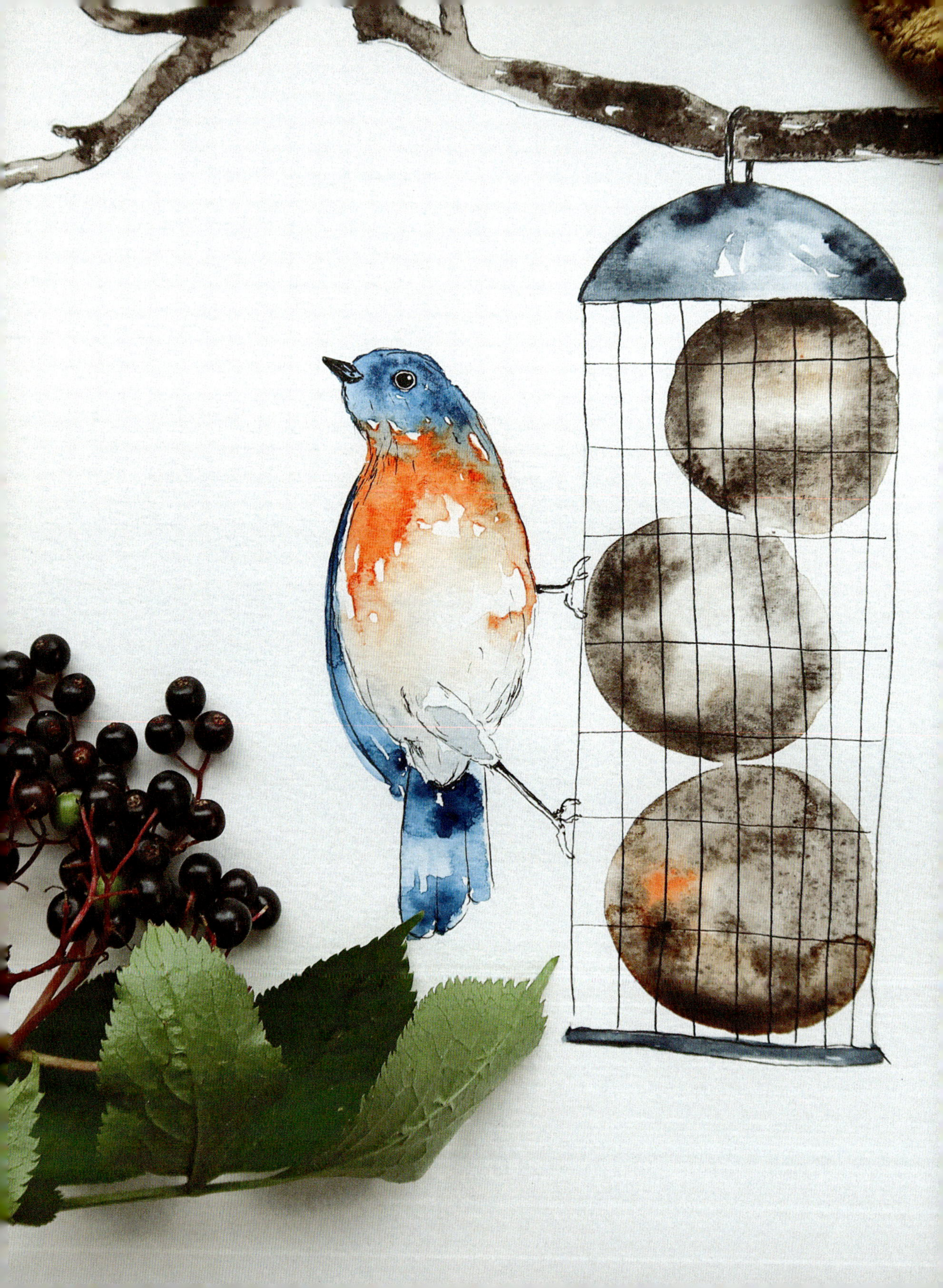

bluebird
a little bird with good news

The bluebird has so many meanings. Actually, a lot of birds have meanings. And this little bringer of joy is no exception. Let me just say that if you spot one of these cuties, you are in for a treat. Apparently, good news will be arriving soon! Maybe it's someone seeing your sketches on Instagram and just loving what they see or maybe finding a cookie you forgot about—you never know.

In this step-by-step tutorial, we find the little fella going to the restaurant for a quick bite. You will learn how to place the birdie on the bird feeder, and then you will learn how to control the colors when working with two bright colors up against each other.

Materials

Pencil and eraser
Paper: Canson Montval 300gsm (140lb) cold press
Watercolor brush: size 7
Water and cloth
Palette
Fineliner: size 01, 005 and 02

Colors

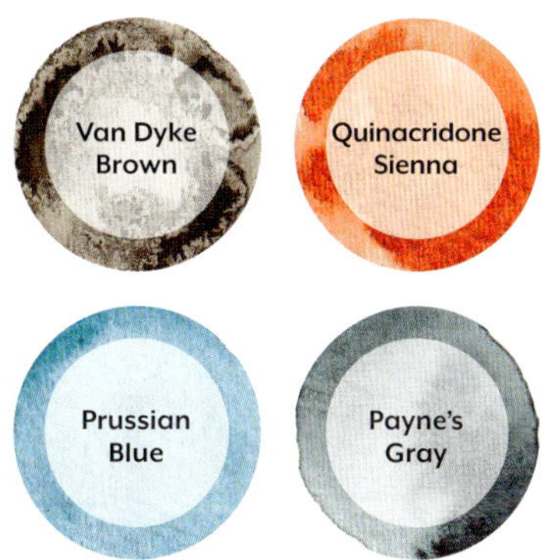

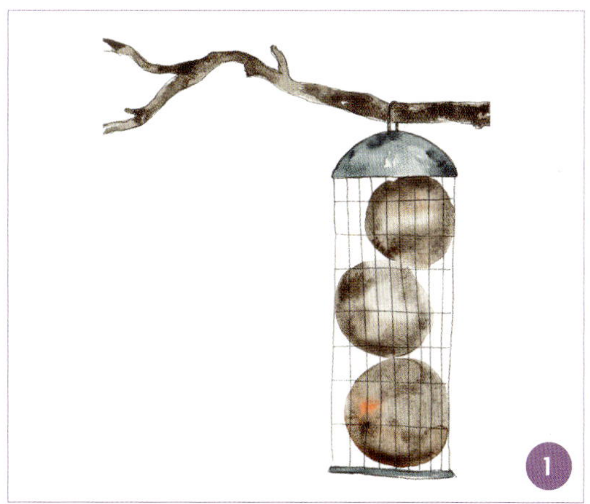

Step 1: To make it easy to place the bird, start with the Bird Feeder (page 31) and a Simple Branch (page 35). For the fat balls, I used Van Dyke brown and a bit of quinacridone sienna to tie it together with the bluebird.

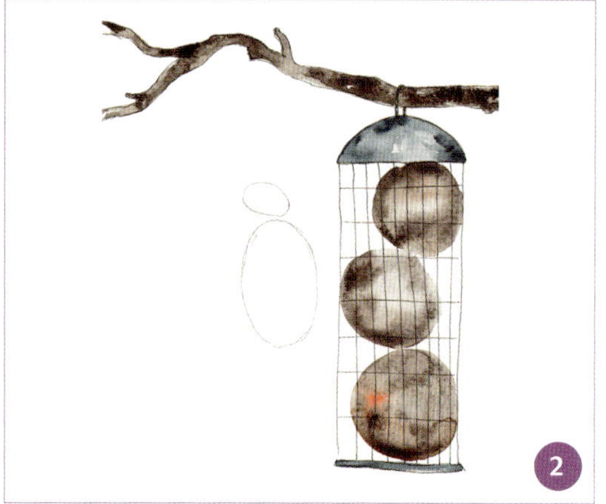

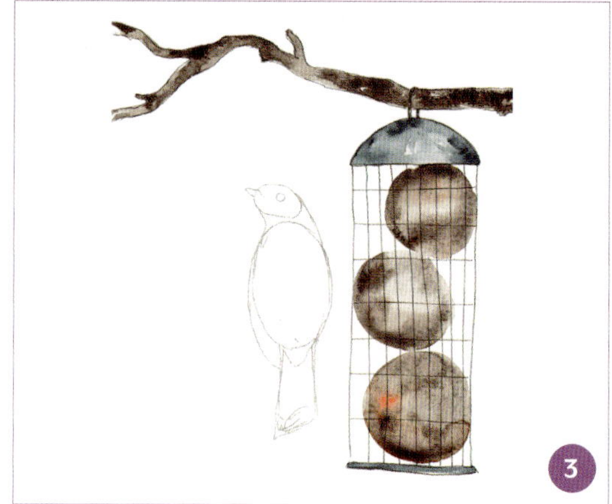

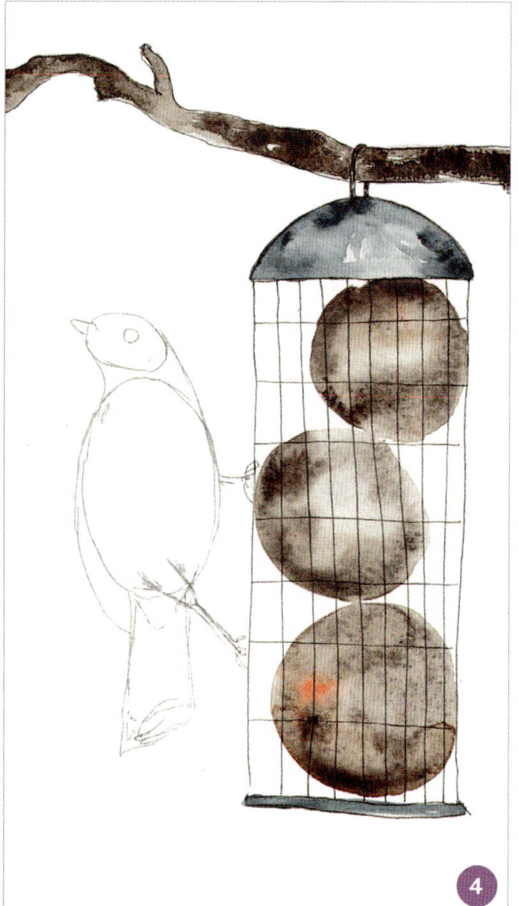

Step 2: When you are happy with the feeder, we are ready for the bluebird. Sketch a small oval on top of a big one with the pencil. The small one should point away from the bird feeder—a bluebird head trying to spot his friends. The big oval should be placed close enough to the feeder so the bird can reach it.

Step 3: Sketch the rounded neck, a pretty big eye, a small beak pointing a bit upwards, a wing on the left side of the body and a tail.

Step 4: Sketch the back leg halfway up the body, covered mostly by the belly. This goes directly to the feeder. The other leg is almost wearing a short pant and has a long leg angled so it reaches the feeder below the body. Sketch the claws grabbing onto the feeder so the bird doesn't fall down. If you have pencil lines you don't want, you can erase them now.

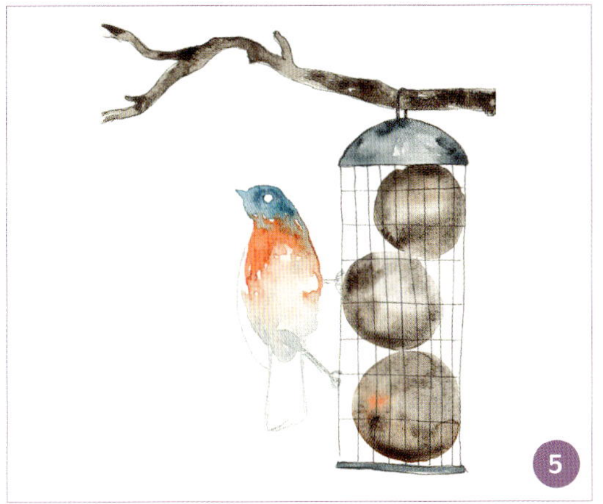

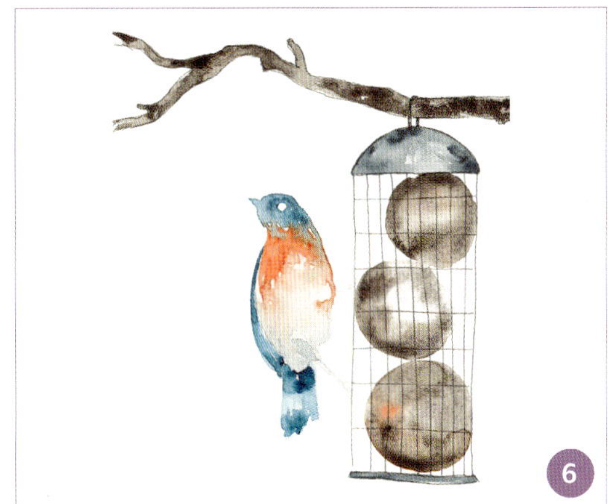

Step 5: Now we can get some color on the body. With Prussian blue and the size 7 brush, paint the head and all the way out on the beak wet-on-dry. Stay clear of the eye. Count to ten, then load your brush with quinacridone sienna and paint the orange part of the breast close to the blue, but without touching it. Then make small water bridges as explained in Bridging Colors (page 15) so the paint mix will be a bit more controlled.

Keep the bottom part of the belly free of the orange. Count to five, and then add clean water to the bottom belly. Let the water kiss the orange of the breast so it runs into the white a bit, giving a pretty transition between the two. In the white belly, drip a watery Payne's gray to make it less white and tie the colors together with the feeder.

Step 6: When that is dry, you can paint the wing and tail wet-on-dry using Prussian blue. Drip in a bit of extra dense color where the tail meets the body for a bit of shadow.

Step 7: This little guy is starting to look so cute. But before we finish, we want to add a bit of personality. Draw the beak and eye with the 005 fineliner. Keep the white space on the eye so we still have a highlight and a ring around the eye.

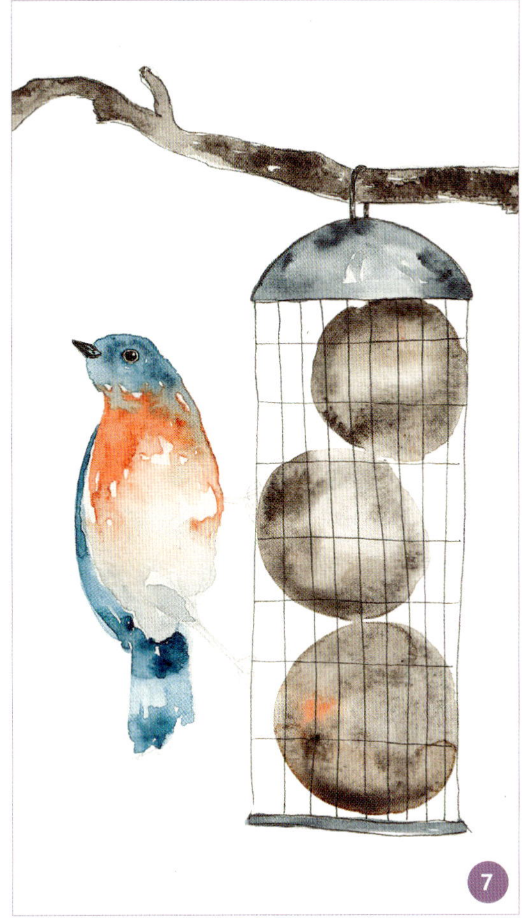

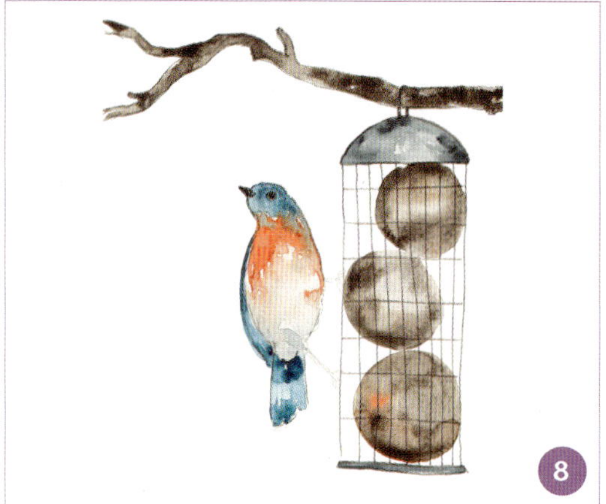

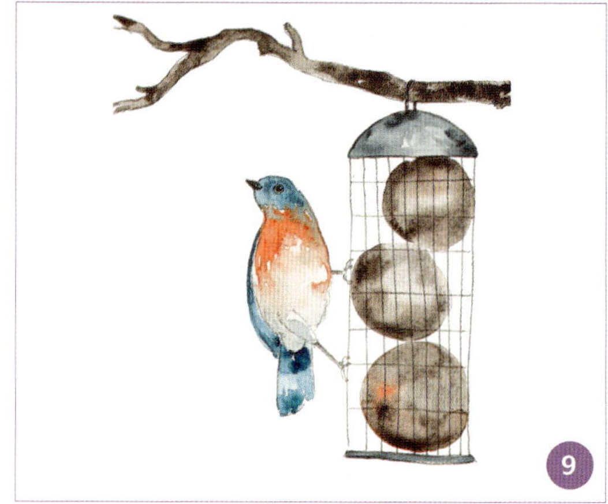

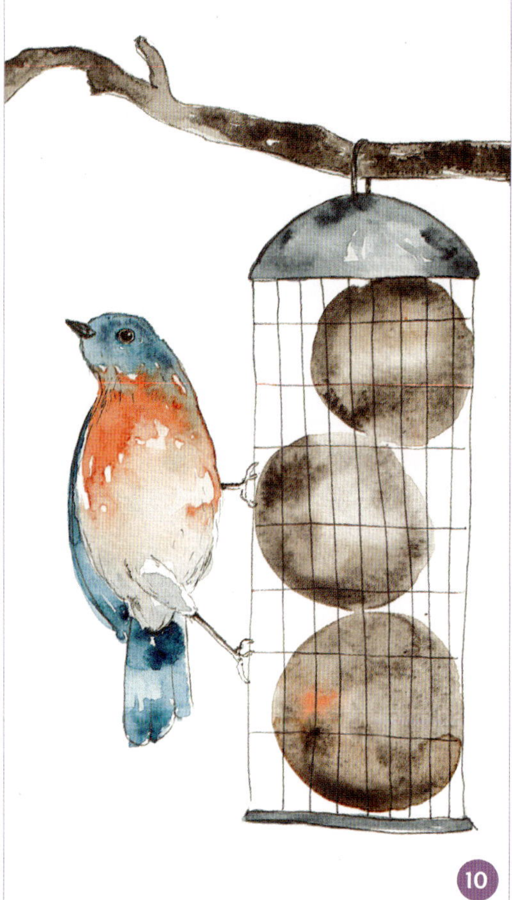

Step 8: Make a quick outline of the body, wing and tail using the 005 fineliner.

Step 9: Outline the legs. You can add a bit of shadow on the legs by drawing a few lines on the top part of the legs. Just make sure the entire leg does not turn black. Draw claws holding onto the feeder, and finally, erase the remaining pencil lines.

Step 10: We are here at the finish line. Add a bit of detail to the feathers with the fineliner. Make sure the marks follow the movement of the body and show that the bluebird is looking to the left.

Now he is ready to have friends over for dinner! And you are ready for your next birdie, which is also a blue one!

blue jay
a stunning bad boy

I have actually never seen a blue jay before. But I really want to because, wow, they are pretty! Those blues are just glowing, and this bird must light up an entire garden. I have heard that blue jays are quite the bullies of the garden, always picking on the other birds. So, to soften up this bad boy, we will pair him with a Cherry Blossom Branch (page 39). And to make the blues shine even more, we are only using cool colors on the branch to draw the attention towards the star of the show.

Materials

Pencil and eraser
Paper: Canson Montval 300gsm (140lb) cold press
Watercolor brush: size 9
Water and cloth
Palette
Fineliners: sizes 01, 005 and 02

Colors

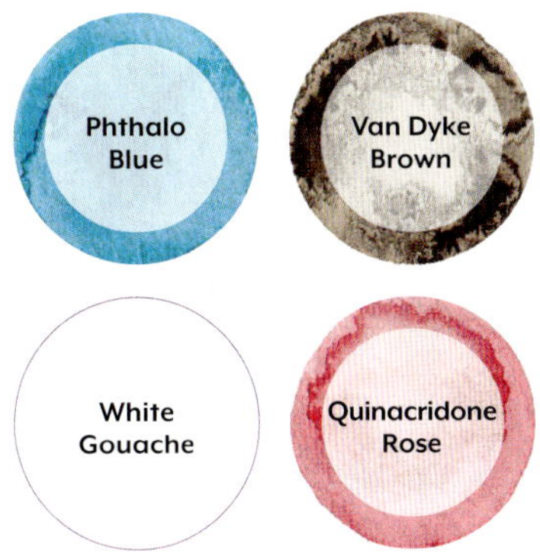

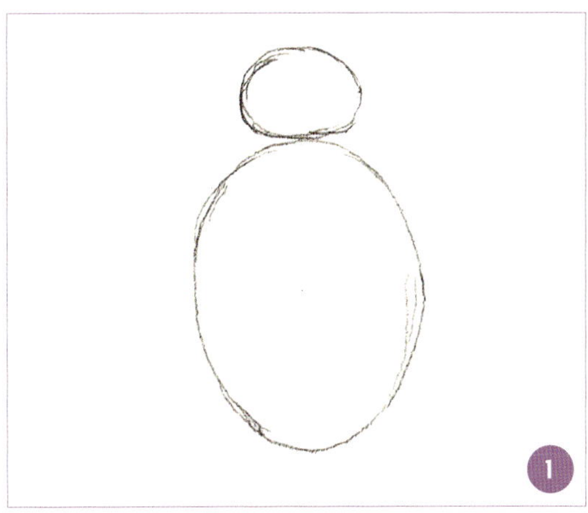

Step 1: Let's start with a small guide. Grab your beloved pencil and draw two ovals. Start with the bigger body oval, and then place the smaller head on top.

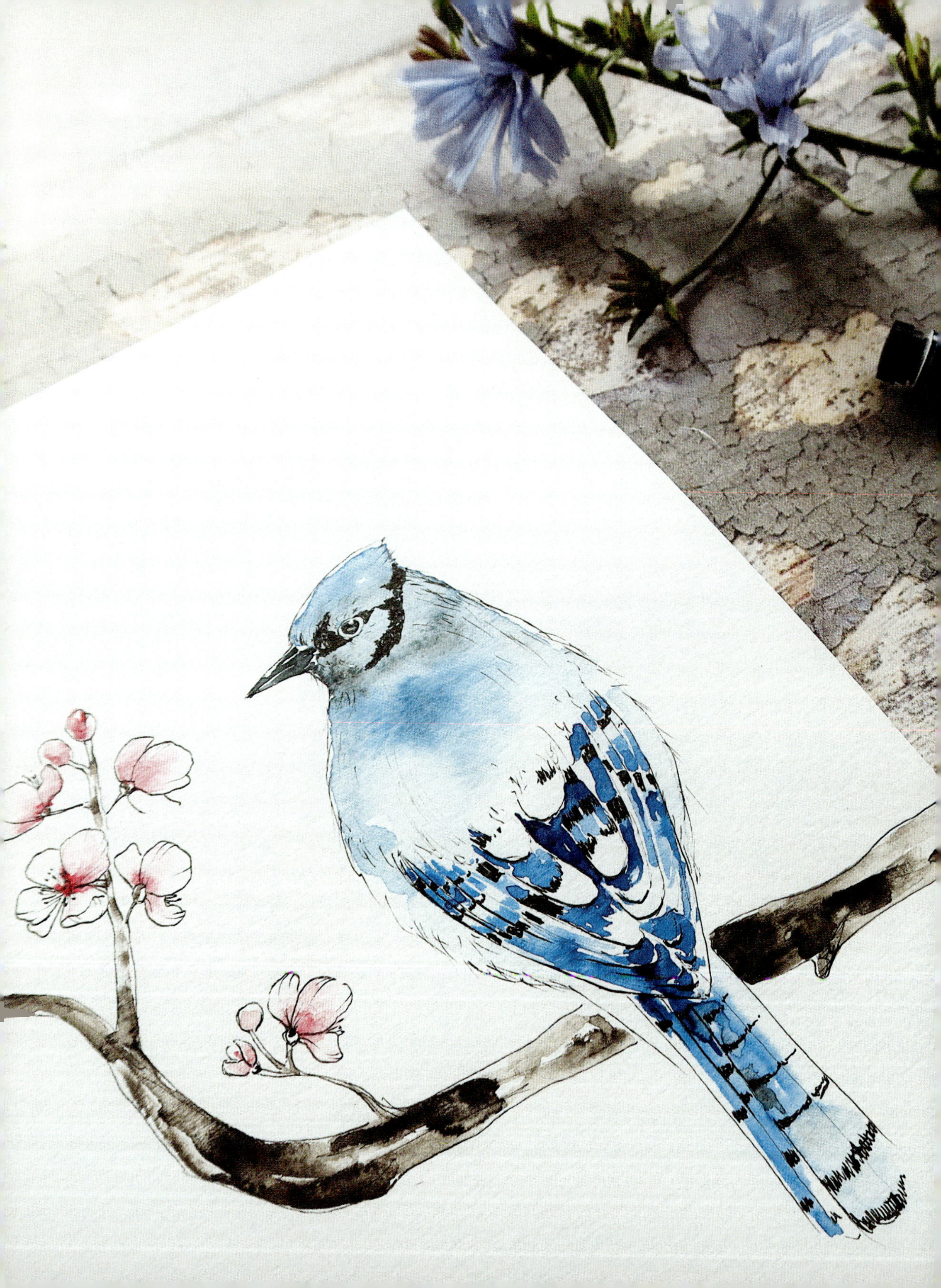

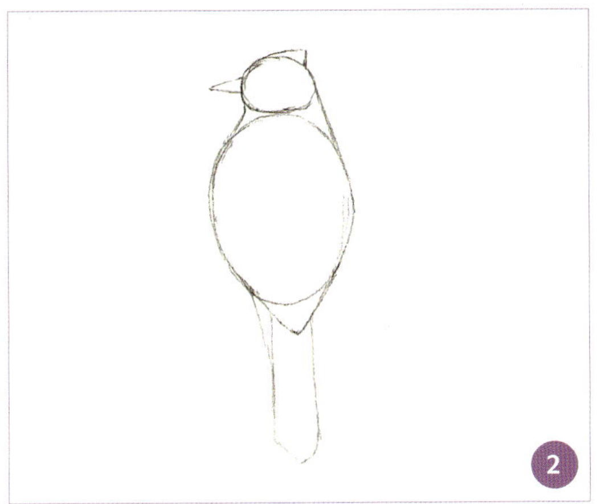

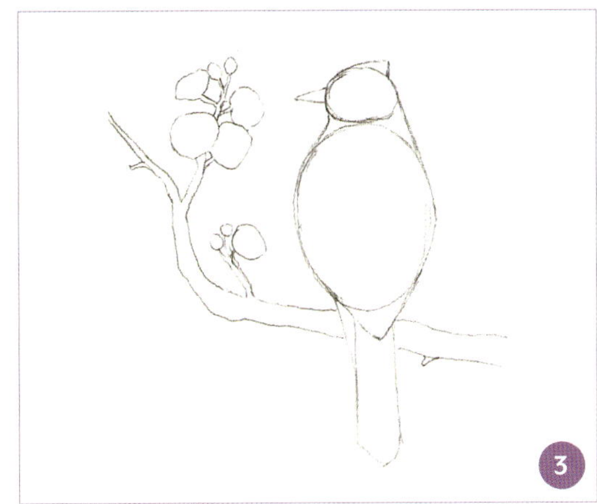

Step 2: Attach the two ovals with a neck and throat. We're envisioning this bird from the back, so you can give it those bird features like a tail, wings going down and ending in a point, a beak looking to the left and a beautiful triangular crown.

Step 3: Sketch the Cherry Blossom Branch (page 39). Erase the lines you don't need anymore.

Step 4: Wet the body of the blue jay with the size 9 brush. Drip in phthalo blue on the head and top of the back and a bit of Van Dyke brown around the neck. Try to keep the lower part of the body free of paint. If the paint runs down, you can lift it with a bit of tissue.

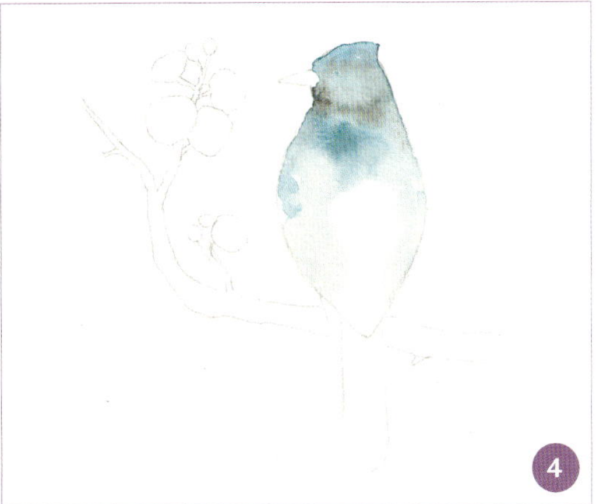

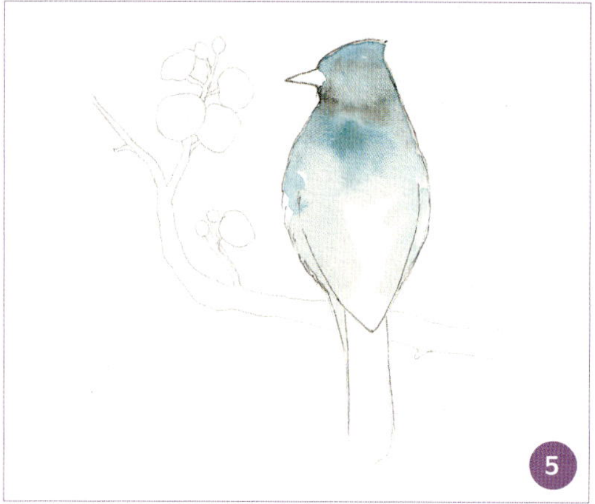

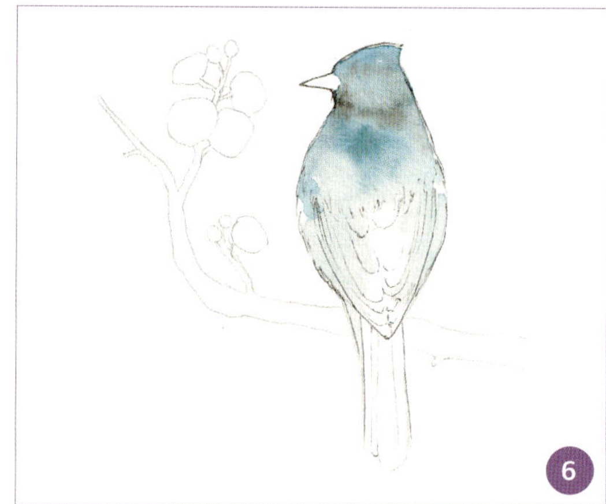

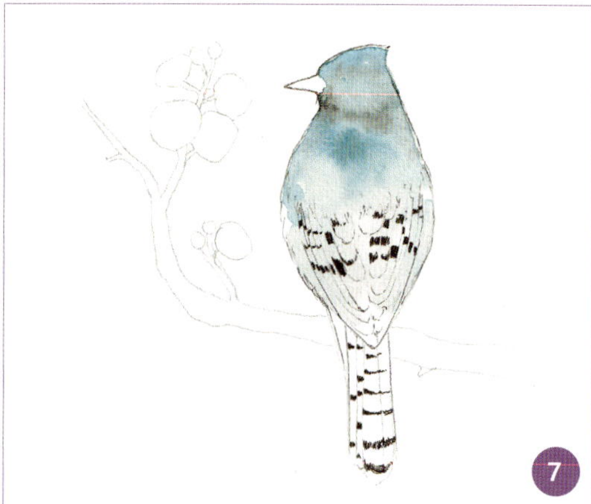

Step 5: Draw the outline of the body with the 01 fineliner, showing a bit of a feathery texture on the edges. Then quickly outline the wings, tail and beak.

Step 6: Loosely draw details on the wings with the 005 fineliner. Closest to the edge, the wings have big, long feathers, and when moving towards the middle, they become wider, shorter and more rounded—almost stacked on top of each other. The lines on the tail are long and centered around a big rounded feather in the middle.

Step 7: Draw the black marks on each feather with the 02 fineliner. Let these marks spread across the wings and tail. They start small on the sides and get bigger towards the middle.

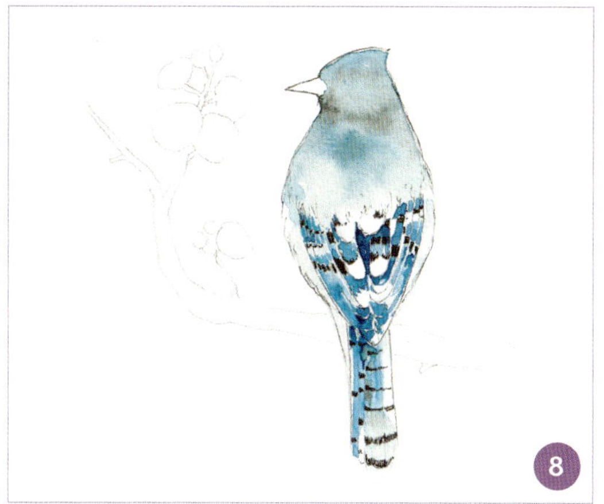

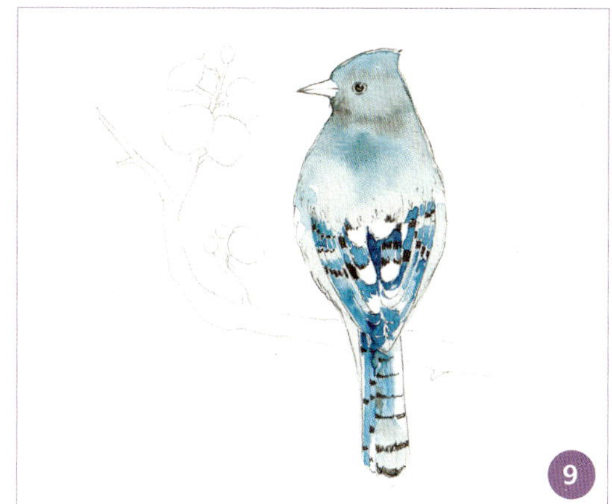

Step 8: Now it's time to add a pop of bright blue. Paint wet-on-dry using phthalo blue on the wings and tail. Leave some areas without paint, and leave white space between the feathers. The tail is also painted wet-on-dry, but here you drip in a bit of Van Dyke brown as well to make it a bit more neutral.

Step 9: Draw the oval eye with the 005 fineliner and white gouache, as shown in A Few Sketching Tips for Our Birdie Friends (page 22).

Step 10: Paint the beak Van Dyke brown with a tiny bit of phthalo blue. Make sure to keep a highlight at the top of the beak.

Step 11: Outline and add details to the Cherry Blossom Branch as shown on pages 40 and 41.

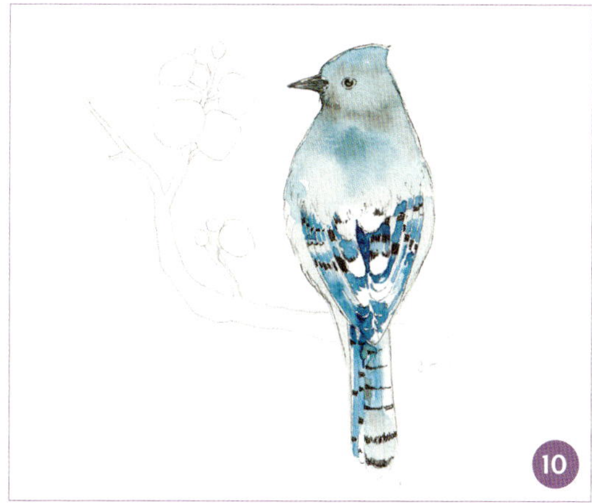

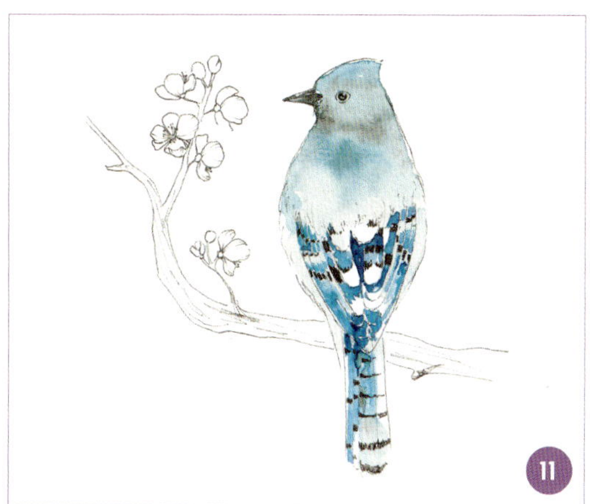

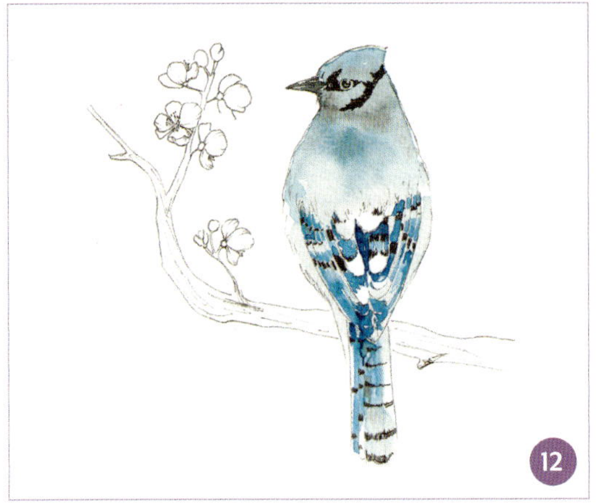

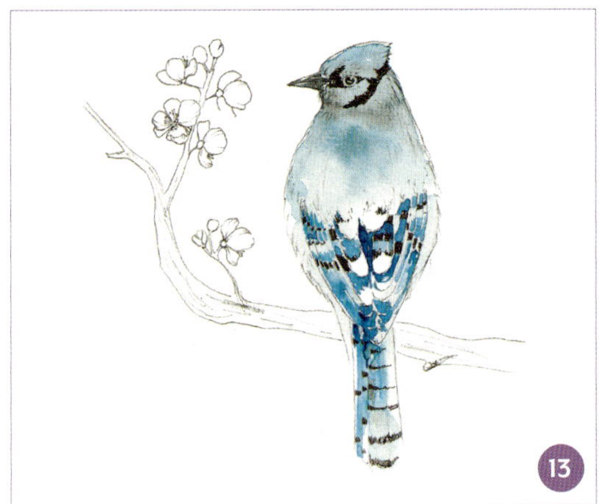

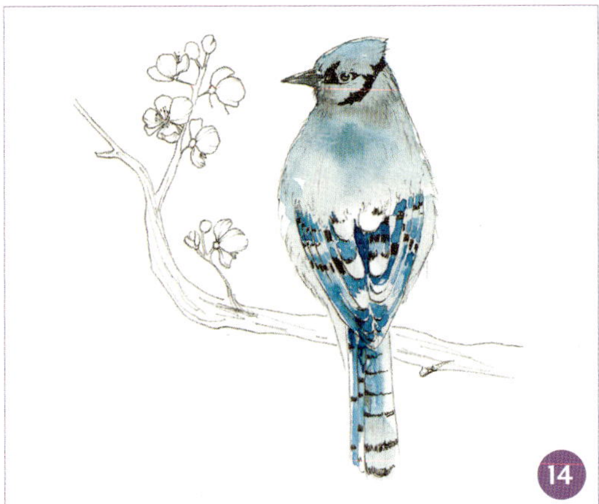

Step 12: This is looking pretty! We are ready for the final touches on the blue jay. So, pick up your 02 fineliner, and draw the dark marks around the eye and down the neck.

Step 13: Add a few final details to the feathers on the neck and body with the 02 fineliner. And just to make it look a bit more "bad boy," you can draw a few wild and beautiful feathers that are just breaking free of the body.

Step 14: With the 02 fineliner, add a few dark lines between the feathers on the wings and tail to create some shadow.

Step 15: Finally, paint the branch in Van Dyke brown and the blooms in bright quinacridone rose like on pages 41 and 42, and you are good to go! This little blue jay is so handsome. It's almost like he's up to no trouble at all.

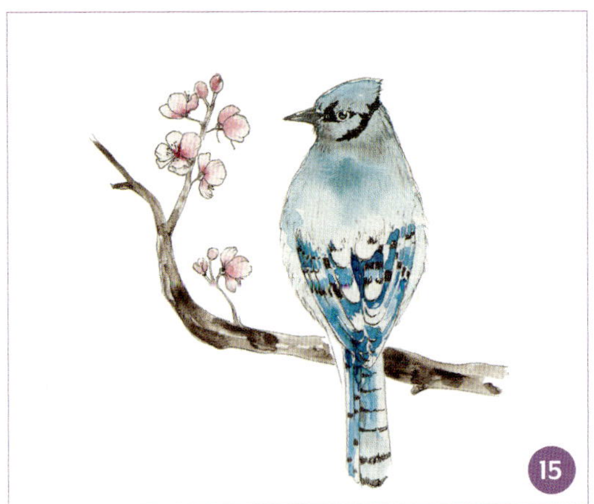

red cardinal spreading holiday cheer

I have a feeling that the first time I see a red cardinal in real life, my heart will skip a beat. That's because this bright red bird is just stunning. And oh, so bright! No wonder some countries have this as their all-time favorite Christmas bird and also see them as good luck. Why not take all that good luck and spread it out over the next tutorial. Here you will learn to paint this punk daddy bird sitting on his nest looking out for the two little ones while mom is out getting Christmas presents.

Materials

Pencil and eraser

Paper: Canson Montval 300gsm (140lb) cold press

Watercolor brushes: sizes 4 and 9

Water and cloth

Palette

Fineliners: sizes 005, 01 and 02

Colors

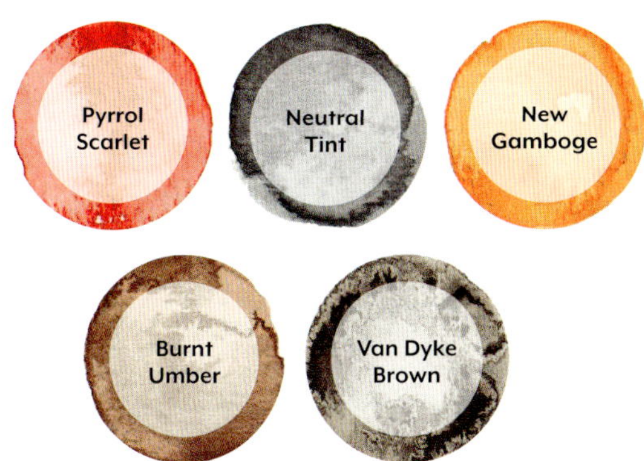

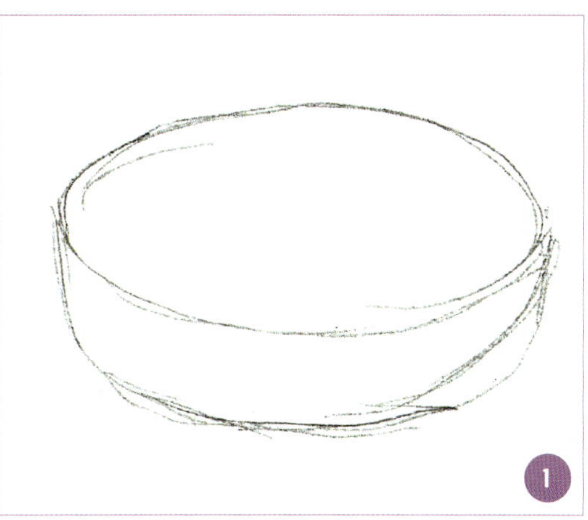

Step 1: Start by sketching a nest with the pencil. We want to be able to peek into it, so make it a wide oval with a bottom.

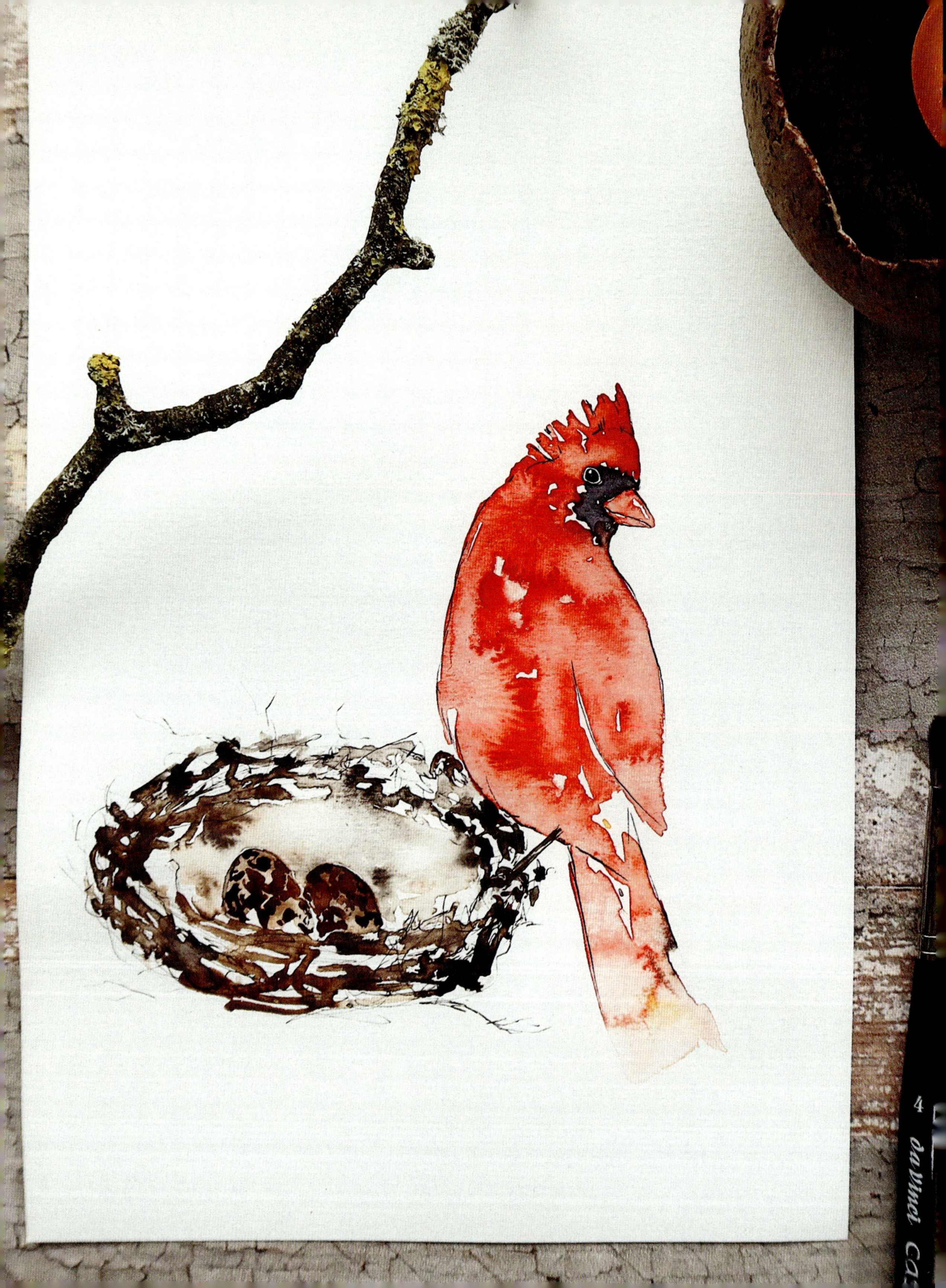

4
da Vinci ca

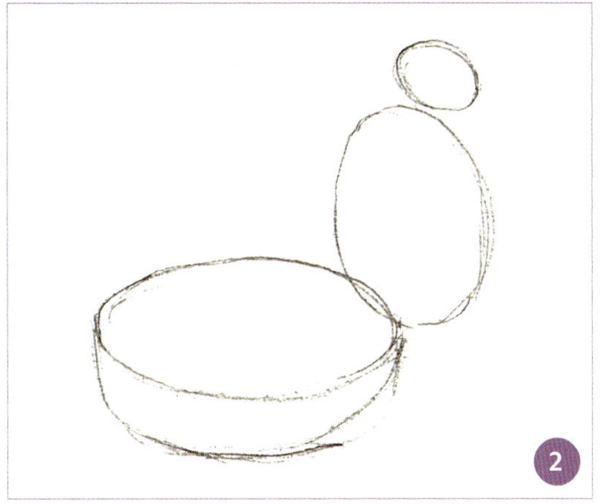 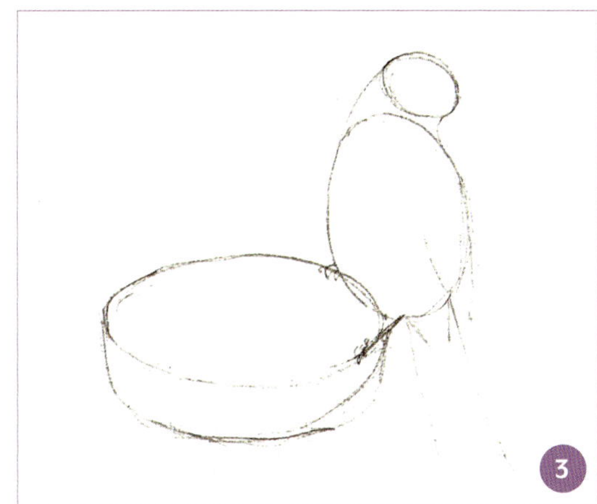

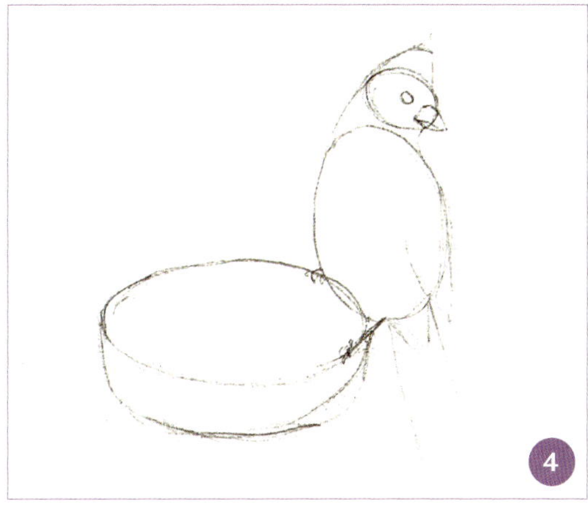

Step 2: Now you can place the bird on the nest. Start by sketching a big oval that overlaps the nest a bit. Then draw a small oval on top of the big one. This way you make sure the bird is close enough to grab the nest with its claws. We want the cardinal to be looking for mom, so tilt the head a bit to the right.

Step 3: Sketch the rounded neck and throat, a tail, a wing on the right side of the body, legs and feet. The back foot should only be visible as a few claws grabbing the side of the nest. Attach the front foot to a leg that meets the body around the top of the tail.

Step 4: Draw its oval eye, a big beak pointing a bit down and a cool mohawk. Erase the pencil lines you don't need.

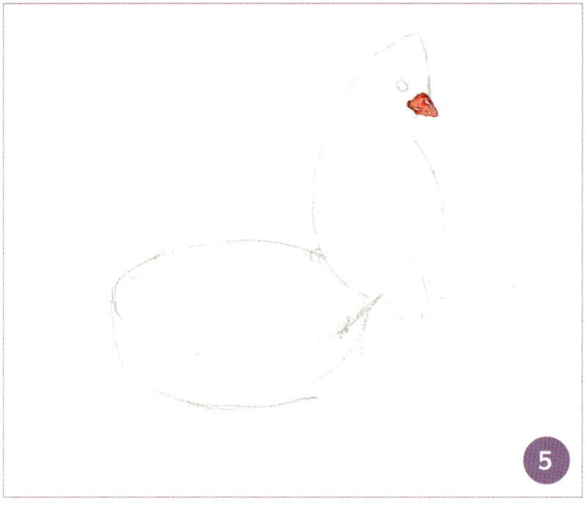

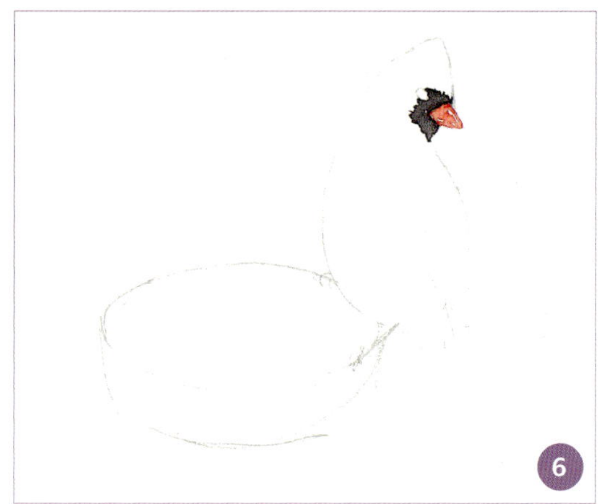

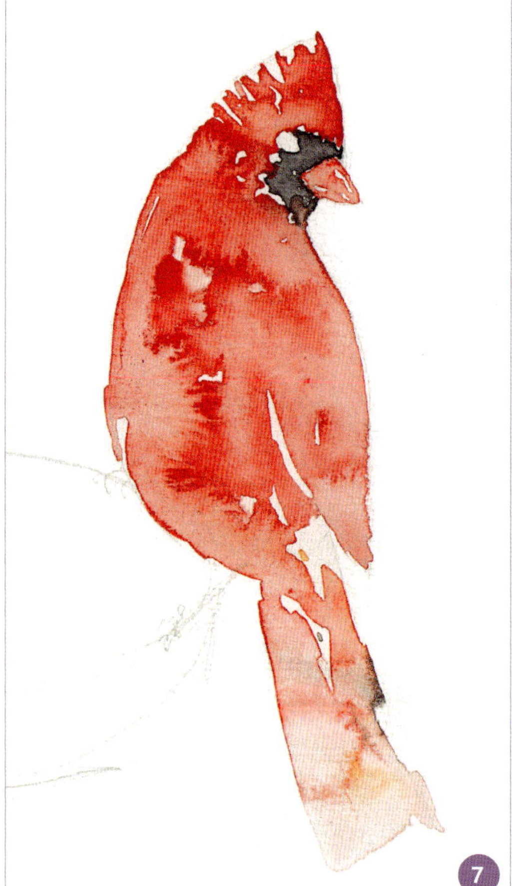

Step 5: Paint the beak with the size 4 brush. Start with a soft outline of the beak in pyrrol scarlet, and then fill in the area. Keep some white space.

Step 6: With the size 4 brush, paint the dark area around the beak all the way to the throat and eye using neutral tint. Keep the edge uneven to show the feathery texture.

Step 7: Now, take a deep breath because we are going to paint the cardinal in one go. Grab your size 9 brush and start at the head, adding the feathers on the top using pyrrol scarlet—but drip in a bit of new gamboge. Then work your way around the back and stomach. Paint the wing in one quick stroke on the right. Keep a bit of white space, and then paint a tail below the body. Connect the tail to the stomach. You can also drip in a bit of neutral tint at the tail. Drip in clean water for texture.

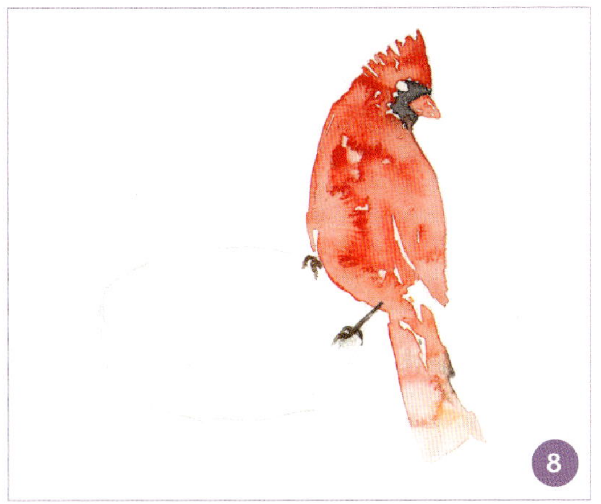

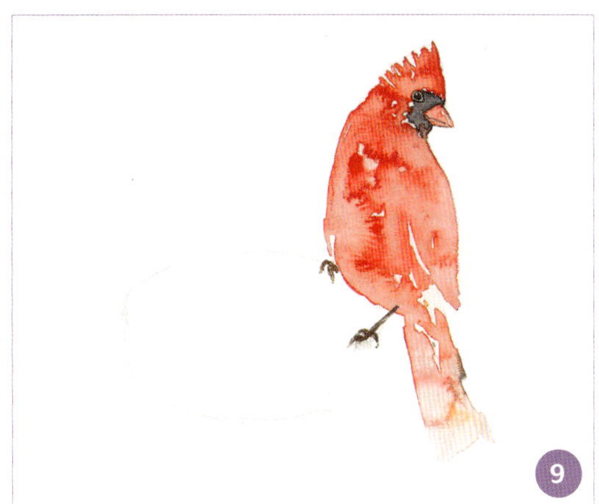

Step 8: When the body is dry, paint the legs using burnt Umber with the size 4 brush. Drip in a bit of Van Dyke brown closest to the body.

Step 9: Outline the beak and draw the eye with the 005 fineliner so we know who this cardinal actually is. Well, hello there!

Step 10: Sketch a few details with the 01 fineliner. Outline the body and make a few light strokes to the mohawk on the top of the head. Also draw a few details on the feet to give it a bit of texture.

Step 11: Now take a look at A Cute Bird's Nest (page 59) and Colorful Bird Eggs (page 65) to finish this. I used neutral tint, Van Dyke brown and burnt Umber for the nest and burnt Umber and neutral tint on the eggs.

And that's it! You have made the perfect illustration for a holiday card. Next time, you can even add small Christmas hats to the eggs. That would be so adorable.

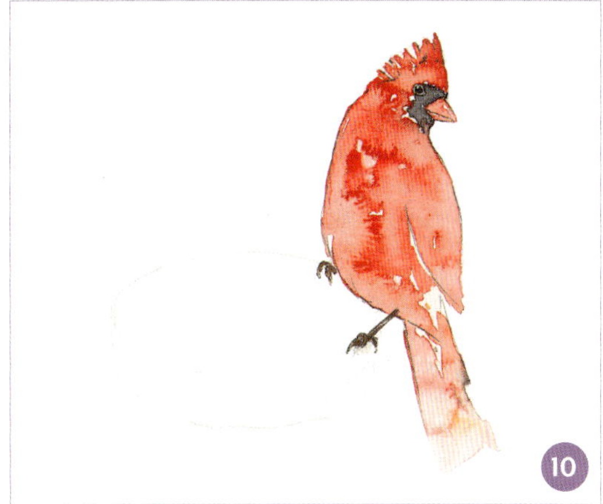

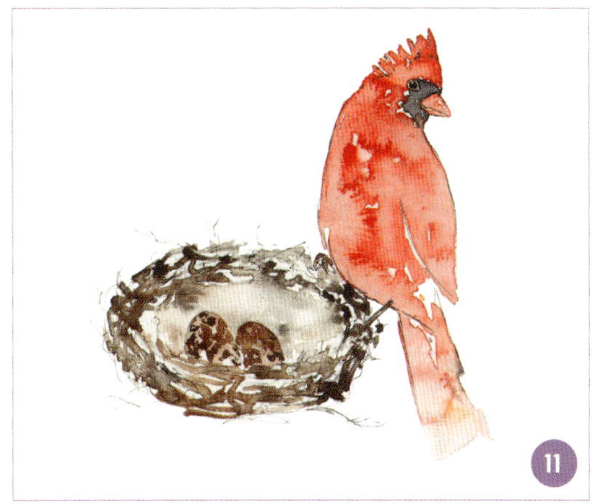

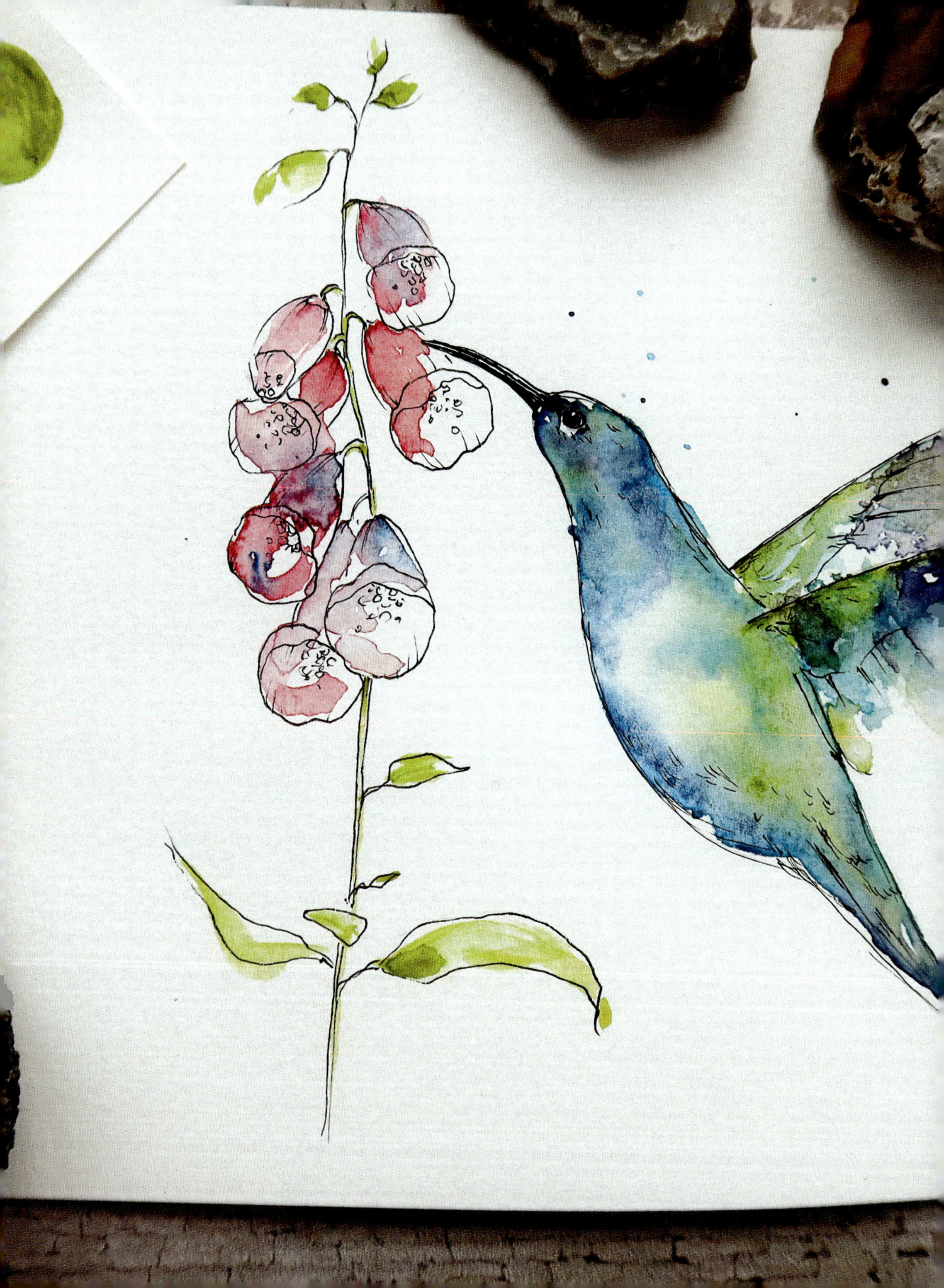

hummingbird
a bird of beauty and grace

One of the most fascinating birds to me is the little hummingbird. I feel like it's almost in the space somewhere between bird and butterfly with that long beak that looks almost like the butterfly's straw.

Did you know hummingbirds can hover perfectly still in the air? That is really cool! So, in this step-by-step, I wanted to share with you a really cool way to paint flying wings. (Hint: You'll be playing with water.)

Materials

Pencil and eraser
Paper: Canson Montval 300gsm (140lb) cold press
Watercolor brush: size 9
Water and cloth
Palette
Small water mister
Fineliners: sizes 01, 005 and 02

Colors

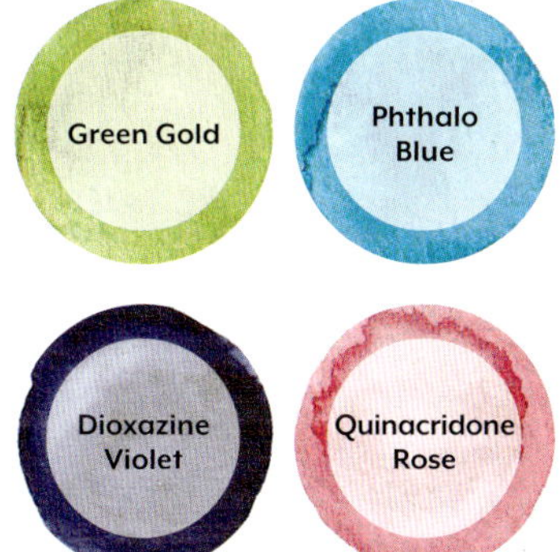

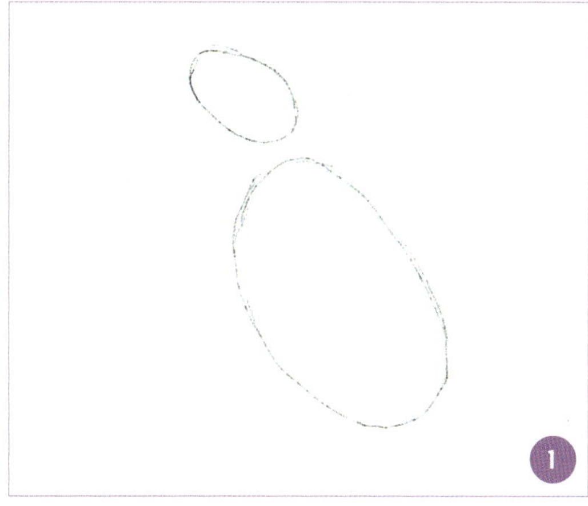

Step 1: This time we are going to do a flying bird facing to the left. So, with the pencil, draw two ovals: a small head tilted left and upwards and a body tilting a bit to the left.

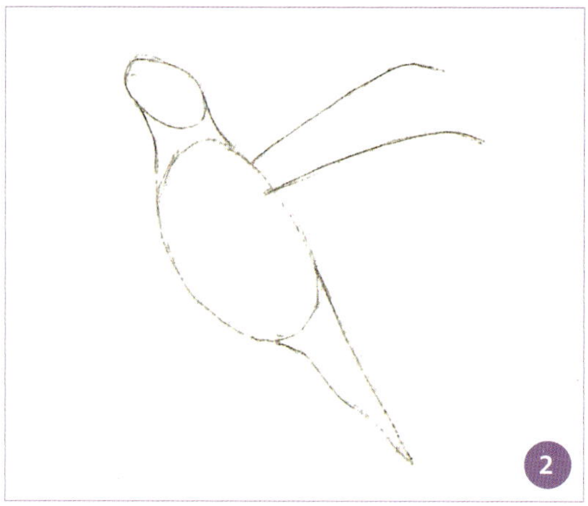

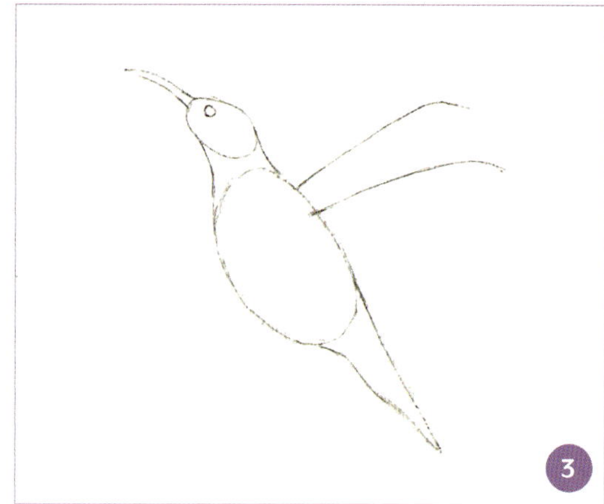

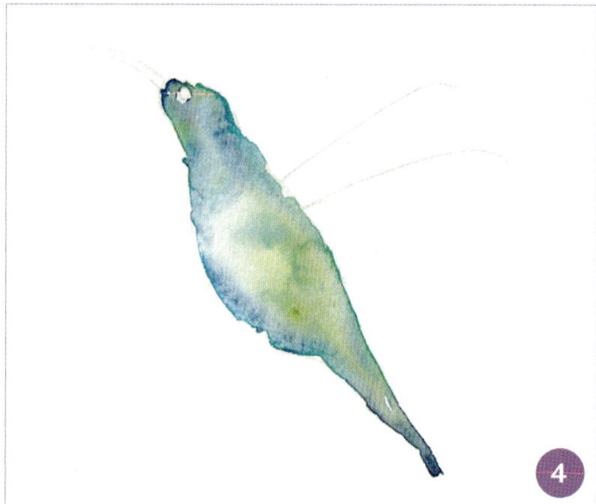

Step 2: Sketch the long pointed tail, throat, neck and two lines with a small curve at the end showing the top edge of the wings.

Step 3: Finish the sketch with a long pointy beak and an eye, and erase the pencil lines you don't need.

Step 4: Wet the body, and with the size 9 brush, drip in green gold, phthalo blue and dioxazine violet close to the head. Stay clear of the eye and try to let the water do the mixing so you don't muddy up the bright colors.

Step 5: Now we are going to try something fun! Spray clean water underneath the wings with the small water mister. Try to avoid spraying above the wings. In the droplets, drip in green gold, phthalo blue and the dioxazine violet. It's perfect if you can let the paint run into the droplets and spread out. Wait for this to dry completely. There is a lot of water, so go for a walk or maybe draw one of the other projects in this book while you wait.

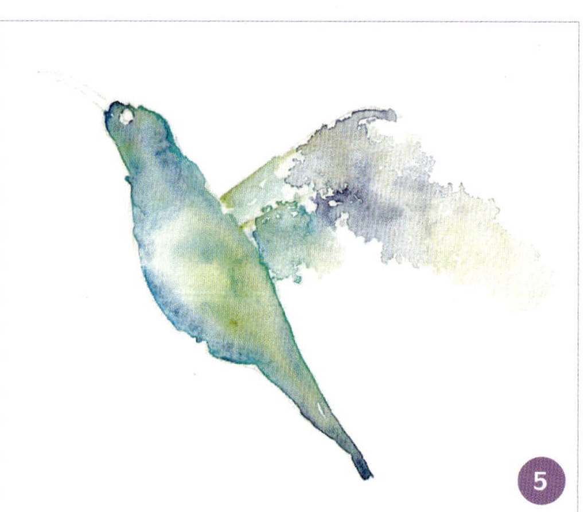

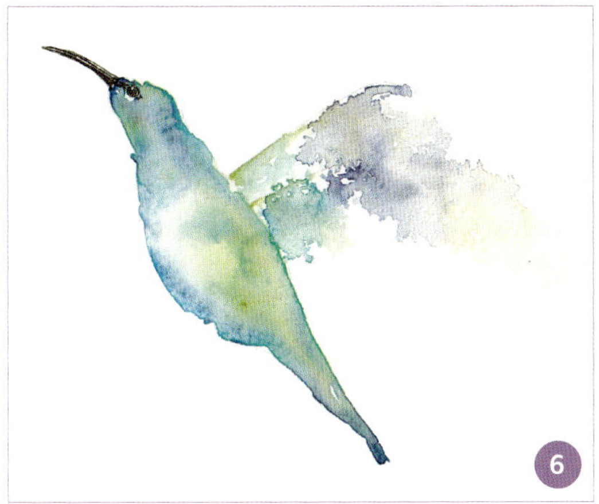 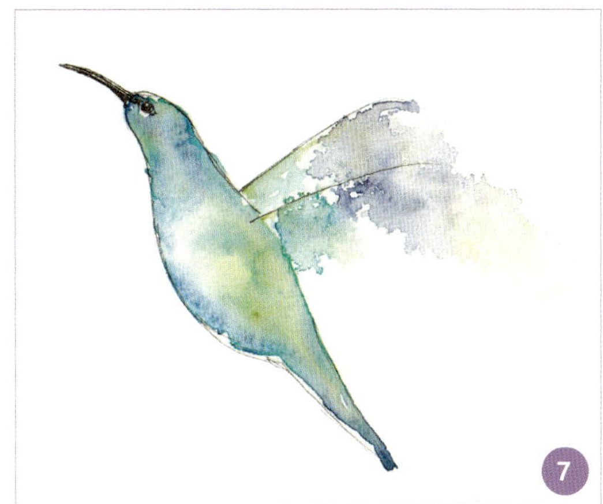

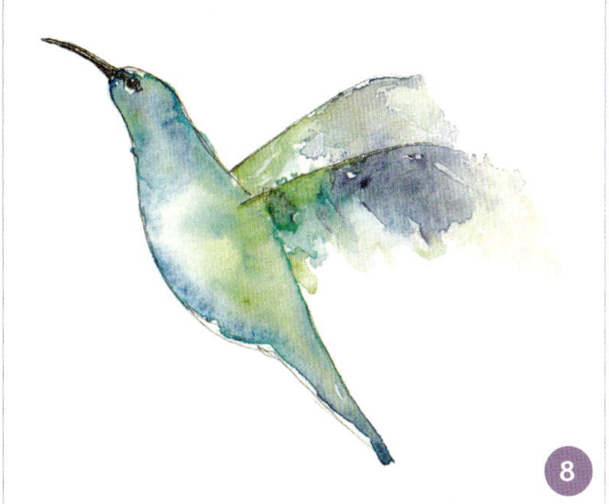

Step 6: Draw the beak and eye with the 01 fineliner. Keep the highlights long on the beak since it's . . . well . . . a very long beak.

Step 7: Draw a quick outline of the body with the 005 fineliner. Also, draw the top edge of the wings. Draw the line of the front wing a bit into the body with the back wing tucked behind.

Step 8: To get a bit more color to the wings, add a new layer of paint. This time keep it wet-on-dry using the same colors but with less water. Create brushstrokes going in the direction of the feathers, and keep it loose with very little detail. Let it dry.

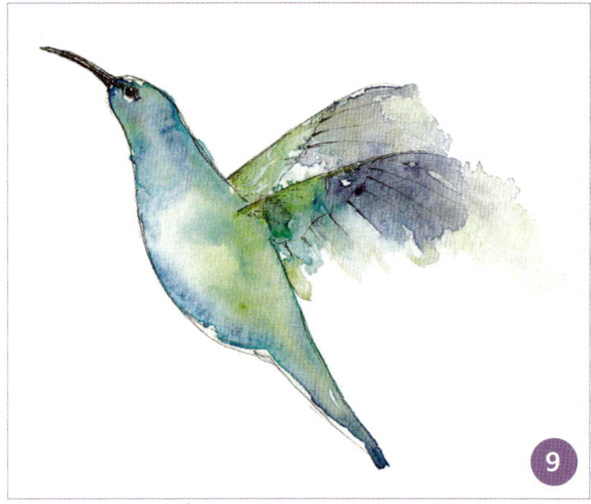

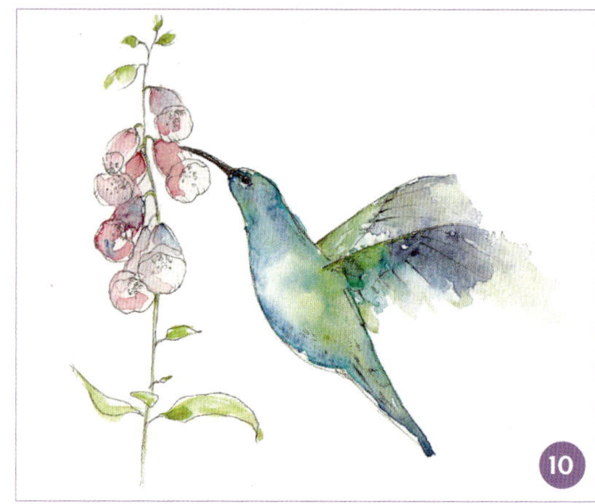

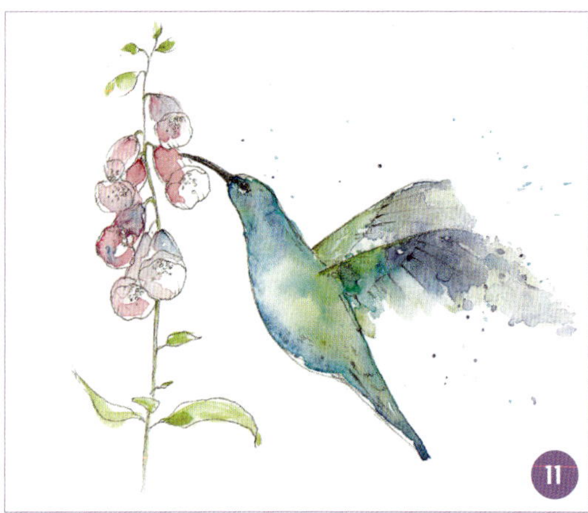

Step 9: With the 005 fineliner, draw a small irregular triangle on the top part of the wings where they attach to the body. Then make lines on the wings going from that triangle in the direction of the feathers, fading out into the color burst.

Step 10: We are almost there, but I feel like it is a bit lonely there on the page. So, paint the Foxglove (page 55). To tie the flower with the bird, drip in a bit of phthalo blue (instead of the French ultramarine from the earlier tutorial) into the rosy blooms. If you feel you need a bit more focus on the bird, add a bit more texture to the feathers on the body.

Step 11: This tutorial was very much about playing with water and creating movement. So why not end it with some fun splatters! Use dioxazine violet and phthalo blue at the wings, and then splatter with clean water to spread it out a bit more.

I absolutely adore this little birdie! And now you can use this technique to make all your other birds fly! After all, they fly quite a lot when they are not chilling in the garden.

pigeon
a bird of prosperity and fertility

I have a very close relationship with this cute but also kind of clumsy and loud bird. In some kind of personality test I took years back, I was a pigeon. I had no idea what that meant, but it did make me want to perfect sounding like one. I'm pretty sure that was not what the teacher intended with the test, but what can you do!?

In this tutorial, we will play more loosely with water to create some interest to an otherwise gray bird. And then we will give it a dash of color because it deserves a bit of glam too.

Materials

Pencil and eraser
Paper: Canson Montval 300gsm (140lb) cold press
Fineliners: sizes 01, 005 and 02
Watercolor brush: size 9
Water and cloth
Palette

Colors

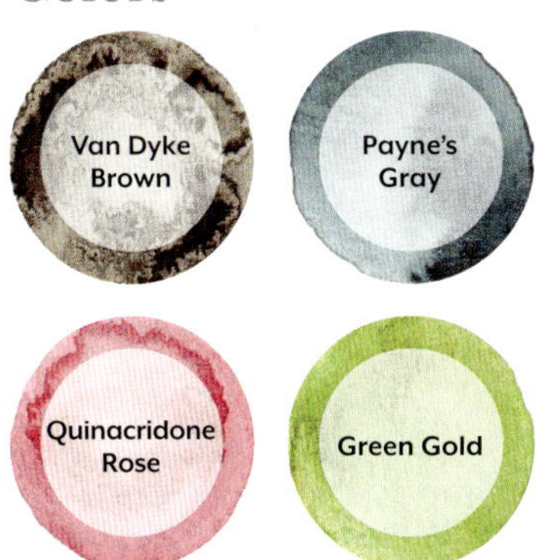

Van Dyke Brown

Payne's Gray

Quinacridone Rose

Green Gold

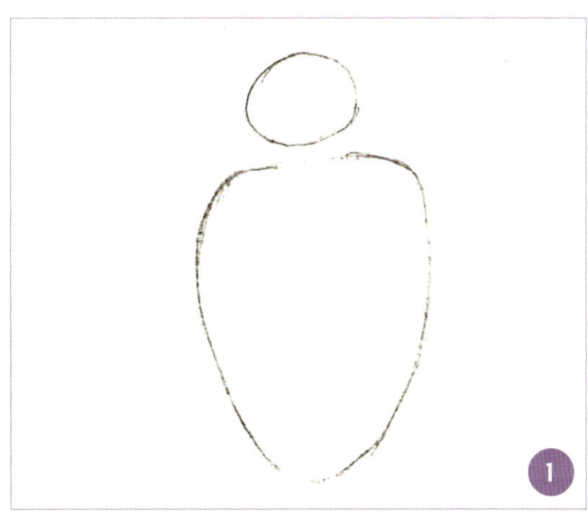

Step 1: Sketch a small circle floating above a chubby carrot figure in pencil. This will become a pigeon as seen from the back.

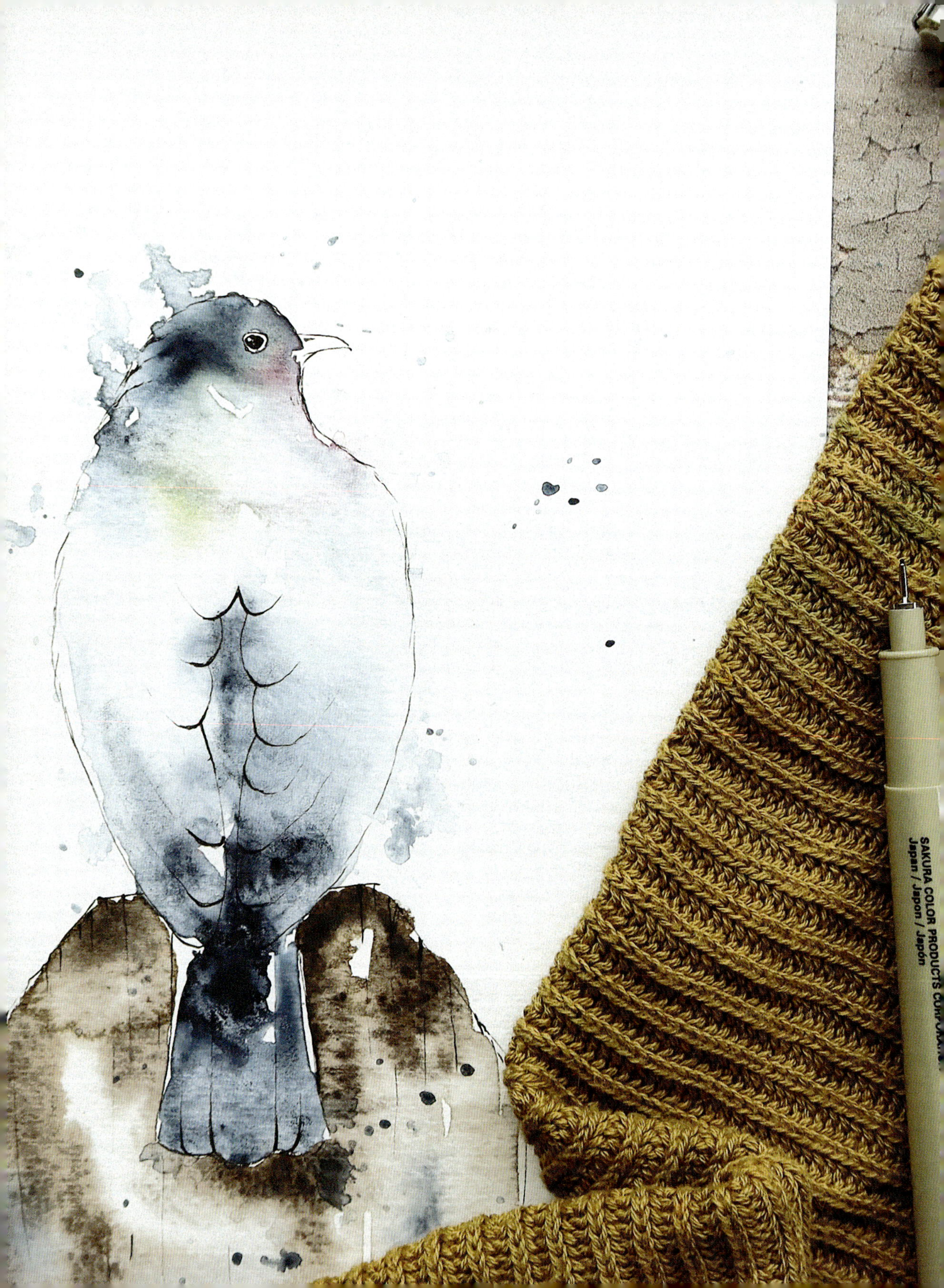
SAKURA COLOR PRODUCTS CORPORATION
Japan / Japon / Japón

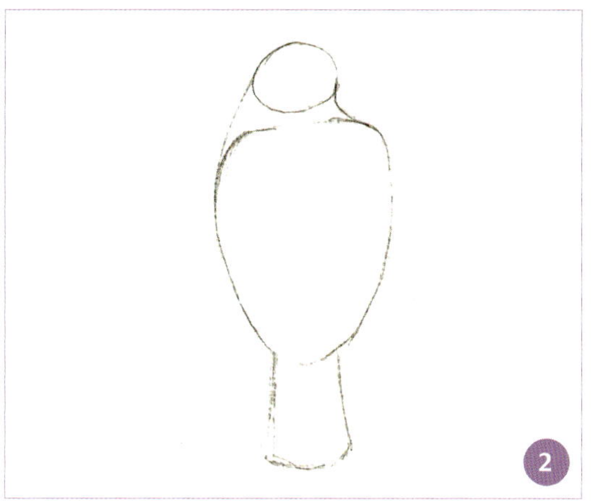

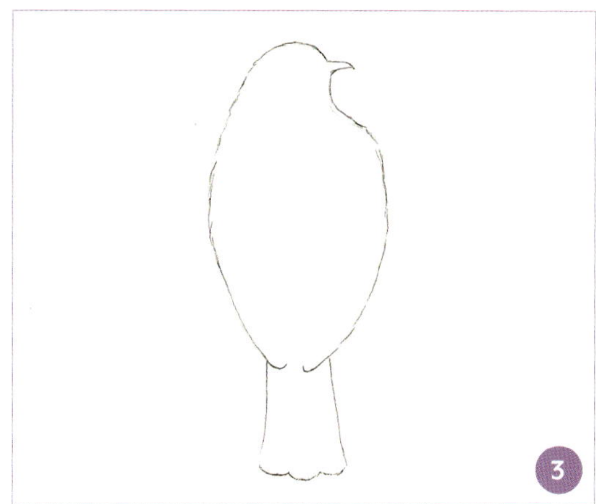

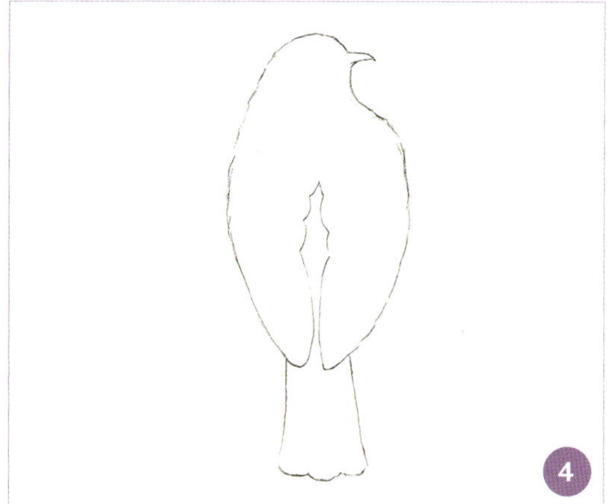

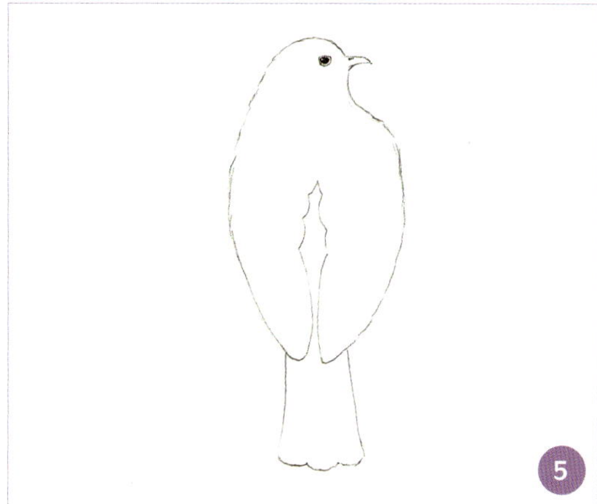

Step 2: Add lines for the neck and tail. Sketch the pigeon looking to the right, and then erase the lines you don't need anymore.

Step 3: Draw a sketchy outline with the 01 fineliner showing the outer edge of the wings on the back as well as the head, beak and tail ending in three round shapes. Keep the outline of the body broken to show some of the feather texture on the edge. Draw a slightly bent pointy beak as well.

Step 4: Take your 005 fineliner and sketch the rounded details on the wings.

Step 5: Sketch an oval eye with a highlight and a bit of detail to the beak. Just a small line on the top will do the trick. Then, when you are ready, you can erase the pencil lines.

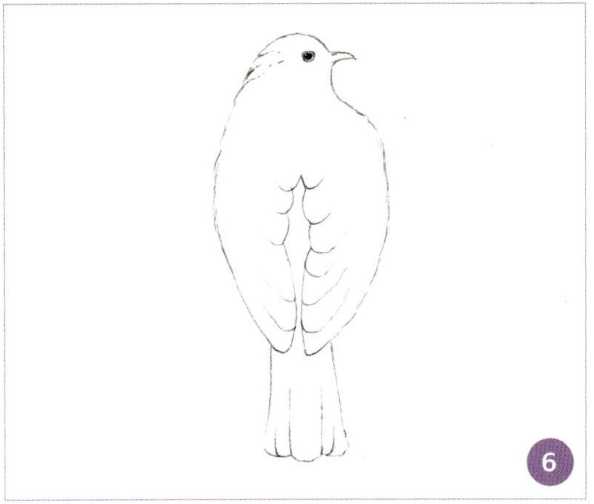

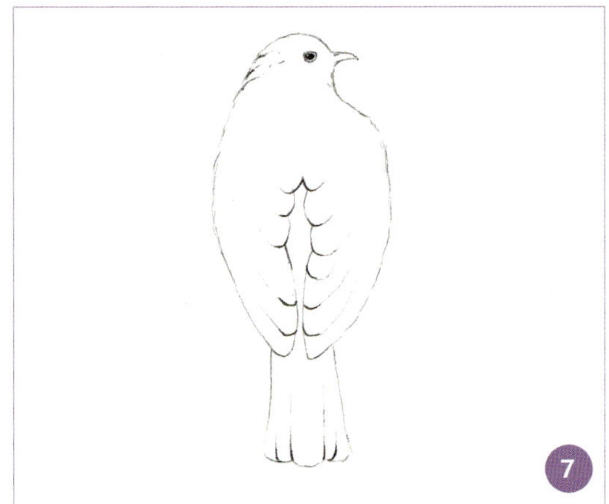

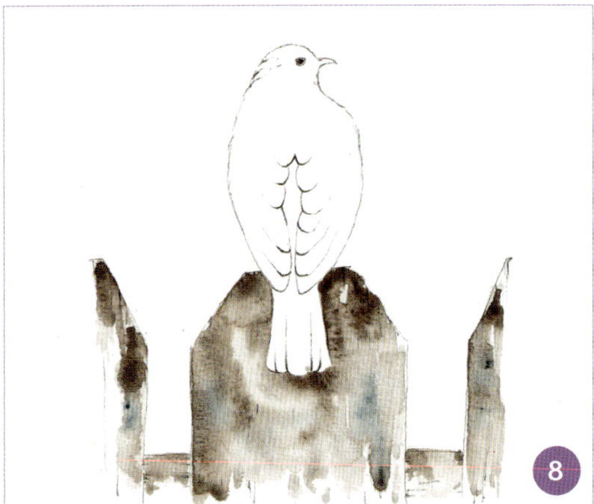

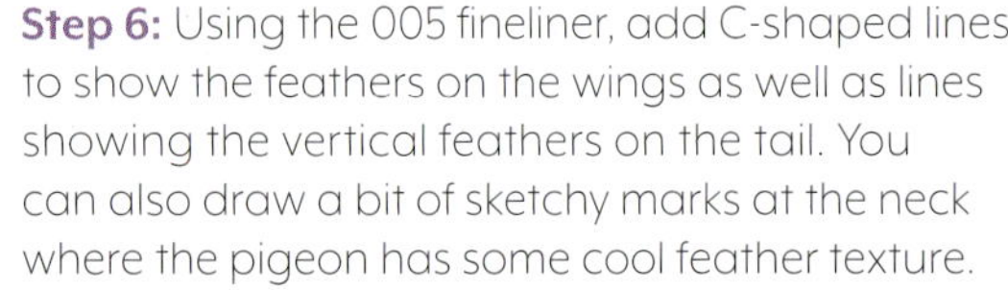

Step 6: Using the 005 fineliner, add C-shaped lines to show the feathers on the wings as well as lines showing the vertical feathers on the tail. You can also draw a bit of sketchy marks at the neck where the pigeon has some cool feather texture.

Step 7: Dig deep in your pencil case to find your 02 fineliner to add darker details. Draw a bit below the overlapping wings and feathers for some nice depth.

Step 8: Pigeons are often sitting on things as they observe the world. So, sketch a Picket Fence (page 27) for this birdie to sit on, and paint it in Van Dyke brown and Payne's gray.

Step 9: Paint the pigeon very loosely wet-on-dry using Payne's gray. Drip in a bit of quinacridone rose at the throat and chest and green gold at the shoulders. While it's still wet, splatter clean water on the edges of the bird so the paint runs out there a bit. And don't hold back on the splatters—just give it a flick or two with the size 9 brush to make some splatters using Payne's gray as well.

Now this otherwise gray Pigeon is all set to hit the dance floor—well done!

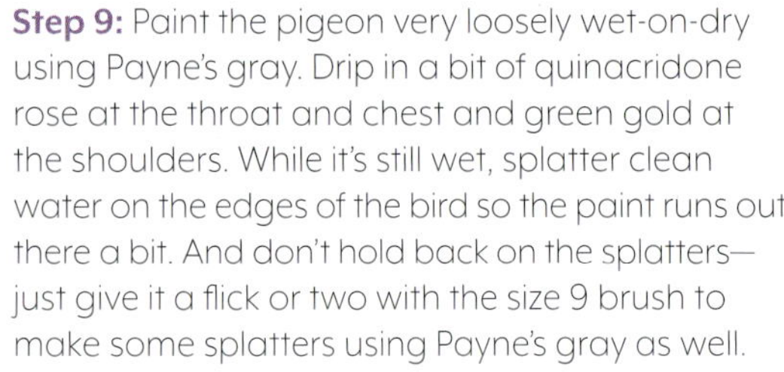

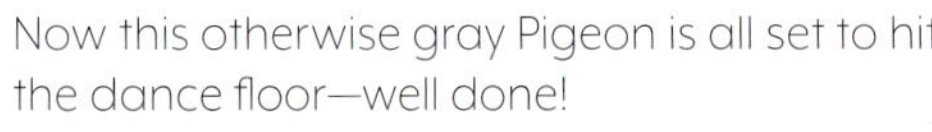

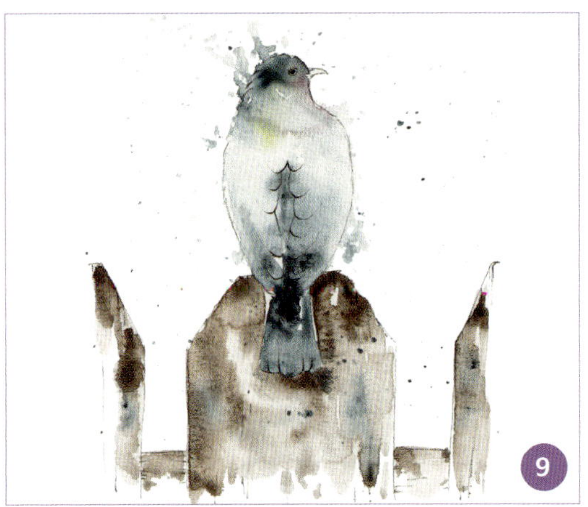

house sparrow

the friendly bird of community and teamwork

When I see house sparrows in the garden, there is never just one. There are always at least ten flying around, chatting and having the best time. I always imagine they are having a party or a family celebration of some kind.

In this tutorial, I wanted to give you yet another way to get these birdies flying because these sparrows rarely sit still for a second! Unless they hear a sound, and then they all fly into a bush and hide.

Materials

Pencil and eraser

Paper: Canson Montval 300gsm (140lb) cold press

Fineliners: sizes 01 and 005

Watercolor brush: size 4

Water and cloth

Palette

Colors

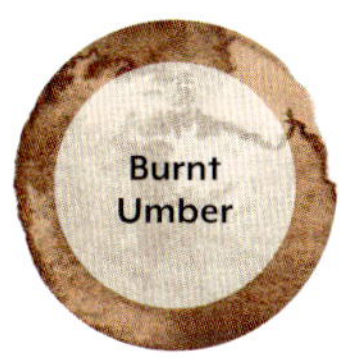

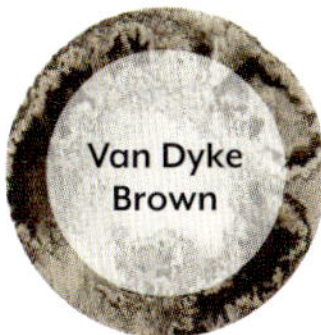

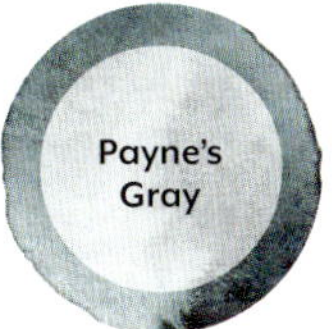

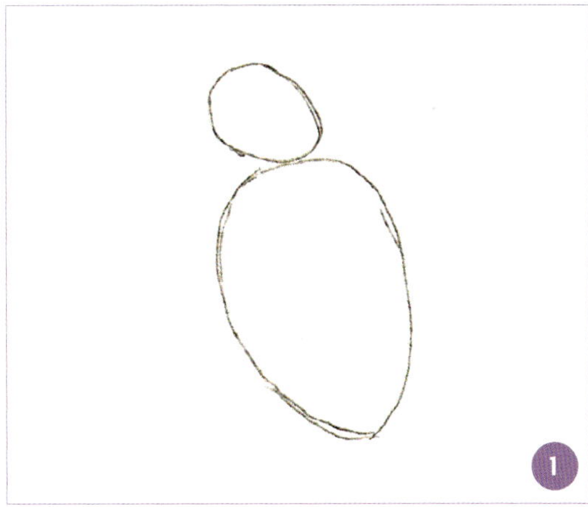

Step 1: Sketch the oval head and body with the pencil, tilting the bird a little to the left.

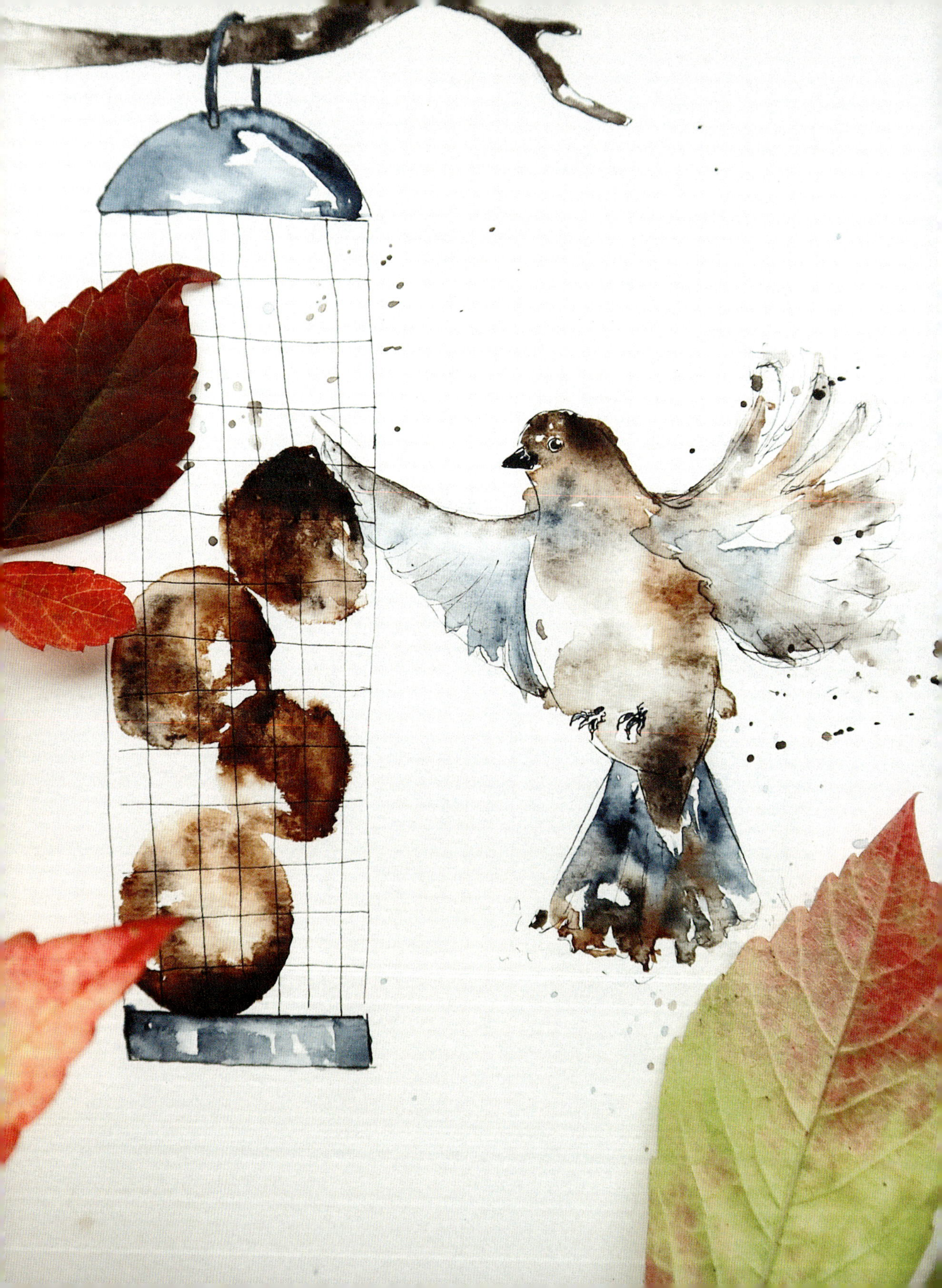

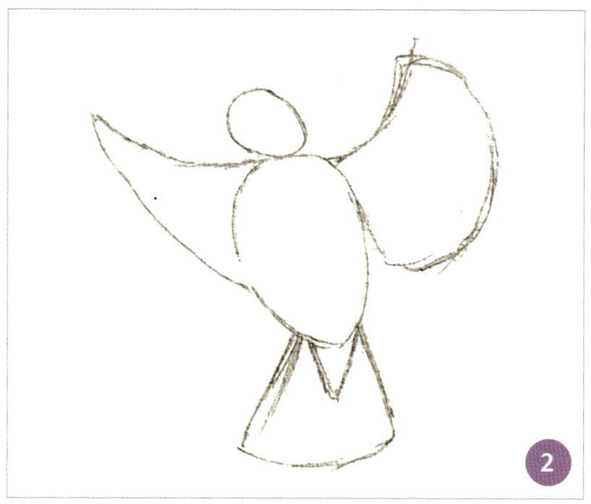

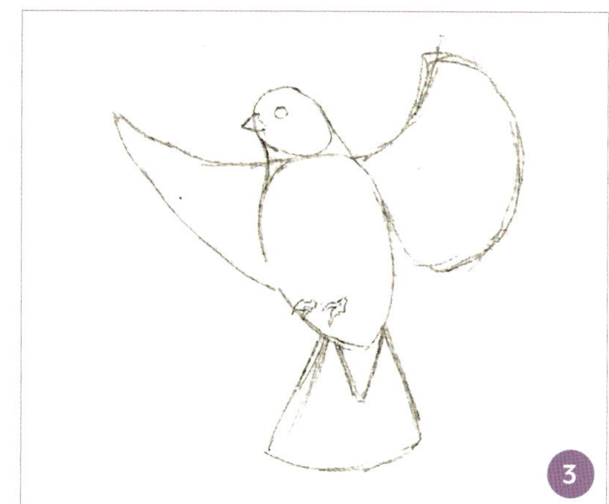

Step 2: Sketch the wings and tail. Shape the back wing almost like a triangle pointing to the left and the front wing big and rounded to the right. Since this birdie is about to land, the tail should point forward a tad, which means the lines will lean a bit to the left.

Step 3: Sketch the eye, a small beak, the neck and the feet. The feet are almost hidden in the feathers, so you can only see the toes and very little of the leg. Erase the lines you don't need when you love the sketch.

Step 4: Draw an outline of the body and the outer edges of the tail and wings with the 01 fineliner. Keep it sketchy. For the wings, it's totally cool if you draw a couple of lines on the same spot.

Step 5: Outline the beak, eye and feet with the 005 fineliner.

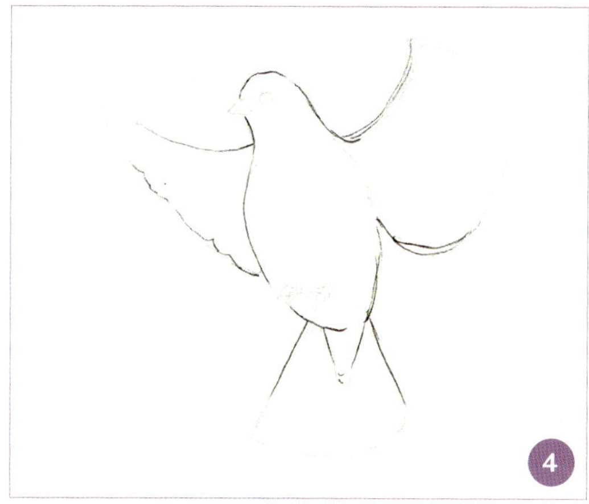

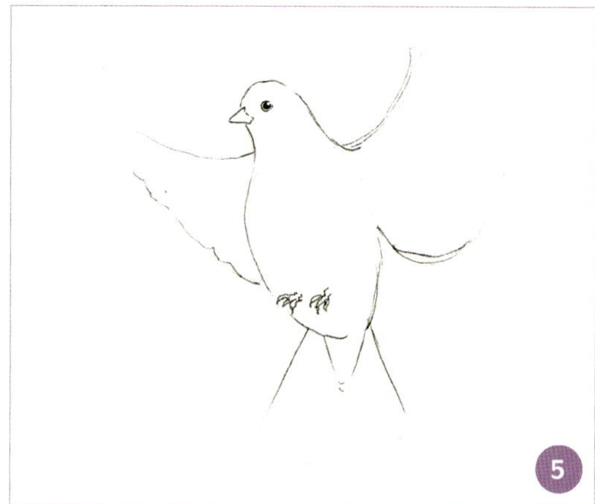

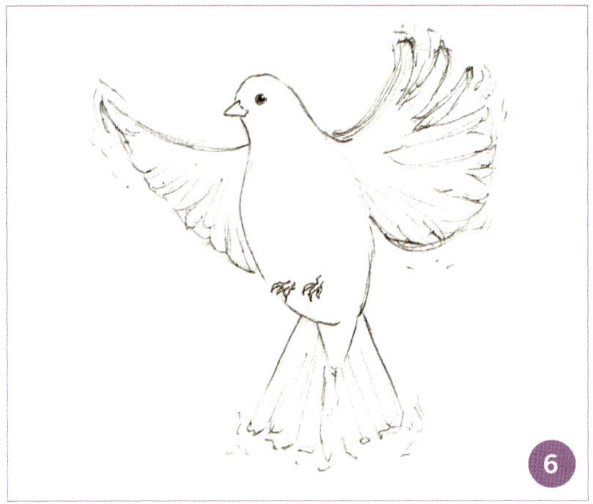

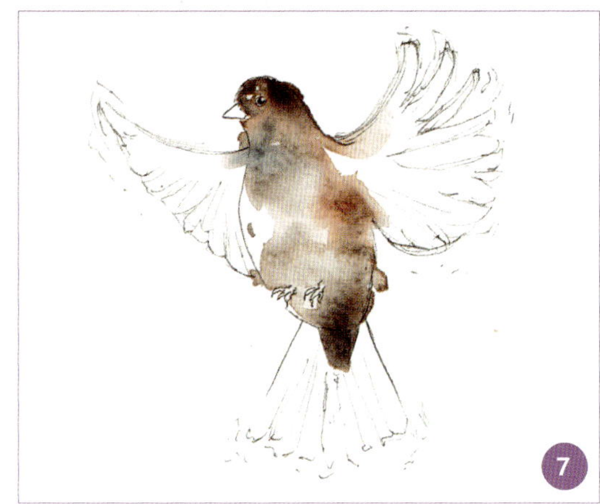

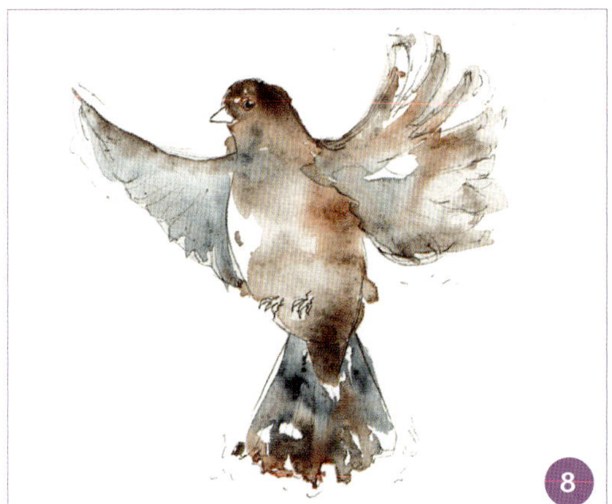
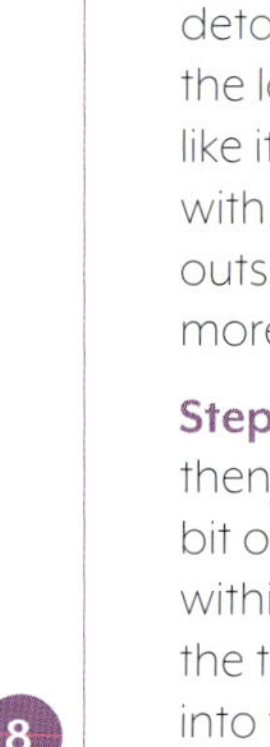

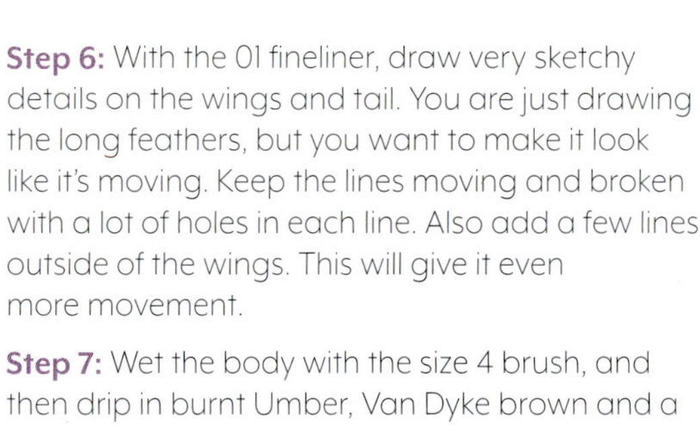

Step 6: With the 01 fineliner, draw very sketchy details on the wings and tail. You are just drawing the long feathers, but you want to make it look like it's moving. Keep the lines moving and broken with a lot of holes in each line. Also add a few lines outside of the wings. This will give it even more movement.

Step 7: Wet the body with the size 4 brush, and then drip in burnt Umber, Van Dyke brown and a bit of Payne's gray. Keep it very sketchy and not within the lines. Add a fine line of clean water at the top of the wings so a bit of the paint can run into that. Don't be scared of white space.

Step 8: Once the breast and belly are dry, wet the wings while randomly leaving some white spaces dry, and then drip in Payne's gray close to the body and on the lower part of the wings. Then use a bit of Van Dyke brown on the tip of the feathers. Don't stay within the lines—keep it sketchy. You only need to see one or two feathers to know it's a wing in flight. Paint the upper part of the wings in Van Dyke brown. Then do the same with the tail. Wet it and drip Payne's gray closest to the body. Then drip Van Dyke brown at the lower part of the tail. While everything is still wet, drip a few droplets of burnt Umber onto the front wing and the tail.

Step 9: Once the previous layer of paint is dry, paint the beak and feet using Payne's gray.

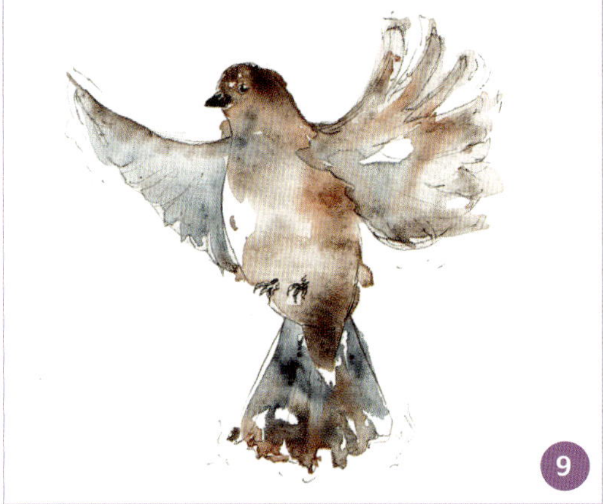

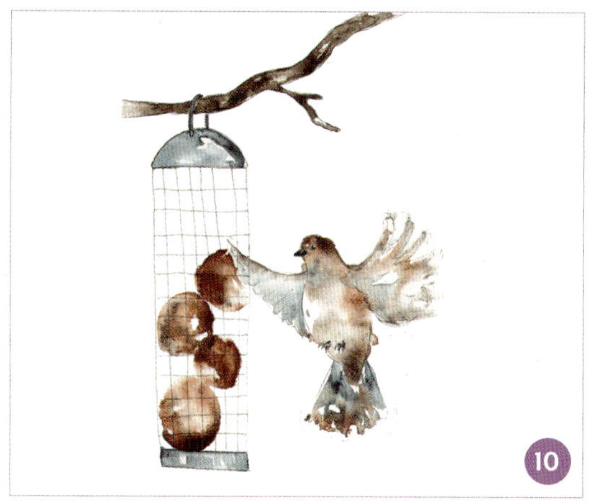

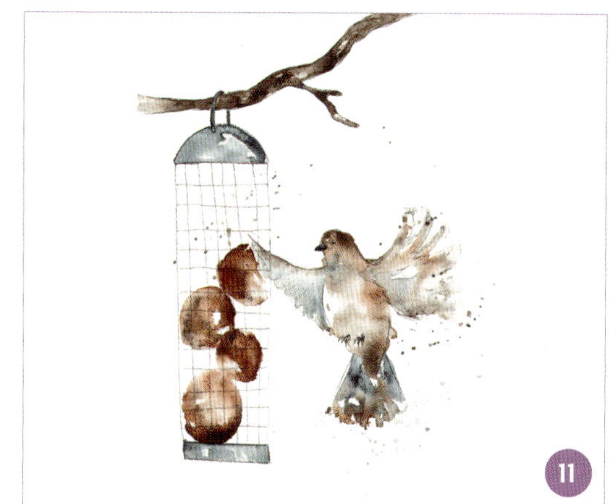

Step 10: Now you can feed the hungry sparrow with the Bird Feeder on page 31. Let it overlap the wing a bit, so you'll be able to see the wing through the netting. Paint the balls of birdfeed using burnt Umber and Van Dyke brown.

Step 11: Drip a few splatters of watery Van Dyke brown and Payne's gray, especially at the front wing and tail.

Step 12: We're at the end here, and I thought the wing behind the feeder needed to be pushed back farther. So, I just gave the top ball a second layer and let it overlap the wing a bit. Remember, you can always adjust as you go—nothing is set in stone, not even watercolor.

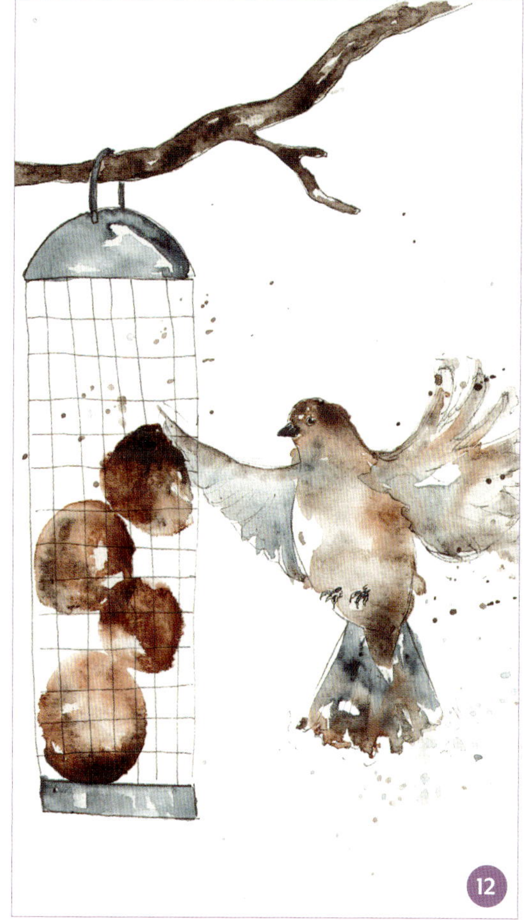

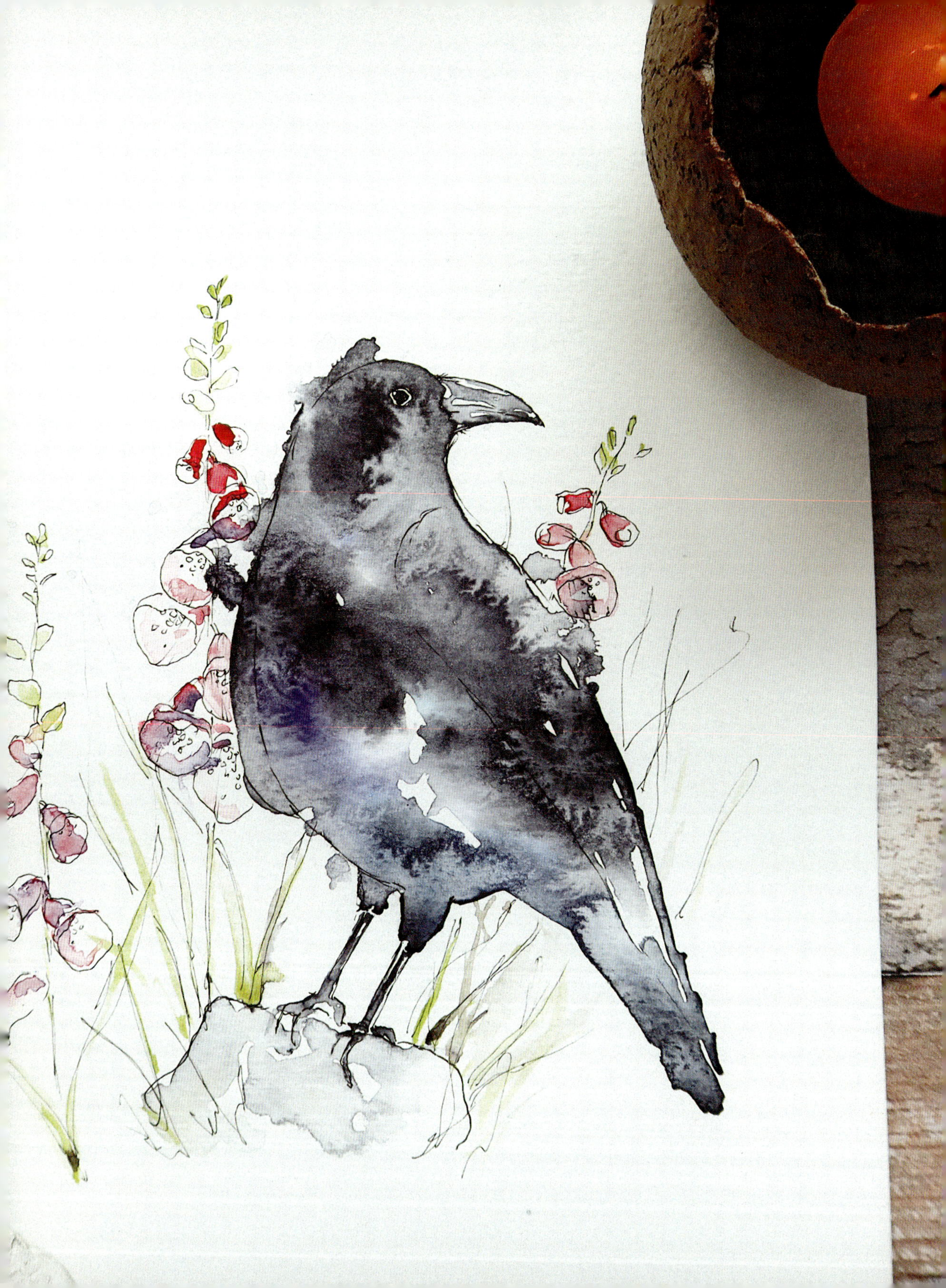

raven
a bird of mystery, prophecy and insight

This might just be the mightiest of the birds. Also, they can seem a bit scary with their dark colors, but don't make the mistake of thinking they are boring and only belong in *Game of Thrones*. When you look closely at their feathers, they are actually shining with blues and violets.

Here, in this final illustration of the birdies, we are going to play with the raven standing on the ground surrounded by beautiful foxgloves, which will hopefully take the edge off the spookiness of this bird.

Materials

Pencil and eraser
Paper: Canson Montval 300gsm (140lb) cold press
Watercolor brushes: sizes 9 and 4
Water and cloth
Palette
Fineliners: sizes 01, 005 and 02

Colors

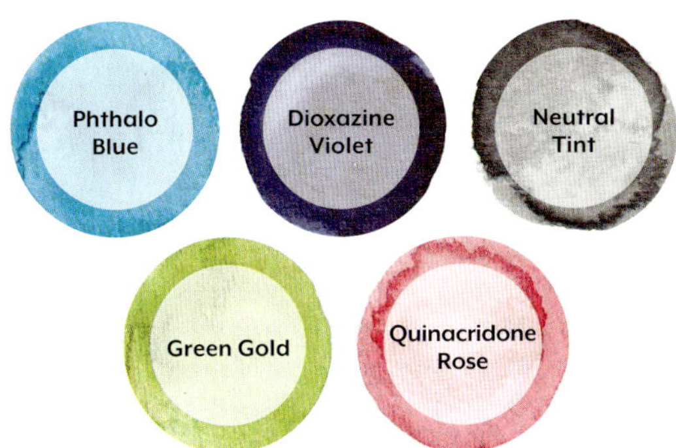

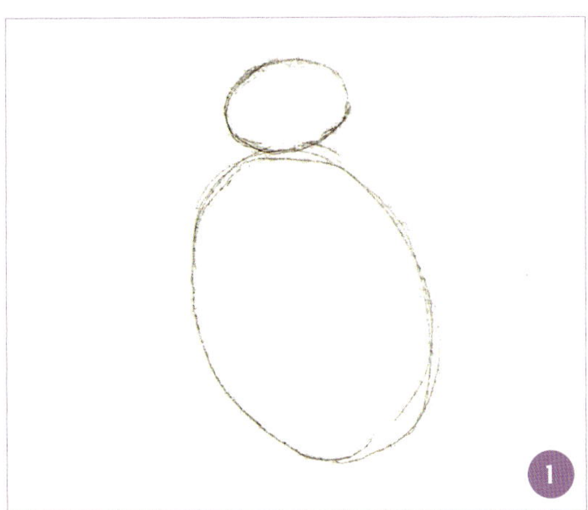

Step 1: Sketch a big oval with a smaller one on top with the pencil. Tilt the top oval to the right as if he is looking out for someone he can guide and be all wise around.

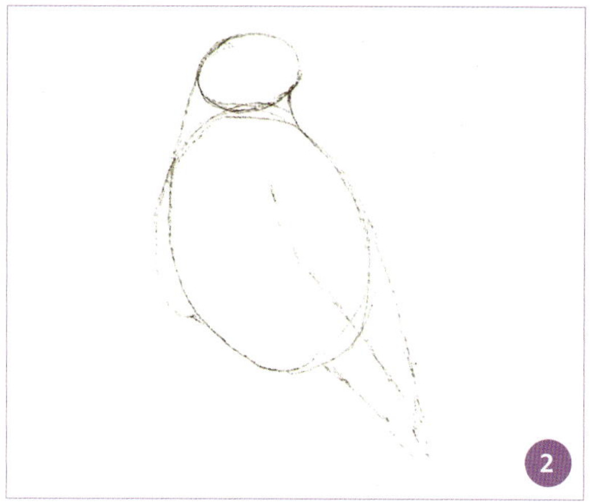

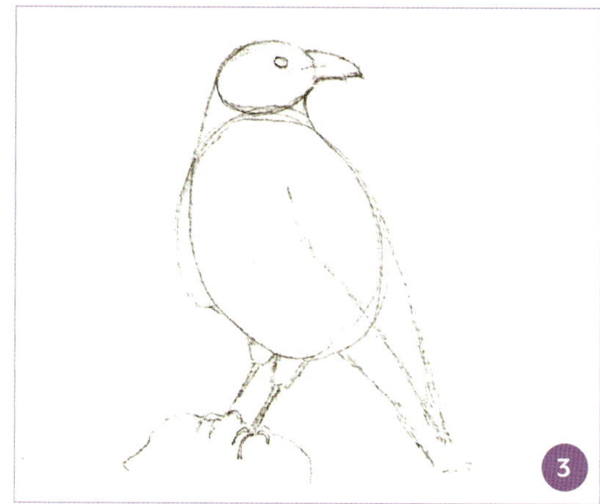

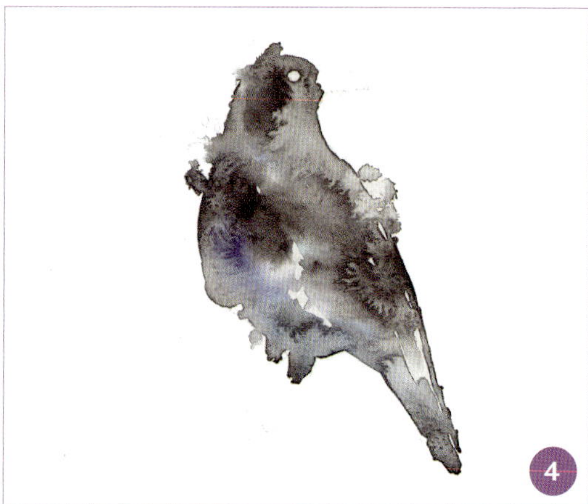

Step 2: Add a big wing on the right side of the body and a small one tucked behind the body on the left. Then draw lines to show the neck, throat and tail.

Step 3: Draw a big beak. This is a lot bigger than the ones we sketched up till now, but I promise you, it's that big! Draw an oval eye and give him two legs with thighs pointing to the left and a rock to stand on. (After all, ravens are a bit too mighty to be sitting on the ground.) You can now erase the pencil lines you don't need.

Step 4: Paint the entire body with clean water using the size 9 brush, avoiding the beak, eye and legs. Then drip phthalo blue and dioxazine violet into it.

Step 5: With the size 4 brush, paint the beak and legs using neutral tint while leaving plenty of highlights.

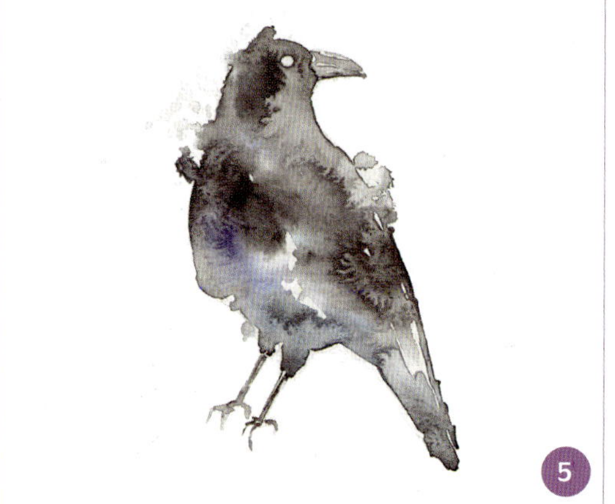

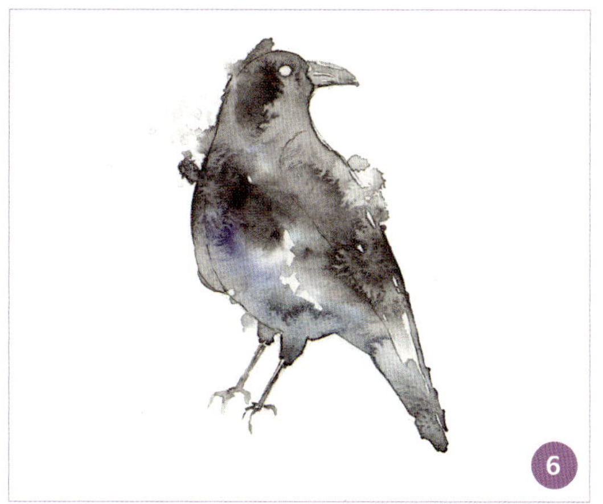

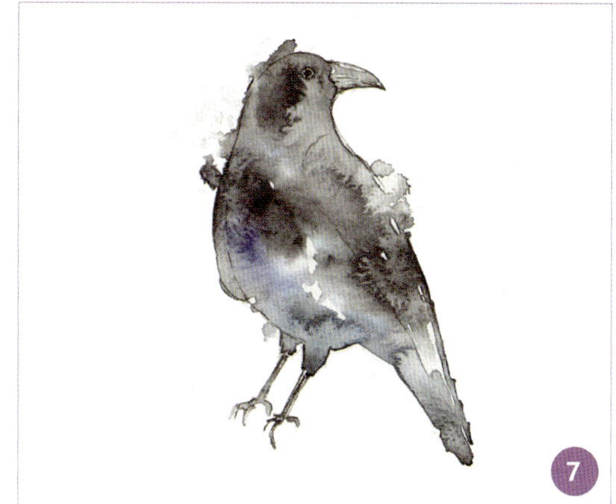

Step 6: Wait for everything to dry completely, and then sketch the outline of the body and wings with the 01 fineliner.

Step 7: Then grab your 005 fineliner, and sketch the smaller details like the eye, beak and legs.

Step 8: Now you can have fun sketching and painting the flowers from Foxglove on page 55 surrounding the raven. Make sure to keep some flowers behind it for a bit of depth. And when you add fineliner details, try to give the most detail to the flowers closest to the raven, which will lead the viewer's eye.

I used green gold for the stems and quinacridone rose for the flowers. While the blooms are still wet, you can drip in a bit of dioxazine violet in the quinacridone rose as well as in the green gold to tie the colors together. Finally, finish with adding a few grass straws with the tip of your brush.

Step 9: Wet the rock and carefully drip in neutral tint and green gold.

And that is it—you finished that last birdie! What an accomplishment. Give yourself the gift of putting all the sketches out on your bed and admire the work you've done. Congrats!

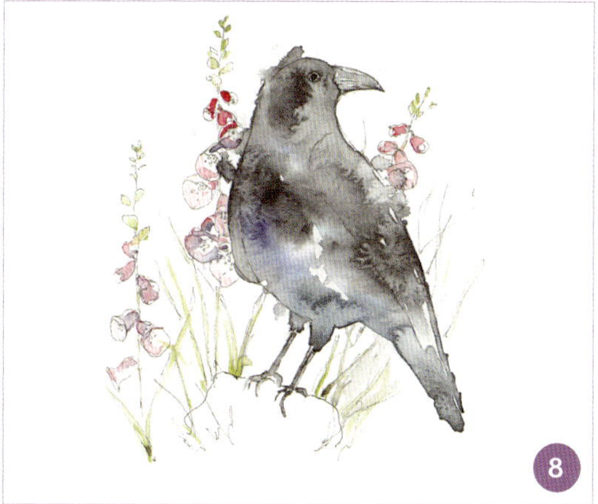

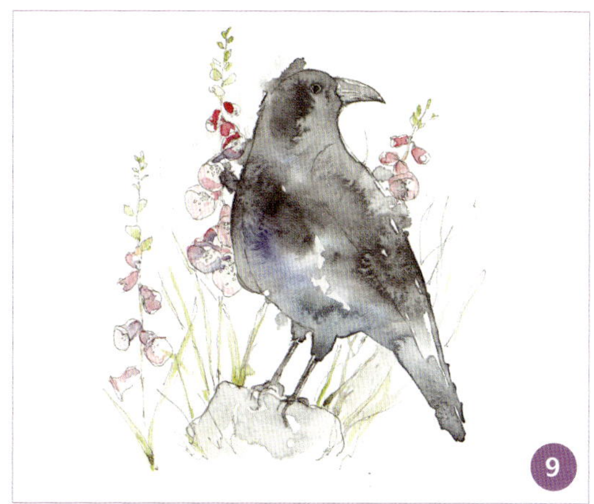

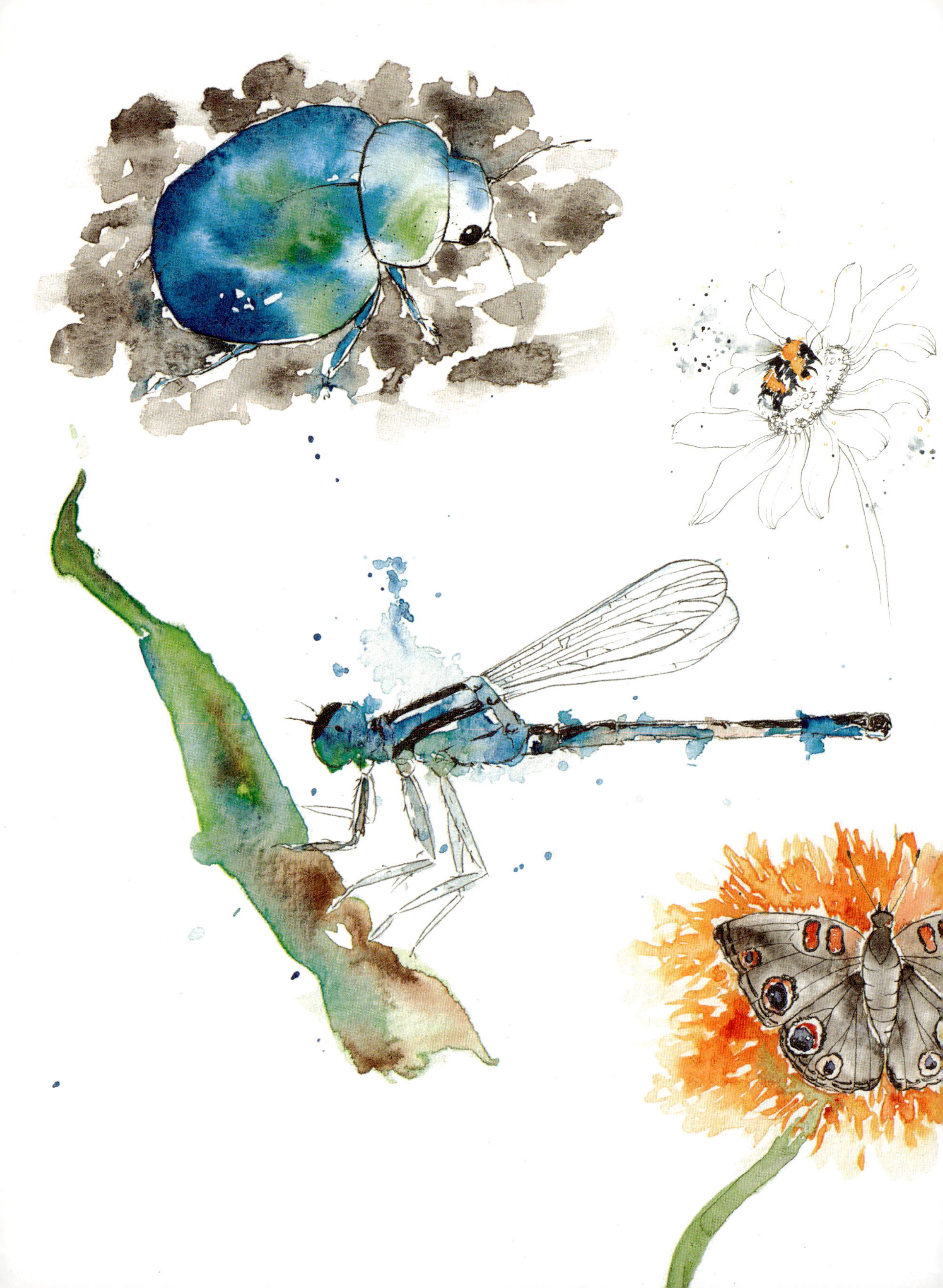

eleven butterflies, bumblebees & other cute bug tutorials

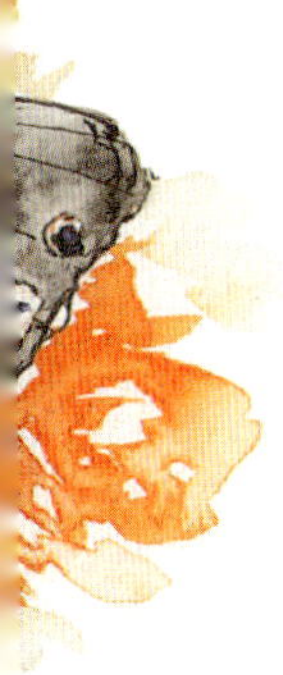

I just love sketching birds, but if you zoom in even more into the garden, there are actually so many other beautiful winged creatures. And in this chapter, we are going to show them some love. Insects are often a bit overlooked (okay, maybe not the butterfly), but we are going to make them the star of the show now. Because when you think about it, how cute is a small ladybug or grasshopper?

The funny thing is that a lot of these insects are quite similar. So, when we get the hang of the basic shapes, it's super easy to get cracking on more and more. You can just sketch a head, a body and a tail. Throw in six legs and antennas, and then adorn it with wings. It's actually that simple. We will start with the small Butterfly Caterpillar (page 131), emerge into a beautiful butterfly, and when we feel comfortable enough, we can move to some of the lesser-known insects.

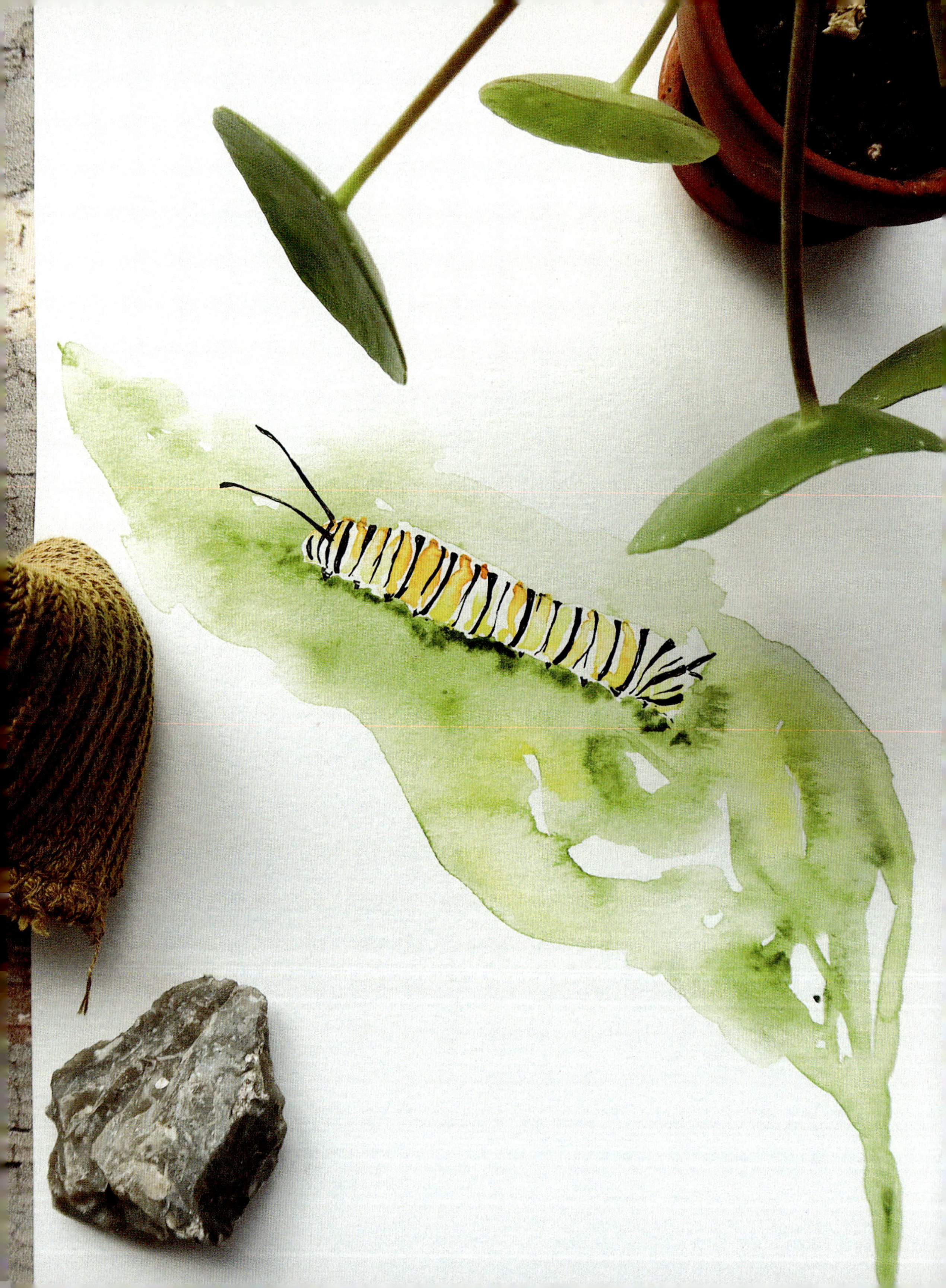

butterfly caterpillar

the cute little baby monarch

When I find a caterpillar in the garden, I always call the kids to gather around the little creature. They either say "Aaaw, Mom, that is so cute" or "Eeew, gross! A worm!" And then we talk about the process it goes through from caterpillar to cocoon, and then finally into a beautiful butterfly. And while doing that, mommy tries to hide those happy tears when I look at my own little caterpillars (not worms) slowly transforming too.

This is actually the only animal in the book without wings. It does have some striking colors, though, because it already looks a bit like its grown stage.

Materials

Pencil and eraser

Paper: Canson Montval 300gsm (140lb) cold press

Watercolor brushes: sizes 4 and 9

Water and cloth

Palette

Fineliner: size 01

Colors

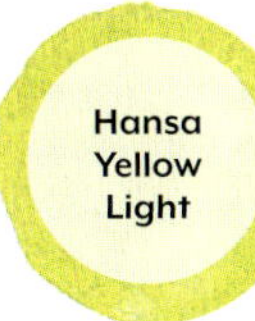

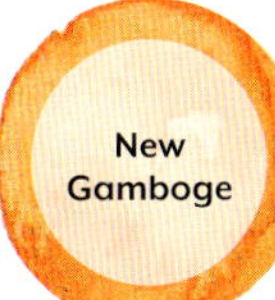

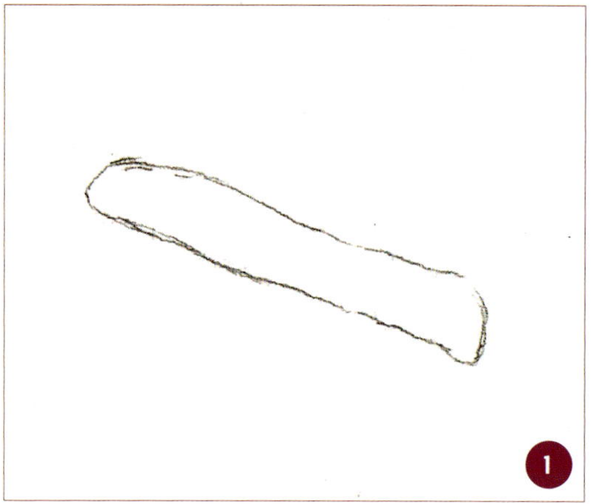

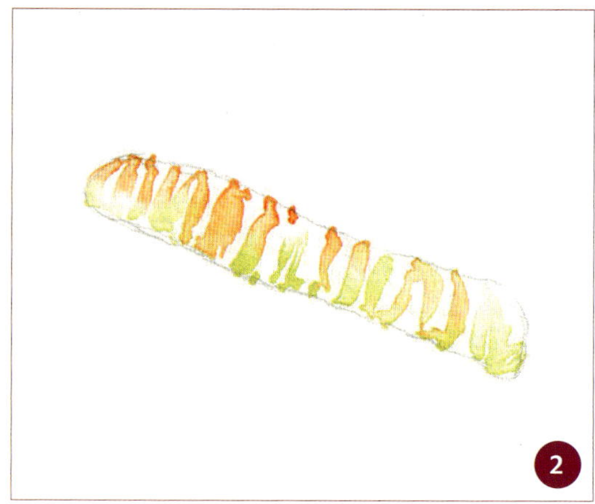

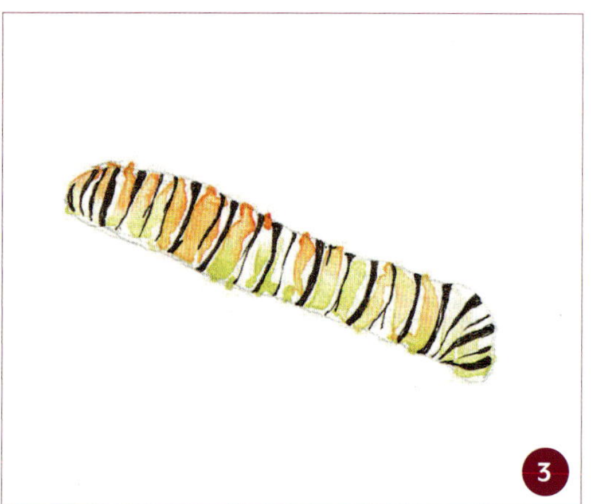

Step 1: Sketch the caterpillar in pencil. It very much looks like a worm, but it's not.

Step 2: Draw vertical lines with clean water across the body using your size 4 brush. At the bottom of the watery line, drip in Hansa yellow light, and at the top of these lines, drip in a bit of new gamboge. Wait a while for it to dry.

Step 3: Add dark lines with the 01 fineliner. Leave white space and yellow lines between the dark lines so it gets a stripey look. Keep some of the lines thin and some thick. Bend them a bit at the ends by making them shorter and letting them meet at the same point.

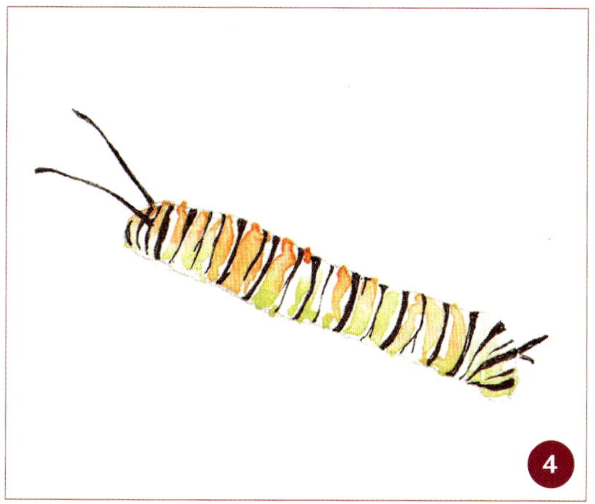

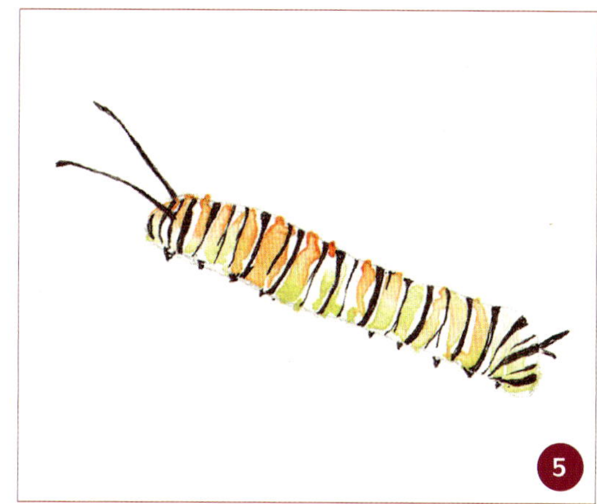

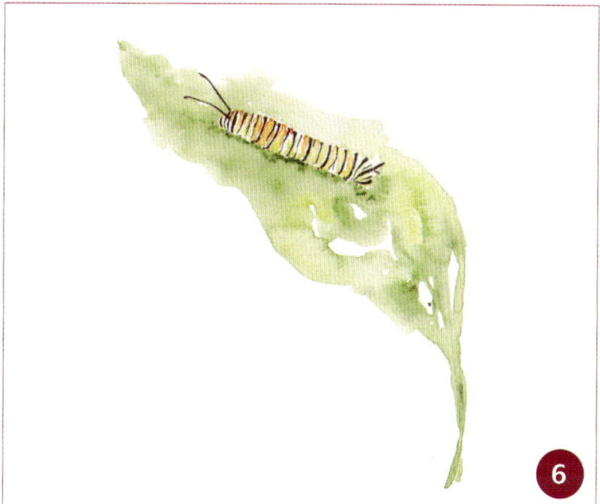

Step 4: With the fineliner, add long antennas to the head and short antennas at the back.

Step 5: Draw very small triangular legs beneath the body with the fineliner. After that, erase the pencil lines.

Step 6: Paint a leaf with the size 9 brush wet-on-dry using sap green. Drip in a bit of the Hansa yellow light while it's still wet. Now grab your smaller size 4 brush, and add a denser sap green underneath the caterpillar's body for a bit of shadow.

And now it's ready to eat this leaf and the surrounding ones before taking a nap and turning into a beautiful butterfly. And personally, I am super curious to see how it turns out, so flip the page and start sketching the Monarch Butterfly (page 135).

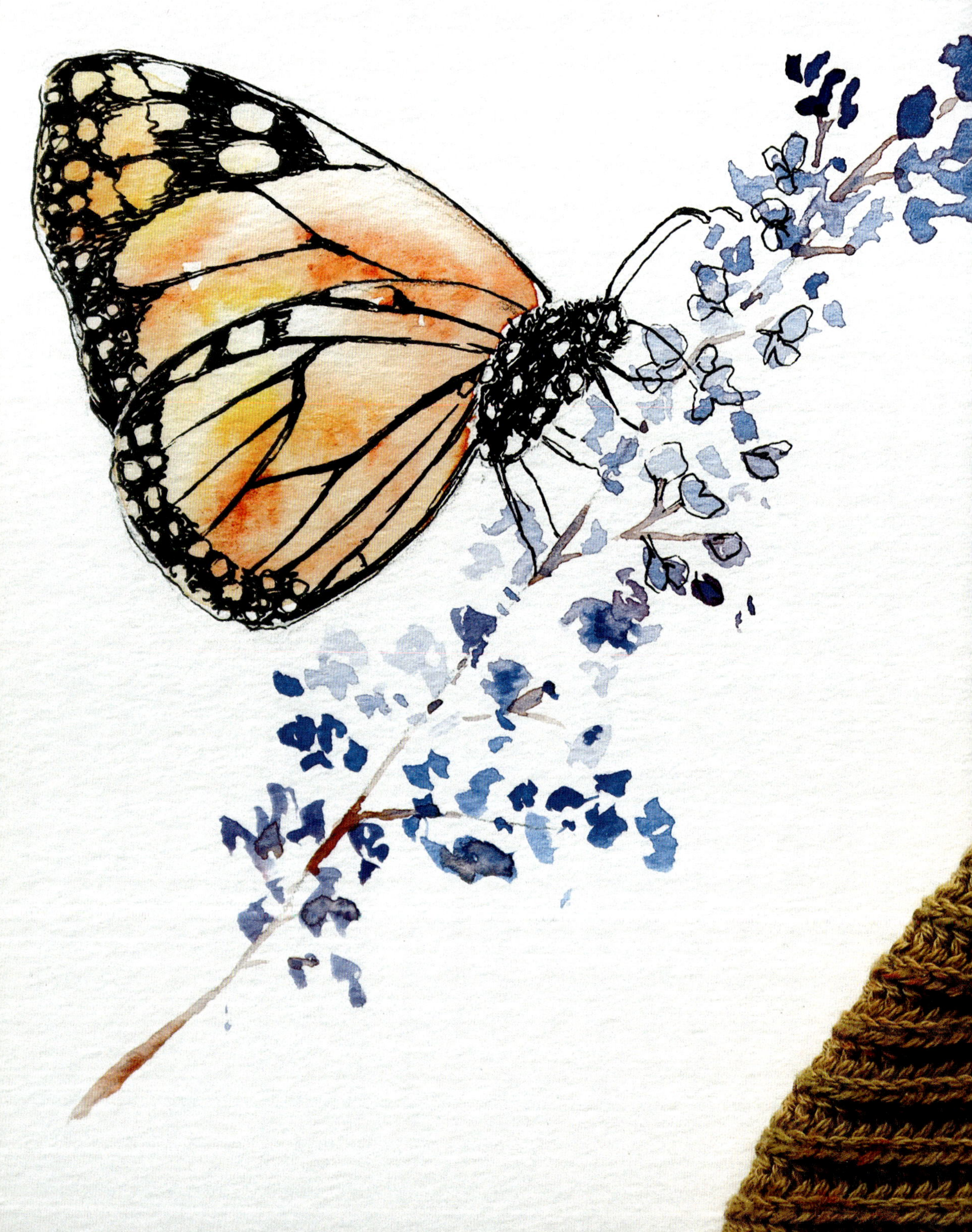

monarch butterfly
the king of butterflies

I heard someone once say that butterflies are like flowers flowing in the wind. I absolutely love that image because that is exactly how I see it too.

The first butterfly we are going to sketch is the king of butterflies, the monarch. (Yes, we're starting out strong!) We will sketch it from the side so you can really enjoy the pattern on the wings. And here, the mix of watercolor and fineliner just becomes so impressive with the soft colors and the dark graphic pattern. This is going to be so much fun!

Materials

Pencil and eraser
Paper: Canson Montval 300gsm (140lb) cold press
Watercolor brush: size 9
Water and cloth
Palette
Fineliners: sizes 005 and 01

Colors

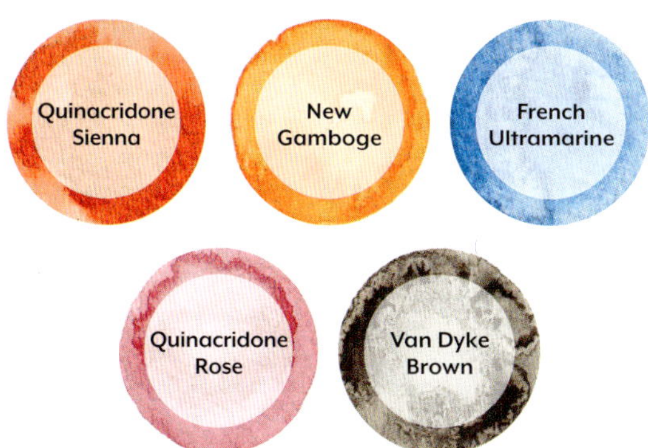

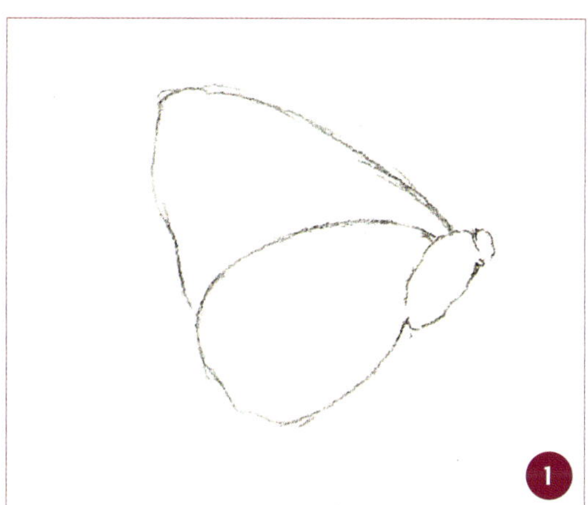

Step 1: With your pencil, sketch an oval body with a small head turning to the right and wings. It's easiest if you place the bottom wing first and then the upper wing. The bottom wing starts at the top of the body and goes all the way to the tail, looking almost like a balloon. The top wing is more like a triangle with soft edges that starts closer to the head and tucks behind the bottom wing.

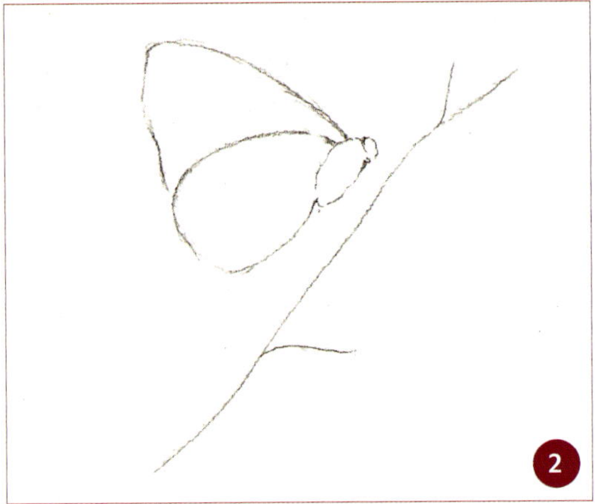

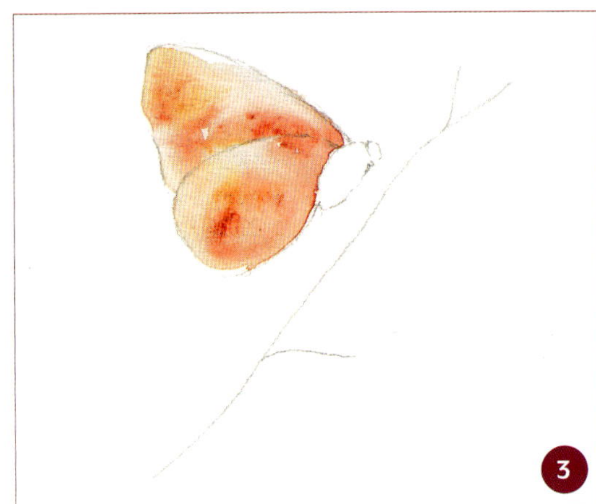

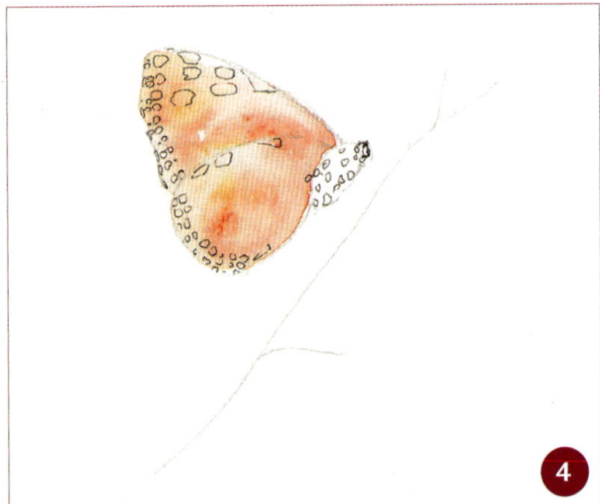

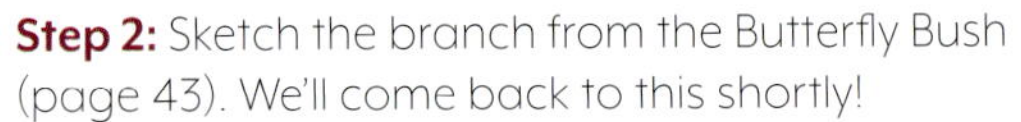

Step 2: Sketch the branch from the Butterfly Bush (page 43). We'll come back to this shortly!

Step 3: Grab your size 9 brush and wet both wings with clean water. Then drip in quinacridone sienna and new gamboge. While you wait for it to dry, you can take a look at a garden website to see if you should update your own garden with a few pretty blooms for the butterflies.

Step 4: With the 005 fineliner, sketch the different uneven marks on the butterfly wings and body. This is to frame all the places that need to be preserved from the black in the next steps. Make big marks on the top of the wings and small on the body and on the tip of the wings.

Step 5: Now grab your 01 fineliner and color in the body. It's actually a bit furry, so keep some white space, and stay clear of the marks you made in step 4.

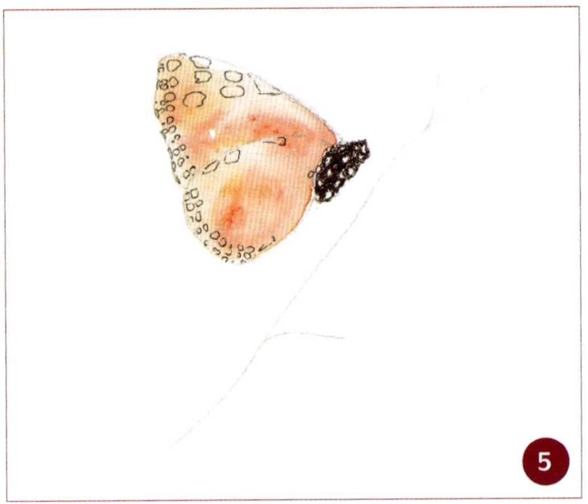

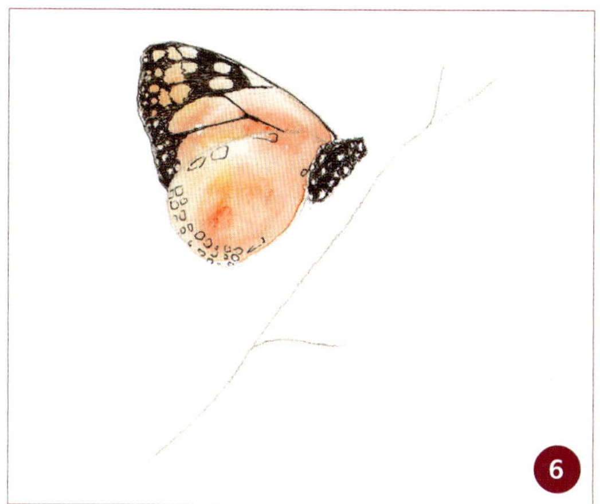

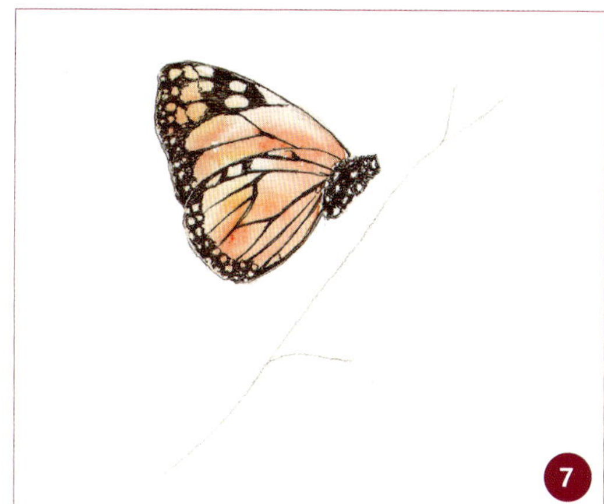

Step 6: Color in the marks made in step 4 on the first wing with 01 fineliner. You can also give the wing a few dark veins and a dark outline.

Step 7: Draw around the marks on the other wing, and create some veins going from the body and towards the outer edge of the wing. Let a few of them spread out like branches on a tree before reaching the edge.

Step 8: Turn to the Butterfly Bush on page 43 to see how you can make a throne worthy of a monarch. For the blooms, I used French ultramarine in a mix with quinacridone rose. For the branch, I used Van Dyke brown.

When you feel like it's a pretty wonderful place to rest, use the 005 fineliner to add two antennas and six legs, and you are done!

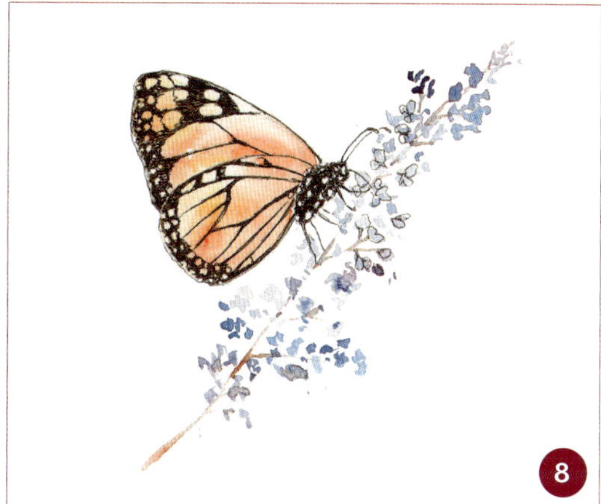

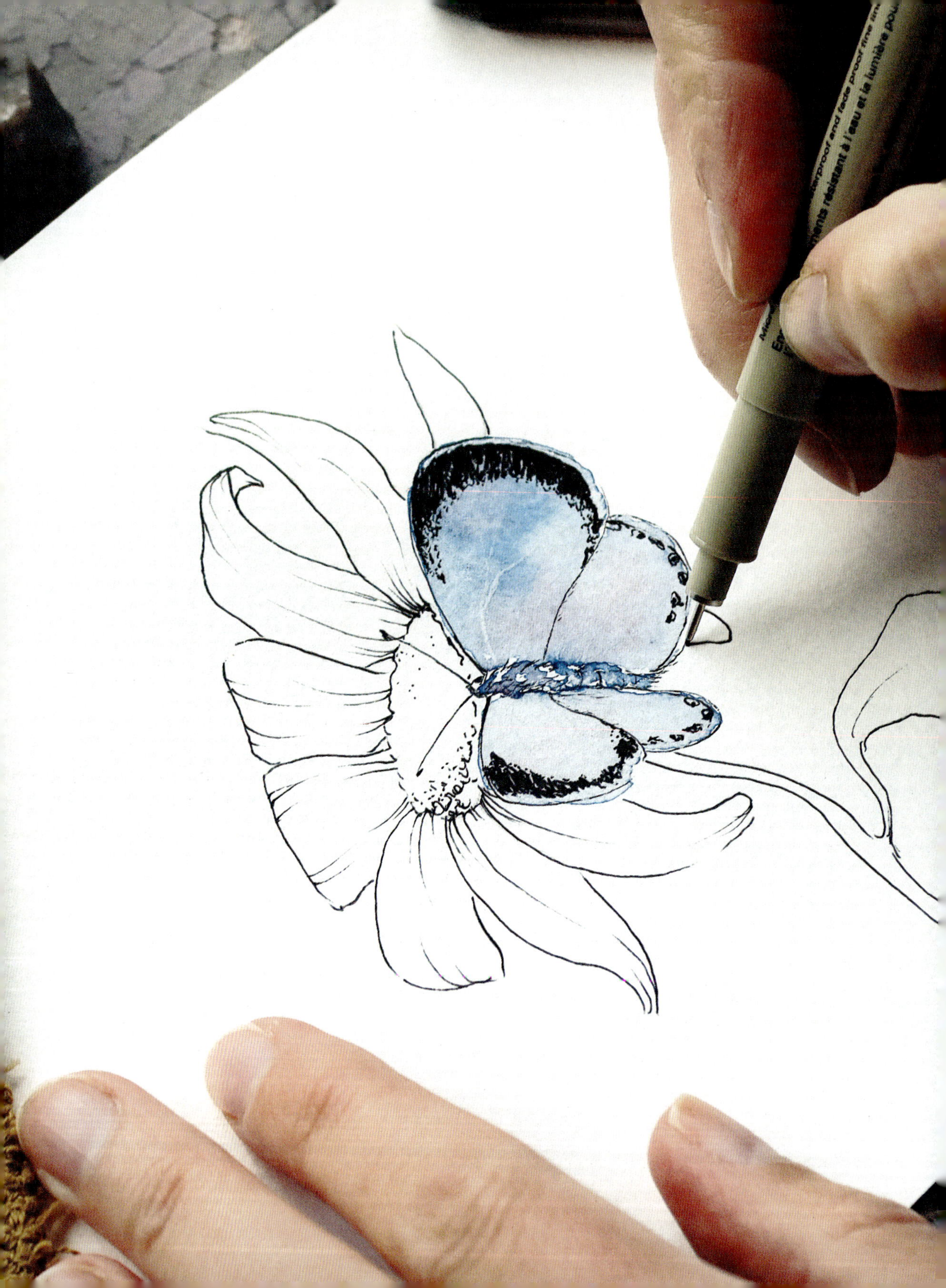

holly blue butterfly

the wish granter

Make a wish when you see a holly blue, and it will take it with them as they fly away. Isn't that great!? It's like the Santa of butterflies! But I have a feeling it is bearing gifts and messages from nature and not so much from elves. That might not be a bad thing.

In this tutorial, I want to show you a different way of combining ink and watercolor. Here, we are going to keep the flower without any color so the focus is all on our blue friend.

Materials

Pencil and eraser

Paper: Canson Montval 300gsm (140lb) cold press

Fineliners: sizes 01, 005 and 02

Watercolor brush: size 4

Water and cloth

Palette

Colors

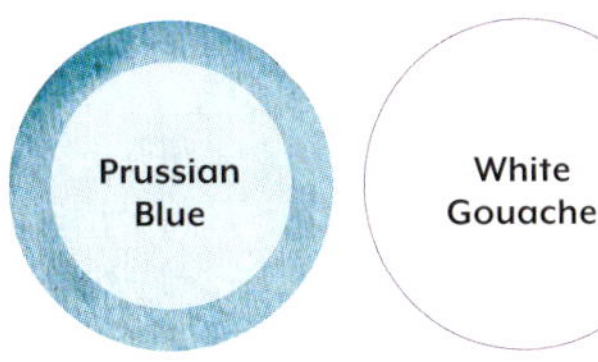

Mixes

Mix the Prussian blue with a bit of quinacridone rose for the color that drips into the blue.

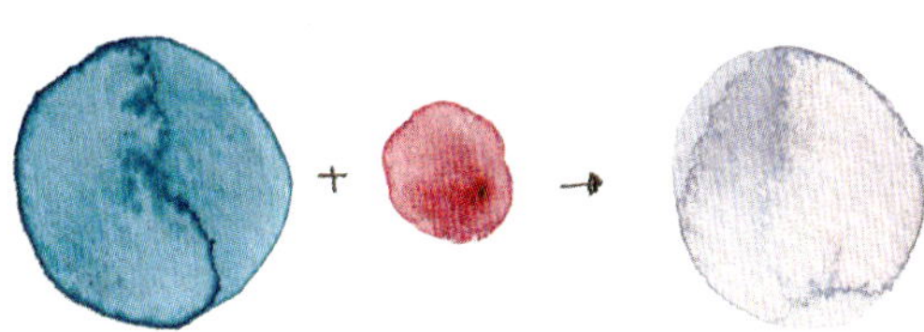

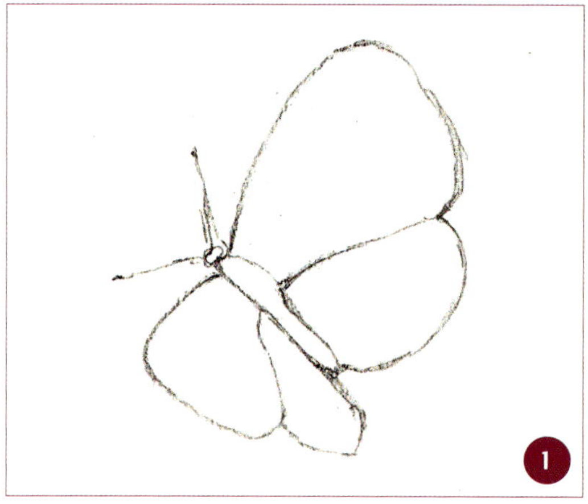

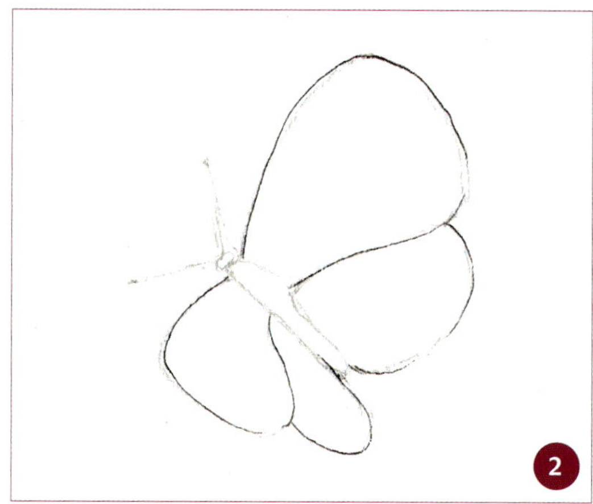

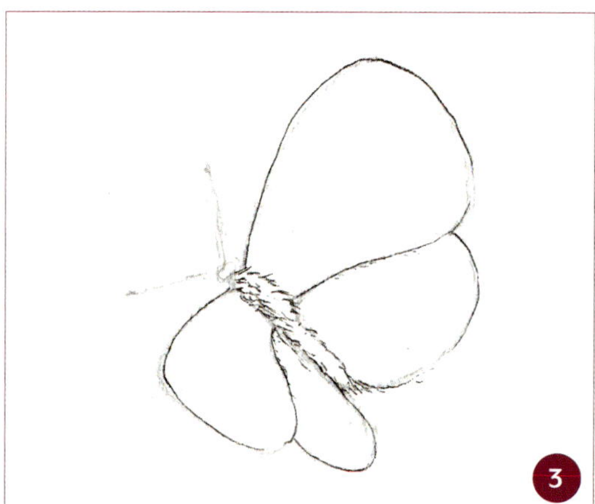

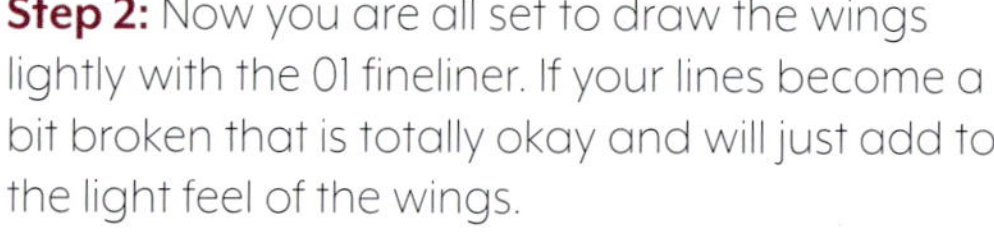

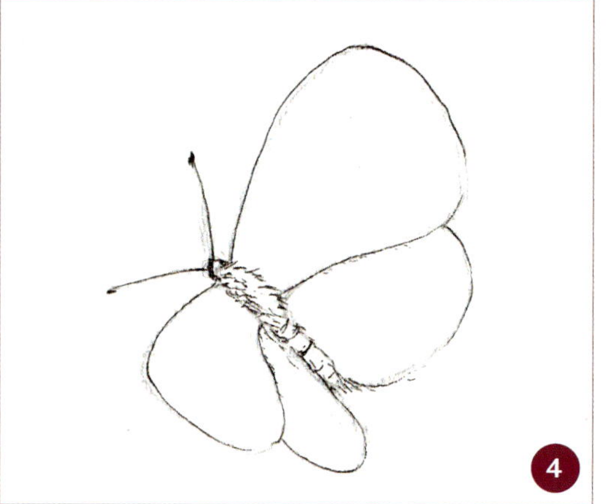

Step 1: Sketch the butterfly in pencil. Its body is almost like a thin carrot with a small round head and two antennas pointing in different directions. The wings on the right are bigger than the ones on the left to show it at an angle. Start with the top wings on both sides of the butterfly, and tuck the lower wings underneath the top wings.

Step 2: Now you are all set to draw the wings lightly with the 01 fineliner. If your lines become a bit broken that is totally okay and will just add to the light feel of the wings.

Step 3: This butterfly is a bit furry, so draw short, sketchy lines going from the head down toward the body with your 005 fineliner.

Step 4: Draw a small head, antennas and lines on the lower part of the body with the 005 fineliner. Erase the pencil lines before moving on to painting.

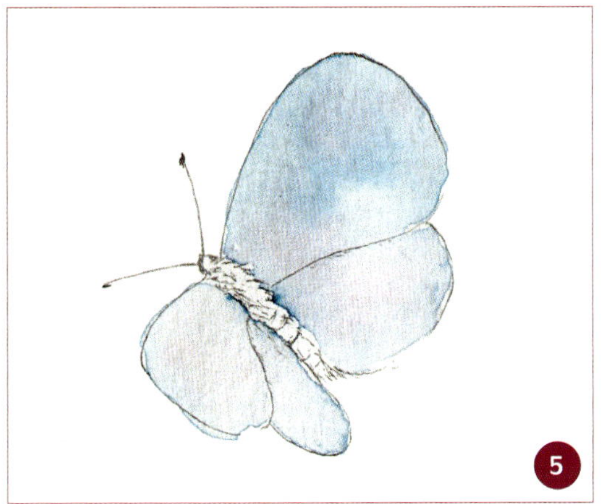

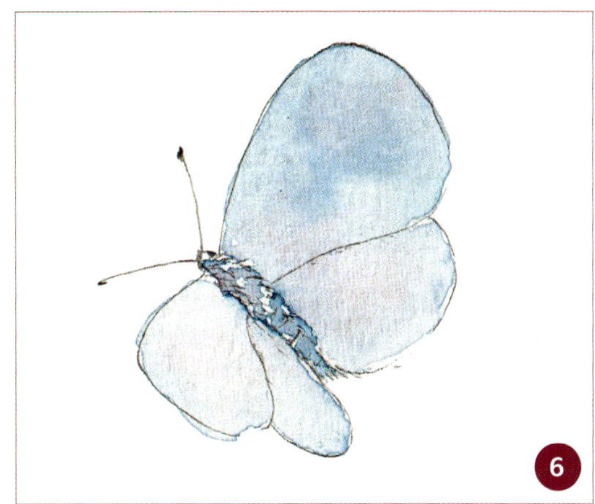

Step 5: Wet the wings with the size 4 brush and drip in Prussian blue. While it's still wet, drip in a bit of the rosy mix. Don't do too much. Add a bit more intense blue close to the body to give it a bit of depth.

Step 6: Once the wings are dry, paint the body wet-on-dry using Prussian blue and a bit of the rosy mix.

Step 7: Now let's get out the gouache because it's time to add very fine white veins to the wings. Only do a few lines going from the body towards the edge of each wing, branching out like a tree. If you feel the white is too strong, dab it lightly with your finger to lift some off.

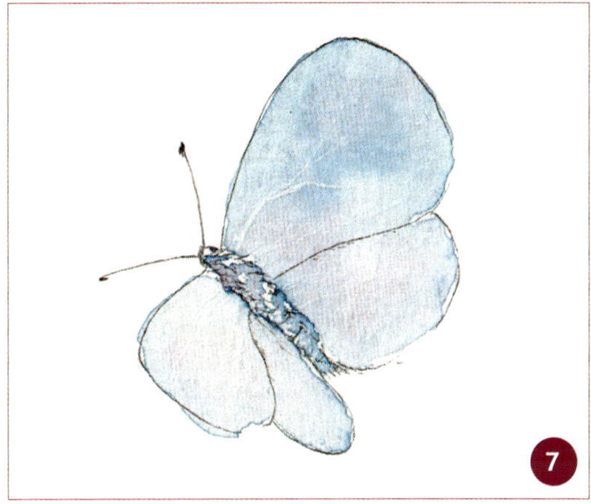

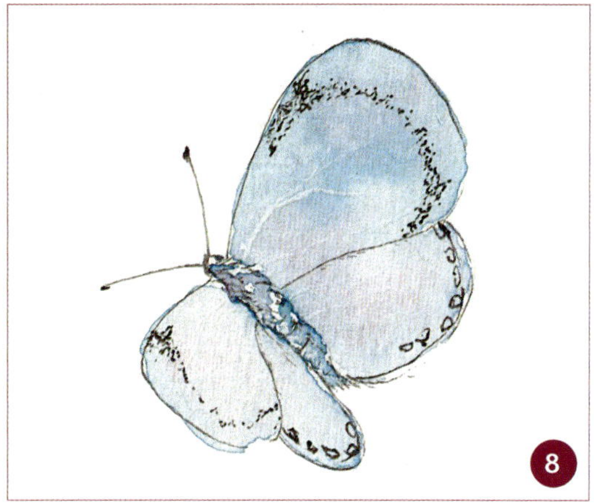

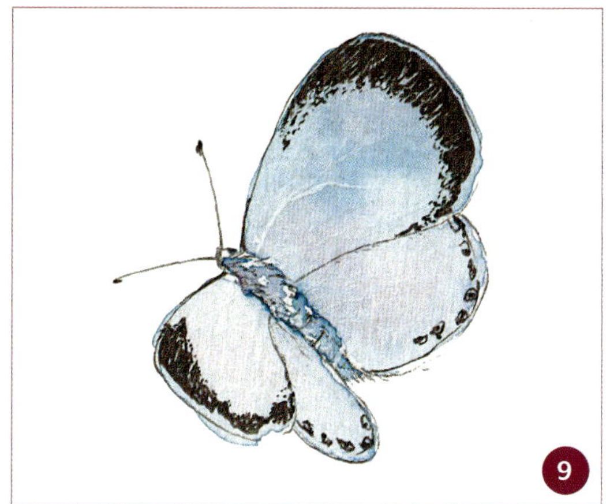

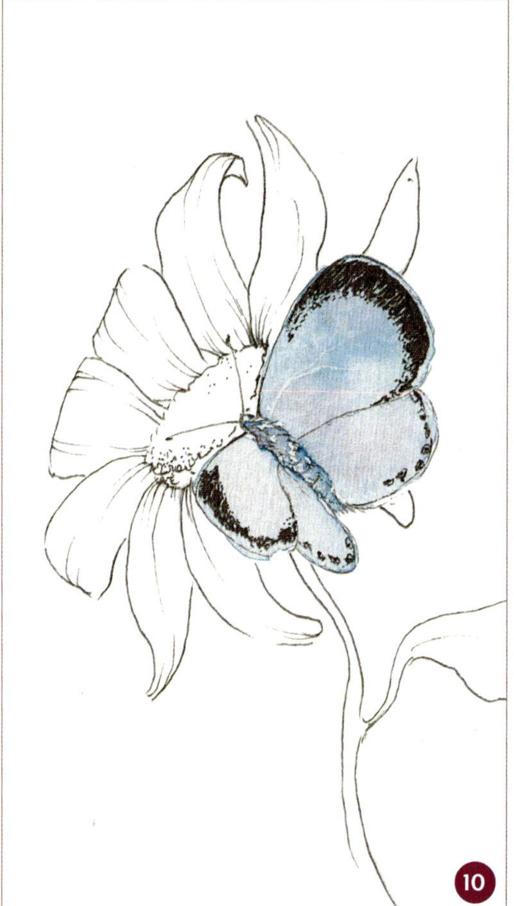

Step 8: To make the dark areas on the wings, we need to add marks to show where the areas start. Draw small dots on the two top wings and bigger, uneven oval-like shapes on the lower wings using the 005 fineliner.

Step 9: Fill out the wing tips of the two top wings with the 02 fineliner. On the lower wings, just add a few dark spots inside the marks for a bit of depth.

Step 10: Finally, we need a bloom for this little one. And I am going to challenge you a bit, because here, I made a variation of the White Oxeye Daisy (page 51). When you follow the tutorial, draw fewer petals but keep them wider. And then finish it off with a normal leaf.

And that's it. Not completely painting everything in a composition is a pretty incredible look. It gives it an entirely different feel, focus and lightness.

swallowtail
a butterfly of hope and grace

When I was a kid, I vacationed in France with my family. One of the highlights was running through fields filled with wildflowers to look for butterflies. The ones we found were so different from the butterflies at home, and it felt like we were part of a fairytale just watching how they danced around the flowers. But one butterfly made us all stand still for a moment. And that was (and still is) the swallowtail. It is gigantic compared to other butterflies, and it is just so graceful. It felt almost like seeing a unicorn! So, I just had to include this beauty in the book.

Here you will experiment with focal point and also how to use paint to make a softer version of the dark spots on the wings.

Materials

Pencil and eraser

Paper: Canson Montval 300gsm (140lb) cold press

Fineliners: sizes 01, 005 and 02

Watercolor brushes: sizes 4 and 9

Water and cloth

Palette

Colors

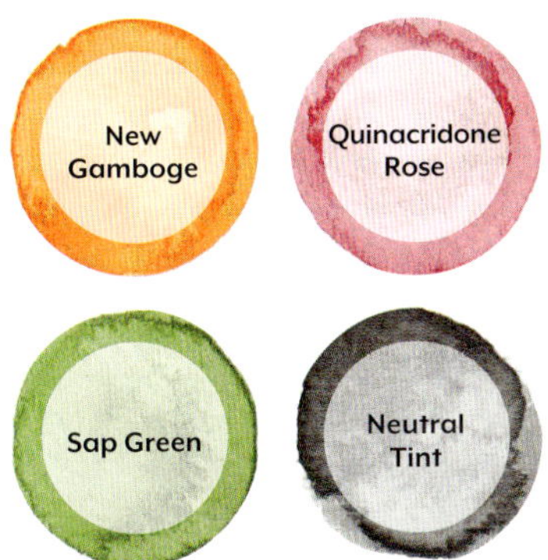

New Gamboge

Quinacridone Rose

Sap Green

Neutral Tint

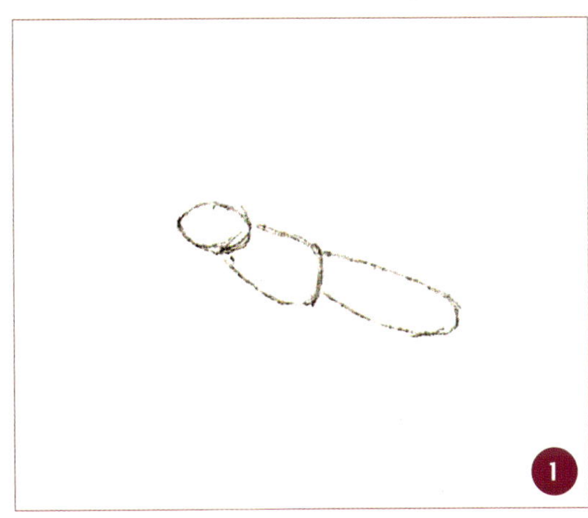

Step 1: Draw a pencil guide of the head, body and tail.

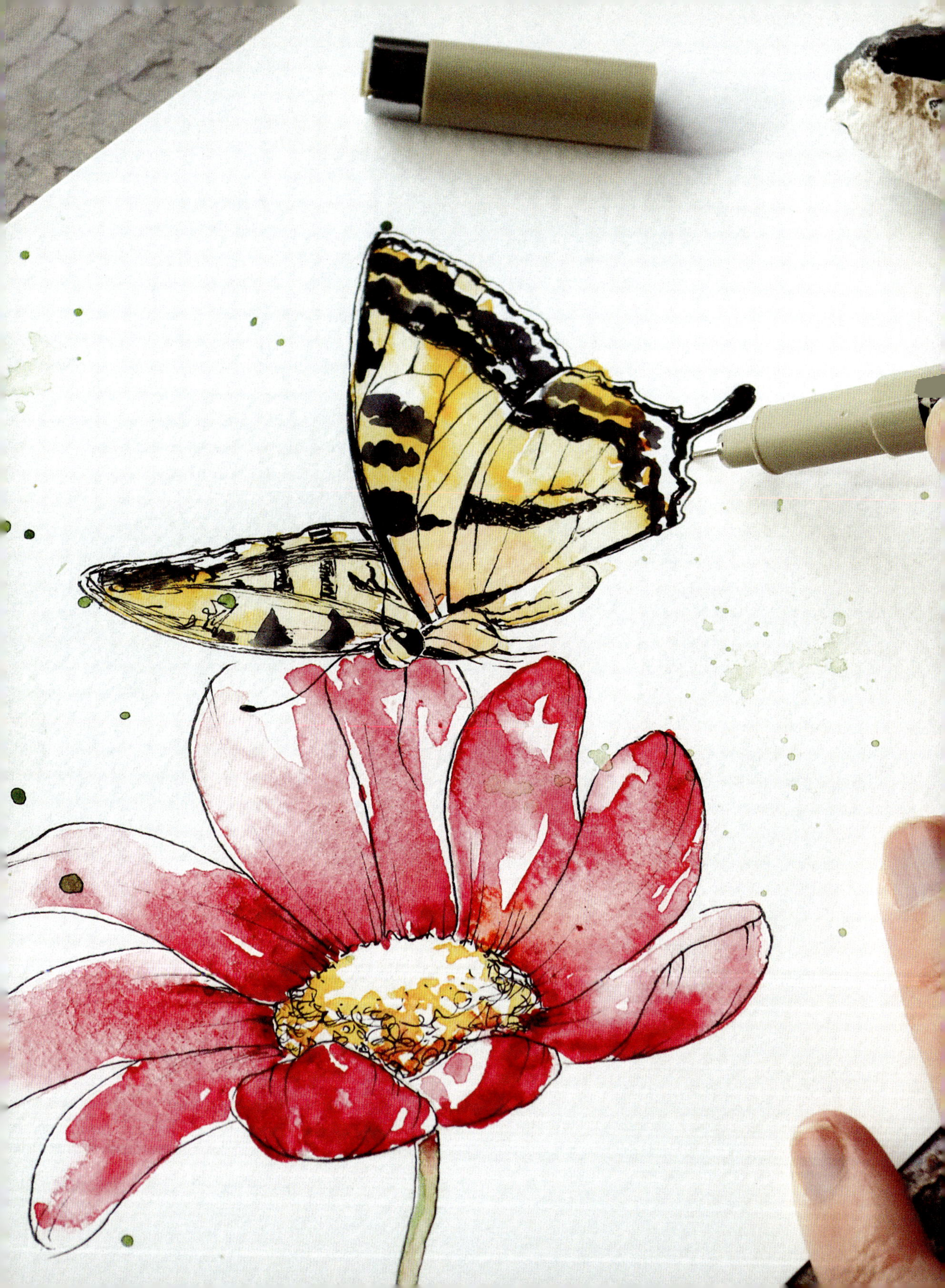

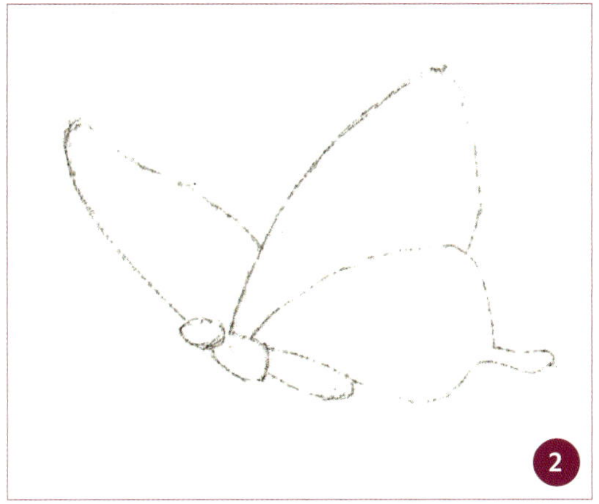

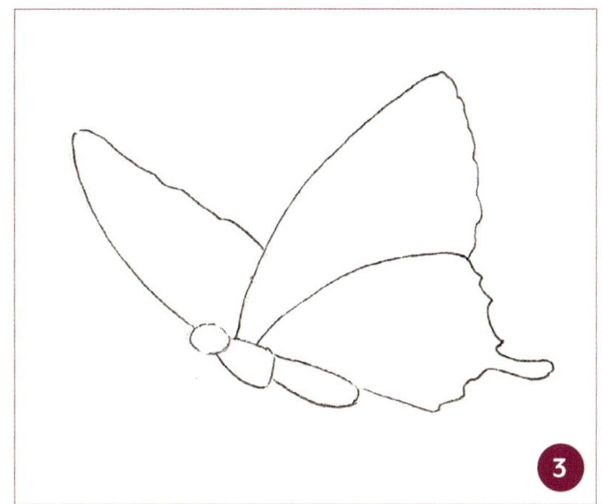

Step 2: Draw the big, beautiful wings. Start with the lower wing in front and give that a small tail at the bottom. Then draw the upper wing tucked in behind the lower one. Then, draw the wing on the other side that is hidden a bit behind the body.

Step 3: When you love your pencil sketch, outline the body and wings with your 01 fineliner. Give the edge of the wings a few dents, and then erase the pencil lines.

Step 4: Draw dark marks on the wings with the 01 fineliner. Give the front wings the darkest marks and veins and keep it lighter and sketchier on the back wing. Swallowtails have a lot of different patterns, so you can Google some of them if you want. What is important here is that you don't fill up all the dark areas just yet. We are going to do that with paint in a second.

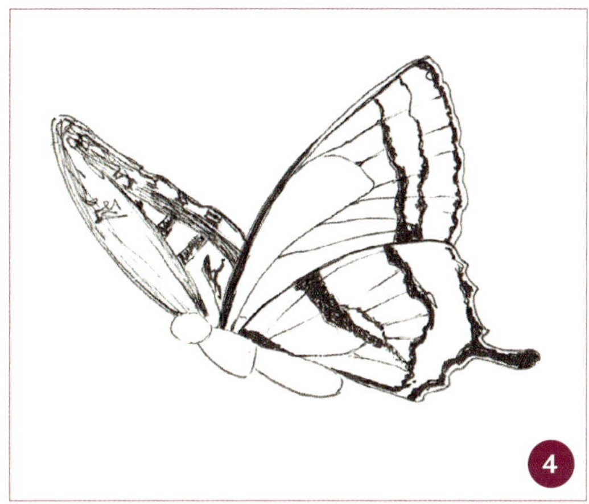

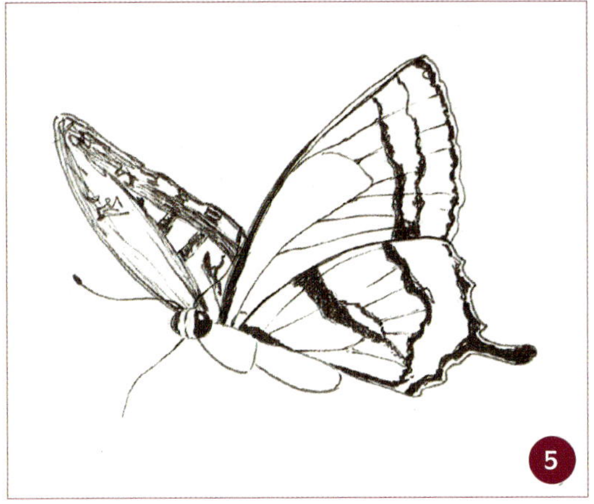

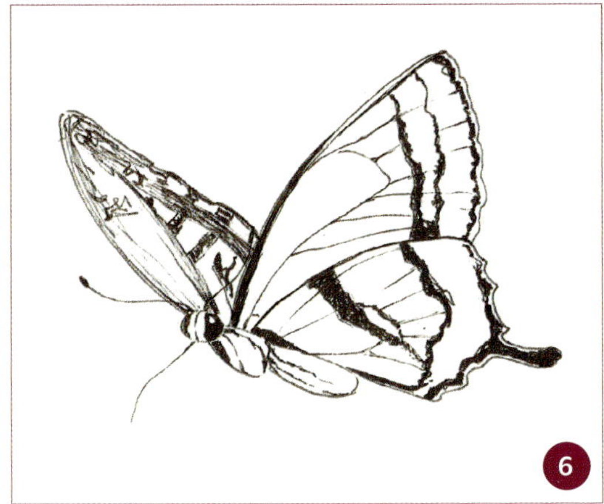

Step 5: With the 005 fineliner, draw two big eyes with highlights and a line between the two. Then draw a thin line that will be the proboscis it uses to drink nectar and two antennas ending in small ovals.

Step 6: Use the same fineliner to draw a few lines following the length of the body.

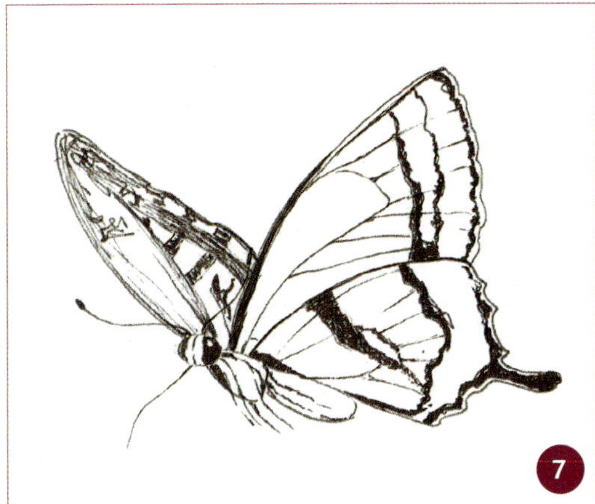

Step 7: Draw legs pointing back with the same fineliner. Sure, it has six legs, but they are not all visible from this angle.

Step 8: Before you add paint, draw a variation of the White Oxeye Daisy (page 51), sort of like the one you did for the Holly Blue Butterfly (page 139) with the thick, shorter petals, but this time, we will give it some color.

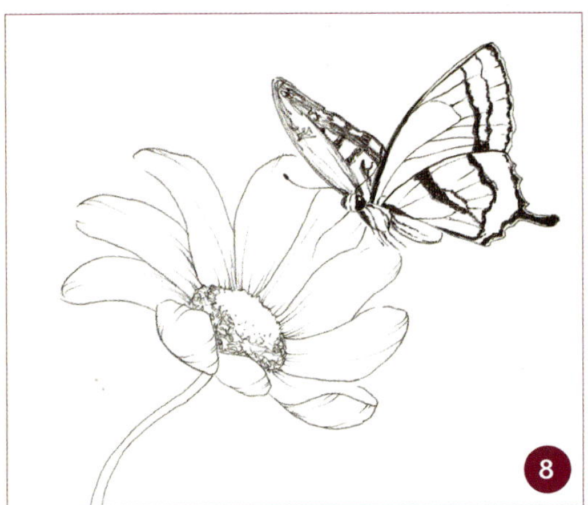

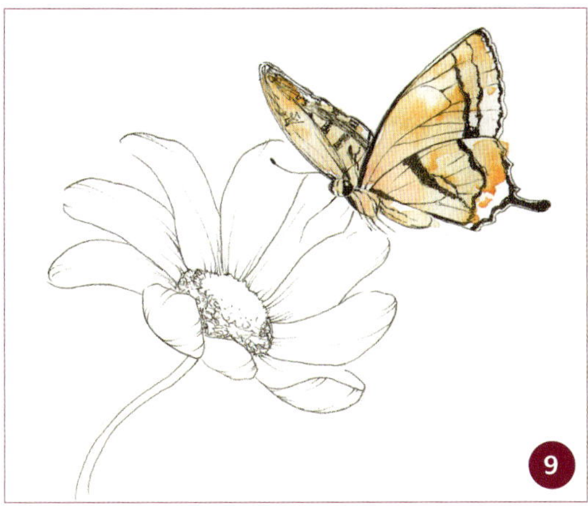

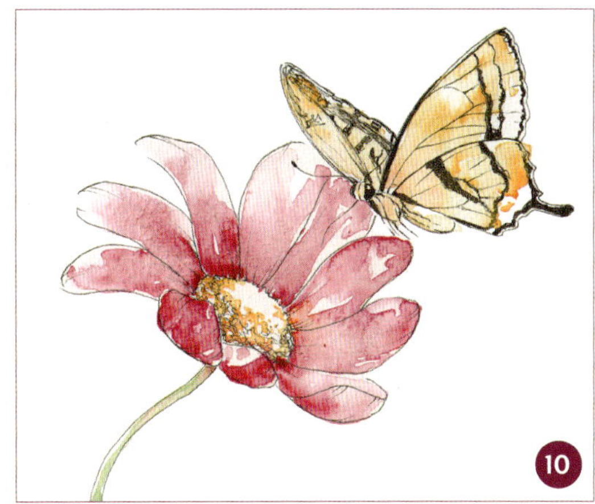

Step 9: I feel so very ready to get started painting now! Wet the entire butterfly with clean water using the size 4 brush, and then drip in new gamboge. While it's still wet, drip in a bit of quinacridone rose on the butterfly's underbelly and the low part of its wing. This color is the flower reflecting onto the butterfly.

Step 10: Now we paint the flower. First, paint the center using new gamboge and a bit of quinacridone rose. For a highlight, leave the center white. While that is drying, paint the stem in sap green, and at the top, drip in a bit of quinacridone rose for a nice color play. When all that is dry, paint the petals in quinacridone rose.

Step 11: Paint a few dark areas of the butterfly using neutral tint, and make sure to vary the amount of paint you use. That way some of the marks will look more transparent than others, making the wings feel light and airy.

Step 12: Top off the sketch with a few splatters around the graceful butterfly in sap green and clear water.

Well done! You just sketched my childhood unicorn! And there are so many different swallowtails out there, so just go searching for variations in patterns and colors. Just know that it can be a bit addicting when you first get started.

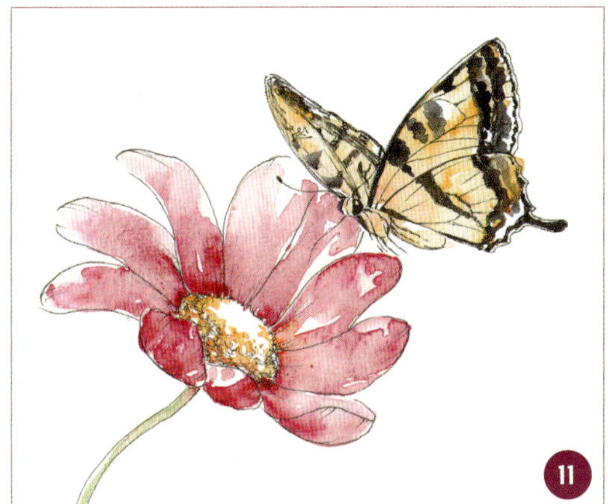

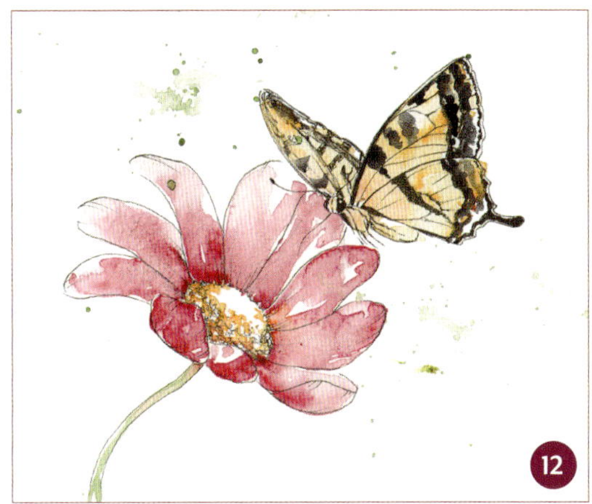

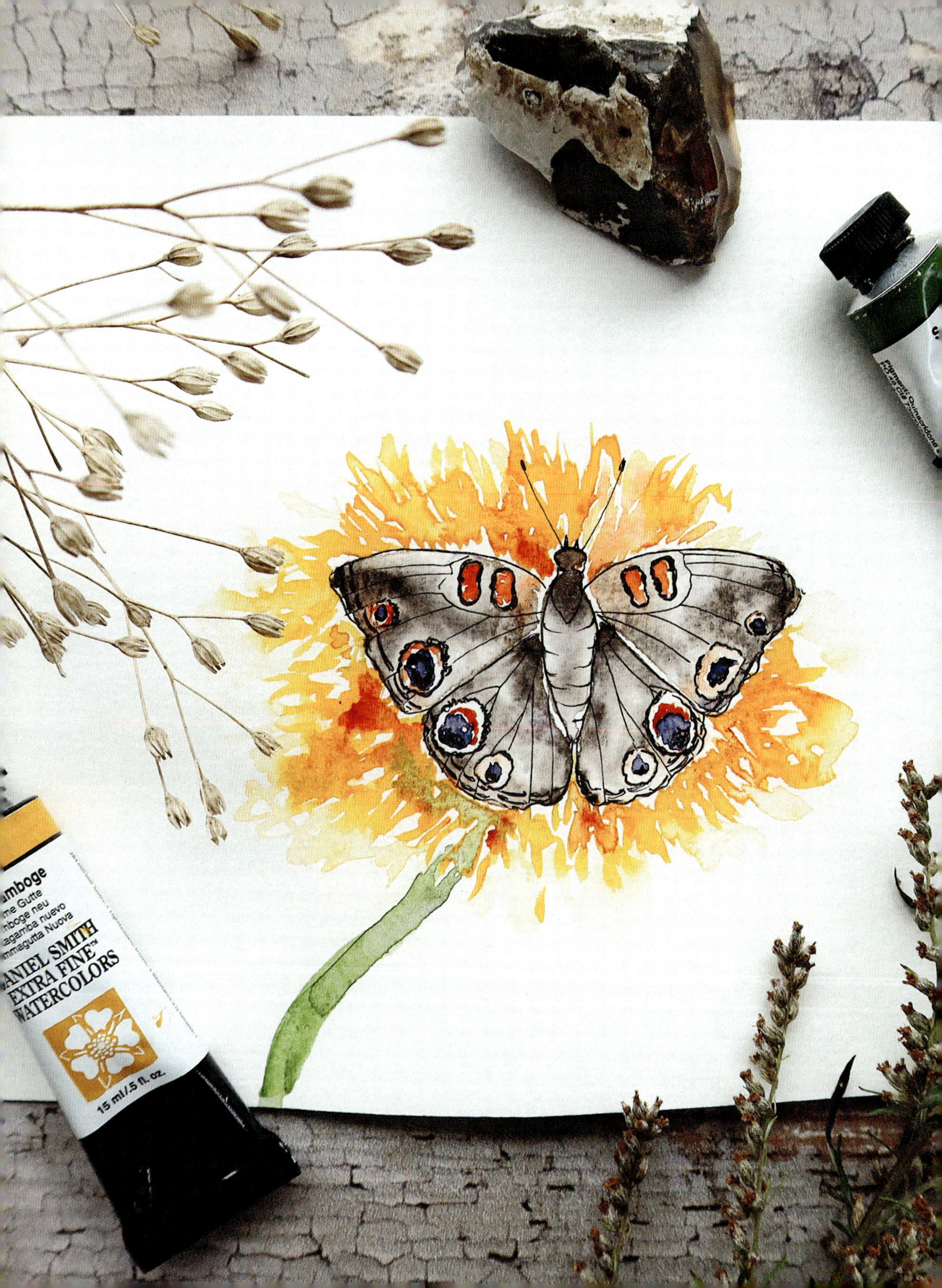
amboge
me Gutte
mboge neu
agamba nuevo
mmagutta Nuova
DANIEL SMITH
EXTRA FINE
WATERCOLORS
15 ml/.5 fl. oz.

common buckeye butterfly

a butterfly disguised as a moth

Not all butterflies are colorful, but they are all interesting, each in their own way. And that is why I wanted to include a brown butterfly. It looks like a moth but is actually a butterfly with the most incredible skills of disguise. It has pops of color to dazzle and potentially scare away potential danger.

The buckeye's favorite pose is with wings wide open to get as much good use out of the sun as possible. So, we will place it like that resting on the Dandelion (page 47).

Materials

Pencil and eraser

Paper: Canson Montval 300gsm (140lb) cold press

Watercolor brushes: sizes 4 and 9

Water and cloth

Palette

Fineliners: sizes 01 and 005

Colors

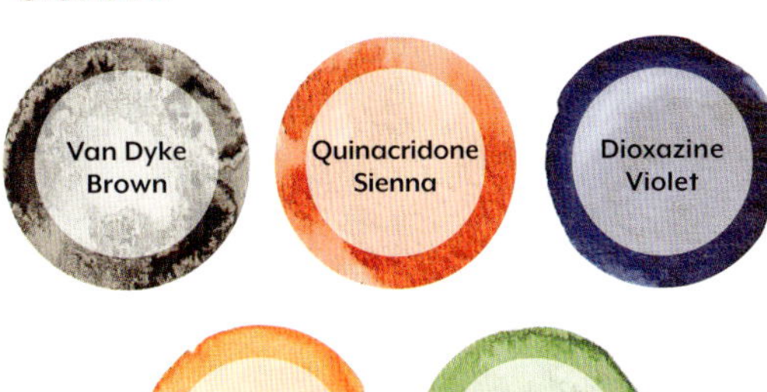

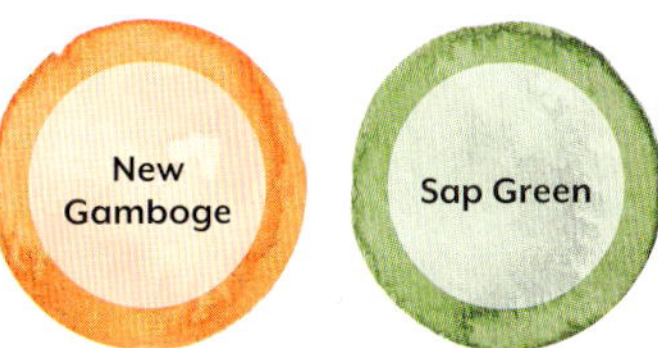

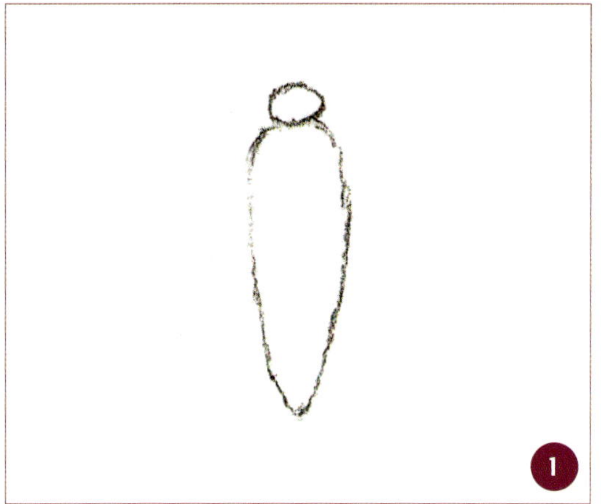

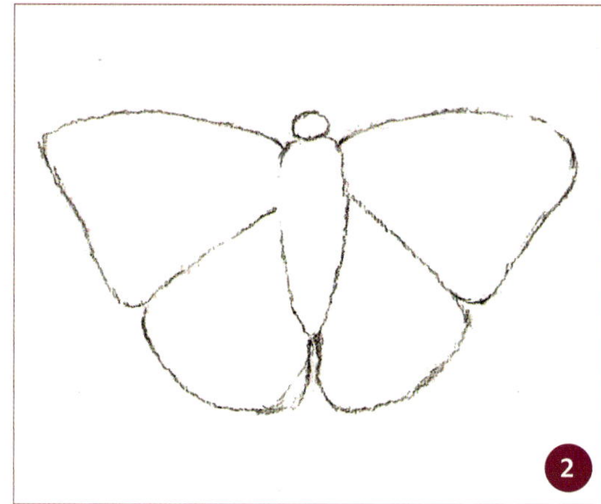

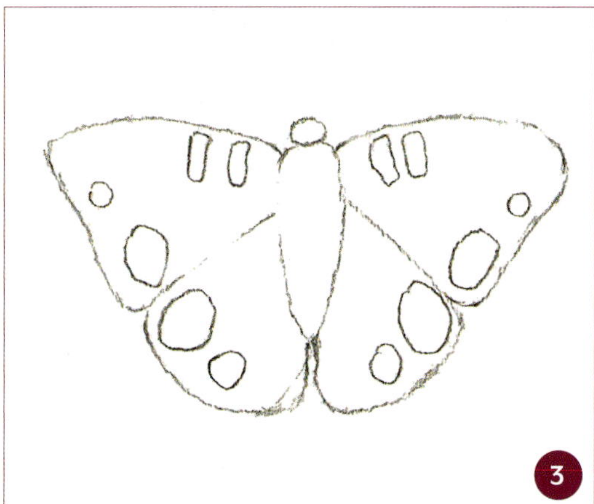

Step 1: Draw a carrot shape for the body with the pencil. Draw a small circle on top for the head.

Step 2: Draw the lower wings, which almost look like teardrops. Then draw the upper wings as rounded triangles that are slightly tucked behind the lower wings.

Step 3: Now draw all the beautiful marks on the wings: There are two small rectangles on each side of the top wings, and then there are pretty round circles and ovals on the edges of all the wings.

Step 4: Using your size 4 brush, paint the body and head with clean water. Drip Van Dyke brown into the water, and then drip in a single drop of quinacridone sienna at the neck and a tiny bit of dioxazine violet on the body.

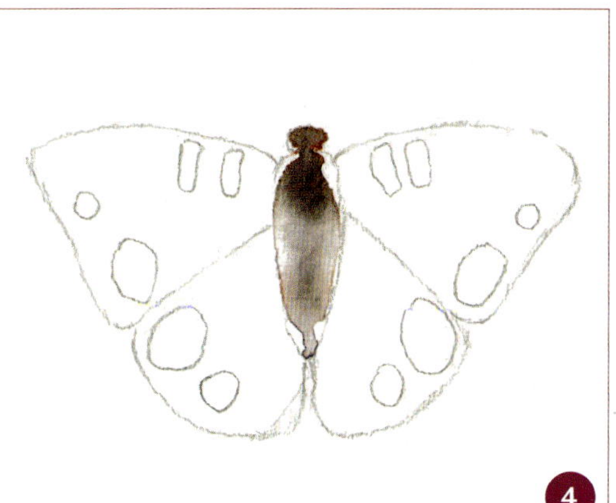

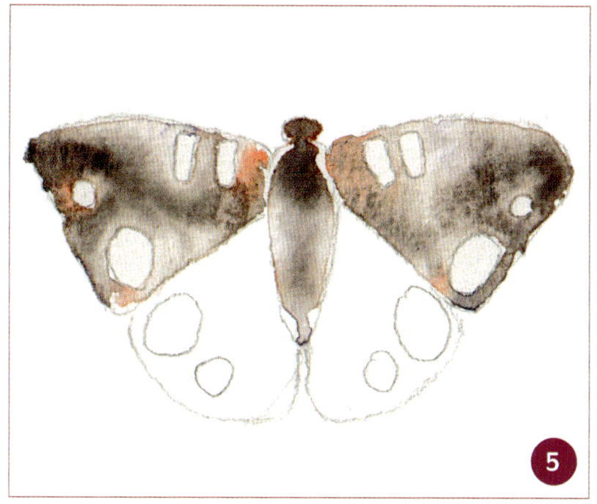

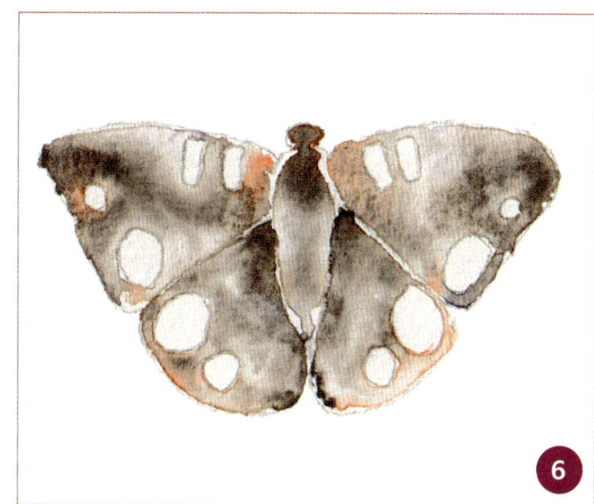

Step 5: Wet the top wings and drip in Van Dyke brown. Then drip a bit of quinacridone sienna close to the body and at the tip of the wings. It's important that both wings are the same, so take your time here and be careful around the marks you made earlier. For a bit of variation, you can also drip in a bit of dioxazine violet in the wing.

Step 6: Do the same with the lower wings. Here, you keep the quinacridone sienna close to the edges of the wings and the violet to the part of the wings that are close to the body. When everything is dry, you can erase the pencil lines.

Step 7: Using the size 4 brush, paint the rectangular marks on the top wings wet-on-dry using a bright quinacridone sienna. Do the same thing for the inner outlines of the circle and oval marks. For the two largest oval marks on the lower wings, try to leave a white outline between the quinacridone sienna and the brown of the wings.

Step 8: Dip your brush in the dioxazine violet, and paint the white areas left in the circular marks. Try to keep a bit of white space.

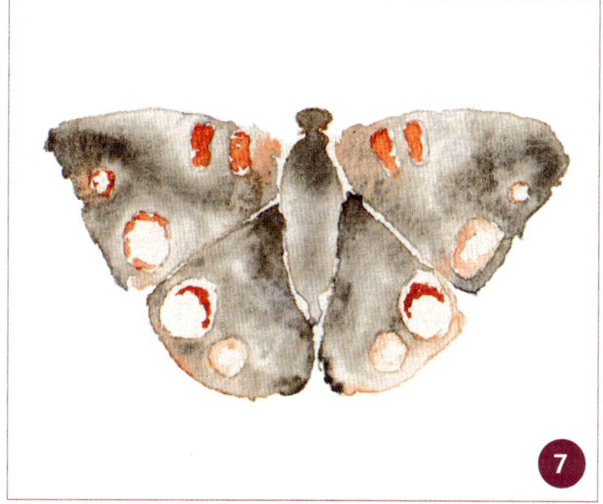

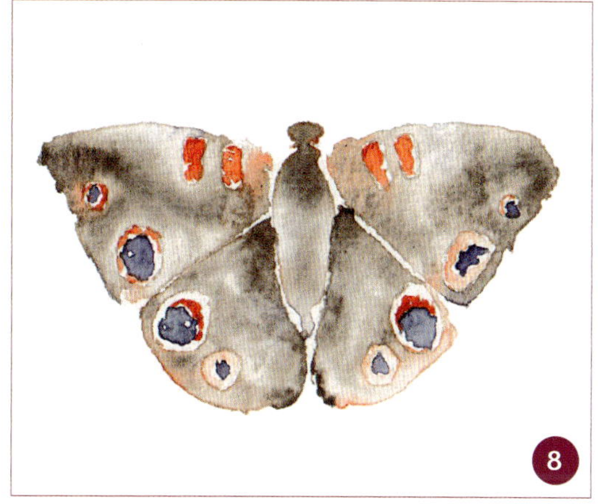

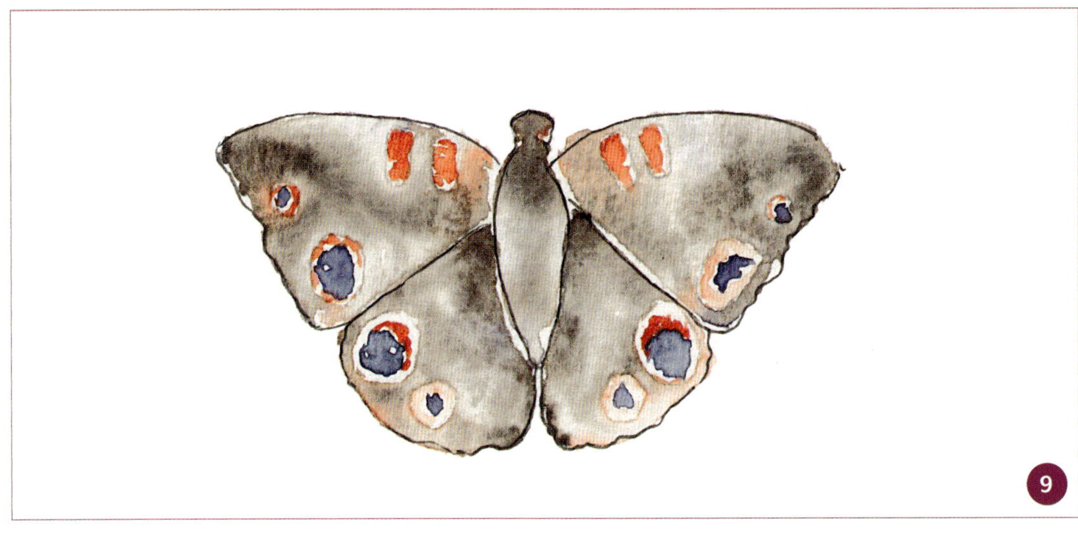

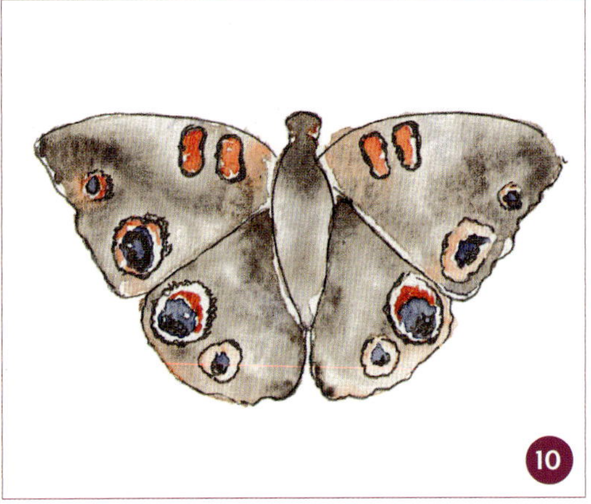

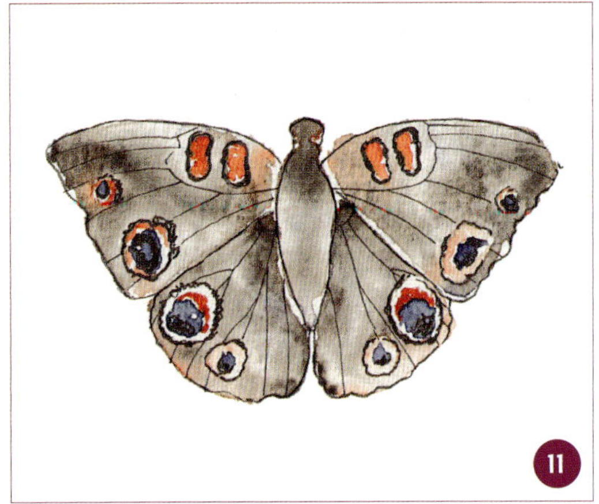

Step 9: When the buckeye is dry, you can admire its colors, and then grab your 01 fineliner and outline the wings.

Step 10: Draw dark marks around the rectangular and circular marks on the wings. On the biggest ovals, add a bit of dark to the bottom of the violet.

Step 11: Shake your hands now because we are going to loosen up and draw long veins with the 005 fineliner. Make sure both sides look the same, and have fun making a beautiful pattern.

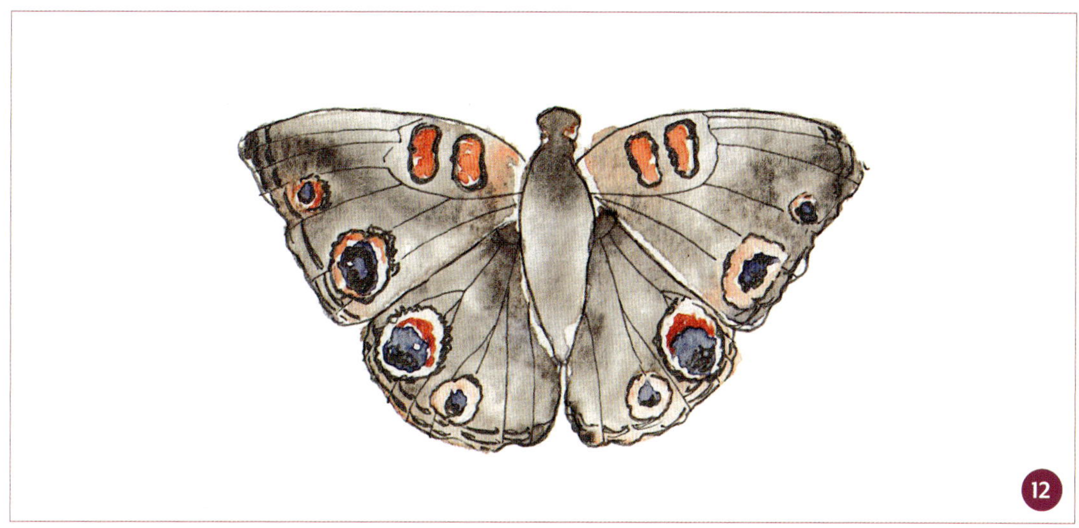

Step 12: With the same fineliner, draw small C shapes around the edges of the wings.

Step 13: The last thing we need to finish this guy is the two antennas ending in a small oval, two pointy mandibles and a few marks across its body to show its shape.

Step 14: Paint the Dandelion (page 47) beneath the butterfly using a size 9 brush and the tutorial. Use new gamboge and quinacridone sienna to make the colors work with this butterfly, and then use a bright sap green for the stem.

That was the last of the butterflies. Now you are ready to spot more butterflies out in the wild and bring them home as sketches. Or you can jump to the next winged friend, which is kind of a magical one.

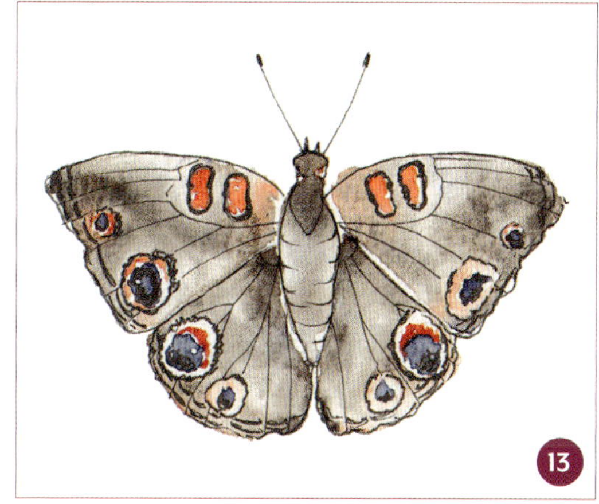

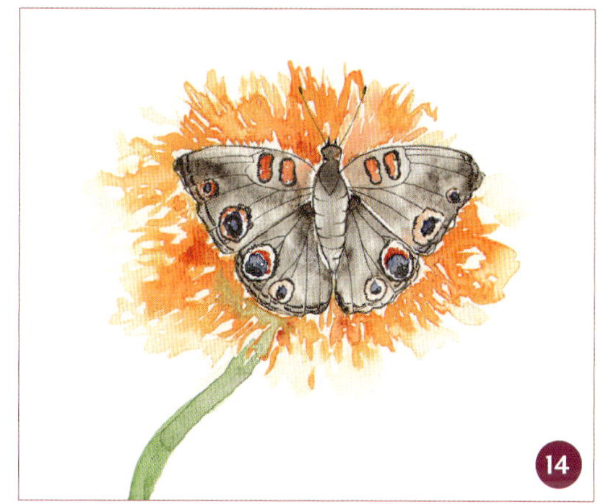

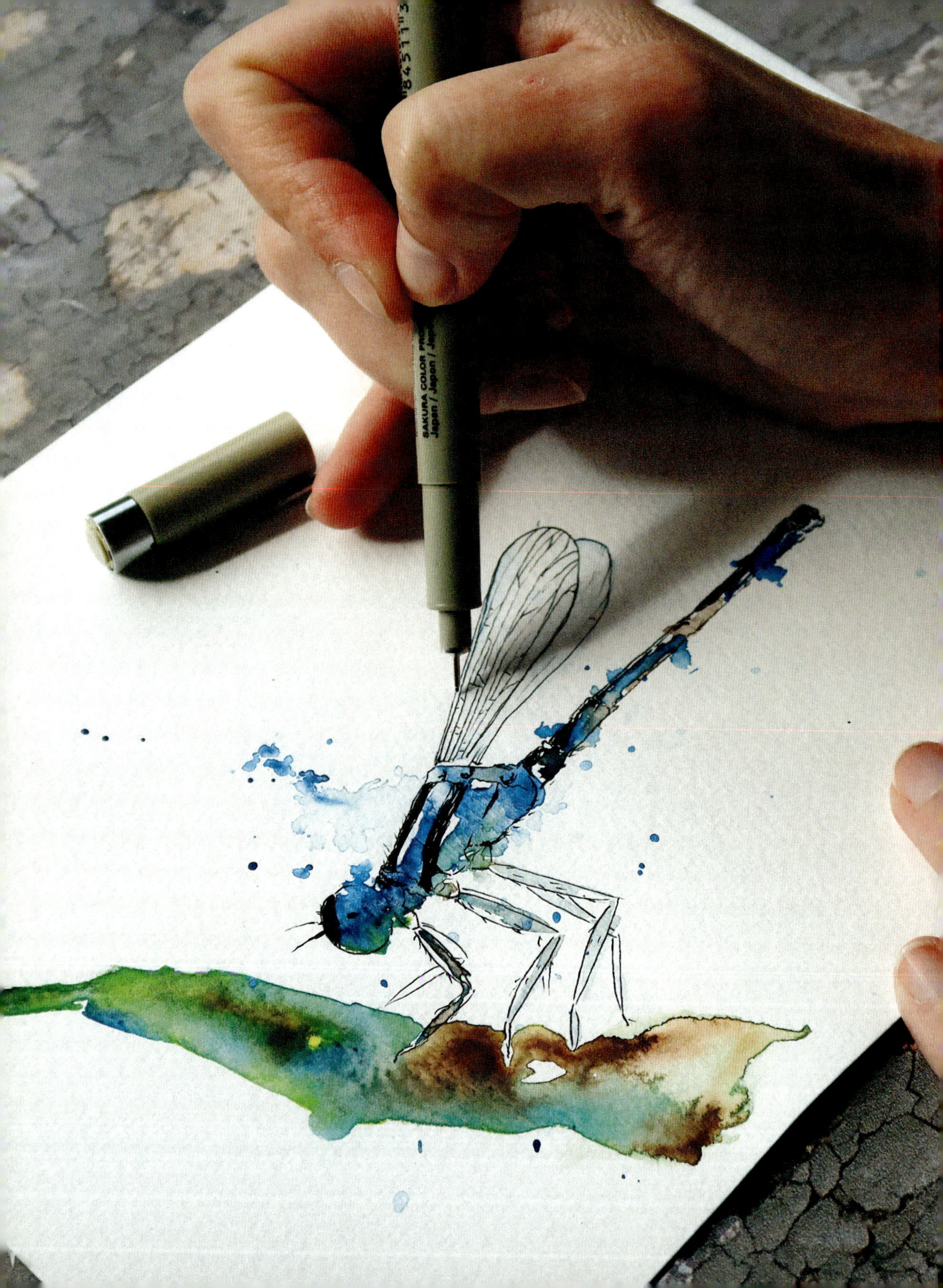

dragonfly
a sign of change and self-realization

If you are here to learn ink and wash or maybe improve your techniques, then see this dragonfly as a sign that you are on the right path. After all, each and every sketch we do is part of our personal development. On top of that, the dragonfly is actually said to symbolize living life to the fullest. So, this is a way of saying don't hold back. Mix, splatter and paint with big brushstrokes! So, let's dive in filled with dragon energy.

Materials

Pencil and eraser
Paper: Canson Montval 300gsm (140lb) cold press
Fineliners: sizes 01, 005 and 02
Watercolor brushes: sizes 4 and 9
Water and cloth
Palette

Colors

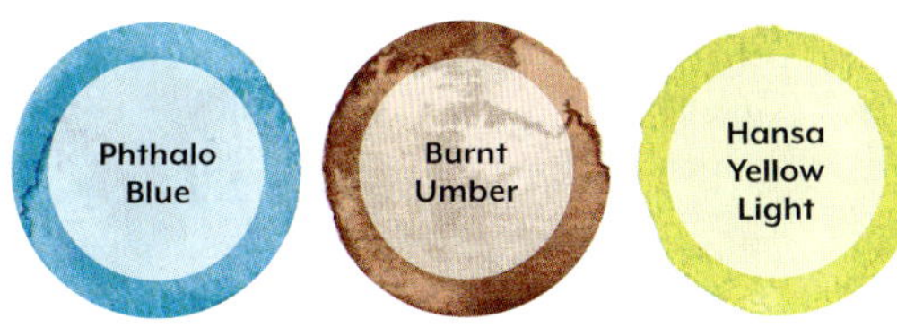

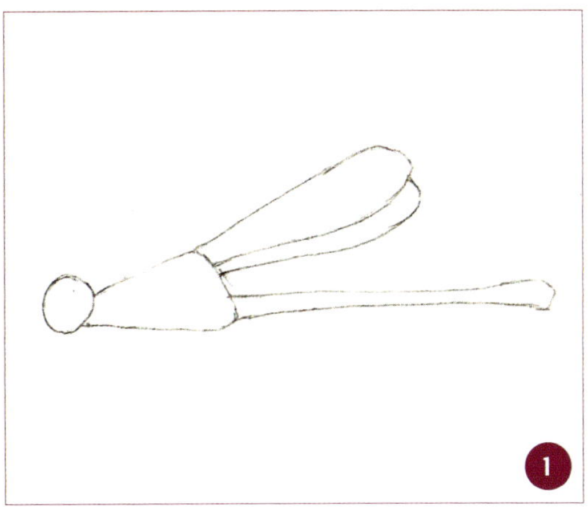

Step 1: Sketch a round head with your pencil. Then, sketch a triangular body. Attach a long, thin tail to the lower-right section of the body, and give it a little bump at the end. Sketch two elongated wings floating over the tail.

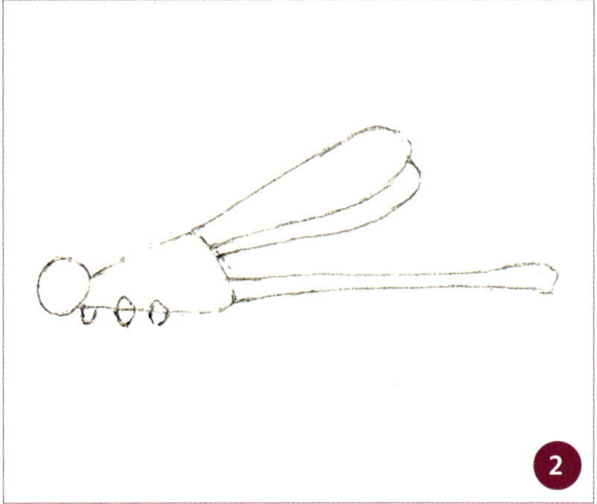

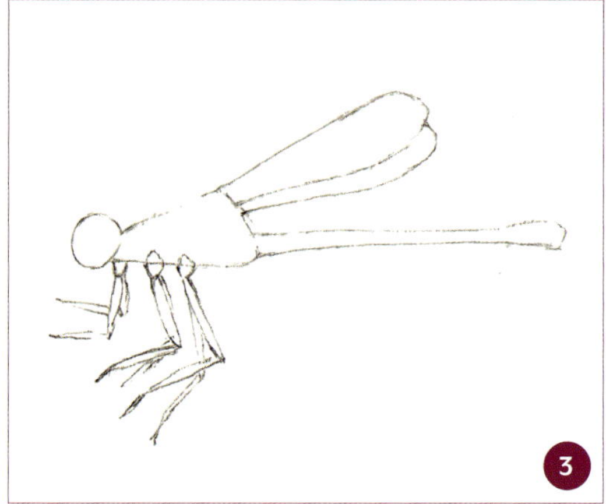

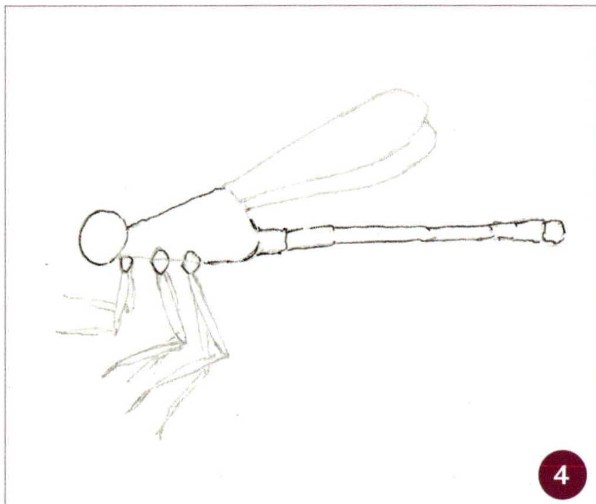

Step 2: Draw three small, rounded diamond shapes at the bottom of the body.

Step 3: Draw the legs starting at the diamonds. You will only be able to see the ones in front completely; the others are hiding and barely visible. The legs are made of two parts divided at a knee and ending in a small, narrow foot.

Step 4: Now grab your 01 fineliner. Sketch the outline of the body, the diamonds, head and tail. When you draw the tail, give it a few small dents to show off its texture.

Step 5: Use the 005 fineliner to outline the legs and wings. Erase the pencil lines.

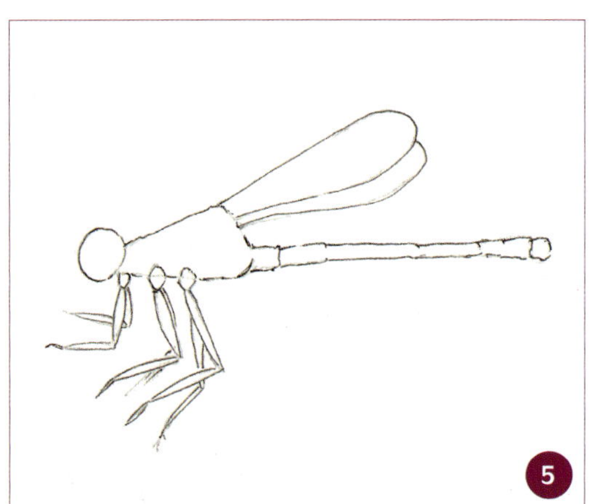

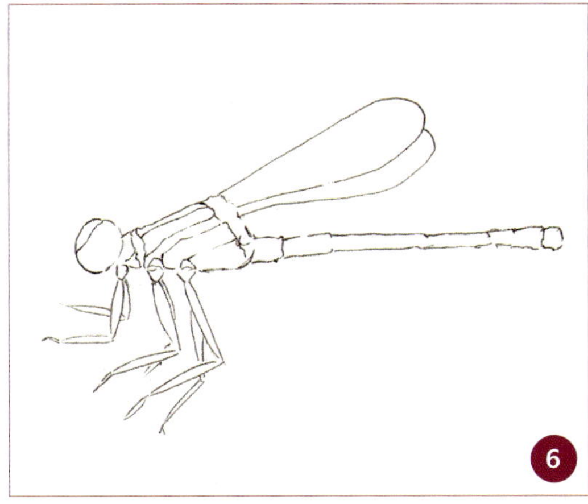

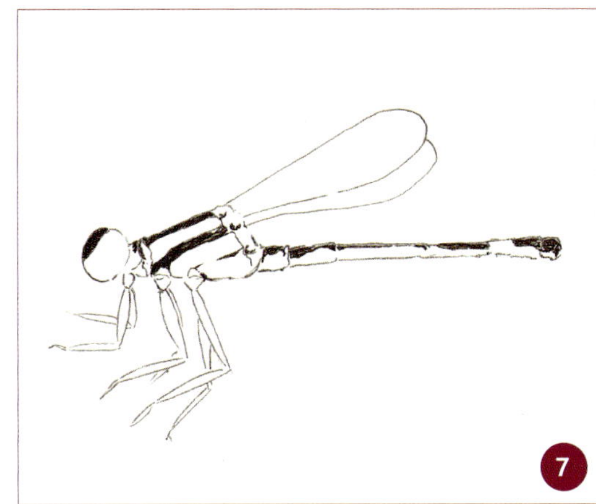

Step 6: Using the same fineliner, draw a small hat on the head. Add two roughly diagonal lines on the body, dividing it into two parts: a small section closer to the head and a larger section closer to the wings. Draw a few lines across these body sections ending at the rough lines. These will be guides for the dark marks in the next step.

Step 7: With the 02 fineliner, fill in the hat and the marked areas on the two sections of the body. Then, fill in the top half of the tail. Let the dark marks on the tail be thin in some spots and thicker in others.

Step 8: Use the 005 fineliner to add the final touches to the body: small hairs, short antennas and a small eye.

Step 9: Add lines to the wings with the 005 fineliner. Let most of the lines go from the body to the edge of the wing, and then have a few go across, creating a random pattern of veins.

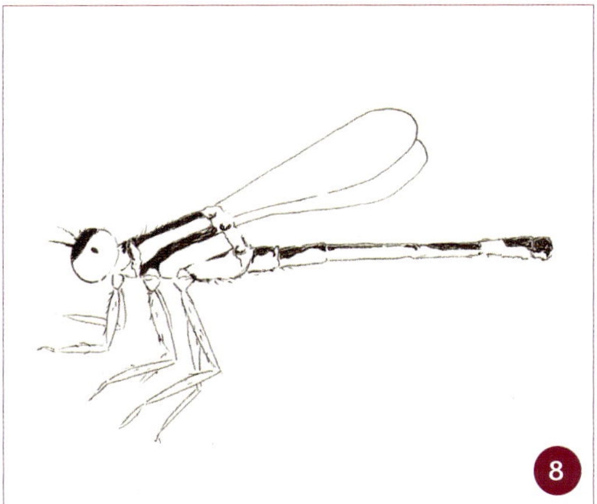

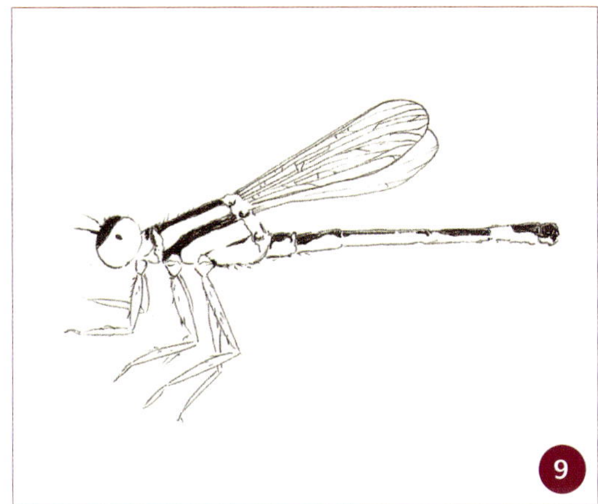

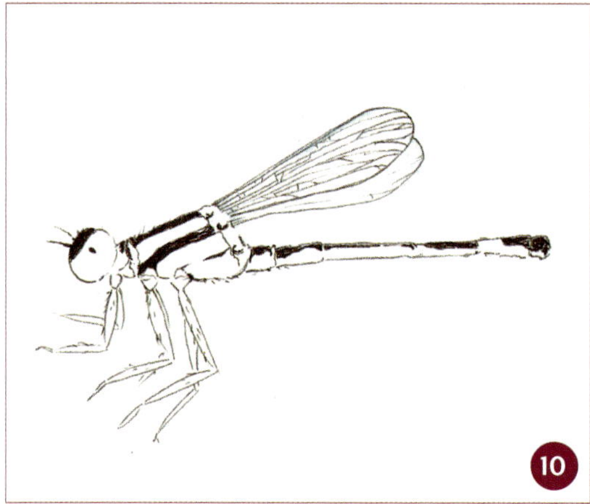

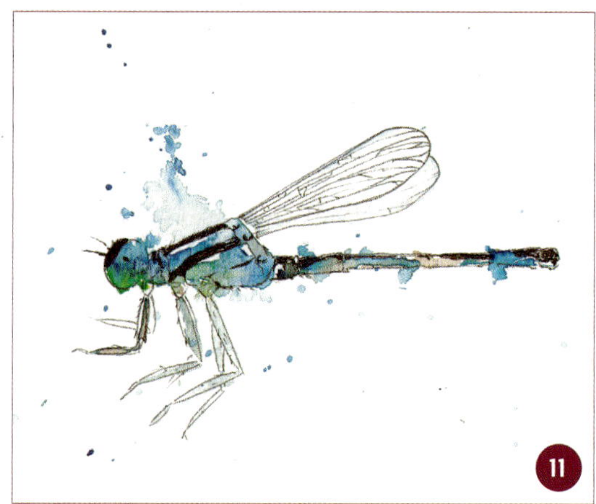

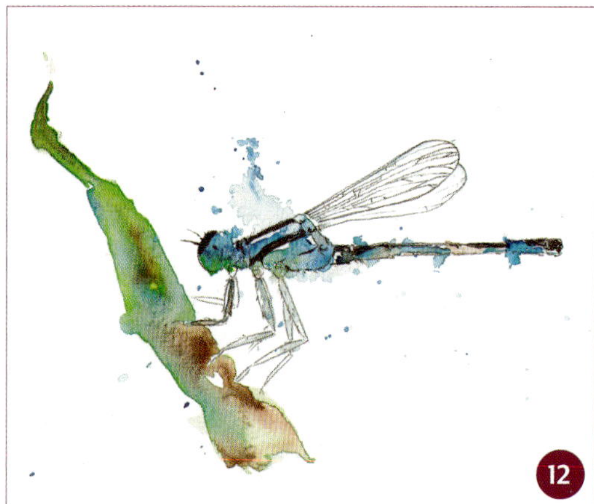

Step 10: We want the wings to look very light and transparent, so wet the wings with your size 4 brush and drip in phthalo blue and burnt Umber. Count to five, and then drip in a bit of clean water. Now use a damp brush and lift as much paint as you can from the wings. They will look super transparent but still have a blue tone.

Step 11: Now wet the entire body and paint it using phthalo blue. Drip in a bit of Hansa yellow light at the stomach and the bottom part of the head. Let a bit of burnt Umber be a part of the tail. While your dragonfly is still wet, load the size 9 brush with phthalo blue and make a bunch of splatters around the insect. Then load the brush with clean water and tap it so the clean drops land on the paper as well as on the body you just painted. This will help it flow a bit, making it look looser and airier.

Step 12: Paint a quick leaf for it to sit on with the same colors you've used for the rest of this project.

And you are done! Can you feel that change is in the air? Maybe it will lead you to a grasshopper. You never know.

grasshopper
an insect symbolizing taking a leap of faith

Grasshoppers chirping is one of those sounds that holds a ton of memories for me—and maybe for you too. The second I hear the first little chirp, I'm instantly reminded of warm summer vacations.

In this tutorial, we are going to find a balance between the hard exoskeleton (yes, a pretty cool word for armor) and the delicate, transparent wings. So, we are going to work a bit with the superpowers of watercolor, which are transparency and layering.

Materials

Pencil and eraser
Paper: Canson Montval 300gsm (140lb) cold press
Fineliners: sizes 01, 005 and 02
Watercolor brushes: sizes 9 and 4
Water and cloth
Palette

Colors

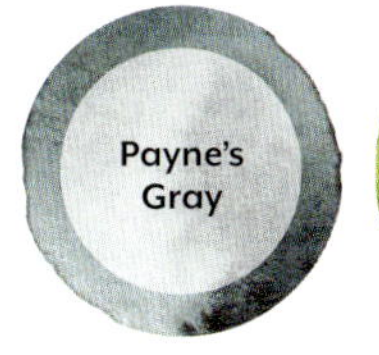

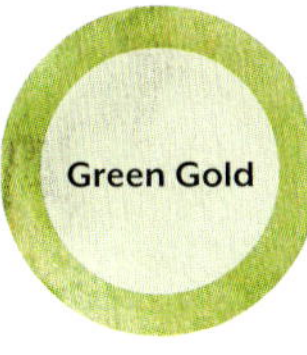

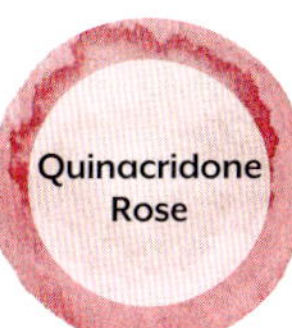

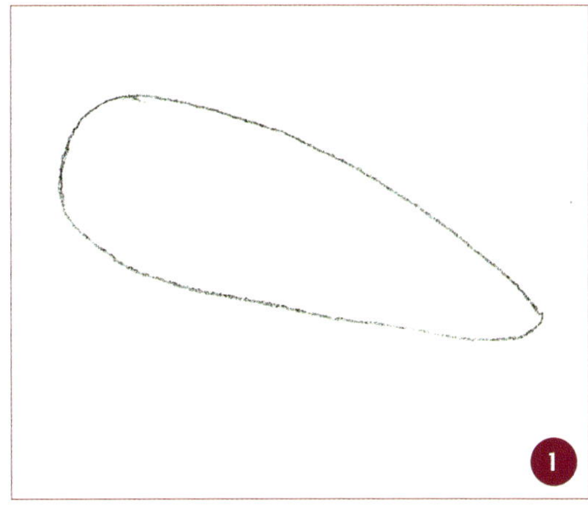

Step 1: Draw a carrot shape for the body with the pencil.

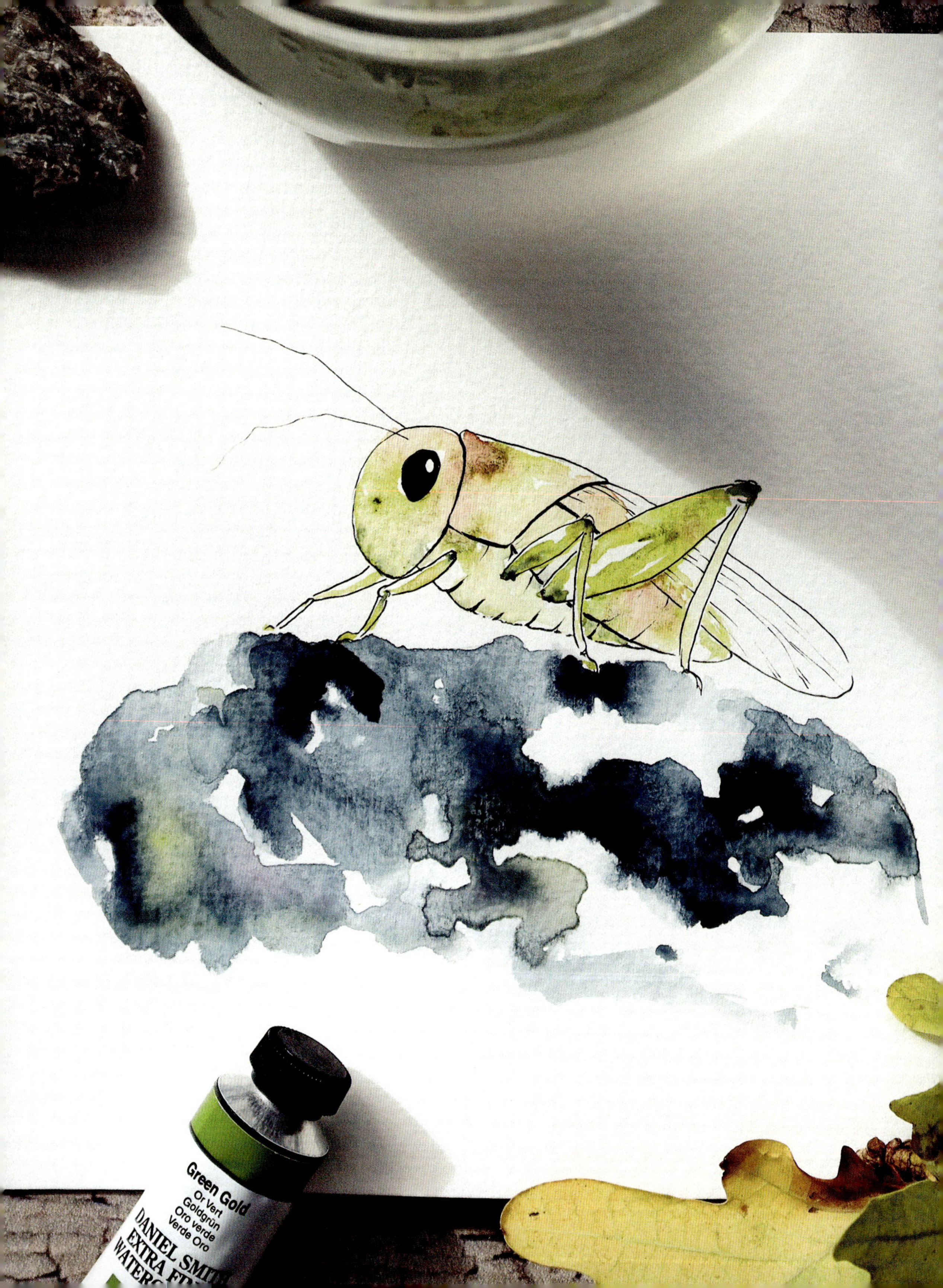

Green Gold
Or Vert
Goldgrün
Oro verde
Verde Oro
DANIEL SMITH
EXTRA FINE
WATERCOLOR

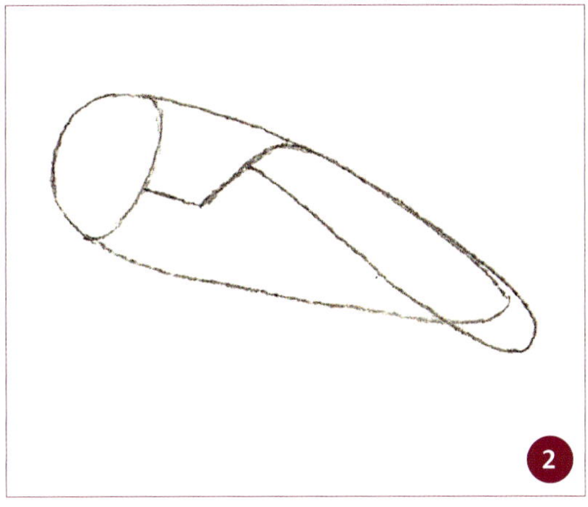

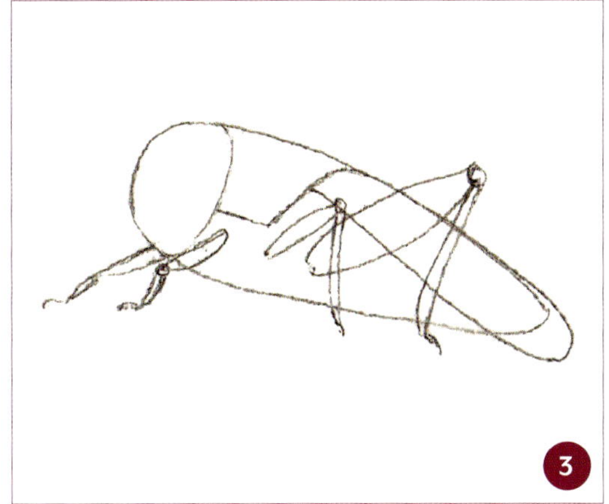

Step 2: Turn the thickest part of the carrot into an oval head by drawing a curved line. Then draw a shield on the back and a wing that extends from it to the edge of the body at the bottom.

Step 3: No grasshopper is complete without those iconic legs. Start with the biggest one, placing it in the middle of the body close to the belly. Make the thigh thicker than the rest of the leg so it's ready to jump. Draw a small circle for the knee.

The second leg is a smaller version of the hind leg you just drew. It's great if you can get it to overlap the back leg a bit. Give both legs a small foot that points backward.

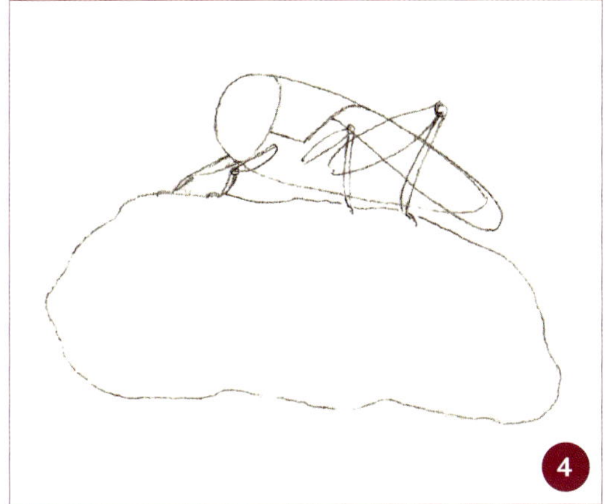

At the front, just beneath the head, you can place the front leg. It's also divided into three parts, but it's pointing forward. Behind the head, draw the far-side leg that is peeking out. These front feet should point forward.

Step 4: Draw a rock with a rough edge where the grasshopper can play its song.

Step 5: Before diving in with the fineliner, add a few more details to the body in pencil. Round the breast and give it more armor between the wings and legs.

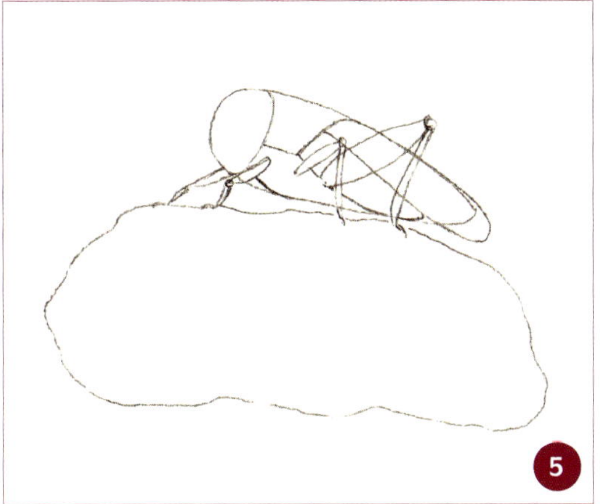

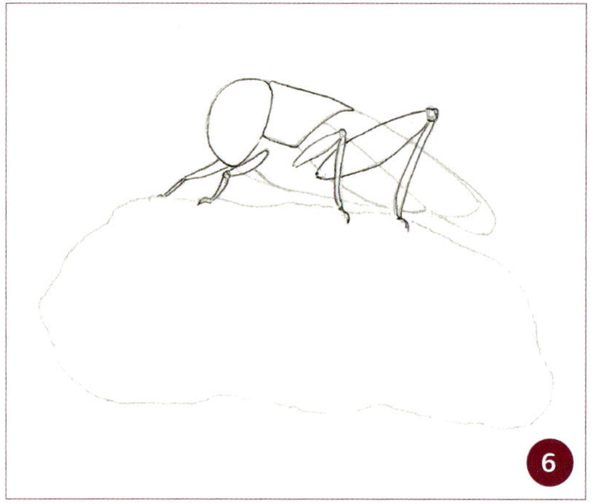

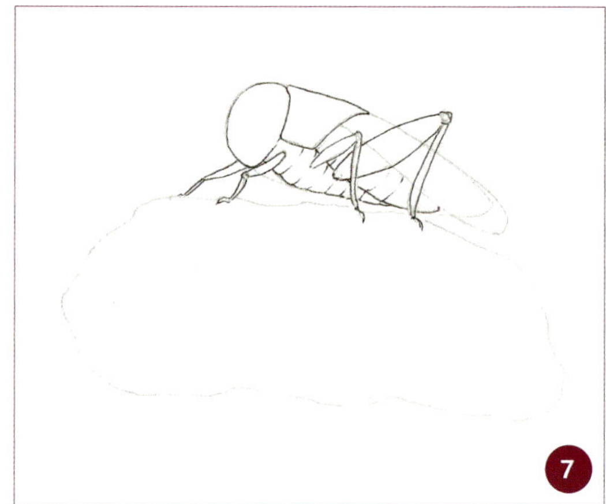

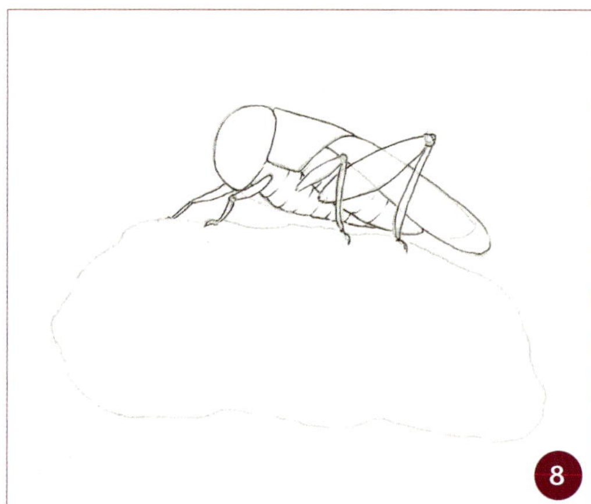

Step 6: Now you can find your 01 fineliner and outline the head, shield and legs.

Step 7: Continuing with the same fineliner, give the belly some details. Draw C shapes from the bottom towards the body and down again. You can also add a few lines to the armor below the wing.

Step 8: To make the wing lighter, outline it with your 005 fineliner. Make sure to keep the wing behind the legs. Erase the pencil lines for the grasshopper.

Step 9: Now you want to locate your 02 fineliner for some darker details. Draw the eye first. It's big, teardrop shaped and has a highlight in the upper-right corner. Draw some shadow where the plates and shields meet by thickening those lines.

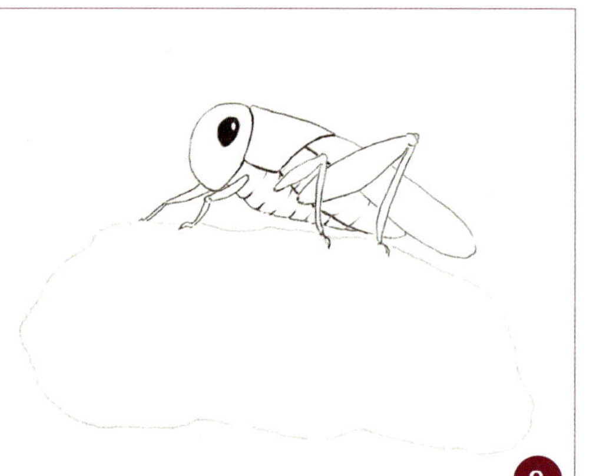

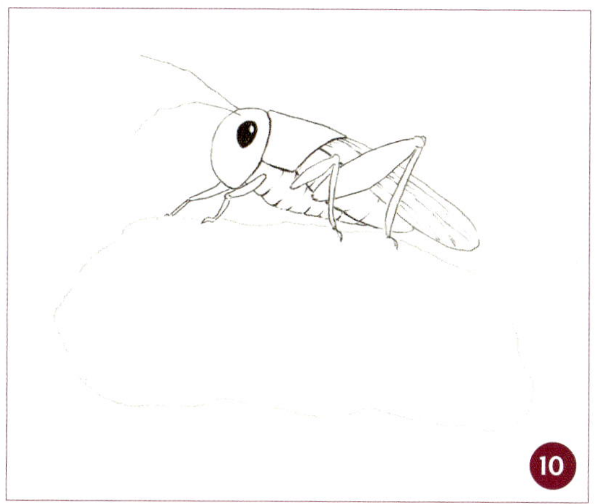

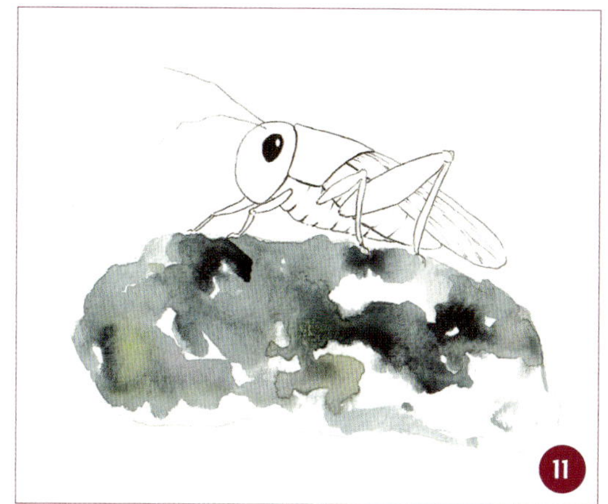

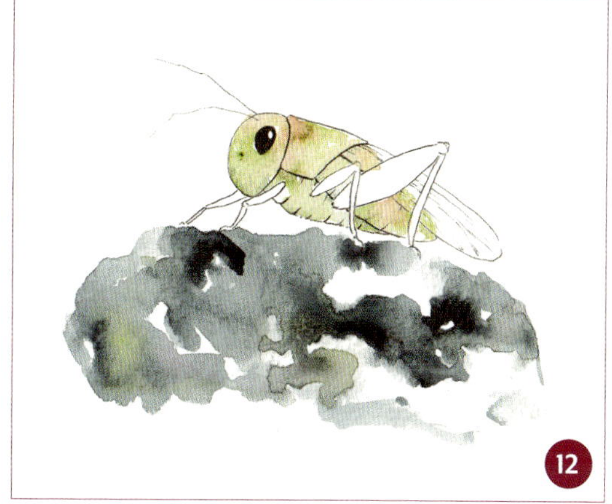

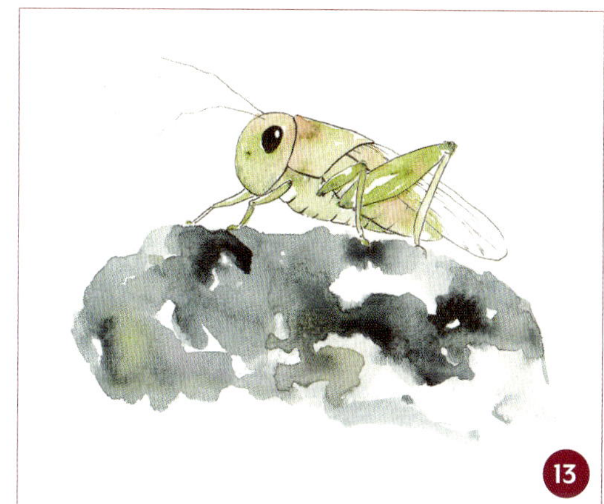

Step 10: With the 005 fineliner, draw a few veins in the wing, and draw antennas pointing forward from the top of the head.

Step 11: Paint the rock with the size 9 brush wet-on-dry using Payne's gray and a few drops of green gold and quinacridone rose. Leave lots of white space.

Step 12: Erase any remaining pencil lines, and let's add some color to this guy! Using the size 4 brush, wet the body and head with water and drip in green gold and a few drops of quinacridone rose at the top and on the exoskeleton. Don't paint the wing—just the part where you can see the body through it.

Step 13: Paint the legs wet-on-dry using green gold and a bit of Payne's gray at the joints.

Now he is all set to start singing his grasshopper blues. Well done!

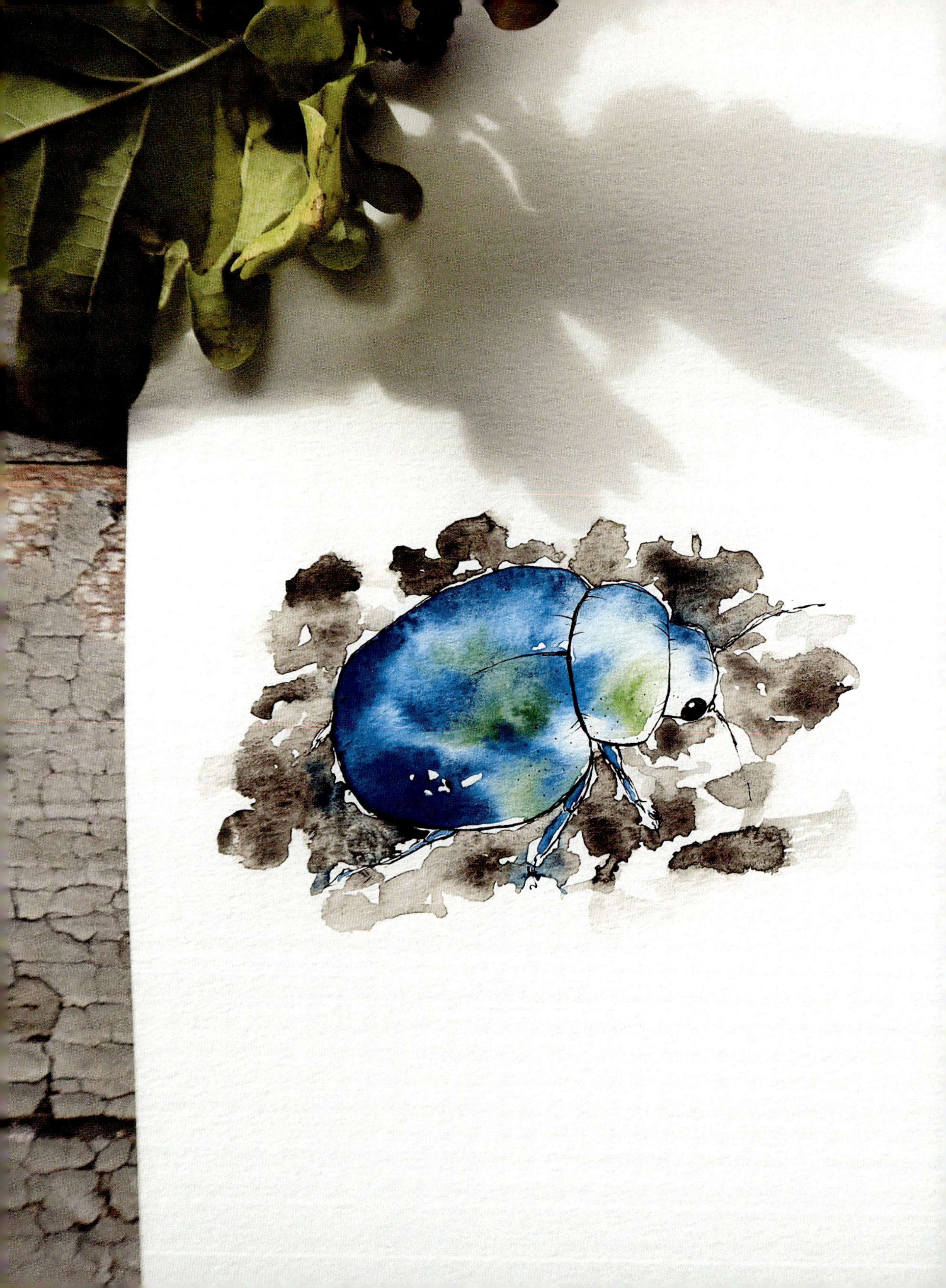

beetle
an insect centered in its own strength

The beetle is a pretty impressive little thing. Its entire body is covered in a hard armor, and under that armor, it can unfold delicate wings that will take it anywhere in the world. The beetle truly is centered around its own strength and reminds me of a very colorful Vanagon. (Don't ask me why.)

In this tutorial, we are going to have fun making this beetle shine with color so it's ready to fly out and have a good time.

Materials

Pencil and eraser
Paper: Canson Montval 300gsm (140lb) cold press
Fineliners: sizes 01, 005 and 02
Watercolor brushes: sizes 9 and 4
Water and cloth
Palette

Colors

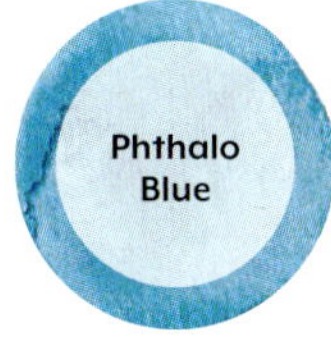

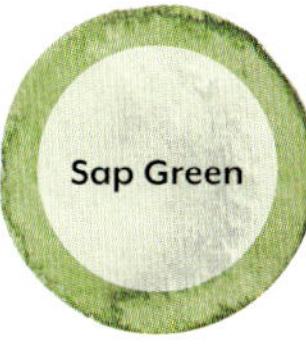

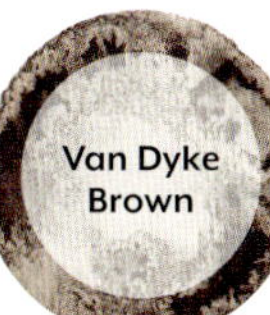

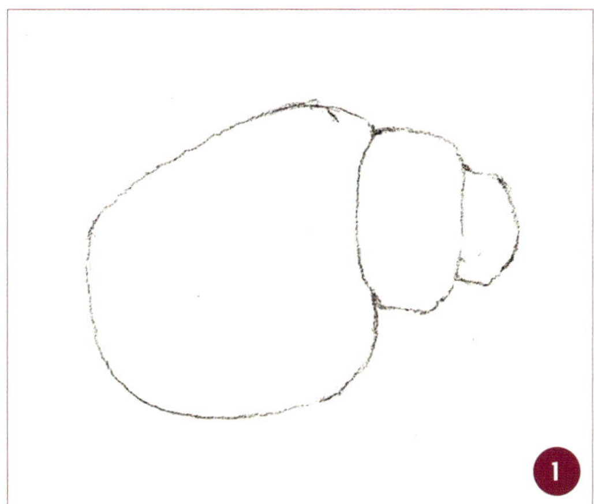

Step 1: With the pencil, sketch the body, which in this case, includes the folded-up wings at the back and then the thorax and a head facing to the right.

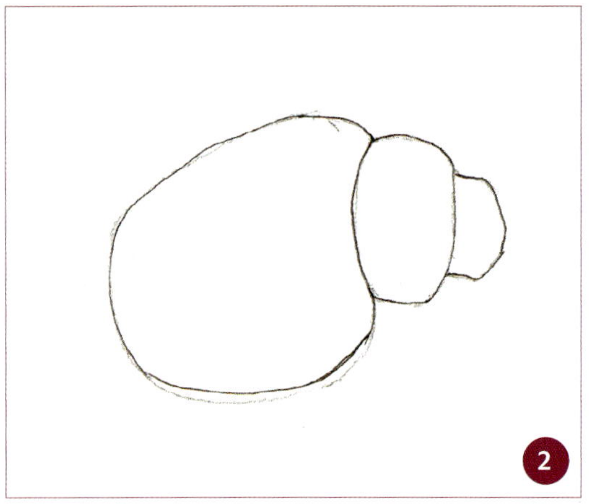

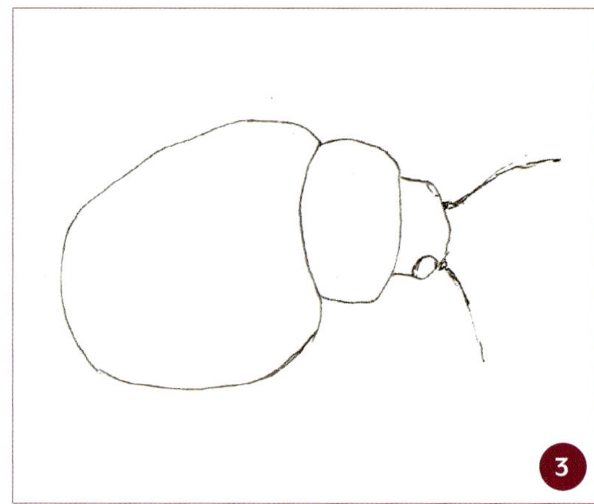

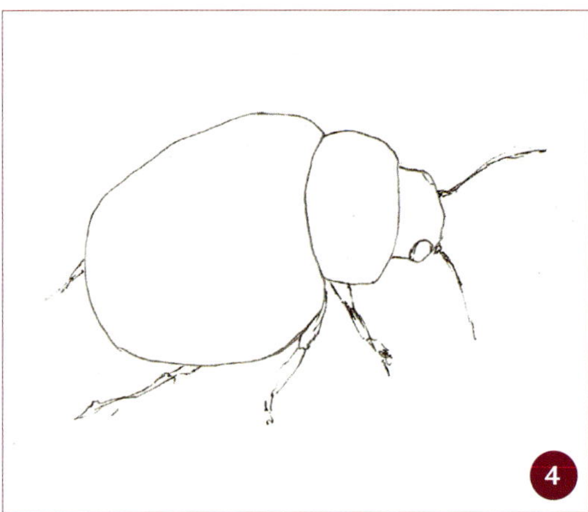

Step 2: Outline the three shapes with the 01 fineliner, and then erase the pencil lines.

Step 3: Draw two antennas and the outline for the bulky eyes using your 005 fineliner. The back eye is barely visible, but it's there.

Step 4: Draw the legs. All legs are made of three parts: a short, thick thigh section, a second longer leg section and then the delicate foot. The visible front leg points forward and the three visible back legs point backward.

Step 5: And now let's make it shine! Wet the body with the size 9 brush. Drip in phthalo blue and sap green. Let the color be darkest on the backside of the body. If you can, leave a few white spots on the armor covering the wings.

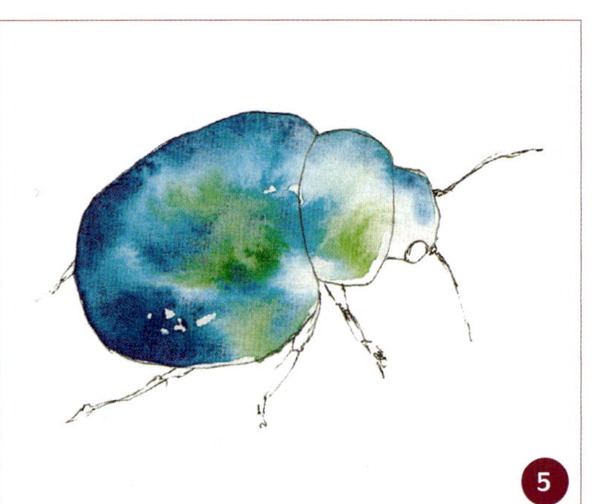

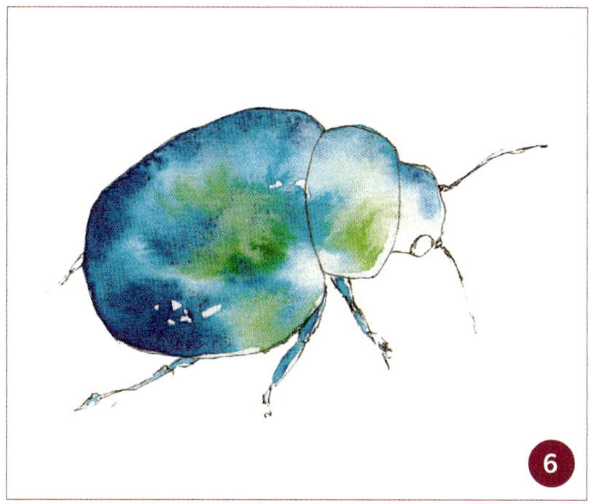

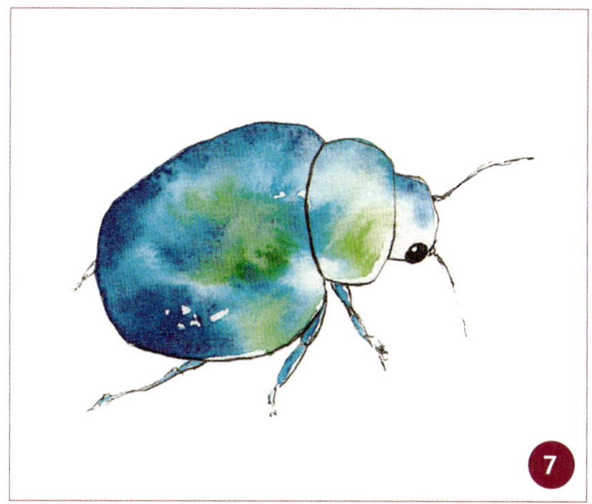

Step 6: Paint the legs with the size 4 brush wet-on-dry using phthalo blue. While you wait for the beetle to dry completely, take a walk (or grab a piece of chocolate from the bottom of the drawer).

Step 7: Now you are ready to draw in the eye with the 02 fineliner along with the dark lines at the bottom of the body and where the body parts meet.

Step 8: Add a few details with the 005 fineliner. I added dots to the armor plates covering the wings and some shaping lines going from the area where the body parts meet and outwards. You can also draw a line showing the middle of the backplate so you know where the beetle will open its wings to fly.

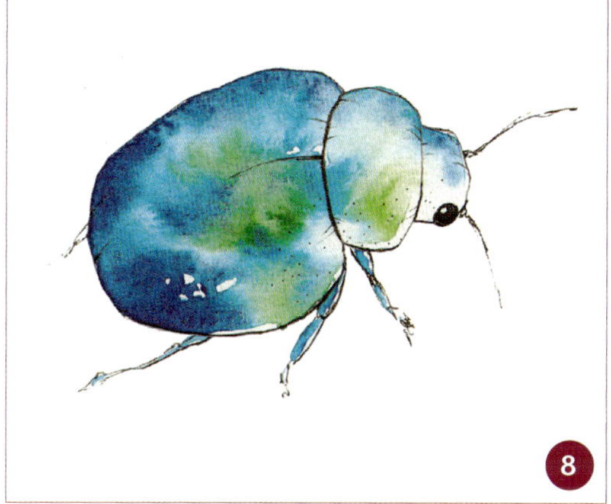

Step 9: To ground the little guy paint a bit of . . . well . . . ground in Van Dyke brown and drip in a bit of phthalo blue in the brown below the beetle.

Hmm, somehow this tutorial made me dream of traveling the world in a big van. Funny how animals of all kinds give us associations like these.

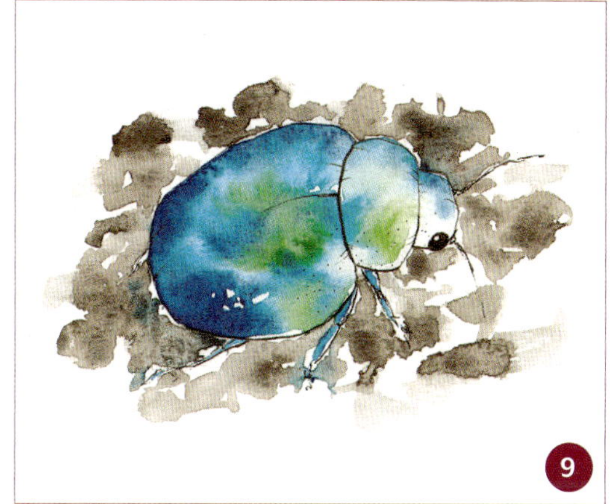

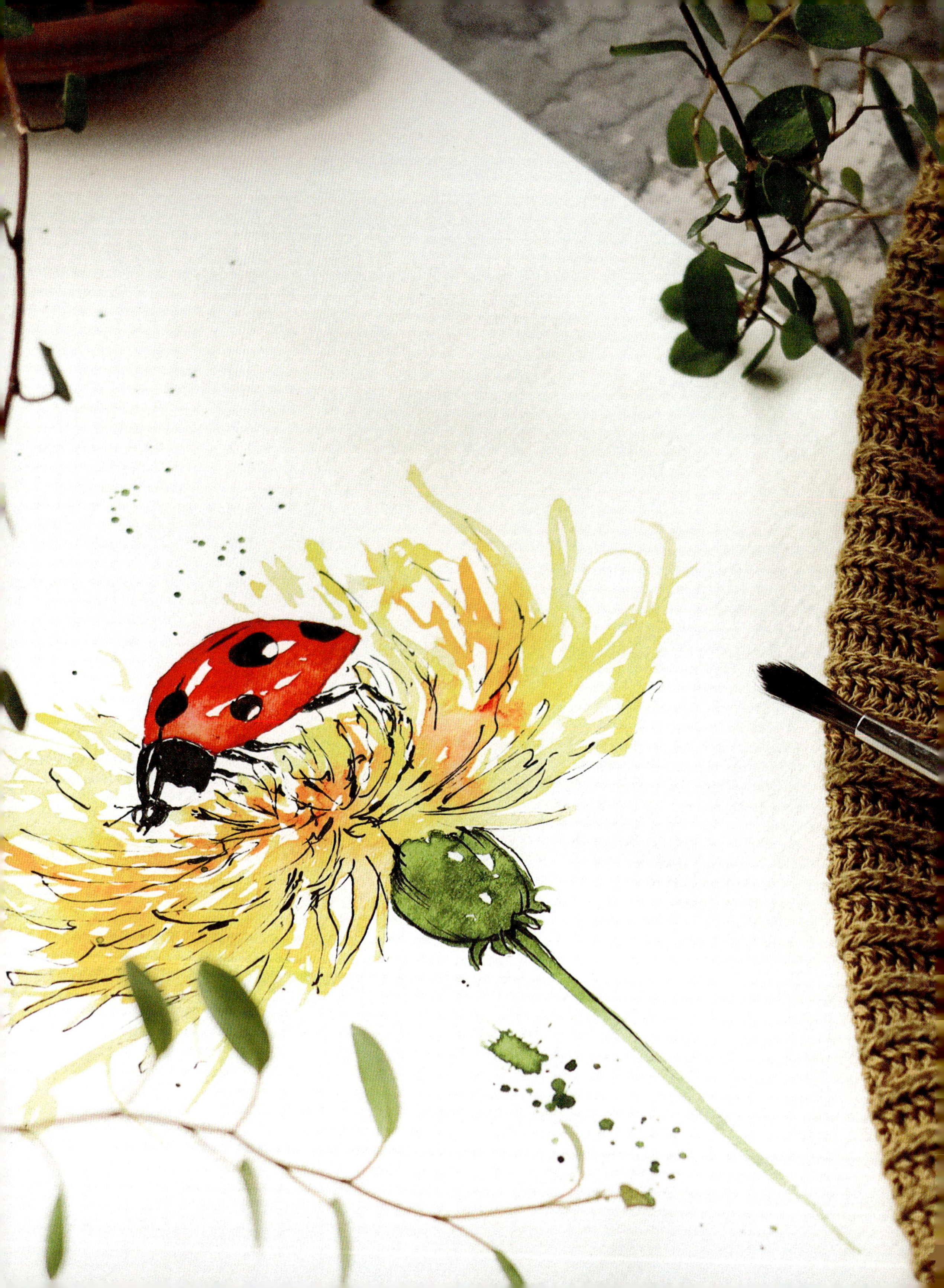

little miss ladybug

a cutie that is always looking for sunshine

Here in Denmark, when we find a ladybug, we hold it carefully and when it takes off, we ask it for good weather tomorrow. I think it's such a cute little ritual and kind of works perfectly with this cutie.

In this step-by-step, we are going to draw a ladybug sitting on a Dandelion (page 47). We will create magic using a loose watercolor technique for the dandelion combined with the graphic elegancy of the ladybug.

Materials

Pencil and eraser
Paper: Canson Montval 300gsm (140lb) cold press
Fineliners: sizes 01, 02 and 005
Watercolor brush: size 4
Water and cloth
Palette

Colors

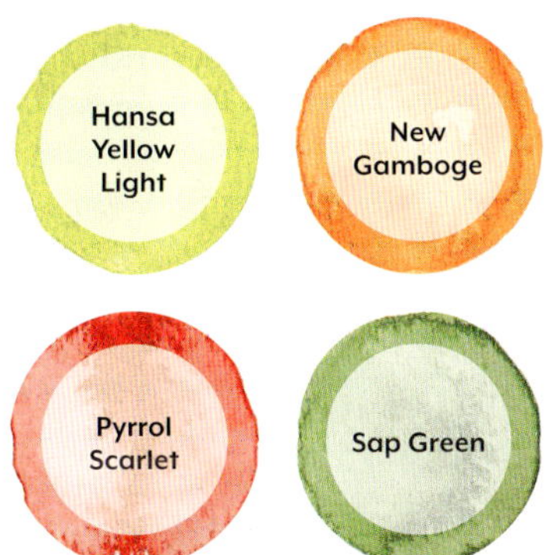

Hansa Yellow Light

New Gamboge

Pyrrol Scarlet

Sap Green

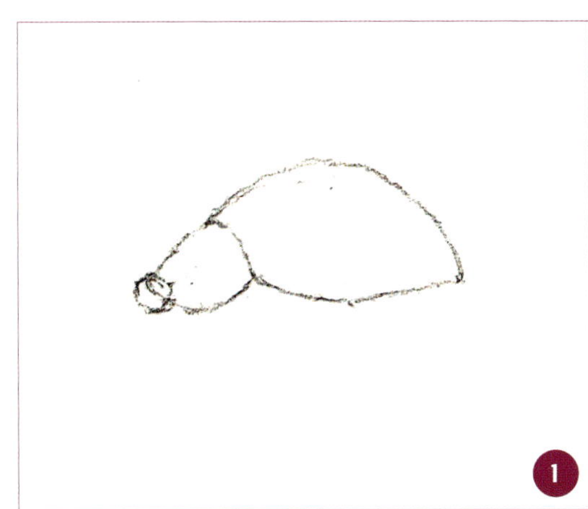

Step 1: With the pencil, sketch the thorax and head facing to the left. The back of the body with the red wings is an oval shape with a sharp corner at the end. The breast part is almost a rounded square with a small head at the end.

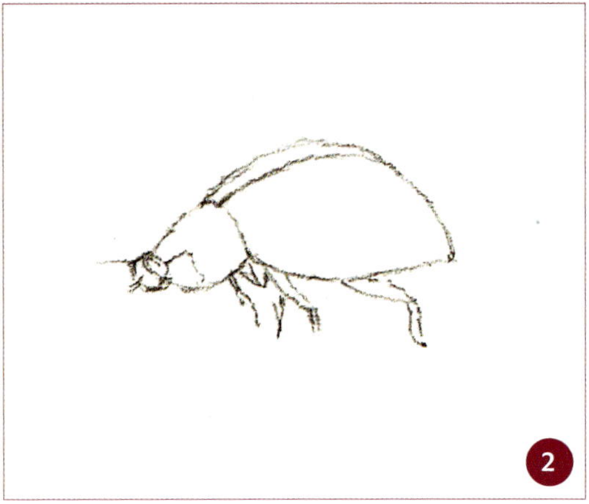

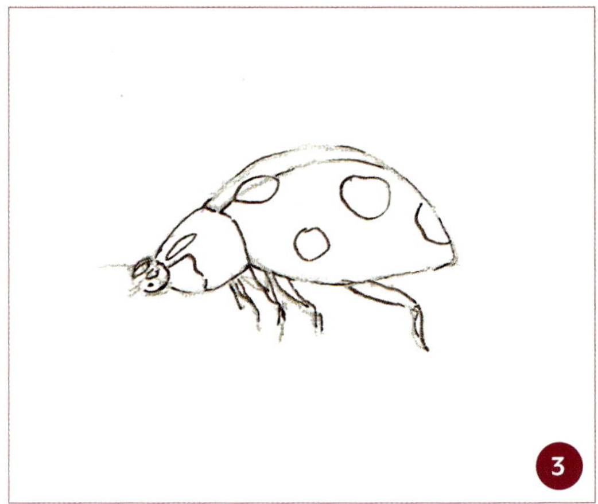

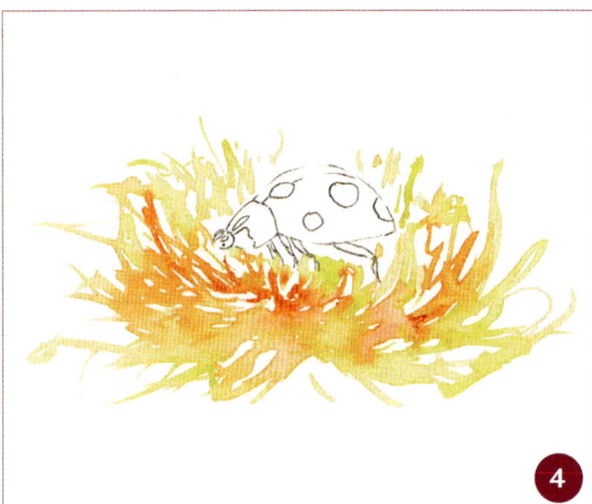

Step 2: Add legs, the line on the top of the bug and a highlight on the breast.

Step 3: Use the 01 fineliner to outline the bug and sketch in a few dark circles on the back as well. Let some hide on the side, and keep them organic-looking and in different sizes. You can erase the pencil lines and enjoy how cute it's already looking.

Step 4: With the size 4 brush, paint the Dandelion (page 47) using Hansa yellow light and new gamboge. Drip in a few drops of pyrrol scarlet in the center to tie the flower together with the ladybug. Consider how big a ladybug will look on a bloom like this. To put the ladybug front and center, I made my flower pretty small, letting the ladybug be around one-third of the length. But if you want to put the flower in focus, you can do it differently.

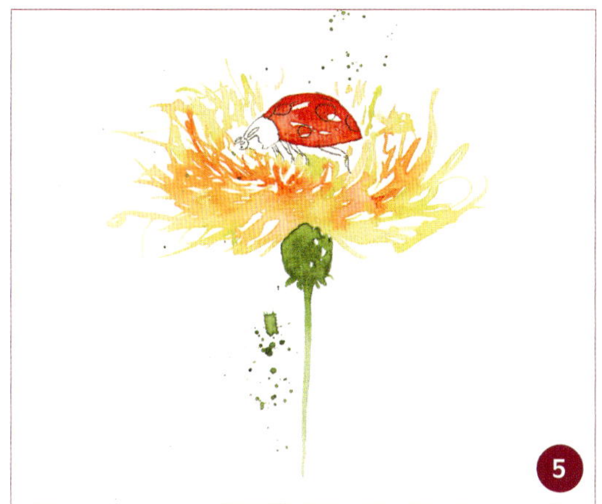

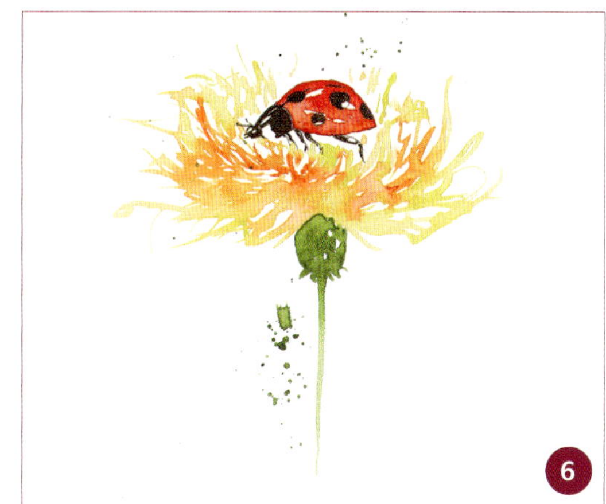

Step 5: Paint the stem using sap green. You can do a few green splatters because that just looks really cool. Paint the wing part of the body using pyrrol scarlet. Leave long, flat highlights to make the body shine.

Step 6: Grab your 02 fineliner, and when the body is completely dry, draw in the black areas on the rest of the body, along with the head, spots and legs. Make sure to keep white space. You can always add more dark, but it's harder the other way around. Also draw small antennas and a mandible made out of two little lines.

Step 7: Finish off the dandelion with a bit of fineliner detail like on page 49. Keep details in front as well as in the back of the ladybug so she is framed—almost like a pretty painting.

Well done sketching this beauty! And by the way, did you notice I dropped my brush in step 5? I continued on anyway. Leaving this mistake in the book was done very much on purpose. (Though dropping the brush wasn't.) Why? We all make mistakes in our sketches (yes, me too!), and you get to choose if you want to get frustrated or just figure out how to use it. I think the last way is more fun. Don't you?!

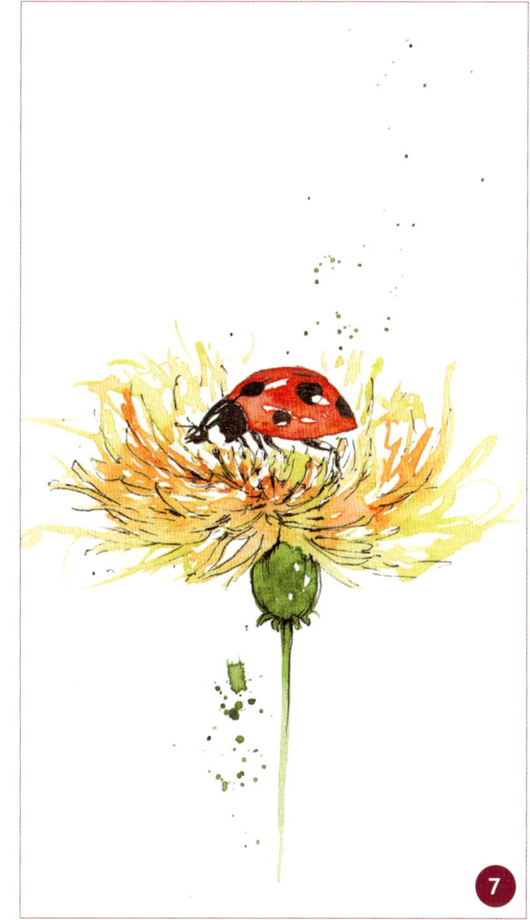

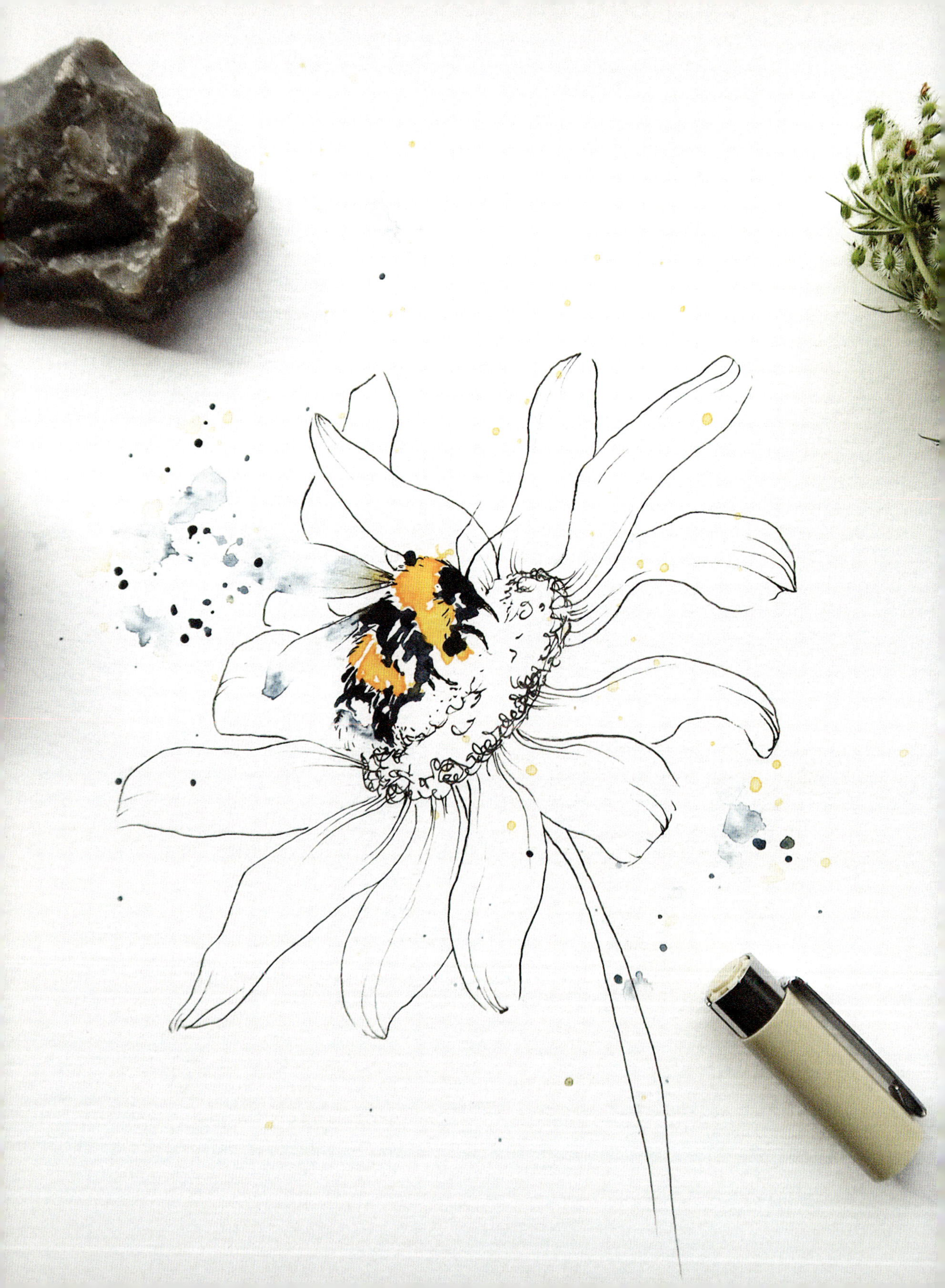

bumblebee
reminding you to trust your instincts

Did you know that technically a bumblebee should not be able to fly?
Crazy, right?! And there it is, anyway, flying from bloom to bloom.
I can't help but get so inspired by this. If your head says you can't fly
but your instincts say you can, then maybe you should just give it a go!
That goes for this tutorial as well. Here you will paint a bumblebee
almost entirely in watercolor, and it's going to be so cute. Just trust your
instincts, and you'll be fine.

Materials

Watercolor brush: size 4

Paper: Canson Montval 300gsm (140lb) cold press

Water and cloth

Palette

Pencil and eraser

Fineliners: sizes 005, 01 and 02

Colors

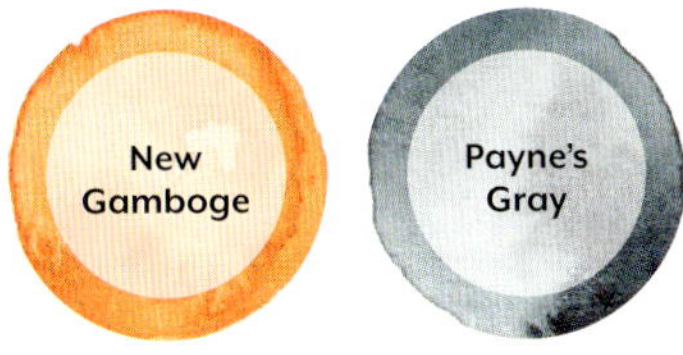

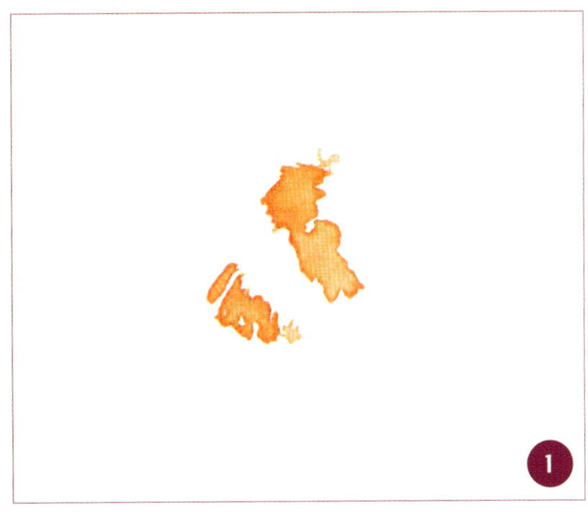

Step 1: Grab your size 4 brush and paint two yellow stripes wet-on-dry using new gamboge. Keep it light with white spaces and a bit of feathering along the outer edges.

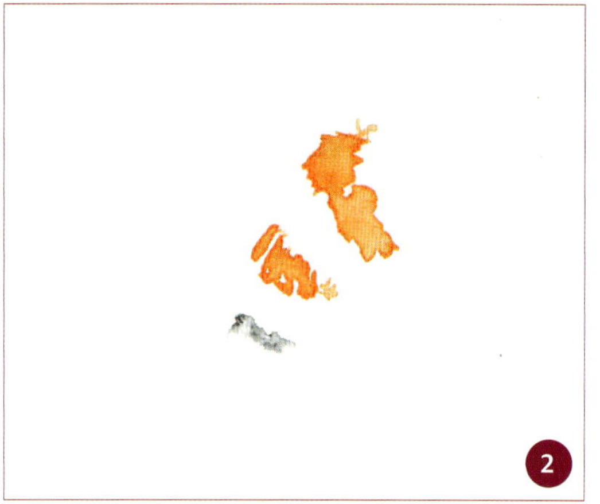

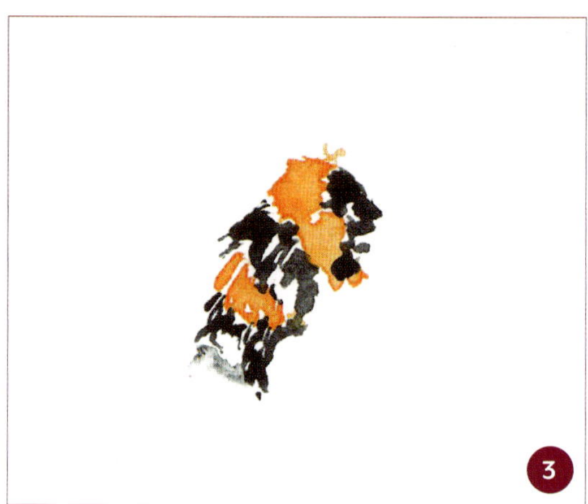

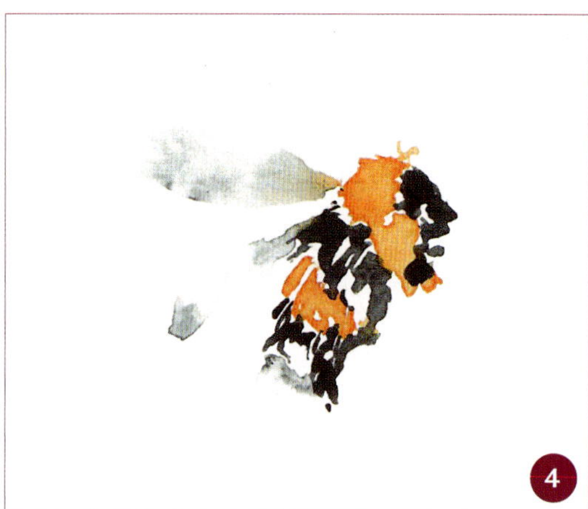

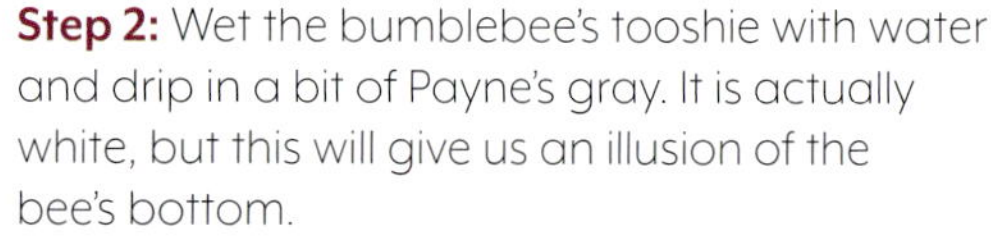

Step 2: Wet the bumblebee's tooshie with water and drip in a bit of Payne's gray. It is actually white, but this will give us an illusion of the bee's bottom.

Step 3: When the stripes are dry, paint the dark stripes and the head in Payne's gray. Keep it very light with lots of white space.

Step 4: Paint two wings in clean water and drip in a bit of Payne's gray with some new gamboge close to the body and on a few places on the edges of the wings.

Step 5: Again, we are going to do a variation of the White Oxeye Daisy from page 51. You can start by sketching it out in pencil so you know how it's going to be placed.

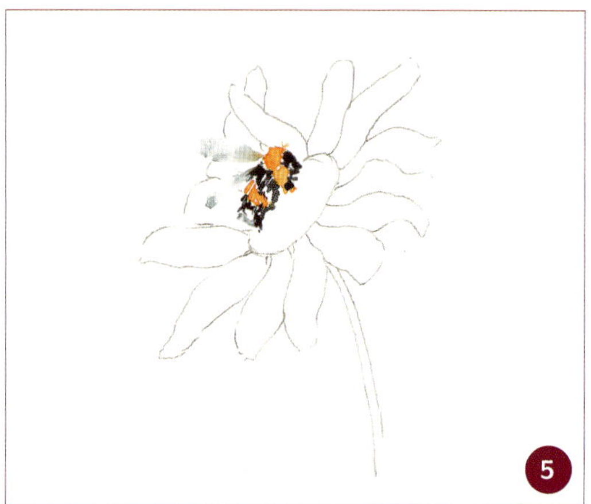

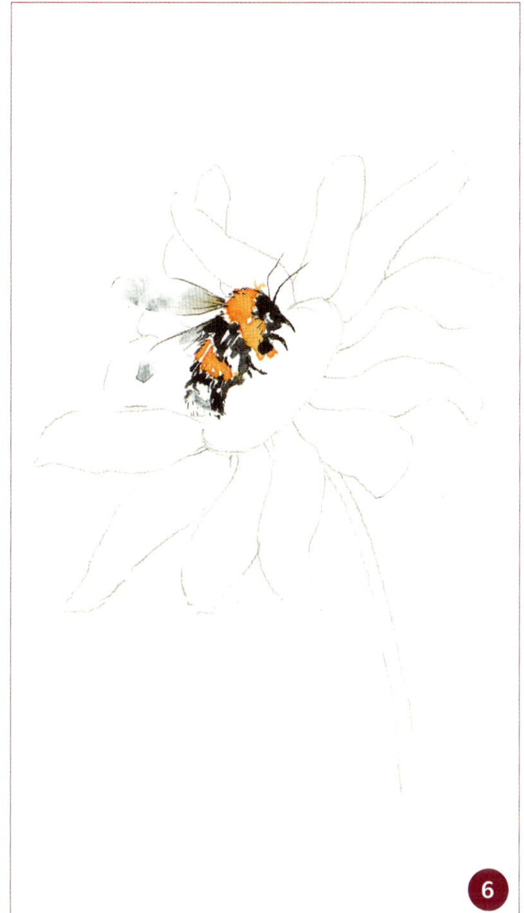

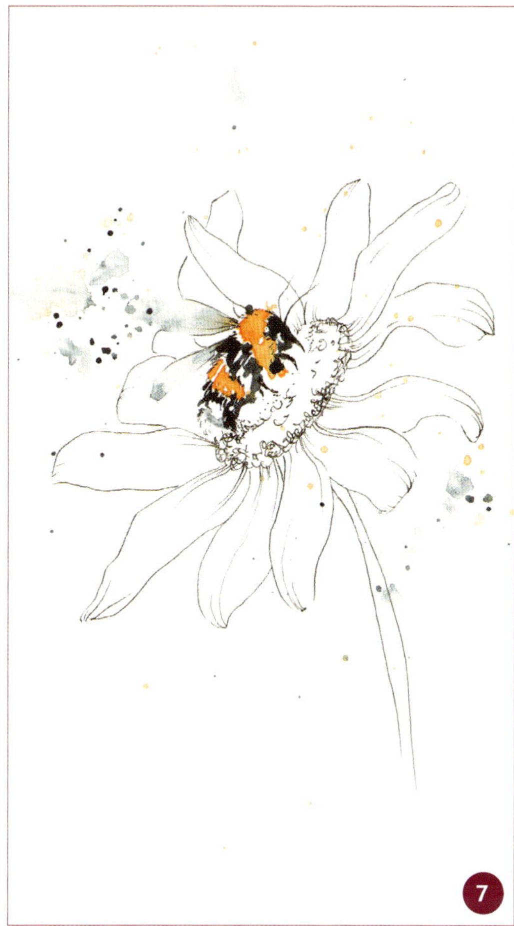

Step 6: Add a bit of fineliner detail to the bumblebee. Draw the legs and antennas with the 005 fineliner and also some furry texture on the body. Then carefully add a few lines to the wings. Don't outline it when you get to the outer edge— just let the paint shine for itself.

Step 7: Finish the flower with an outline and detail lines with the 01 fineliner. And to top off the sketch, you can add some lovely splatters using Payne's gray and new gamboge to make it a bit wild.

I love this little, optimistic bee. It can make you very happy and inspired to try something you actually don't think you can do! And that leads us to the last tutorial. (Though I am very confident you CAN do it!)

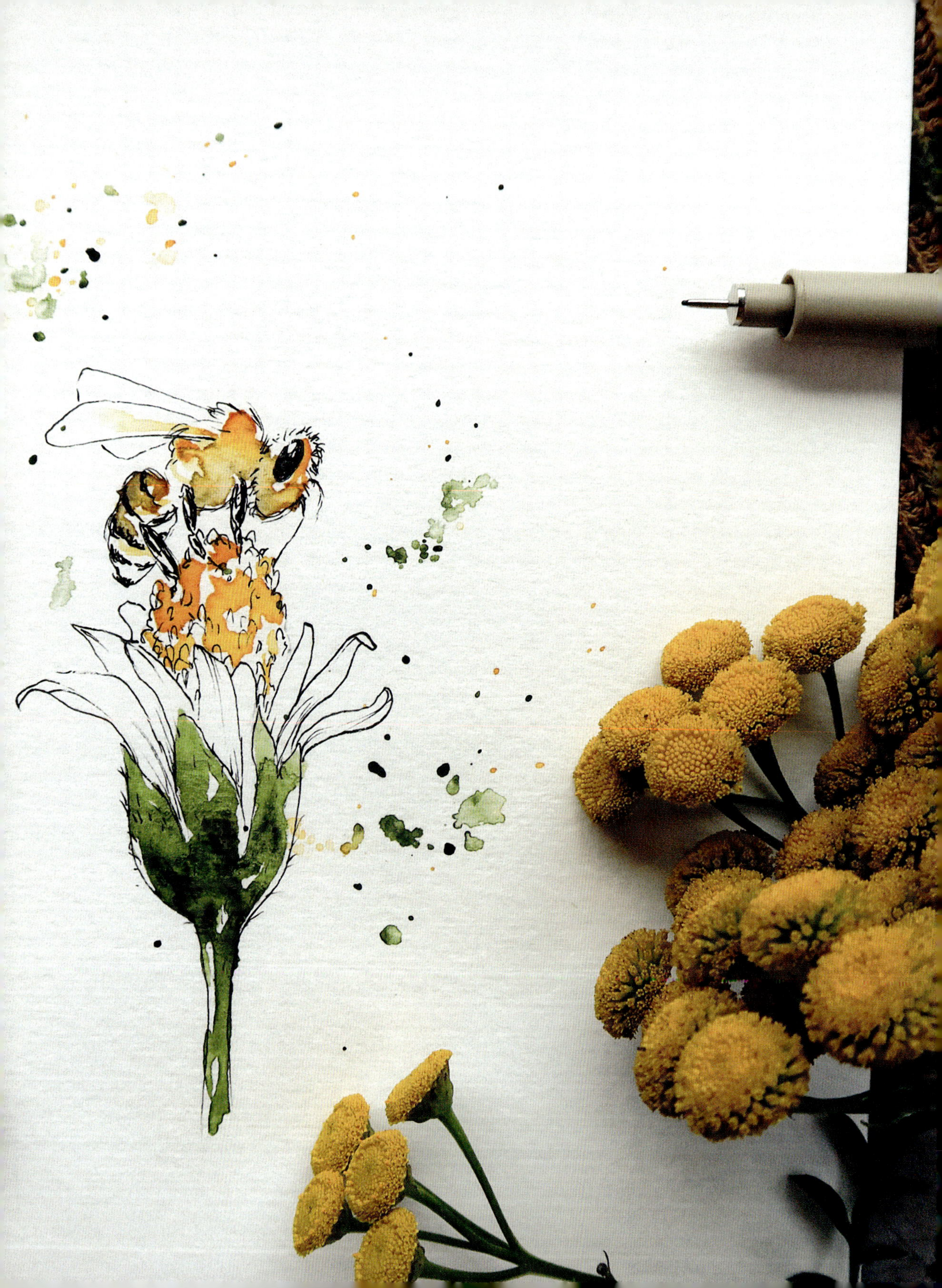

honeybee
guardian of the garden

The honeybee might just be one of the most important insects in the garden. They are really what keeps it all together, spreading pollen so the garden grows from year to year while providing honey as a gift. How wonderful is that?! Every year, my kids and I go to a nursery to find new flowers for the bees to enjoy, and every time a bee gets caught in the house, we carefully help it out to the blooms.

I've chosen this as the last tutorial because it's challenging, and I'm actually also challenging you a bit with the flower. Why? Because now you are ready to fly for yourself. This is still a variation of the White Oxeye Daisy (page 51) but in a closed version with a big center, almost like a coneflower. You can do it!

Materials

Pencil and eraser
Paper: Canson Montval 300gsm (140lb) cold press
Fineliners: sizes 01 and 005
Watercolor brush: size 4
Water and cloth
Palette

Colors

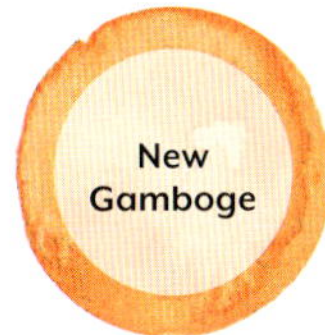
New Gamboge

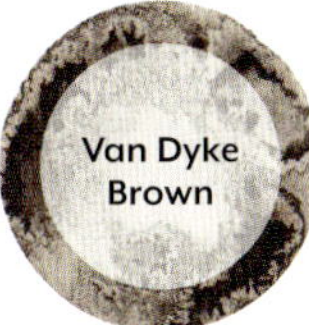
Van Dyke Brown

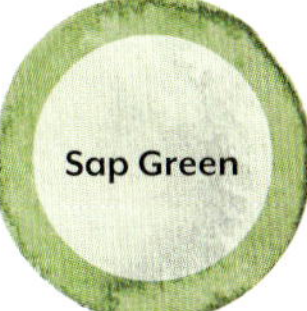
Sap Green

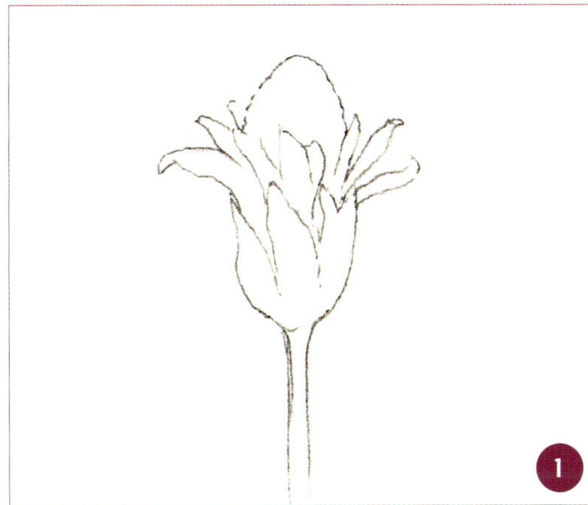

Step 1: Sketch the flower with the pencil. Draw the bottom of the flower first, then add the petals hugging the center and the rounded cone at the top.

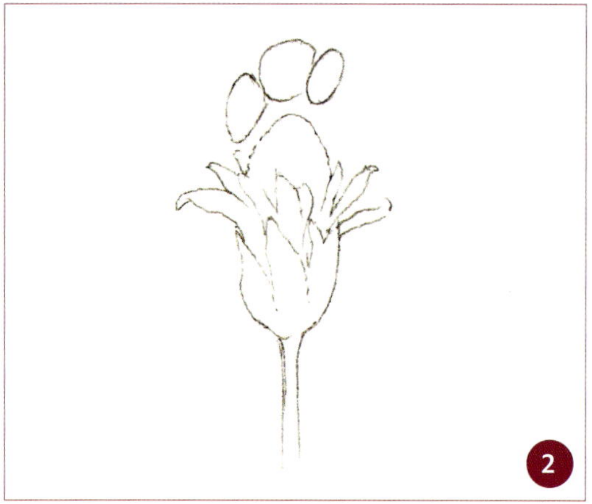

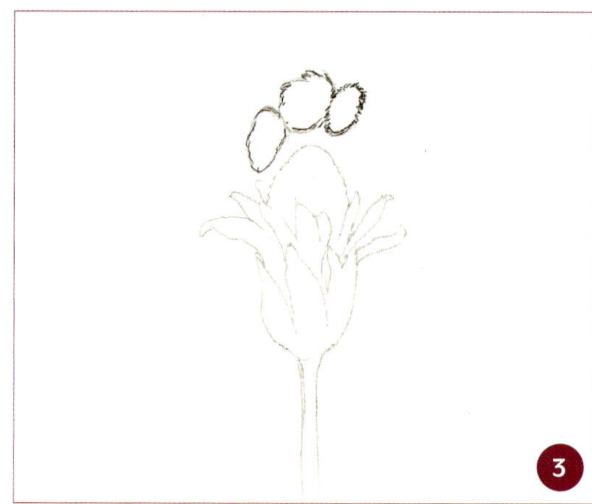

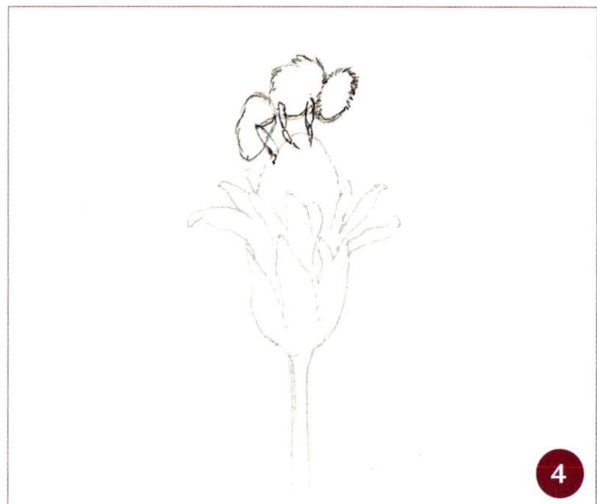

Step 2: Sketch three shapes for the bee: an oval head, a square with rounded edges for the body and a short carrot shape for the tail.

Step 3: With the 01 fineliner, draw the edge of the body and head using small lines that look like fur. You can leave a little gap with no fur markings where the body meets with the tail.

Step 4: With the same fineliner, draw the legs. As with all the other insects, the legs are made of three parts with the thigh being the thickest. If you want to see this in more detail, flip to page 20 for a closer look at insect anatomy.

Step 5: Draw the wings with the 005 fineliner. To add depth, I made one in front of the other.

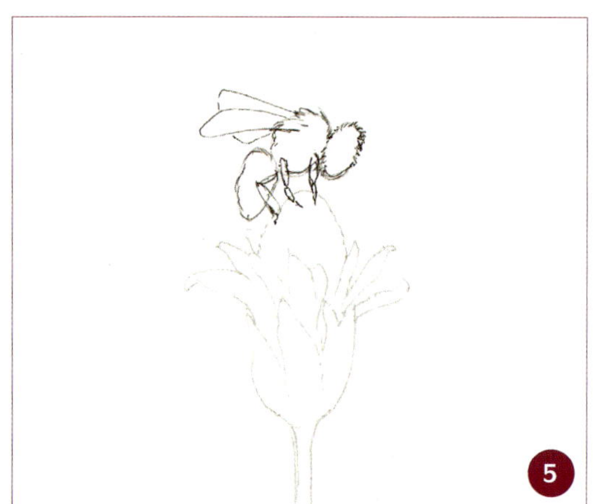

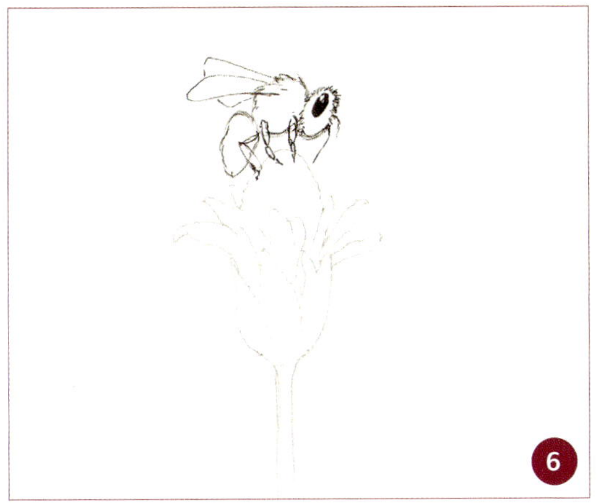

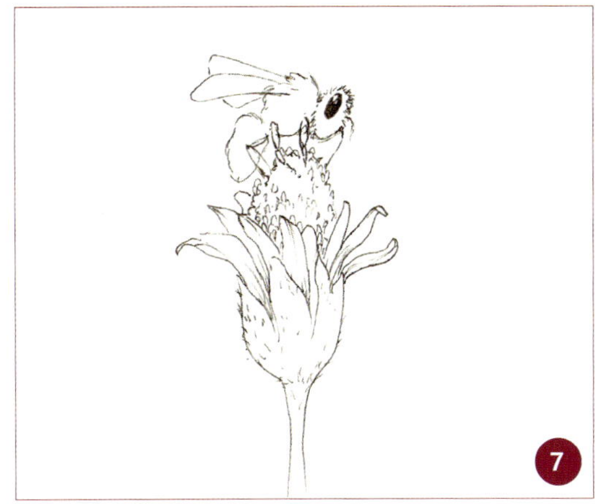

Step 6: Switch to the 01 fineliner to draw an eye with two highlights (one larger and one smaller). Add two antennas searching for pollen.

Step 7: While you have the 01 fineliner in hand, finish the flower with an outline and some details, then erase the pencil lines.

Step 8: Draw the dark areas on the bee's body with the same fineliner, and add dark shadows to the legs while keeping a few highlights.

Step 9: Paint the honeybee using new gamboge with the size 4 brush. While still wet, drip in a bit of Van Dyke brown on the honeybee's belly. While it dries, you can give the center of the flower a bit of the new gamboge as well, while keeping plenty of white space. When the body has dried a little, you can wet the front wing so the yellow can flow into it, making it look transparent.

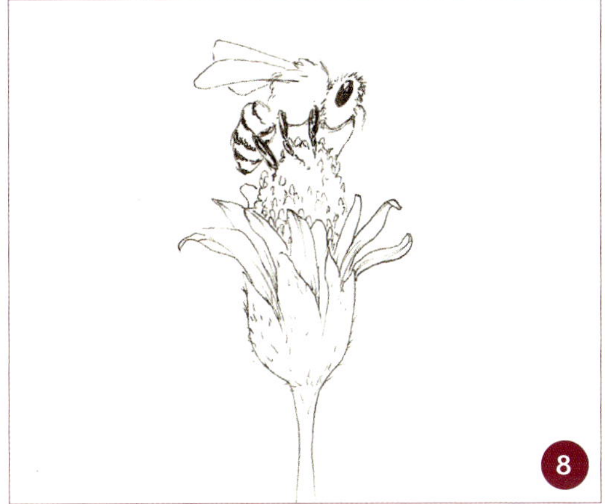

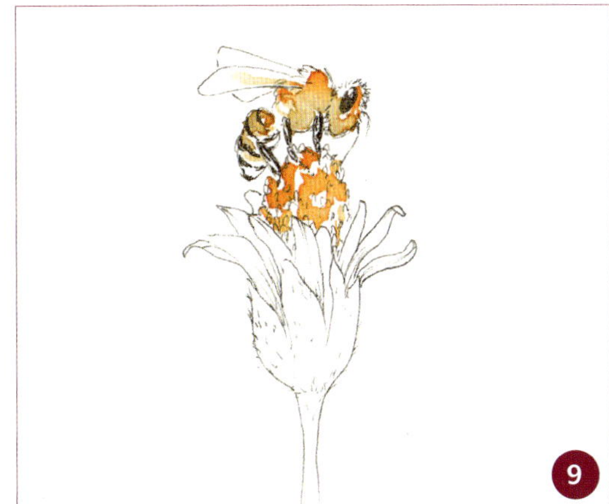

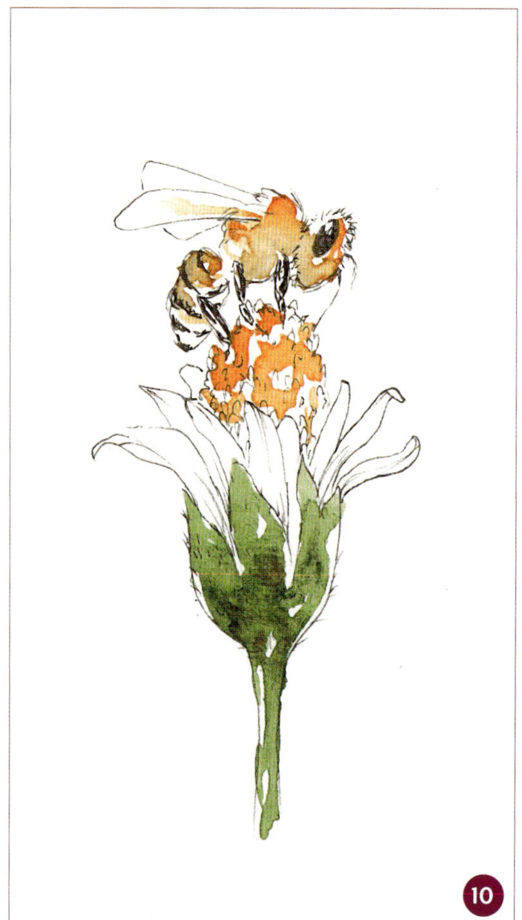

Step 10: Paint the stem using sap green and drip in a bit of Van Dyke brown to tie it all together.

Step 11: And let's finish this off with a bang! Using one color at a time, load your brush with sap green and new gamboge and give it some nice splatters. Don't hold back!

going into the wild

Woo-hoo! You are done, my friend! Start by congratulating yourself—this is extremely impressive! Now you can, of course, do the book all over again (or my first book, *Ink & Wash Florals*), but you can also turn to Finding Your Own Style (page 183) to see what your next step might be. Maybe you feel ready to fly solo now? I, for one, believe in you! You are amazing!

And that leads me to this next chapter because you are ready to be set free. And if you want to dive even more into birds and bugs, the next step for you, my friend, is going into the wild. Because, sure, you can definitely just find photos online, but you can also pack a bag and go outside where the birds and bugs actually live! How cool is that?!

They Move So Fast I Can't Sketch Them!

Yes, I know birds and insects move really fast, but what you want to do is bring a phone and take photos. Start this way so you are sure to have something to sketch when you get home. Then, observe the birds. How do they move? How are the tail, wings and body moving in relation to each other?

Or, if you want to start sketching right away, start with something slow, like a beetle. Just make sure to be careful with all insects and birds. You are here to observe, not interrupt.

Make quick sketches in a sketchbook with fineliner—or maybe even just pencil in the beginning. Then you can always add watercolor when you get home. Make sure to make note of the surroundings. Do you want to include flowers or other things in your sketch? And yes, it's totally cool if you feel a bit like a scientist. I did too when starting out. And by the way, if you feel like you don't have enough wildlife around, you can attract some by planting things they love like flowers with tons of nectar. It's a win for you and for our winged friends.

What to Bring into the Wild

Here is a small packing list for when you venture out:

- Sketchbook
- Pencil, eraser and sharpener
- Fineliners
- A few brushes and paint
- A bottle of water and a cup
- Cloths
- Backpack to put it all in
- Something to sit on
- Phone to take photos and update your Insta story
- Snacks and something nice to drink
- And to be a real science pro, bring binoculars and books about birds and insects
- Sunglasses if it's sunny
- Sunscreen
- If it's raining, bring an umbrella or just go back inside to redo a sketch from the book.

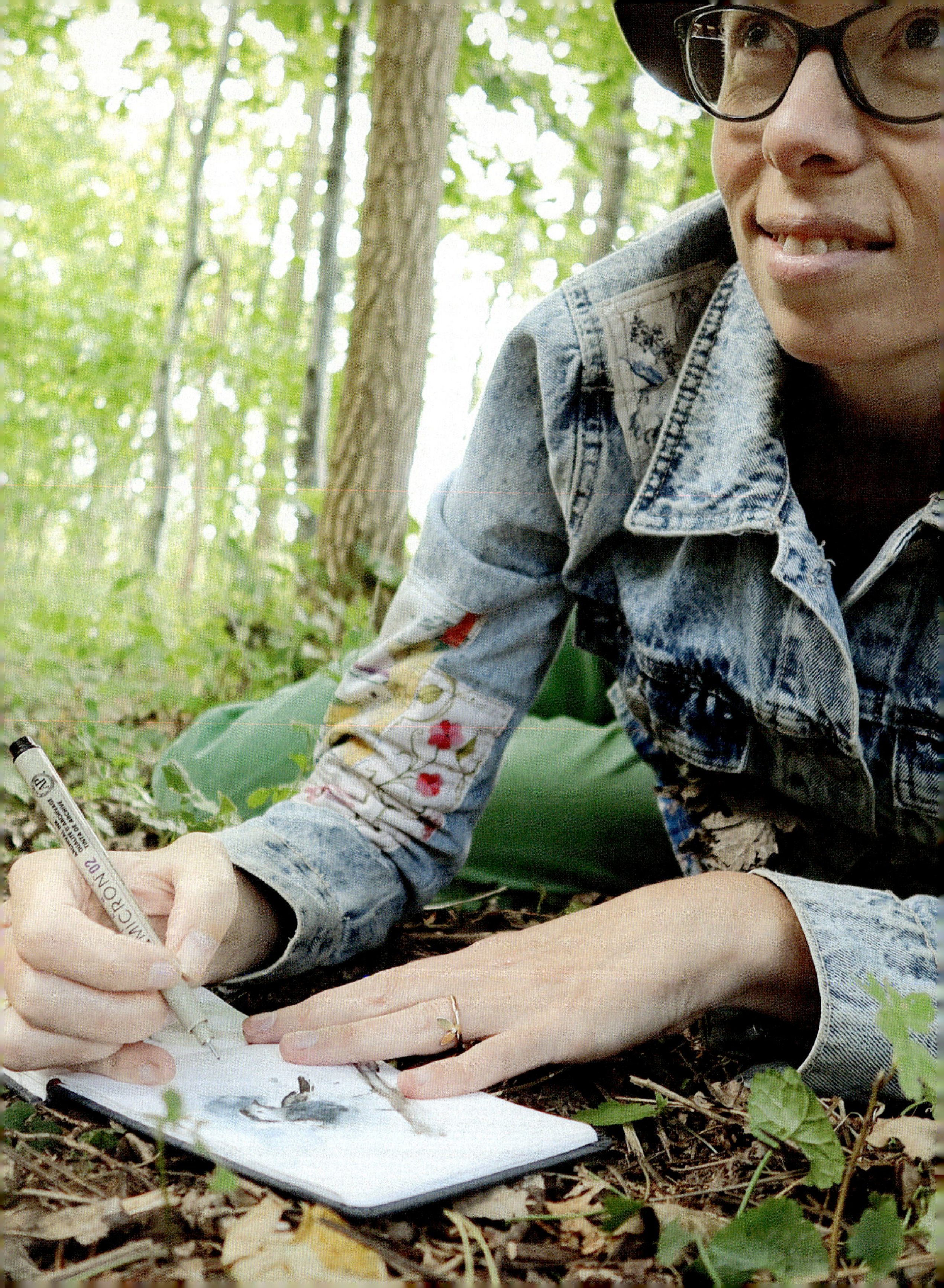

finding your own style

As you can see throughout the book, there is no right or wrong way to do this. You don't HAVE to start with watercolor and you don't HAVE to start with a 01 fineliner. You just go with what feels natural. When you start to do that, you start to develop your own style. But of course, if you are ever in doubt, sketch a project or two from this book to get a feeling of the technique.

So how do you find your own style? Well, some say you can look at other people's art and take what you like. Some people say you just have to work hard, trying out tons of combinations to see what works for you.

I say, start at day one. Just do one sketch. Then another. Slowly, your style will develop. But it's not really about finding your style; it's really about the process. Your style will change over the years as you grow in skill, interests and mood. Personally, my style just six years ago was super cartoony and dreamy, and now it's much looser and semi-realistic. Both are my styles. And I love both. As long as you keep creating, you have a style, and that style is changing with you. Isn't that wonderful? No more need for wild goose chases; just enjoy the moment.

So here, at the end of this, I want to challenge you. You read the book and made the sketches. Now you know everything you need to know to step into the deep water. You are ready; I promise.

A Small Challenge

Find three images of birds or butterflies and just start. Do three sketches of each of the photos. You can keep developing them as you go. But you will feel more and more comfortable in this as you move along. Maybe you want to do it differently with the second photo. What do you feel like? Just go with your intuition. It is ready to stand on its own a long time before we are.

acknowledgments

I think by now you noticed how much these wonderful winged friends mean to me. But there are humans as well who also mean the world to me and deserve so much gratitude.

My two little Caterpillars who agreed to let mommy paint while they played with magnetic sand and listened to children's books on the radio. My incredible husband who always takes care of the kids when I go to writing retreats or just need a painting break. I am sending you a Beetle because you always stay centered in your own strength—you are my rock!

I want to send a very special Swallowtail to my parents and siblings. If it hadn't been for those summer days enjoying the butterflies in southern France, I'm not sure this book would have been the same.

And then of course, a big thank-you to my mother-in-law. She gave me binoculars and a bird book for my birthday to research for this book, and she supports my every move. I am sending you a colorful Goldfinch for your motivation and inspiration.

I also want to send a big, warm flock of happy House Sparrows to my wonderful team at Page Street Publishing: Aïcha, Sadie, Sarah, Meg, Katelynn and everybody else—you are incredible!

Finally, I want to send out the biggest, most adorable Bumblebee to my followers, students and readers of my books. The Bumblebee trusts its instincts and flies, even if it is told it can't . . . and you can too! I believe in you.

about the author

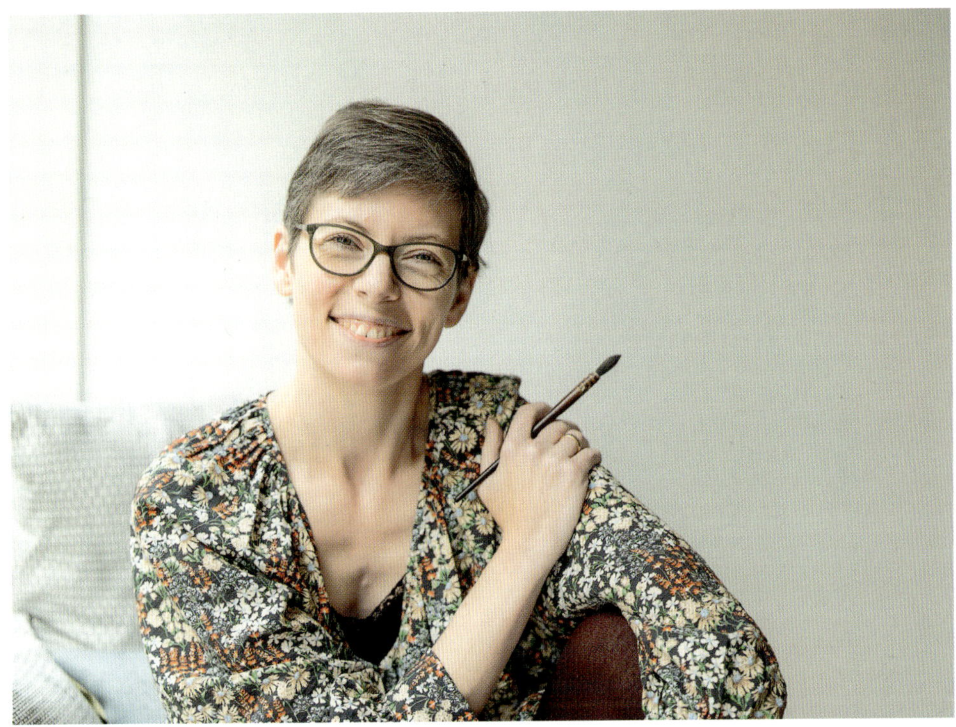

Camilla is an artist, mom, wife, bestselling author, educator, tree hugger, cat lady, flower girl and big fan of chocolate croissants and drinking menthe tea in her garden. She lives with her family in Denmark, out in the country, and from her little red house, she teaches watercolor and ink to students from all over the world. When she is not teaching or painting, she is enjoying her garden, birdwatching with the kids and buying butterfly-friendly flowers. And no, you can never get enough flowers—period.

You can learn more from her in her online courses, on her YouTube channel and in her first book *Ink & Wash Florals*.

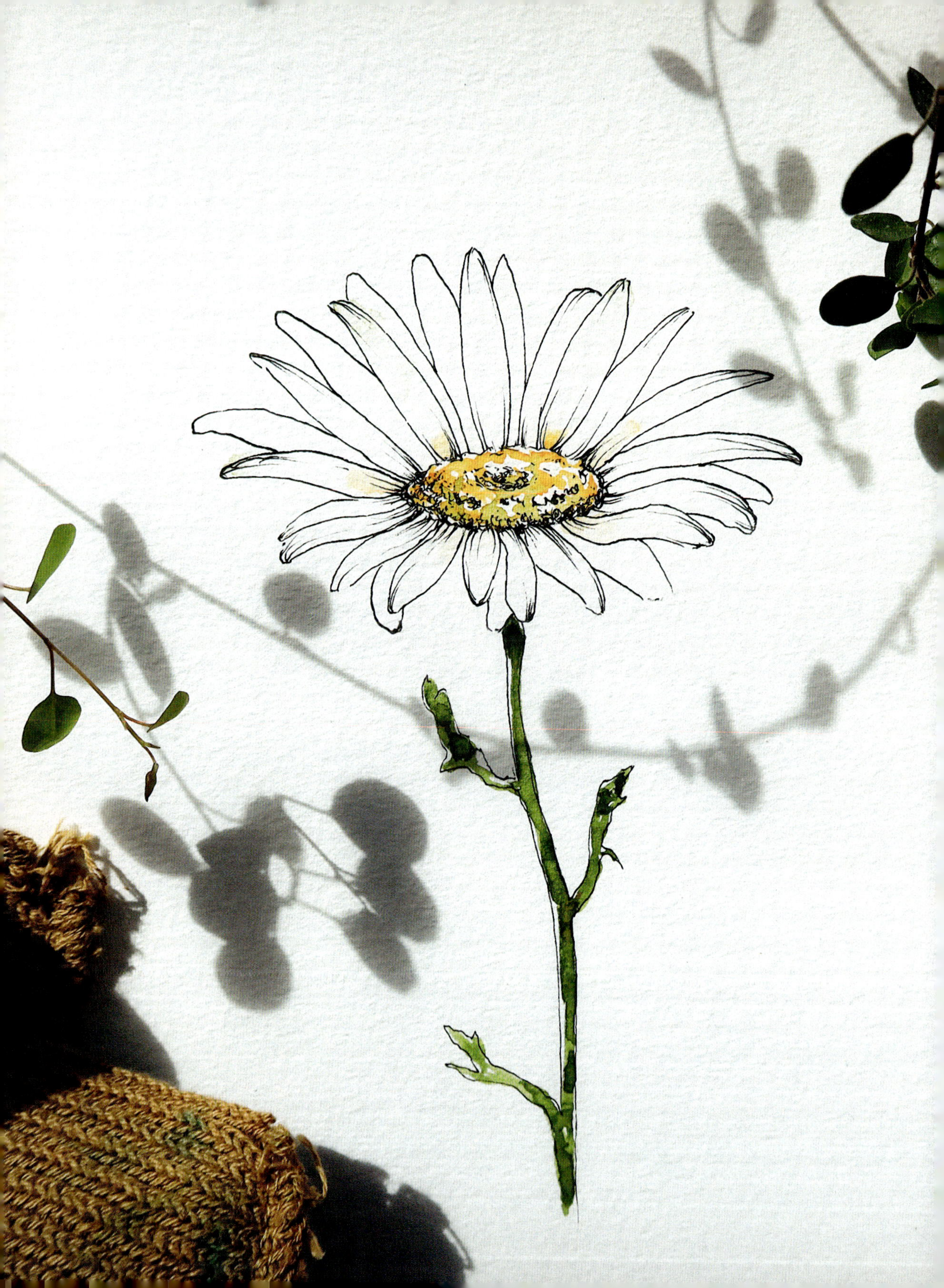

index